Sounds of War

Comparatively little is known about the musical cultures of the British armed forces during the Great War. This groundbreaking study is the first to examine music's vital presence in a range of military contexts including military camps, ships, aerodromes and battlefields, canteen huts, hospitals and PoW camps. Emma Hanna argues that music was omnipresent in servicemen's wartime existence and was a vital element for the maintenance of morale. She shows how music was utilised to stimulate recruitment and fundraising, for diplomatic and propaganda purposes, and for religious, educational and therapeutic reasons. Music was not in any way ephemeral: it was unmatched in its power to cajole, console, cheer and inspire during the conflict and its aftermath. This study is a major contribution to our understanding of the wartime realities of the British armed forces during the Great War.

Emma Hanna is a lecturer in the School of History at the University of Kent. She is the author of *The Great War on the Small Screen: Representing the First World War in Contemporary Britain* (2009).

Studies in the Social and Cultural History of Modern Warfare

General Editor
Jay Winter, *Yale University*

Advisory Editors
David Blight, *Yale University*
Richard Bosworth, *University of Western Australia*
Peter Fritzsche, *University of Illinois, Urbana-Champaign*
Carol Gluck, *Columbia University*
Benedict Kiernan, *Yale University*
Antoine Prost, *Université de Paris-Sorbonne*
Robert Wohl, *University of California, Los Angeles*

In recent years, the field of modern history has been enriched by the exploration of two parallel histories. These are the social and cultural history of armed conflict, and the impact of military events on social and cultural history.

Studies in the Social and Cultural History of Modern Warfare presents the fruits of this growing area of research, reflecting both the colonisation of military history by cultural historians and the reciprocal interest of military historians in social and cultural history, to the benefit of both. The series offers the latest scholarship in European and non-European events from the 1850s to the present day.

A full list of titles in the series can be found at:
www.cambridge.org/modernwarfare

Sounds of War

Music in the British Armed Forces During the Great War

Emma Hanna

University of Kent

CAMBRIDGE
UNIVERSITY PRESS

CAMBRIDGE
UNIVERSITY PRESS

University Printing House, Cambridge CB2 8BS, United Kingdom

One Liberty Plaza, 20th Floor, New York, NY 10006, USA

477 Williamstown Road, Port Melbourne, VIC 3207, Australia

314–321, 3rd Floor, Plot 3, Splendor Forum, Jasola District Centre, New Delhi – 110025, India

79 Anson Road, #06–04/06, Singapore 079906

Cambridge University Press is part of the University of Cambridge.

It furthers the University's mission by disseminating knowledge in the pursuit of education, learning, and research at the highest international levels of excellence.

www.cambridge.org
Information on this title: www.cambridge.org/9781108480086
DOI: 10.1017/9781108609449

First published 2020

Printed in the United Kingdom by TJ International Ltd. Padstow Cornwall

A catalogue record for this publication is available from the British Library.

Library of Congress Cataloging-in-Publication Data
Names: Hanna, Emma, author.
Title: Sounds of war / Emma Hanna.
Description: New York : Cambridge University Press, 2020. | Series: Studies in the social and cultural history of modern warfare | Includes bibliographical references and index.
Identifiers: LCCN 2019042103 (print) | LCCN 2019042104 (ebook) | ISBN 9781108480086 (hardback) | ISBN 9781108609449 (ebook)
Subjects: LCSH: World War, 1914–1918 – Great Britain – Music and the war. | Music – Social aspects – Great Britain – History – 20th century. | Music – Political aspects – Great Britain – History – 20th century. | Popular music – Great Britain – 1911–1920 – History and criticism.
Classification: LCC ML3917.G7 H3 2929 (print) | LCC ML3917.G7 (ebook) | DDC 781.5/99094109041–dc23
LC record available at https://lccn.loc.gov/2019042103
LC ebook record available at https://lccn.loc.gov/2019042104

ISBN 978-1-108-48008-6 Hardback

For my beloved Grandma, Jean Ward-Penny.

Thank you for a lifetime of love and laughter.

Contents

Figures

Acknowledgements

If it takes a village to raise a child, then it takes a small state to write a book. Over eight years of researching and writing, a number of people have assisted and supported me, and I wish to thank as many of them as possible here.

I am grateful to the archivists and librarians of the following collections: Borthwick Archives (University of York), British Library, Cadbury Special Collections (University of Birmingham), Commonwealth War Graves Commission, Imperial War Museum, Liddle Collection (University of Leeds), Liddle Hart Centre for Military Archives, Museum of the Royal Logistics Corps, National Archives, and the Royal British Legion. I would particularly like to thank Barbara Gilbert (Fleet Air Arm Museum), David Blake (Royal Army Chaplaincy Museum), Esther Mann (Royal Army Music School, Kneller Hall), Frank Bowles (Library, University of Cambridge), George Malcolmson (Museum of the Royal Navy), Jo Baines (Special Collections, University of Kent), Karim Hussain (British Red Cross), Kathy Adamson (Royal Academy of Music), Ken Reeves (George Edwardes Musical Comedy Society), Ken Montgomery (YMCA England), Lucia Stuart (Seymour Hicks Museum), Nina Hadaway (Royal Air Force Museum), Norman Gilham (Royal Flying Corps Association), Rob Illingworth (Kent History and Library Centre), Robert Fleming and Penny Hutchins (National Army Museum), Robert McIntosh (Museum of Military Medicine), and Ruth MacDonald and Steven Spencer (Salvation Army International Heritage Centre). I am also very grateful to Anna Farthing, Janet Snowman, Katrina Henderson, Laura Boyd, Mary Kemp, Malcolm Doolin, Mark Warby, Nick Hiley, Oliver Dunn, Paul Taylor-Holland, Peter Howson, Stephen Smedley, Steve Bartlett, Stuart Bell, Thomas Greenshields, Tony Lidington, Victoria Carolan, Rear Admiral James Goldrick and Colonel Simon Vandeleur of the Coldstream Guards Association.

All my colleagues on the *Gateways to the First World War* and *Reflections on the Centenary* AHRC projects have been immensely supportive throughout. I am privileged to have the most positive teammates anyone could wish for in Alison Fell, Brad Beaven, Catriona Pennell, James Wallis, Helen Brooks, Lucy Noakes, Mark Connelly, Sam Carroll and Zoë Denness. I owe an enormous debt of thanks to the staff of the School of History at the University of Kent for their boundless support, advice and friendship, particularly Jackie Latham, Jenny Humphries, Juliette Pattinson, Karen Jones and Kenneth Fincham.

I am thankful to many fellow historians who have informed my work in various ways including Angela Byrne, Adrian Gregory, Adrian Smith, Alastair Lockhart, Andrew Maunder, Barbara Kelly, Chris Kempshall, Clare Makepeace, Dan Todman, David Welch, Dominiek Dendooven, Edward Madigan, Gary Sheffield, Gavin Rand, Glyn Prysor, Heather Jones, Helen Barlow, Helen McCartney, James Pugh, Jane Potter, Jay Winter, Jeffrey Reznick, Jenny Macleod, Jessica Meyer, Jim Beach, John Horne, Jonathan Boff, Jonathan Lewis, John Mullen, Kate Kennedy, Laura Seddon, Linda Parker, Lynsey Shaw Cobden, Martin Wilcox, Michael Hammond, Michael Snape, Michael Walsh, Michelle Meinhart, Nick Hiley, Oliver Wilkinson, Peter Grant, Quintin Colville, Richard Grayson, Ross Mahoney, Sarah Palmer, Sophie de Schaepdrijver, Stefan Goebel, Stephen Badsey, Tim Bowman, Tim Godden, Toby Thacker, Tony Lidington, Virginia Crompton and Will Butler. Colin Wagstaff, James and Susan Brazier, and everyone at the Western Front Association has been wonderfully supportive, in addition to all those who attend the events for *Gateways*, and students past and present.

I am very glad to have the most patient and supportive agent, Anthony Haynes at Frontinus. I am also grateful to Michael Watson and everyone at CUP involved in getting this book into print. My wonderful friends, particularly Eleni, Eva, Jill, Lee-Anne, Liz and Michelle have always provided help and humour on our adventures through life and motherhood. I am immensely grateful to my family for their perseverance and support, and I am indebted to my Mum, Christine Ward-Penny. She has helped with everything from research to childcare, sitting through hours of me talking about this project which she has endured with the patience of a saint. Above all, I owe the biggest thanks to my husband Steve, and my son Arthur. I could not do this without the bedrock of their love and support. No expression of thanks will ever be enough to explain how grateful I am to be sharing my life with them.

Emma Hanna

Abbreviations

AEF   Australian Expeditionary Force

ADS   Advanced Dressing Station

ANZAC   Australian and New Zealand Army Corps

ASC   Army Service Corp

BEF   British Expeditionary Force

BRC   British Red Cross

CCS   Casualty Clearing Station

CLC   Chinese Labour Corps

CO   Commanding officer

DSO   Distinguished Service Order

EFC   Expeditionary Forces Canteens

ENSA   Entertainments National Services Association

FANY   Field Army Nursing Yeomanry

HQ   Headquarters

MT   Motor Transport

MWC   Music in Wartime Committee

NAAFI   Navy Army and Air Force Institutes

NACB   Navy and Army Canteen Board

NCO   Non-commissioned officer

NMMU   Naval and Military Musical Union

NSL   National Service League

OBE	Order of the British Empire
PCWRC	Professional Classes War Relief Council
PoW	Prisoner of war
PRC	Parliamentary Recruiting Committee
QAARNC	Queen Alexandra's Army Nursing Corps
QMAANC	Queen Mary's Army Auxiliary Corps
RAM	Royal Academy of Music
RAMC	Royal Army Military Corps
RFC	Royal Flying Corps
RMLI	Royal Marines Light Infantry
RMSM	Royal Military School of Music
RNAS	Royal Naval Air Service
RNSM	Royal Naval School of Music
RNVR	Royal Naval Volunteer Reserve
RUSI	Royal United Services Institute
SEF	Soldier's Entertainment Fund
VAD	Voluntary Aid Detachment
VC	Victoria Cross
WAAC	Women's Army Auxiliary Corps
WEC	Women's Emergency Committee
WEE	War Emergency Entertainments
YMCA	Young Men's Christian Association

Introduction

In parallel with studies of the poetry of the Great War, Britain's musical history of the conflict has focused on a small group of elite composers.[1] Comparatively little is known about the musical cultures of the British armed forces despite music's quotidian nature in the British Army, Royal Navy and Royal Flying Corps/Royal Air Force. This book will examine the formal and informal applications of music in the British forces on land, sea and air, during their periods of work, rest and play, in military camps, on ships, in aerodromes, on the battlefields and in hospitals and prisoner of war camps, theatres, cinemas and canteen huts. It will explore how music of all kinds, live and recorded, was utilised to stimulate recruitment and fundraising, for diplomatic and propaganda purposes, and for religious, educational and therapeutic reasons. It will observe how the unprecedented expansion of Britain's armed forces by the recruitment and conscription of approximately 6 million British civilians brought elements of continuity and change to the musical cultures of each service. It will show why the musical cultures of Britain's armed forces should be examined in the social, cultural and military contexts in which they developed.

Music was a staple of family and community life across the social spectrum. Singing and the playing of instruments were appreciated and there was an expectation that those who were capable should entertain. In 1914, there were approximately 3 million pianos in Britain, one for every fifteen people.[2] Street singers were common, and in 1900, there were more than 30,000 brass bands in the UK, often subsidised by local employers, regularly competing in high-profile competitions.[3] The Great War occurred at a time of significant social and cultural change in the British military services as well as in civilian life. After the inglorious performance of the British Army in South Africa (1899–1902) the service was subject to a series of reforms, culminating in the recommendations of Lord Haldane between 1906 and 1913.[4] In parallel with the Army, Admiral John 'Jackie' Fisher, as First Sea Lord between 1904 and 1911, did much to modernise the operation of the Royal Navy. The Royal Flying Corps was founded by the Aerial Navigation Act on 1 April 1912. It operated under the dual command of the War Office and the Admiralty, and comprised two wings, naval and military, to support the Navy and the Army as required. In parallel with the developments in Britain's armed forces, the quality of their music was of concern to the Naval and Military Musical Union. Established by leading military figures in 1909, it sought to raise the tone of Navy and Army concerts by 'popularizing the fine old soldier and sailor songs, which have been somewhat neglected of late'.[5]

In Britain, a cultural war simmered between the forces of traditionalism and modernity.[6] Forms of popular music, particularly music hall songs and 'ragtime', were seen by some as signs of cultural decadence which were polluting British cultural life.[7] There were tensions between what middle-class observers considered to be 'the true music of the people, namely folk music' and what we now recognise as the actual music of the people, commercial popular songs disseminated via the gramophone.[8] The outbreak of war exacerbated cultural tensions which had been present in peacetime; the old versus the young, the old fashioned versus the modern, the national versus the foreign. Added to these 'conflicts of values' were charges of decadence. The war, some argued, had been sent to put England right.[9] The British sculptor, W. R. Colton, expressed the widely held view that Edwardian England had become degenerate, slothful and corrupt. It was, he said 'high time that war should come with its purifying fire' because 'so-called Art had grown in Europe like unto a puffed-out fungus of enormous size, without beauty, without delicacy, without health'.[10] For those who agreed with Colton, Modernism did not start with post-impressionism and the twelve-tone scale, it was the symptom of an infection from the time of Nietzsche and Wagner. These links between German culture and perceived decadence were one and the same sickness. This sense of needing to be cleansed, and of war as a social and cultural disinfectant, was expressed by Rupert Brooke, the most published and read poet of the wartime generation. Serving with the Royal Naval Division during the evacuation of Antwerp in October 1914, Brooke implored his peers to 'Leave the sick hearts that honour could not move/And half-men, and their dirty songs'.[11] Furthermore, there were hopes in 1914 that the war would serve to develop a recognisably British elite musical style. The nineteenth century had been a time of musical internationalism; Italian music dominated opera, German composters led the orchestral field and the French the operetta.[12] There was considerable prejudice against British music in Britain. *The Strad* magazine claimed that war 'except so far as it crushes individual talent, is not in principle inimical to art', asserting the conflict would arouse 'the best and truest feelings of our race'.[13]

Several leading professional performers were quick to identify the problems and the possibilities the war presented. Before the outbreak of war there were approximately four hundred touring musical theatre companies in Great Britain, and in the Autumn of 1914, this decreased by more than half.[14] In August 1914, a National Relief Fund was established to assist any person whose livelihood was negatively affected by the war. However, there were limiting caveats, such as the stipulation that if performers were unemployed on 4 August 1914 – the date of Britain's declaration of war – they were deemed ineligible for assistance.[15] Perhaps in response to the difficulties caused by such stipulations, *The Era* started its own War Distress Fund, chaired by the actor-manager of the Kingsway Theatre, Lena Ashwell, who saw that as men could enlist in the forces it was the employment prospects of female performers that would be worst affected. Ashwell's fund explained that it existed 'for the purpose of assisting ALL WORKERS . . . who suffer through the war'.[16] Lena Ashwell also established the Three Arts Club in Marylebone, one of many organisations established by higher profile women in the first few weeks of the war. Ashwell was also heavily involved in establishing the Women's Emergency Corps, which was set up on 9 August 1914 by Evelina Haverfield and Decima Moore with the Women's Social and Political Union. The WEC headquarters were located at the Little Theatre, London. Moore was an actress and soprano who had performed with the D'Oyly Carte Opera Company and the George Edwardes Company, and, like Ashwell, she had connections to the Suffragette movement.[17] The primary aim of the WEC was to train women as doctors, nurses and motorcycle riders in order to support the war effort.[18] Professional performers needed to balance their desire to contribute to the war effort in addition to protecting their careers and livelihoods. It should not be forgotten that the industries involved in publishing printed music and producing gramophones and records were required to generate profits to survive. The expansion of Britain's armed forces, and the desire of those at home to support – and sometimes forget – the everyday realities of war, meant that the desire for music of all kinds created an enormous market for these commodities. However, the work presented here is not intended as a definitive history of British military music, nor does it seek to act as an encyclopedia of every servicemen's troupe that performed in the Great War. This book examines servicemen's musical encounters, illuminating why, where and how music was provided and experienced by performers and servicemen alike.

Historiography

During the Great War, many men and women were involved in music-making on the fighting fronts as enlisted servicemen or civilian volunteers. However, the majority of these individuals are absent from the histories of the conflict. While established entertainers such as Harry Lauder, Lena Ashwell and Ellaline Terriss published their wartime memoirs, too many voices are missing.[19] As Sir Walter Raleigh's official history *War in the Air* underlined in 1922, official records do not in themselves make history, that they are 'colourless and bare'.[20] This lack of texture was still felt in 1963, when veteran RFC pilot Sholto Douglas complained that books written about the war were 'lacking in a feeling for the temper of that time' which have reduced the most intense experiences 'to the dull level of clinical research'.[21] However, the words of R. H. Mottram should also be kept in mind. In 1924, in the preface to his *Spanish Farm Trilogy,* Mottram warned that studies of the conflict should beware of making the war appear as 'fabulous, misunderstood and made romantic by distance'.[22] Nevertheless, servicemen's songs and music which were widely sung and played during the Great War form key topographical features in the landscape of Britain's memory of 1914–18.[23] They have become *lieux de mémoire* (sites of memory).[24] However, certain creative interpretations including Great War songs, such as the stage play and subsequent film *Oh! What a Lovely War* (1969) have twisted the musical memory of the conflict away from the history of the music concerned, telling us more about the social, cultural and political conflicts of the 1960s than the songs and music of 1914–18.[25] *Tipperary* for example 'was never greatly sung', highlighting the fact that it was propagated by the *Daily Mail* correspondent, George Curnock, who reporting from Boulogne heard soldiers of the BEF singing the song 'instead of another equally popular, which the same troops started up a few miles farther on'. As a result, 'a hitherto unknown and unwanted song of such mediocre worth . . . was never Tommy's song'.[26] A visitor to the fighting fronts was much more likely to hear the strains of *Annie Laurie.*[27]

The musical lives of servicemen were studied during the course of the conflict. Some already understood that the voice of British soldiers, sailors and airmen were distilled in the songs that were sung on the fighting fronts, for example Second Lieutenant Frederick Nettleingham's *Tommy's Tunes* (1917) and *More Tommy's Tunes* (1918). Interest in servicemen's music continued after the war. In 1927, *Air Force Songs and Verses* was published to raise money for the RAF Memorial Fund and featured 54 RFC/RAF squadron songs with another 27 from the period of the Great War and Armistice. In 1930, Western

Front veterans John Brophy and Eric Partridge published *The Long Trail:
What the British Soldier Sang and Said in The Great War of 1914–18.*[28]
Their survey of soldiers' songs found that most came from private soldiers, songs of 'homeless men, evoked by exceptional and distressing
circumstances; the songs of an itinerant community, continually altering
within itself under the incidence of death or mutilation'.[29] The desire to
collect and preserve servicemen's songs continued after the Second
World War. Published in 1945, the *Airman's Song Book: Being an
Anthology of Squadron, Concert Party, Training and Camp Songs and Song-
Parodies [. . .]* aimed to preserve the songs and therefore 'the traditions
reflected in them'. The author stated that as 'the sailors had their shanties
and the "brown types" their marching refrains' the airmen 'had written
their own history' in their songs. These are songs and ditties purely
composed by, for and about airmen.[30] In 1960, Brophy and Partridge's
work enjoyed a second edition which featured more accurate lyrics to
many of the songs than had been permitted by their publishers thirty years
earlier.

The histories of the military music schools during this period are also
key to our understanding of the role of music in Britain's military
culture. There are just a handful of existing histories of music in
Britain's armed forces. While many of them are well-written, with
evident access to sources held in personal collections, few of them are
fully referenced works providing signposts for future scholars looking to
write the histories of Britain's military music institutions. The work of
Henry Farmer, Bandmaster of Portsmouth Division 1884–1917, and
Hector Adkins, of the Royal Military School of Music 1921–43, are still
acknowledged as the authorities on military music.[31] Former Army
bandsmen produced two histories of the Royal Military School of
Music, Kneller Hall; Lieutenant Colonel P. L. Binns's *A Hundred
Years of Military Music* (1959), and Gordon and Alwyn W. Turner's
The Trumpets Will Sound (1996). The study of the history of music in
the Royal Navy was opened by John Trendell's *A Life on the Ocean
Wave: The Royal Marines Band Story* (1990) and more recently John
Ambler's *The Royal Marines Band Service* (2003). Ian Kendrick's *Music
in the Air* (1986) contains relatively little information about the early
years of music in the RFC/RAF. The most authoritative recent work,
Trevor Herbert and Helen Barlow's *Music in the British Military* (2013),
examines the formal role of music in the British Army up to 1914 from
a musicological perspective.

In the last thirty years, some historians have opened studies into the
cultural life of Britain's armed forces. J. G. Fuller's *Troop Morale and
Popular Culture* (1990), Alex Revell's *High in the Empty Blue* (1995) and

Maryam Philpott's *Air and Sea Power in World War I* (2013) have shown that cultural history and military history are not mutually exclusive. Histories of the music of imperial troops, and non-British servicemen who fought for Britain in the Great War, have begun to appear. Music in the Canadian and Australian/New Zealand forces has been examined by Jason Wilson and Robert Holden.[32] The work of Anne Sampson, Dominiek Dendooeven and Santanu Das is also greatly contributing to this field.[33] Historians need to venture further into uncharted territory of the Great War, and music of all kinds is an area which has long been neglected. Historians should recognise the significance and usefulness of music because it is an intrapersonal process, a social phenomenon and a product of cultural influences and traditions.[34] Contemporary criticisms and analyses of music help us to locate musical practices, values and meanings in their cultural contexts. Recent studies of popular forms of music have proven to be particularly illuminating in terms of the genre's commercial, entertainment and leisure value.[35] Musical industries – encompassing the theatres, cinemas, music halls, music publishers, instrument makers and gramophone firms – were employing hundreds and thousands of people and making a significant contribution to the national economy.[36]

However, in today's archives items related to music are generally classified as 'ephemera'. Even in the largest national collections, those whose task it has been to make some order of the millions of items relating to the Great War have inadvertently consigned the historical traces of music and musicians to the margins of historical interest. The record keepers in post-Armistice Britain prioritised the maps, memoranda and battle-plans laid out by Commanders during those tumultuous, but ultimately victorious, years. This is eminently understandable. Britain had won a costly victory in 1918, and after the Treaty of Versailles was signed in June 1919, Britain hoped never to go to war again. Whatever records relating to music and musical entertainment which survived the culls of the 1920s and 1930s and were stored in the Public Record Office in Central London may have been among those destroyed by the Luftwaffe in the second world conflagration. The records of the various military music schools suffered from a different kind of attrition. As the British armed forces went through successive restructures in the post-1945 period, the documents relating to their activities in the Great War were lost or discarded along the way. Whatever survived was at the mercy of archivists' selective preferences throughout the twentieth century. Written in 1977, for example, the regimental journal of the Royal Engineers, *The Sapper,* is preceded by the disclaimer: 'References to some articles published has been omitted because, although providing good experience for the participants, the events can hardly be classified as being of historic value worthy of being referenced.'[37] Because of these selective practices and assumptions, surviving primary source material which documents the formal and informal musical activities of British servicemen during the Great War is scattered far and wide.[38]

However, the research presented here indicates that the War Office and Admiralty may have had very little to do with the organisation of musical activities; they were fighting the considerable might of the German Empire on land, at sea and in the air, and British civilians were for the first time being killed on British soil by German bombers and battleships. The music of the troops, not least for ceremonial, entertainment and recreational purposes, was not high on the government's priorities. The war was expected to be short, so there was no anticipation of any need to change the ways in which the British armed forces operated. No one in August 1914 could imagine how the war would develop into four years, three months and fourteen days of attrition, at incalculable human cost. Musical activities are rarely mentioned in official documents, for example unit war diaries, so the traces of music on the fighting fronts are mainly found in servicemen's letters, diaries, photographs, local and national press and regimental magazines. Oral testimonies are also useful. This is one of the reasons that it is very difficult to examine the musical cultures of non-white servicemen, such as the Labour Corps workers from India and China. With high rates of illiteracy, these men were not keeping diaries, and no one interviewed them to record their wartime experiences.[39] The main traces of their music have been found in the collections of voluntary-aid organisations that worked with these men. It was these agencies, such as the Salvation Army, British Red Cross – with the Order of St John of Jerusalem, and the Young Men's Christian Association (YMCA) – that filled the gaps that the British War Office and Admiralty were unable or unwilling to fill. They became the largest enablers and providers of music to the battlefronts as a natural extension of their work in camps, canteens, rest huts and hospitals. However, they were by no means the only organisations of their kind to be working in the battle zones. Other charitable groups active before the Great War extended their reach, such as the Seamen's Rests, the Church Army, the Dominion Comforts Fund, the Church of England Soldiers' Home, Army Scripture Readers, the Navy Mission Society and the British Soldiers Institute. The Salvation Army, British Red Cross and the Young Men's Christian Association, however, were the three largest groups both by their reach and by resources and personnel in serving the British forces wherever in the world they were fighting. A good deal of musical activity was encouraged, enabled, inspired or created by these organisations according to their own priorities. However, very few military historians have mentioned music or the work of voluntary organisations.[40] General aspects of the YMCA's wartime work have recently been subject to academic attention by historians such as Michael Snape and Jeffrey Reznick.[41] While these studies have done much to uncover the enormous efforts the voluntary-aid organisations made during the war years, this book builds on their work to examine the full extent of the provision of music for servicemen.

To the servicemen of the Great War, music was not ephemeral. It was entirely desirable, if not vital, to have both formal and informal music in all wartime contexts. The more we seek to understand the everyday wartime existence of British servicemen and women at war, the greater is the need to appreciate all aspects of their lives during the conflict. So many veterans spoke of the brass bands playing near recruiting stations, and as they went to war from camps, barracks and train stations. Many more recalled with great accuracy the words, both official and unofficial, to their regimental march, and who could sing the more respectable song lyrics to oral history interviewers in the 1960s and 1970s. We can now listen to these men singing their songs via online collections. We can hear how they edited and altered lyrics to suit their mood and identity, how the men could let officers know if they were dissatisfied with their leadership by the choice of their songs on the march, of the hymns that were sung to offer comfort (or comedy when the tunes were appropriated), tunes that reminded them of home, and of the songs composed as memorials to remember lost comrades. From the trenches, to aerodromes and ships, in medical settings and in prisoner of war camps, the power of music to amuse, reassure, inspire and to heal was recognised and valued.

That the fighting fronts were full of all kinds of music may come as a surprise. Private Charles Jacques, who served in Macedonia, wrote that many soldiers recalled 'happy evenings spent around an ancient and dilapidated piano in some billet or estaminet' when 'even the poorest singer was received with as much acclaim as if he were a very Caruso'.[42] Furthermore, as Coldstream Guards Bandmaster, John Mackenzie-Rogan underlined, music 'plays a great part in our lives at all times, . . . especially in great times of stress that its influence can be almost overwhelming'. Rogan maintained that 'the effect on the hearts and minds of the hundreds of thousands who heard the music was magical'.[43] As Scott Hughes Myerly's *British Military Spectacle* (1996) showed how military traditions such as uniforms and parades played a powerful role in the maintenance of soldier's morale and espirit de corps up to the Crimean War, we can see how in the Great War military bands continued to provide a central focus of a unit's tribal identity.

They were a major source of pride and enjoyment for the soldiers as well as anyone who witnessed the spectacle of a band leading a column of servicemen on the march, on parade, or showing off their prowess by 'beating the retreat'. Furthermore, recent works of history have reached previously unexplored areas of Great War history showing how sport and theatre were taken to servicemen to maintain morale.[44] Studies of music in the Australian and Canadian armies have been recently published.[45] Glen Watkins's *Proof Through the Night: Music and The Great War* (2003) studied predominantly American music during the time of the Great War, and John Mullen's *The Show Must Go On! Popular Music in the Great War* (2015) focused largely on popular music at home in Britain. This study will show that, much to the chagrin of some commentators from Britain's musical elite, music from home was highly prized in servicemen's concert halls, recreation huts, hospital wards, prisoner of war camps and mess rooms.

Chapter Overview

The structure of this book is organised to examine the formal and informal applications of music at work, at rest and at play. Chapter 1 will provide the context of how and why military music was coordinated in the period immediately before the outbreak of the Great War. It will briefly trace the beginnings of Royal Marines Divisional Bands in the Royal Navy during the late eighteenth century, as well as the founding of the Royal Military School of Music at Kneller Hall, and the Royal Naval School of Music at Eastney Barracks, explaining how bandsmen were recruited, trained and deployed, and why music was a vital element of the services' daily, ceremonial and wartime operations. This chapter will also engage with pre-war concerns expressed about the lack of music in Britain's armed forces, and the wider debates about the quality and direction of British music in the Edwardian period.

The second chapter will examine the use of music in recruitment and fundraising. It will show how military musicians were mobilised in the early days of war, and the ways in which commanders had to cater for the newly expanded forces. It will look at how the civilian music industry responded to the start of the conflict, and the ways in which bands, concerts and other musical events were used for the purposes of supporting the war effort. This chapter will also provide a survey of the work of various committees established to support both the music industry and individual musicians, all of whom sought to both protect and maximise performers' employment opportunities during the early years of the war.

Chapter 3 will move with the military bands, pipes, drums and Buglers to the fighting fronts. It will show the practical uses of music in the field and on board ships as an important marker for servicemen's daily schedules. This section will also outline musicians' roles in battle. It will show that while Bandsmen in regular infantry units often acted as stretcher bearers, those who enlisted from August 1914 and served in Territorial battalions did a great many other jobs. It will also show that the formation of bands was driven largely by the men themselves.

The fourth chapter will show how music played a key part in the unit's identity on land, at sea and in the air. The squadron songs of the RFC, for example, tell us a great deal about how airmen dealt with combat stress and fear.[46] The singing of songs on the march or at rest was a vital component of regimental identity as well as discipline.

Chapter 5 will demonstrate that music was a vital part of the daily routines of those interned in prisoner of war camps. The forming of orchestras and theatrical revues were a popular way of passing the time and maintaining morale, but in many cases musical activities were used by prisoners of war to conceal attempts to escape. This chapter will give examples of how prisoners of war used music as a means of keeping up their morale to stave off feelings of 'mouldiness', later identified as barbed wire disease.[47]

Chapter 6 will examine the role of music in religious worship and pastoral care on the fighting fronts. It will show how the singing of hymns was a central feature of several organisations' work in drawing men towards their religious services and pastoral care, and of how the hymns were deployed in times of great stress. It will show how many of the voluntary-aid organisations combined their own brands of practical Christian philanthropy and pastoral care to servicemen as a 'counter-attraction' to keep men away from less salubrious pursuits, as well as to educate and civilise servicemen and labourers fighting for Britain.[48] The seventh chapter will provide an overview of the ways in which music was used in medical settings during the war. It will outline how the British Red Cross, which was tasked by the War Office to coordinate the organisation and supply of British hospitals, ensured that provision was made for live and recorded music in the majority of their facilities. This chapter will also consider how the medical profession came to recognise that music was an aid to servicemen's recovery and convalescence. The experiences of civilian entertainers in military medical settings will also be examined.

Chapter 8 will look at the use of the Gramophone for both educational and recreational purposes, showing how this developing technology was used on the fighting fronts in the maintenance of servicemen's morale, as well as for medicinal and therapeutic uses in hospitals and convalescent homes.

The ninth chapter will provide a survey of the principle civilian concert parties which travelled to entertain servicemen throughout the war. The frontline tours undertaken by well-known entertainers such as Ellaline Terriss, Seymour Hicks and Harry Lauder will be examined, showing how their appearances on the fighting fronts boosted servicemen's morale but also how they played into a wider political agenda. Lena Ashwell's collaboration with the YMCA will be explored through the diaries and correspondence of a myriad of performers and war workers, providing a deeper analysis of personnel who were key to the success of the Ashwell productions.

The tenth chapter will examine the growth of servicemen's concert parties in the context of the rapid expansion of the fighting forces, and of the significant figures who were key to the provision of music for the purposes of recreation and amusement. This chapter will show that Britain's armed forces each had a strong tradition of musical entertainments solely by servicemen for their comrades which was much bolstered by men who had been professional performers before they enlisted. Furthermore, this chapter will show that servicemen used the pantomime form to reinforce their belief that they were fighting in a just war. Chapter 11 explains what happened to musicians and music in the British armed forces after the signing of the Armistice. As the true cost of war was counted, the individuals and organisations who had worked to raise the status and quality of servicemen's musical experiences throughout the conflict continued much of their work in the immediate post-war period. The book ends by showing how music was used to remember the dead, and explains the genesis of the first Festivals of Remembrance 1923–27.

It is time to recognise the wartime endeavours of British musicians who served King and Country during the Great War. This book will show that amongst so much fear and death, music exuded life, purpose, identity and belonging. The following chapters will demonstrate that music was not ephemeral; in all its different forms music was an essential and highly valued part of everyday life in Britain's armed forces during the Great War.

1　Music in Britain, 1914

Military Music

In February 1867, Queen Victoria 'received the sworn services of four-feet-seven of enthusiastic band-boy'. On a pay of eight pence per day, he joined the 11th (North Devon) Regiment of Foot and was posted to the depot companies at Parkhurst on the Isle of Wight. Like many others before and after him, the boy had followed his father into the ranks after hearing tales of adventure in distant lands. His great-grandfather had fought under Marlborough, his father joined the year before Waterloo, and his older brother had served in the Crimea and at the Indian Mutiny. With the other band boys, he shared his barrack room with many of the men's families, and his time was occupied with band practise, recruit drills on the square, route marches and the playing of the daily Tattoo.[1] Fifty-three years later, this band boy – John Mackenzie-Rogan – would attain the rank of Lieutenant Colonel, Senior Regimental Director of Music to the Brigade of Guards and the British Army.[2]

When Rogan enlisted, the average regimental Depot band consisted of flutes, drums and bugles massed together.[3] In some units, a bandsman was referred to as a 'Windjammer', a man 'whose mission in life was to apply wind to a musical instrument'.[4] Military music was mostly written by non-British composers. The foundations of the modern military band had been developed in Germany with the 'Harmonie-Musick' combination of two oboes, two clarinets, two horns and two bassoons. The Royal Artillery Band was formed along these lines in 1762 during the Seven Year's War where the Prussian army featured bands who could play wind instruments on the march. By the 1770s, most British infantry bands had groups of eight to ten players based on Germanic instrumentation. By the end of the eighteenth century, the side drum, played by a Marine, replaced the trumpet as a means of communicating orders aboard British naval ships.[5] In the period immediately before the Battle of Trafalgar, the captains and officers of the larger fighting ships recruited their own bands of string and woodwind players. The officers would pay for the instruments and the musicians' wages at the rate of an able sea-man. In 1801, the Earl of St Vincent, First Lord of the Admiralty, had a band of twenty-six musicians, most of whom came from Malta or Rome.[6] By 1800, three of the Divisional Bands of the Royal Marines had been established, and after the invention of the Kent Bugle in 1810, brass instruments could be played chromatically and took more promi-nent roles in the bands.[7] German musicians were held in high esteem. They were actively recruited during the mid-eighteenth century, repla-cing British bandsmen in the newly created bands of the Grenadier and Scots Guards.[8] Foreign bandmasters were also highly desirable. However, the War Office was resistant to the introduction of formal musical training owing to the costs involved. Apart from the bandmasters of the Royal Artillery and the Royal Military College, who were paid from central funds, the remaining bands were, as in the Royal Navy, under the jurisdiction of the officers of each regiment who recruited and paid for their bands privately. Furthermore, bandmasters at this time remained of civilian status and were not officially members of the regiment.

During the first half of the nineteenth century, Britain's military bands attained high standards. The Guards and the Artillery bands, being permanently based in London, could attract the best bandleaders, and their bandsmen could also work as players in leading orchestras. However, for the regiments of the line, whose existence policing Britain's imperial interests meant they were more peripatetic, the bands were the first to suffer. When the Crimean War began in 1854, large numbers of bandsmen sought alternative appointments, and only four of the twenty regiments who paraded at Scutari had a bandmaster. More chaotic, however, was that, owing to the decentralised structure of British military music, there was no standard instrumentation or tuning. At a Grand Review in Scutari in honour of Queen Victoria's birthday, the massed bands of the British Army played the National Anthem in front the General Staff of the allied forces. The performance was a disaster as individual bands played in different keys and even different arrange-ments. The Duke of Cambridge, the most senior member of the royal family present, was deeply embarrassed. As a lover of music, he decided that something needed to be done to improve the performance of British military bands. Various voices within the British military establishment agreed that the British were falling behind, particularly as the French army had already established a central college of music in 1836, the *Gymnase de Musique Militaire*. When the Duke of Cambridge became Commander-in-Chief of the British Army in 1856, he believed that a subscription system would be a more economical way to pay for the training of military bands at a designated location. In March 1857, the

Figure 1.1 Kneller Hall in the late nineteenth century. © Royal Military
School of Music.

first music students arrived at Kneller Hall (Figure 1.1) in Whitton,
Middlesex.[9] Despite some public criticisms about the cost of the scheme,
by July 1866, a report published by the *Journal of the Society of Arts* stated
that 'The objects contemplated in the foundation of the Military School
of Music have been successfully attained'. However, it found that while
the school had created a constant supply of trained performers for the
regimental bands, it was still deemed to be inadequate to the needs of the
service. Nevertheless, bandmasters were seen to have developed a greater
sense of permanency within the regiments and sharing in their espirit de
corps.[10]

However, in the Royal Navy, bandsmen were still being trained on the
job. The title 'Master of the Band' is in common usage from the 1830s,
but the additional rate of bandsman was not created until 1847. In 1863,
the senior ratings of Chief Bandmaster and Bandmaster (1st class Petty
Officer) were established but no qualifications or training were required.
However, later in 1863 the government granted £200 for the purchase of
instruments, and the first sixteen boys were entered for training as band
boys on wooden Boys' Training Ships where they were given elementary
musical training and formed into bands. When they were deployed to the
fleet they would also serve as magazine and powder men.[11] In 1867, the
Admiralty began to give grants to purchase instruments, thereby lightening the financial load of the band from ships' officers. In the annual

Figure 1.2   Musical drill on boys' training ship *Exmouth*, 1899.

report of 1871, seventy-two band boys were in training.[12] Bandmasters were given the rank of Petty Officer and band boys and bandsmen were designated 2nd class ratings. By 1874, Chief Bandmasters were present on most training ships and they were charged with carrying out the boys' musical examinations or 'inspections' twice a year. Life on a training ship for young boys was hard, and many, like Charles Sanderson, who joined the Training Ship *Exmouth* (Figure 1.2) at Grays, Essex, in 1900, came from orphanages. Practise took place in the sand lockers of the ship, ballast rooms located above the bilges. The sand was boarded over to prevent the boys sinking and light was provided by an 'eight-hour candle'. Practise was from 9 am until 11 am and from 1 pm until 3 pm each day.[13]

Many of the organisational changes that occurred in the bands of the British Army during the second half of the nineteenth century were mirrored by similar developments in the bands that served the Royal Navy. The designation of 'Bandmaster' had been introduced in both the Army and Navy in 1863, and, in 1874, it was instructed that civilians were no longer to be enlisted as bandmasters. Only men who had trained at Kneller Hall, or those in possession of the certificate of qualifications from that institution, could be designated as bandmasters. In the Navy, the Admiralty ordered the Adjutant General of the Royal Marines to inspect the bands of the training ships twice a year and grant certificates of competency to the Chief Bandmasters.[14] In 1889, the German conductor and composer Jacob A. Kappey was appointed as the official examiner of Student Bandmasters at the Royal Military School of Music, Kneller Hall. He had been selected by the officers of the Portsmouth Division as 'Master of the Band' in 1857, having previously served in the German Army before moving to England to take up the role of civilian bandmaster to the 89th Regiment of Foot, later called the 2nd Royal Irish Fusiliers.[15]

Meanwhile, in 1884, Vice Admiral Prince Alfred, Duke of Edinburgh, the Commander-in-Chief of the Channel Squadron, recognised that the standard of musicianship of bandsmen waiting allocations for ships was deteriorating due to the lack of opportunity to practise whilst they were held in Depot Ships. He suggested that bandsmen awaiting draft should be attached to the band of the Commander-in-Chief at one of the Home Ports. He went even further and suggested that a rota system be set up so that all men took their turn at sea service. The latter suggestions did not endear the Duke to commanders at the Home Ports since they were cultivating their own bands on the pattern of the Guards, the Royal Artillery and the Royal Marine Divisions – stable bands that offered inducements and privileges to the finest players, such as teaching or performing in leisure hours. His third suggestion was for a training school for music for the training and qualification of Bandmasters'.[16] However, musicians were not held in high esteem by the majority of the Royal Navy. They were regarded as 'idlers' and often given other work to do on board ship – such as midshipman's servants. Ships' Bands were the cause of growing unrest in wardrooms at the turn of the century as Royal Navy officers were still responsible for the financial upkeep of the bands, and in some cases the Bandmaster. In addition, many of the foreign Bandmasters and musicians 'were disinclined to take part in, or notice of, RN custom, tradition and discipline'.[17] It was the alienation of Royal Navy officers which drove the changes, combined with the realisation that the Army held music and musicians in much higher esteem and was therefore likely to recruit better musicians. In October 1902, an officer on the training ship *Mercury* outlined the differences between perceptions of music in the Army and Navy:

Boys are sent from here into the Army Bands, in preference to the Navy Bands. Some of the reasons being that the prospect for a Military Bandsman is far in advance of that of the Navy. Kneller Hall which is a military institution is a great advantage and there is no similar institution in the Navy. . . . The two services will not compare until the Bandsman afloat is placed on a similar footing to those on shore. . . . The Bandsman on board is generally an annoyance to everyone, except just at the time he is taking part in the Band. The Army Band boy is far better looked after and cared for. Also there are many opportunities for private engagements, which never come in the way of the naval men.[18]

In the British Army, the unit's band had come to play a central role in the Army's formal routines. This included disciplinary procedures such as the flogging and 'drumming out' of soldiers found guilty of various misdemeanors. Drummers were trained, as part of their duty, in the regulation manner of flogging. Soldiers charged with minor theft were sentenced to twenty-five lashes with cat-o-nine-tails. Deserters and men of bad character were 'branded' (tattooed) near the diaphragm with 'D' or 'BC' in the orderly room of the corps by the Drum-major (in infantry regiments) in the presence of the Adjutant and Medical Officer.[19] One month after his enlistment, Band Boy Rogan took part in a drumming-out ceremony, 'the last word in military degradation':

The prisoner under escort faced the parade the Colonel and the Adjutant, both mounted, stood close by, while the drums and fifes of the Depot battalion were formed up close at hand. ... The prisoner is handcuffed. A small drummer-boy steps out with a rope, with a running noose to it, and places the noose around the man's neck. The drums and fifes strike up that traditional tune, 'The Rogue's March' – and away goes the procession, the band first, and the rogue behind, led by the drummer-boy and his rope. ... The band makes for the barrack gate, and the rogue ... is given a vigorous farewell kick by the boy. The gate is slammed on him ... There is no more Army for him.[20]

After four years serving with the 2nd Battalion the Queen's (Royal West Surrey Regiment) in Poona, in April 1896, Rogan was appointed as the bandmaster of the Coldstream Guards. His band consisted of thirty-three performers, only eleven of whom were under the authorised establishment. Their duties consisted of playing in Hyde and Green parks, state concerts, drawing rooms at Buckingham Palace, Levées at St James's Palace and regimental or brigade sporting occasions. Private engagements included various shows and concerts in and around London and the big provincial towns.[21] However, Rogan felt hamstrung by smaller band numbers. He underlined that the War Office should 'let Tommy Atkins have his music, because all the bands are primarily *his* bands. They are intended for the soldier; the concert hall is only their secondary place'.[22]

In the aftermath of the Boer War, Britain's Army and Navy undertook various programmes of change and development. The Royal Navy continued to modernise but routine and tradition remained of central importance. Long spells afloat placed significant importance on maintaining the morale of the men. In December 1902, Admiral John (Jackie) Fisher, acted to reform the lack of discipline and poor-quality musical training in the Navy. A keen amateur musician, Fisher was supported by Prince Louis of Battenberg, Director of Naval Intelligence. However, they needed the support of the Royal Marines, specifically the bands of the Royal Marines Artillery and the Royal Marines Light Infantry, for the plans proposed by the Right Honorable the Lords Commissioners of the Admiralty put before the King in a memorandum of 20 May 1903.[23] The recommendations were approved and as a result a permanent Royal Naval Band Service was established as part of the Royal Marines, housed and trained at the newly created Royal Naval School of Music. Existing naval bands were disbanded, and new pay structures were introduced to be borne by the government. The former married quarters at Eastney Barracks, Portsmouth, were provided as a temporary home for the Royal Naval School of Music before a planned move to the permanent quarters at the Melville Hospital, Chatham.[24] On 22 July 1903, thirty-four musicians from the band of HMS *Impregnable* marched into Eastney Barracks and became the first band of the RNSM.[25] By 1913, the Musical Director of the RNSM was Captain Charles Franklin. He visited the charitable training establishments such as the training ships *Exmouth* and *Warspite,* and the Watts Naval School to examine boys for entrance to the RNSM, who would arrive at Eastney in groups of four and five. The boys normally joined at the age of fourteen years and stayed until they were seventeen and a half to eighteen, selected for a Band and sent on to H.M. Ships of War. Royal Marine Bandsman, H. J. Reed, enlisted in April 1913. On receiving his railway warrant on his fourteenth birthday, he travelled down to Eastney and recalled his arrival at the barracks:

Presenting myself ... all 4' 8½" of me – I was greeted with the words 'Move, cannon fodder', by the Sergeant of the Guard and conducted to the Music Director's office. ... I had to be sworn in with the Bible. After the simple ritual I was informed that I had actually signed on for sixteen years ... I had 3 years and 362 days to serve 'boys time', my actual service would start from the age of eighteen. ... So to Musical Stores for our instruments, and to the old Clock Tower near the gate for our uniforms.[26]

The average size of a cohort at Eastney was 150 students. They were housed in barrack rooms which each slept up to twenty-seven boys, where they would also take their meals and practise their instruments.[27] An 'old soldier', usually from the RMLI, helped with the boys' equipment, food and worked 'to make good soldiers' of the young recruits.[28] Pay parade took place every Friday, and the boys were paid 4/8d.[29] After breakfast at 7.15 every morning, the boys went on Parade at 7.55 for inspection and Infantry drill (Figure 1.3). Musical instruction commenced at 9 am on both of the boys' two designated instruments.[30] From the age of fifteen

ROYAL NAVAL BARRACKS, PORTSMOUTH.   *Russell & Sons, Photo,. Southsea.*
(Main Gates, showing Officers' Quarters.)

Figure 1.3 Royal Marines band at church parade at the Royal Marines barracks, Eastney.

and a half, all band boys, together with musicians and NCOs, met in the Concert Hall to practise the larger works of contemporary composers, and for the bandmasters class who took turns conducting the orchestra under the supervision of Captain Franklin. The boys took their GCE classes in the afternoon. Despite the demands of their schedule, at a time when paid leisure time was uncommon, Reed underlined that they were privileged to have three weeks paid holiday twice a year.

Victor Shawyer was born 'within bugle-call range' of the Rifle Depot barracks at Winchester. He followed his father, a Rifleman and bugler in the 1st Battalion, into the army.[31] After the death of his father, Shawyer enlisted as a boy at the age of fifteen years and nine months, and within a few weeks he was posted to Dublin. Shawyer was directed to the band where he observed their practice and parade drills. It was impressed upon him by the bandsmen that they were particularly successful at football, hockey and cricket.[32] Band boys slept eleven beds to a room, with a strict bedtime of 9.30 pm. Shawyer had no say in the choice of his instrument, and was told to play the clarinet with a minimum of five hours practise per day.[33] He gradually got used to army life although he did not much enjoy the food; the Band had separate messing, and a Rifleman from one of the companies was detailed as the Band's cook.[34] The bandsmen were spread over eight companies for purposes of pay and clothing and the occasional parade when they had to parade as Riflemen.[35]

Military discipline was rigorous, and bandsmen were ruled in the first instance by their Bandmasters. Shawyer and his bandmates were at the mercy of a bandmaster who 'was nothing less than a criminal brute to Band Boys. He had one method of instruction only, bash it into them'.[36] Bandmaster Barry had previously served with the band of the 16th Lancers. To the bandsmen of the 1st Battalion, Rifle Brigade, Barry was 'a half-insane, sadistic, murderous, bullying fiend, whose one aim in life was to inflict as much physical pain as he possibly could whilst teaching music'.[37] During band practise, Shawyer recalled that Barry would strike the knuckles of any boy who played a wrong note with the knob end of a soldier's cane. Shawyer emphasised that it was their Band Sergeant, Dimond, who was well respected by the band and held them all together.[38] In the spring of 1913, they were informed that the Band was to be inspected by Hector Adkins, Bandmaster of the 2nd Battalion, Suffolk Regiment, a recent graduate of Kneller Hall. This was one of the first band inspections carried out by representatives of the RMSM. The impending visit was a cause of great concern to Bandmaster Barry who drilled the band with all the test pieces specified, which included the overture to *Mignon*. Even in the early stages of his career, 'Adko' was described as 'a fierce-looking man' who sported a ginger moustache 'set over a pair of tightly-drawn lips which when parted revealed an array of fang-like teeth'.[39] When Captain Adkins arrived, he inspected the instruments, in terms of both the workings and their appearance, moving from the wind to brass section. However, Adkins did not request the band to play the set pieces but selected a random page from the band's programme book and instructed the band to play the pieces from the previous week's church parade. As the band played Adkins kept interrupting and asked them to skip to certain sections. Band boys were then tested verbally by Adkins on 'musical elements', a course of instruction completely neglected by Bandmaster Barry. Despite an evidently uncomfortable day, the band was deemed fit and two men were invited to Kneller Hall for the bandmaster's course.[40]

Edwardian Anxieties

Despite the increasing investment and professionalisation of the formal training of musicians in Britain's army and navy in the Edwardian period, there was a perceived lack of musicianship among the rank and file to the detriment of military morale and *esprit de corps*. In 1906, Surgeon-General George Evatt published the pamphlet *Our Songless Army: A Proposal to Develop the Singing of Marching Songs, Unison Singing, Part-Songs, and Choral Societies by the Soldiers of Our Regular Army, Militia, Yeomanry, Volunteers, Cadet Corps, and Boys' Brigades*.[41] He underlined that while

a great development of efficiency has spread through our army in its various branches, there is one accomplishment which is still quite in the background ... the ability of the soldier to sing a good song, or take his part in a stirring chorus, or on the line of march, or in camp to keep up singing in a really good style.[42]

By not being trained in this direction, Evatt claimed that 'the soldier and the army both suffer'. Evatt maintained that singing 'is essentially the helpmate of comradeship. It teaches the singers discipline, self-control, the power to combine with others for good work, it quickens the eye and the ear'. He went on say that 'if the songs be good, it can act in the highest degree on the *morale* of the individual soldier and on his love of his country and his regiment'.[43]

As a medical man, Evatt emphasised the 'health-giving power' of singing. He described how the act of singing works 'as a means of expanding the whole lung structure, and the breathing power is developed in a most marked degree. Every portion of the air passages is aerated, and oxygen drawn in to kill noxious matter'.[44] That the matter of singing in the army had been neglected for so long 'should be a matter of regret to every soul in the nation. The moment of awakening has ... now arrived'.[45] He repudiated the charge that Britain was an unmusical country by underlining that at the time he was writing there were 18,000 bandsmen in the Salvation Army, and thousands of civilian musicians playing in working men's clubs.[46] However, Evatt specified that soldiers should not sing music hall songs which are 'merely transitory'. As he states that singing and songs should be taught in all army outposts 'as a link to the land he serves and the country to which he belongs', it is preferably only folk songs and 'the traditional melodies which have survived for generations in his countryside ... only songs that have by their essential hold on the hearts of the people survived through long years should be sung by our soldiers'.[47] He insisted that the soldier is 'so intelligent, so awakened, so ready to receive every good influence ... that with proper conditions and suitable teaching the soldier will do his share in this moral and physical effort at betterment'. He appealed to officers to help:

In the far-away camp, in the lonely cantonment, on the distant outpost, on the march, or in quarters, on the troopship or on the convoy, in peace or in war, in the cholera camp or in the barrack room, England feels that every officer will do his duty in this most interesting movement for the awakening of her sons who serve in the army so far away from home and their people.[48]

Evatt pronounced that music 'is no longer the privilege of the few; it is now the heritage of the many'. He underlined that music was 'slowly evoluting within the army' and that it was 'only quite recently that the bands have been entirely State-supported, and in truth national bands', it was the bandmasters' duty to improve the musical life of the whole unit.[49] He recommended that soldiers learn to sing marching songs with the accompaniment of the band, and that it should be a priority for English, Scottish, Irish and Welsh regiments to arrange 'the songs of the country or the county from which the regiment comes'.[50] The matter of songs' musical quality and provenance was of the utmost importance. Evatt warned that 'nothing common, poor or mean should be sung under or around the national flag' and to do so would be 'to wound the Empire in its most vital part'.[51] Evatt also prescribed that every member of a unit should be able to sing the regimental song in unison on parade, and that quartet singing and regimental choirs should be established because 'the soldiers of the Empire should sing *en masse* before their fellow country-men and show of what stuff the army is made'.[52] Songbooks for marching music should be written and published: part one for boys and part two for soldiers. To every bugle call, Evatt recommended that words should be available for singing in camp at the close of the day so that 'in numerous ways, now not even thought of, singing and music can enter into the life of the battalion like sunshine illuminating everything on which it shines'.[53] Senior military figures appeared to agree. Major-General Robert Baden-Powell wrote that he was 'much struck when voyaging home from East Africa . . . with some German troops, to hear them singing patriotic songs and choruses in parts; such practice cannot fail to have good effects morally'.[54] Indeed, in the late 1900s it was 'well known that the Kaiser has done much to encourage the singing of Folk-songs in the German army with considerable success'.[55] Certainly, the efforts to encourage singing amongst the troops was understood as 'a custom almost univer-sally practised in foreign armies, and which tends to keep up a cheerful tone on the march and in camp'.[56]

British military figures such as Evatt expressed a strong desire to raise the tone and standards of British military music as a reflection of the rivalry between countries such as Germany and France. Several song-books were published in this period, including a new edition of the song-book *Scarlet & Blue* for the use of soldiers and sailors in 1909.[57] This was a later edition of John Farmer's *Scarlet & Blue* songbook for soldiers and sailors, which had been published in the 1890s. Farmer, working in Aldershot, had already expressed his concern for the musical life of the services, and he believed that music was something that 'should bind the two Services together in musical combination and friendly competition'.[58] Farmer strongly believed that group singing was an activity which worked to generate 'heartiness, good-fellowship and *espirit de corps*'.[59] This is evidenced by his work from the 1870s as the Music-Master of Harrow where he composed the school anthem *Forty Years On*.[60] In the 1880s, Farmer moved to Oxford to work as the organist at Balliol College where he established the practise of communal singing on Thursdays and published the *Balliol Song Book*. Farmer died in 1900, but the 'Farmerian tradition' was continued by some of his former pupils. This included Colonel B. R. Ward of the Royal Engineers, who had met Farmer as an undergraduate at Oxford, and then continued as his assistant during his work with the Army and Navy.[61]

Ward and several other of Farmer's former students formed the nucleus of the Central Council of the Naval and Military Musical Union (NMMU). A central committee was established in London, and branches were formed in various ports and garrisons. NMMU presidents included Surgeon-Generals George Evatt and Frederick Mott, and Lieutenant-General Sir Horace Smith-Dorrien. Other members of the central council included men from various military branches such as Field Marshal Lord Methuen, Admiral Sir Charles Drury, and Rear-Admiral Troubridge.[62] The Honorary Secretary of the NMMU was the author Major Arthur Corbett Smith. The objects of the NMMU were to promote choral and unison singing throughout the services, and to encourage friendly co-operation in music between the army and navy via singing competitions.[63] To balance the principle of competition between units, 'Glee Parties' would also perform at one another's concerts, and a song would be sung in unison by all competitors at the beginning or end of a contest.[64] The NMMU hoped that those already interested in 'glee singing' would 'draw together by natural gravitation the men whose tastes lie in the direction of music' which would also foster 'social enjoyment'.[65] Winners of the Branch Competitions would proceed to the finals of the annual John Farmer Championship Cup, held in Aldershot. A General Meeting, open to all officers, NCOs and men interested in music was held at the close of the concert season, enabling the Union 'to get in touch with the feelings of the rank and file, and to feel the pulse of democracy'.[66] Branch organisers were encouraged to measure, compare and judge one another's Glee Parties, 'by encouraging the systems that take account most effectively of heredity and provide the best environment' which would also 'ensure the best results attainable being reached in the future by their successors ... to give lance stripes to his fliers, raise the value of the average, and eliminate the unfit'.[67]

The Chatham branch of the NMMU was the first to give a public concert under the auspices of the union, in October 1909, the evening before the anniversary of the Battle of Trafalgar. This was due largely to the work of prominent NMMU committee members Colonel B. R. Ward of the Royal Engineers, and Lieutenant Colonel Charles Hope Willis of RMLI, Chatham Division.[68] At Chatham Town Hall, performances were given by the bands of the Royal Engineers and Royal Marines, the glee clubs of the Royal Naval Barracks, sailors from HMS *Tenedos*, and by solo vocalists and instrumentalists.[69] In 1912, the set pieces for the NMMU's festival at Aldershot for the John Farmer Championship Challenge Cup were announced as a part-song *Soldiers' Chorus* from Gourned's *Faust*, and the unison song *The Lass That Loves a Sailor*.[70] The 1912 competition was won by the Royal Engineers. The NMMU's annual report for 1912–13 recorded that there were four active branches of the Union at Aldershot, Portsmouth, Chatham and the Curragh. Centres had also been formed in other districts and commands, including Dorchester, Bodmin, Exeter, Winchester, Quetta, Weymouth, Cherat, Parkhurst, South Africa, and the China Station, with arrangements for an establishment of a centre at Gibraltar. The various singing competitions which had been held locally throughout the year were felt to have proved 'conspicuously successful'. After one of the London divisions of the Boy Scouts asked to be admitted to membership, the formation of a junior branch of the Union was under consideration. It was expected that the junior branch would also be open to Officers' Training Corps, Boy Scouts, Cadet Companies, and other schools. Requests for enrolment had also been received from several regiments of the Territorial Force.[71]

Royal Patronage for the NMMU was granted, on its second application, in May 1914.[72] The NMMU enjoyed wide support from in the Navy and the Army, and at the outbreak of war 'there were represented upon the central council every military command in the United Kingdom, the several Fleet units and certain of the overseas commands'. However, the majority of NMMU officials were mobilised for active service, even those like Lieutenant Colonel Charles Hope Willis who had retired by 1914 but voluntarily returned to the RMLI at Chatham to serve as a staff officer.[73] By 1915, the work of the union had stalled.[74] Nevertheless, by the outbreak of war, both the Royal Military School of Music at Kneller Hall and the Royal Naval School of Music at Eastney were providing the British Army and Royal Navy with trained bandsmen and bandmasters. It would be another four years before the Royal Flying Corps would establish its own music school once it became the RAF on 1 April 1918.

Civilian Music in 1914

In 1914, there were hundreds of thousands of musicians who earned their living by performing in music halls, theatres and cinemas, in addition to professional orchestras and dance bands. The average musician's wages were only just above those of an agricultural labourer, and working conditions were relatively hard. House musicians were expected to play for up to 4 shows a day plus rehearsals, in smoky auditoria which were often damp. This accounted for a 40 per cent death rate from tuberculosis among professional musicians.[75] When Britain declared war against Germany on 4 August 1914, many musicians joined the forces. There were at this time over 153,000 German immigrants in Britain, and a proportion of these people of German and Austrian origin worked as musicians, who were evicted from orchestras and, from August 1914, the process of arrests and internment began.[76] By May 1915, after the sinking of the *Lusitania*, anti-German sentiment was running high. For example, Edward Euler was a 45-year-old musician employed at the King's Theatre, Southsea. Euler had born in Britain to a British mother and a German father, but he had never been to Germany and nor did he speak German. Nevertheless he was detained under the Defence of the Realm Act for remarks he had made in the theatre, which his colleagues reported to the police.[77] After being held in custody, Euler was discharged on the grounds of insufficient evidence, but magistrates told Euler 'to leave the town at once'.[78]

Any person of Germanic origin had been under suspicion for some time, but the peripatetic nature of the musician's working life placed them under greater scrutiny in a country which had been beset by the fear of spies and invasions since the late nineteenth century. James Pratt described the visits of German musicians who came to play in his home-town of Aberdeen in the summers prior to 1914. The performers, he believed, 'were really spies in disguise . . . busy collecting information . . . about what was happening; fortifications, everything of that sort . . . At that time the Germans were infiltrating into British industry in a most remarkable manner'.[79] Captain Vernon Kell, the head of the Secret Service Bureau – known as MO5(g) and later MI5 – waged an intensive campaign to root out 'conspiracies to commit outrage'. During the first month of the war, the Metropolitan Police investigated 9,000 suspected cases but not one yielded any evidence of wrongdoing. Entertainers came under particular scrutiny. In July 1915, British censors intercepted four sheets of music being sent to Norway. It was discovered that they contained 'secret writing' giving detailed information about various aspects of the British war effort, such as strikes, conscription and possible military targets for German aircraft. One document shows the letter writer, who signed himself 'Cecil', asking his paymasters for more money so that he could gain information from his brother about 'Royal Navy movements'. In October 1915, 'Cecil', whose real name was Courtenay de Rysbach, was sentenced to life imprisonment for espionage.[80] One Home Office memo from July 1916 warned that 'there is reason to believe that the German Government is endeavouring to recruit circus-riders, music-hall performers, and persons on the regular stage for the purposes of espionage in this country'.[81]

The outbreak of war also led to anxieties about performing music by 'enemy' composers, although this proved to be relatively short-lived. The first of the annual Promenade Concerts organised by Sir Henry Wood, then at the Queen's Hall, was scheduled for Saturday 15 August 1914, nine days after the declaration of war. The work of Richard Strauss and other Germanic composers was removed from the programme and replaced by French, Russian and British works including the *Nutcracker* suite and *L'Après-midi d'un faune*. However, after Chappell, the music publishing house who ran the Promenade concert series announced that 'the greatest examples of Music and Art are world possessions and unassailable even by the prejudices and passions of the hour', and the music of Germanic composers was programmed in the remaining wartime Promenade concerts.[82] British piano manufacturers, however, found buoyant opportunities with the removal of new German pianos from the market'.[83]

Musicians and entertainers would experience difficulties caused by the disturbance of war.[84] Overall, musicians' standards of living rose in 1914–18 if they stayed at home which caused tensions between those who were serving in the forces. Music's role in fundraising took its toll on professional musicians, many of whom found themselves out of pocket when they agreed to play for fundraising concerts. The situation became increasingly acute as the war progressed. In November 1917, musicians' unions went on strike to protest against playing in charity concerts without pay, and the issue of performers' patriotic duties and economic value came to the fore.[85] The shortage of players increased demand for musicians, and in many instances Belgian and French musicians who had sought refuge in Britain filled the gaps left by enlistment and eviction. The elite musical scene in Britain became increasingly international. Many Belgian musicians arrived in London, in addition to artists from other nations including the Spanish cellist Pablo Casals and the Polish pianist Karol Szymanowski. Music and musicians from the allies of the British Empire were welcomed in Britain, although the rising number of foreign musicians moving into local house orchestras was a cause of some concern to musicians' unions. British music academies continued to operate. The Royal Academy of Music's magazine said that '[n]otwithstanding the great dislocation caused to our art generally by this devastating war ... the Academy has suffered but little. The entry of new students this term has quite exceeded our anticipations'. At the start of the conflict, two professors had been taken as prisoners of war and a small number of staff and students had enlisted in the forces.[86] The registers of the Royal Manchester College of Music, now known as the Royal Northern College of Music, also recorded buoyant recruitment figures over the course of the war.[87]

Mobilisation

On 18 July 1914, the Reserve Fleet had assembled for a review at Spithead as a test mobilisation. At the Royal Marines Barracks in Chatham, sergeants of the Royal Fleet Reserve arrived for eleven days' training. They enjoyed a smoking concert on 24 July in which vocal and instrumental items were performed by 'members of the mess and a few civilian friends'.[88] On 1 August 1914, buglers sounded the recall in Portsmouth and Gosport. Within days, twenty-four of them were detailed under Bandmaster Faithfull for the Royal Naval Division. Winston Churchill, as First Lord of the Admiralty, noted that for each ship a band 'must be provided' but that 'the quality is not important'.[89] All ships from the Reserve Fleet had a band detailed to them by the staff of the RNSM, and those yet to be allocated were called the 'Ready-men'. Band Boy Reed recalled the buglers 'riding round Portsmouth on their bicycles sounding the mobilisation call, in every street'. Bands, detailed for their various ships, were 'laying on their beds in full uniform, waiting to go'.[90] The Royal Naval School of Music at Eastney continued to ensure the provision of bands for the Fleet. By the end of 1915, the RM Band Service numbered 1,500 men of all ranks.[91] However, sixty-eight miles north, the Royal Army School of Music at Kneller Hall significantly reduced its music teaching. The official diary states, 'At 10.20 pm on this date 4th August the Order to Mobilise was received and arrangements were at once made to carry out the Mobilisation Regulations. All students (except three who belong to the Royal Artillery and Guards) and pupils over eighteen years of age were returned to their units, under War Office authority'.[92] Regimental bands were disbanded and musicians returned to the ranks to serve as stretcher-bearers, medical orderlies and combatants. As Bandmasters were exempt from being transferred to the ranks, thirteen of the most recent bandmaster graduates were recalled to the

RMSM with their band boys.[93] Kneller Hall switched its attention to the recruitment and training of boys from the age of fourteen so they had a few years training before they could be enlisted at seventeen and a half years.[94] In this way, the popular Wednesday concerts, which were open to the public, continued with the programmes reported in *The Broad Arrow: the Naval and Military Gazette*.

Bandmaster Rogan was on the annual summer tour of the provinces with the band of the Coldstream Guards. On 4 August they were performing in Stourbridge at the annual flower show. Rogan had been informed that the declaration of war was due at eleven that night, so he 'addressed the many thousands gathered round the band-stand and appealed to the young men to enlist and go forward to fight for their King and Country. All joined in singing "Rule Britannia" and "God Save the King." It was an impressive scene.'[95] The Band of the 1st Battalion, Rifle Brigade was also busy with public engagements. Bandsman Shawyer was expecting to depart for the bandmaster's course at Kneller Hall. However, on Sunday 2 August the band was rehearsing music from the opera *Maritana* when they were ordered to parade in full marching order at 8 pm. Band practise ceased at once. The bandsmen packed away their instruments and were on parade as riflemen.[96] They were sent to guard duties protecting submarine oil containers at Landguard Fort near Felixstowe.[97] This was Bandsman Victor Shawyer's first sentry duty, as up to that point 'Bandsmen were never called upon for any duty other than that which appertained to a Bandsman'. It was then that he and his colleagues realized that the orders of 2–3 August 1914 were 'no training stunt'.[98] Had it been, the Band would have taken their instruments along to enliven proceedings or, more likely, stayed behind in their various barracks'.[99]

On Monday 3 August, on sentry duty at 10 pm, Shawyer heard a cheer come from the Royal Naval destroyer, HMS *Amphion*, anchored a short distance off the beach. Shawyer thought he was hearing the end of a concert party on board, but when a naval officer landed shortly afterwards he heard him inform his senior officer that war had been declared between Britain and Germany.[100] On Tuesday 4 August, the 1st Battalion, Rifle Brigade marched to Felixstowe to entrain for Colchester, passing cheering crowds of holidaymakers.[101] All servicemen's leave was cancelled; the nation was at war. To break the monotony of confinement to the barracks, sport and music were essential activities which 'helped to pass away the time which would otherwise have hung very heavily. No one left in Barracks will be able to get in a growl about the band, for in addition to its selections on the parade they have taken their part in the concerts that have been arranged almost every other night in the theatre'.[102] However, the influx of reservists caused consternation among some of the regular units. This was particularly marked as regular bandsmen were accustomed to having their own barrack rooms for sleeping and music practice. Bandsman Shawyer and his colleagues were greatly irritated when they returned to their barracks to find that the Band's rooms were now being used by reservists who had 'turned barrack rooms generally accredited as the show piece of the battalion into an apparently old clothes and junk shop in some … bad slum'.[103] In Shawyer's unit, the Bandsmen's pristine review tunics and carefully creased black trousers were strewn into corners, with personal items and pieces of kit going missing. Shawyer was particularly annoyed to find a reservist lying on his bed amidst the mess and chaos, and he recalled that there was 'more than one case of strong feeling and hot words between the newly returned Windjammers and those reservists … and at least one Bandsman had to be forcibly restrained from starting a fight'.[104]

At Colchester, Shawyer was 'annoyed' not to be posted abroad with the battalion. He was one of twelve bandsmen aged eighteen to twenty years old who were kept at the Rifle Depot, and on Saturday 15 August, Shawyer said goodbye to the remainder of the Band departing for France.[105] Shawyer and the remaining bandsmen were sent to Minster on the Isle of Sheppey with the 5th (Reserve) Battalion, Rifle Brigade. The HQ was in the workhouse. Bandsmen were posted to different companies around the island, with Shawyer based at Eastchurch to guard the deserted coastguard station at Shellness. He was then asked to work with the territorials of the Royal Engineers who were operating the telephone switchboard at Shurland Hall. The other bandsmen were given a variety of duties and Shawyer was soon the only bandsmen left on Sheppey.[106] In September, Shawyer was upset to read the first casualty reports from France, seeing his fellow bandsman, the 'quiet, capable' cornet player Percy 'Jack' Merritt listed as killed, just eleven days after Shawyer had bid him goodbye.[107] In mid-September, as the BEF suffered increasing casualties, men like Shawyer who had completed their training were drafted for overseas service. When Shawyer joined the parade at Eastchurch he was delighted to be reunited with his band colleagues. They entrained for Southampton and sailed to France with other regiments including the Guards, Middlesex, the Royal Artillery, Kings Royal Rifles, Seaforths and Gordon Highlanders.[108]

Royal Marines Band concerts were used to give servicemen a good send-off. In Chatham, on 10 September, a concert was arranged by Colonel Marchant as a farewell to the Chatham Battalion. The programme 'was highly appreciated by the vast audience which assembled on this auspicious occasion. Among the artistes were some well-known professional singers who kindly gave their services free'.[109] The reputation and popularity of the Royal Marines band was in itself enough to attract recruits. The *Globe & Laurel* informed its readers that 'A letter was received ... from a civilian bandsman in Western Canada, who ... desired information as to joining the R.M.B. Service. This shows the right spirit, and we hope to see him at Eastney shortly'. Clearly it was an attractive prospect to join up as a Bandmaster of the Royal Marines. Among numerous applications received from prospective recruits, one 'claimed to be competent conductor, and evidently expected to join as a Bandmaster straight away'. They thought that the man 'may imagine that so long as a man can wield a baton more or less effectively, no other qualification is necessary. Nevertheless, we still have hopes'.[110]

In London, the bands of the Brigade of Guards played every day for troops in the London barracks and on the way to the stations, at Horse Guards Parade and in Trafalgar Square. Among the new recruits was the 29-year-old composer George Butterworth. On 1 September 1914, Butterworth had attended the recruiting office at Scotland Yard and enlisted in the Duke of Cornwall's Light Infantry. When the recruits reported for duty the next morning at Horse Guards Parade, they 'marched off triumphantly to Charing Cross Underground Station, headed by a brass band and much stimulated by the cheers of the crowd'.[111] However, this was not the case for every batch of new soldiers. Rogan recalled that 'it was felt, and rightly, that there was not enough martial music; thousands of recruits marched through the streets without even the sound of a drum to cheer them on their way'.[112] Where territorials and new army units were yet to organise a band, the local Salvation Army branch was often called in to give the men a decent musical send-off. On one Sunday morning in early September 1914, for example, the Mayor of Camberwell asked the Salvation Army Nunhead Band to accompany 700 recruits on their march to the station. The scene was described as follows:

The recruits were lined up in marching order ... The Captain and Mayor then spoke a few words of farewell to the men and wished them 'God Speed' after which with lusty lungs and hearty voices, 'God Save the King' was sung, accompanied by the Band. The playing was greatly appreciated by the thousands of people gathered together outside the school and all along the route to Waterloo ... Inside the station yard the Band lined up, and as the dear fellows walked by, some with tears streaming down their faces as they looked back at the loved ones they were leaving perhaps for ever, played 'Auld Lang Syne', several, I noticed, tried to brush the tears aside and joined in singing the well-known words ... but it was only a broken-voiced effort. How the crowds cheered as the final party went by ...

Scores as they passed us murmured 'God bless you' ... One dear fellow shouted
'Pray for us', evidently voicing the feelings of them all.[113]

After the Salvation Army's Regent Hall Band had played to a large crowd
of civilians and soldiers at Oxford Circus, the Band proceeded to the large
new premises of the YMCA off Tottenham Court Road, where
a regiment of the Royal Fusiliers was preparing to leave for Malta. As
the Band approached playing the *Marseillaise*,

the huge crowd congregated in the street and the 'Tommies' on the balconies and
roof and at all the windows gave it a tremendous reception. ... Perhaps the most
striking request was when a stalwart young private pushed his way through the
ring and in a broken voice told the Bandmaster that the soldiers inside were
anxious that the Band should play 'God be with you till we meet again'. This
was done, the whole concourse of civilians and soldiers joining in, many of the
friends with tears streaming down their faces.[114]

However, the outbreak of war also had a marked impact on the activities
of Salvation Army Bands. Younger men who were reservists were called
up, and more were 'taken away from the practice room and the platform
to assist in the task of mobilisation'.[115] Salvation Army Bands in areas
near naval dockyards were particularly badly affected. In Chatham, the
Salvation Army Band 'has suffered considerably as the result of European
complications, as it is almost entirely composed of Dockyard Men'.[116] In
Govan, on returning from their services on Sunday 9 August, 'orders were
received for them to proceed at once to their headquarters and hold
themselves in readiness for service ... hundreds of her citizens being
called on to work night and day, Sundays included, getting warships
ready. Numbers of our Soldiers and Bandsmen are amongst those thus
engaged'. Bandsman Thomson, a member of the Naval Reserve, had
a cordial send-off, his comrades singing *God be with you till we meet
again*.[117] As the first waves of British servicemen went to war, no one
could know how long the war would last, or of the number of men who
would not return. As the casualty rate increased, and the volunteers
dwindled, music of all kinds was used to encourage men to enlist, and
to raise money to fund the war effort. The next chapter will show how
music proved to be a vital ingredient to wartime recruitment and
fundraising.

2   Recruitment and Fundraising

Music was a powerful component of recruitment and fundraising campaigns. Military bands and gramophones playing patriotic music and popular songs were used to attract crowds and encourage men to enlist, and the ability of music to draw attention to the call for both men and money was used throughout the war. As the British armed forces suffered increasing numbers of casualties, considerable social pressure would be brought to bear on men to volunteer, and those who did not risked vilification as 'shirkers' or cowards. However, before conscription was introduced with the passing of the Military Service Act in January 1916, in the earlier stages of the war music could draw men toward the recruiting stations and entice them to join the colours. Indeed, one officer who volunteered admitted that he was not sure 'that the determining factor was not the playing of national airs in Trafalgar Square by the band of the Irish Guards on a sunny morning in June'.[1] Singing would be a feature of meetings to encourage recruitment, for example those arranged by branches of the Parliamentary Recruiting Committee. Established in October 1914, the PRC was chaired by the prime minister, Herbert Asquith, and deployed the techniques of mass advertising used by companies before the war to get more men into the forces. The PRC used local political party associations to form a network that coordinated the circulation of approximately 54 million posters, leaflets and other publications, 12,000 meetings and 20,000 speeches.[2] Their published leaflets included a *Patriotic Song Sheet* that featured the lyrics of a range of songs. In addition to *God Save the King, Rule Britannia, Hearts of Oak, Land of Hope and Glory, Three Cheers for the Red, White & Blue* and *The Old Brigade*, expressly Scottish and Welsh songs were featured such as *Scots, Wha Hae, Auld Lang Syne, Land of My Fathers* and *Men of Harlech.*[3]

As the majority of bandsmen in regular Army units were on active service, the lack of suitably martial music was recognised. By March 1915, it was said that 'in France the inspiration of noble sounds and memories has been needed', that officers 'have been asking for *music*, bands to march the men to battle' because 'thousands have marched off in

Figure 2.1 John Mackenzie-Rogan, Bandmaster of the Coldstream Guards. © Coldstream Guards Association.

silence'.[4] The band of the Coldstream Guards continued to fulfil its private engagements to stimulate recruiting. Rogan (Figure 2.1) stated that he had been asked by the War Office to appeal for men at concerts, so he wrote to town mayors who readily accepted his proposals.[5] Rogan recalled that the programmes were 'mostly of a patriotic kind'. In the middle of each concert, Rogan arranged for a speaker to address audience 'after which I would call on the young men to rally round the flag and support the Government and the King's Navy and Army'.[6] At Sunderland, where recruiting was said to be slow, the Town Clerk asked Rogan 'to put more life into it'. The Coldstreams gave a few concerts to audiences of thousands, then announced they would tour the town on the top of a tramcar between 12 noon and 1 pm. This they did, in a tram 'decorated with the flags of the Allies and playing patriotic airs'. As people 'were pouring in thousands from their workshops and offices . . . on their way home to dinner', Rogan was happy that they had 'intercepted them beautifully'.[7] Local authorities told him that around 50,000 people had attended, and their singing had drowned out the band. The next day, Rogan and the band moved on to South Shields. When he invited the audience to sing *Rule Britannia* he 'caught sight of a large detachment of the British Fleet passing along the coast not far from the shore. At once I drew the attention of the twenty or thirty thousand people to the inspiring spectacle and said that I thought no moment was more picturesquely appropriate for the singing of "Rule Britannia."'[8] In Edinburgh, at the Annual Chrysanthemum Show in Waverley Market, the Coldstream band played to 15,000 people. Rogan underlined that the result of these and many other such visits 'was highly gratifying ... for at the headquarters of the Coldstream Regiment the Colonel Commanding received many letters stating that our work had given a very great stimulus to recruiting'.[9]

There was 'still great need for more bands and more music'. It was widely felt that 'nothing could be more depressing than for bodies of men to be marching about without a note of music to inspire them'.[10] The issue of recruitment was particularly acute as the matter of conscription was still being hotly contested (Figure 2.2). Yet the task of establishing bands for the purposes of recruitment was driven not by the War Office but by private enterprise. In January 1915, Rogan was invited to a meeting at De Keyser's Hotel to discuss plans for recruiting bands and bands for the new armies. Rogan recalled that this first meeting was proposed by the author Douglas Sladen. The attendees included Sherriff Cart de Lafontaine – director of the newspaper *Music Student*, Sir Charles Johnston – the Lord Mayor of London, and many prominent citizens and musicians. Later that month the Lord Mayor called a meeting at Mansion House. Rudyard Kipling was the main speaker, and he gave an insight into the role of a soldier's band:

No one, not even the Adjutant, can say for certain where the soul of the battalion lives, but the expression of that soul is most often found in the Band. It stands to reason that twelve hundred men, whose lives are pledged to each other, must have some common means of expression, some common means of conveying their moods and thoughts to themselves and their world. The Band feels the mood and interprets the thoughts. A wise and sympathetic bandmaster – and the masters I have met have been that – can lift a battalion out of depression, cheer it in sickness, and steady and recall it to itself in times of almost unendurable stress.... Any man who has anything to do with the service will tell you that the battalion is better for music at every turn; happier, more easily handled, with greater zest in its daily routine, when that routine is sweetened with melody and rhythm ... melody for the mind and rhythm for the body.[11]

In February 1915, Johnston published an appeal in the *Daily Telegraph*: 'to shorten the war we wanted millions of soldiers, to get the soldiers we wanted music, and to have the music we wanted money'.[12] The Chairman of the Recruiting Band Committee was Sheriff Cart de Lafontaine.[13] Kipling donated 'considerable sums from his friends' and also the proceeds of an illustrated volume of his *Songs of the English*. William Waldorf Astor, the American press magnate, donated £5,000. The War Office was said to have 'officially sanctioned' the movement and that there 'would soon be a dozen bands in khaki at work in London' with 10 per cent of the money raised given to 'helping country bands'. By early

PUNCH, OR THE LONDON CHARIVARI.—FEBRUARY 3, 1915.

WHO FORBIDS THE BANDS?

[" A band revives memories, it quickens association, it opens and unites the hearts of men more surely than any other appeal can, and in this respect it aids recruiting perhaps more than any other agency."—MR. RUDYARD KIPLING at the Mansion House meeting promoted by the Recruiting Bands Committee.]

Caption: Who Forbids the Bands?
['A band receives memories, it quickens association, it opens and unites the hearts of men more surely than any other appeal can, and in this respect it aids recruiting perhaps more than any other agency.' Mr Rudyard Kipling at the Mansion House meeting promoted by the Recruiting Bands Committee.]
3 February 1915   Credit: Punch Cartoon Library / TopFoto

Figure 2.2 'Who forbids the bands?' *Punch*, 3 February 1915.

March 1915, the fund had raised over £10,000. By spring 1915 there were said to be eleven or twelve bands which each cost £54 per week to maintain, approximately £600 overall. The *Daily Telegraph* asserted that if the National Bands movement was to succeed 'on a scale worthy of the great patriotic object which it is designed to serve – the provision of more money by the public is absolutely necessary'. The need was 'beyond question; can it be doubted that the public ... will yet see to it that our Army shall enjoy the stimulus of good music when any of its units set out upon a march, conscious at the same time that they are providing an attraction which will bring many more men to the colours?'[14]

Rogan served on the Recruiting Band executive committee. Auditions were held to select band and bandmasters, with retired soldiers forming the majority of those who came forward. The main duty of the Recruiting Bands was to play men from recruiting offices to railway stations, and on their journeys to training centres. They also played for wounded soldiers and sailors at various hospitals. Three bands were kept for duty at Whitehall, and the War Office granted permission for the bandsmen to wear uniforms similar to service dress. Rogan examined and conducted the first eleven bands on Horse Guards Parade to prepare for inspection by the King at Buckingham Palace.[15] Meanwhile, they continued to appeal for funds. On 8 March 1915, a concert to raise money for the Recruiting Bands was held at the Egyptian Hall, Mansion House. Tickets were priced at half a guinea each. Lena Ashwell appeared on the bill, along with several professional performers, 'Recruiting Band No.III' and a 'Recruiting Pipe Band'.[16] Ashwell also spoke at a number of other similar patriotic meetings, for example at the 4th Battalion Central London Regiment Volunteers at the Royal Institute of British Architects on 13 July 1915.[17] Henry Walford Davies and his male voice choir gave a concert for the Lord Mayor's Recruiting Bands Fund at the Royal Chelsea Hospital on 17 July 1915. The Coldstream Guards and other Guards' regiments and the massed recruiting bands were also 'helping' with a 'grand military tattoo' planned for the evening.[18] Later that month, there was a large recruiting rally for the London Territorials, the 'Terriers', in Trafalgar Square, 29 July 1915. Approximately 2,000 recruits were on parade, watched by soldiers on leave from the front. It was reported, 'Many bands accompanied the contingents as they marched yesterday through Central and West London, and the rally had a beginning almost more brilliant than the organisers anticipated.'[19]

Bands would play some recruiting songs which dated from 1870.[20] Leslie Stuart's *Soldiers of the Queen* and Rudyard Kipling's *The Absent-Minded Beggar* would have been heard. Many critics wanted soldiers to be singing *Rule Britannia, Men of Harlech, Scots wha hae* or *The Minstrel Boy* depending on where they came from. Some members of Britain's elite musical scene were concerned about the baser nature of popular music. The composer Sir Charles Villiers Stanford tried to get military bands to play old folk songs such as *Lillibulero* – a song made popular during the Marlborough Wars, and the Oxford University Press published six patriotic *Songs of War*, all of which, according to *The Times*, 'ought to have a sure place in every camp repertory'.[21] By September 1915, however, the Recruiting Bands scheme was in danger of collapse. The Lord Mayor Charles Johnston wrote to the national press to appeal to the public to donate further funds to the scheme that was by then 'almost exhausted'. Johnston outlined that it would be 'a calamity' if the Recruiting Bands committee were forced to terminate the bandsmen's engagement which would 'turn adrift some 150 professional musicians' with the effect of depriving soldiers of 'helpful military music' which would also 'materially affect the cause of recruiting'. Reiterating the scheme's slogan, 'To get the soldiers we want music – to have the music we want money', Johnston pleaded with the public to continue donating to the fund.[22]

At this time Rogan was asked by the War Loan committee in London to prepare a scheme of music for the main meetings in and around the capital.[23] He emphasised that 'if you can get a man to *give his life* for his country by appealing to his heart through his national airs, it ought not to be difficult to induce him by the same emotional means to *lend his money* to the country at an unprecedented rate of interest!' The Guards bands played in the City of London 'so that they might be charmed into opening their pockets and putting their savings and their earnings into the great War Loan'.[24] The first fundraising event was held on the steps of the Royal Exchange. As had become his habit, Rogan addressed the crowd and said that the Germans had given them 'a trump card':

I had managed to get hold of a copy of the 'Hymn of Hate' and it had occurred to me that my fellow-countrymen would be both interested and tickled to hear it. . . . I explained to the people that the music was clever and suited the words admirably, but I warned them that neither words nor music had humour. Then the band of the Coldstream Guards played the 'Hymn' – packed full of hate, as the Germans played and sang it.

In the *second* verse, however, I had deliberately garbled the music in such a way that, while the 'Hymn of Hate' was still in progress, it was constantly being interfered with by phrases of the 'Marseillaise,' 'Rule Britannia,' 'Highland Laddie,' 'Dixie,' 'If you want to know the time, ask a Policeman,' 'The Old Kit Bag,' 'Another Little Drink,' and other popular things. This second verse I called 'The reply to the Hymn of Hate from the British and French trenches.' It was received with an uproar of applause.[25]

Rogan addressed the crowd to inform all those who could invest to march behind the band to the Mansion House where they could make their payments. He recalled that 'thousands followed and, while they waited their turn outside the Mansion House, the band kept the enthusiasm at concert pitch by playing patriotic music'.[26] The band moved on to Trafalgar Square as the next 'scene of our operations'. They played in this location several times during the floating of the War Loan. Rogan emphasised that all the bands in London at the time 'took some part in the meetings and this musical propaganda in connection with the War Loan proved highly effective'.[27] In this way, military bands and their music formed part of the theatrical staging of outdoor events in public spaces which produced an ideal atmosphere for recruiting and fundraising purposes.[28]

The bagpipes were valuable recruiting instruments. In 1915, the Scottish music hall star Harry Lauder assembled his own band of pipes and drummers to go on a recruiting drive of Scotland after visiting his son's battalion on active duty. 'What stirs a man's fighting spirit quicker or better than the right sort of music?' Lauder asked. He stated that 'enormous crowds followed my band' and that it 'led them straight to the recruiting stations'.[29] Lauder's band was composed of fourteen pipers and drummers in Highland uniform, and they played old hill melodies and songs of Scotland. Lauder did not travel with the band. Instead he went on tour 'without official standing, going about urging every man who could to don khaki. I talked wherever and whenever I could get an audience together and I began then the habit of making speeches in the theatres, after my performance' (Figure 2.3).[30] Lauder recalled in 1918 that 'I and my band together influenced more than 12,000 men to join the colours'.[31] Lauder's recruiting drive also reached Canada to where thousands of Scots had emigrated in the decades before 1914.[32] The Reverend Lauchlan MacLean Watt also took his bagpipes on a fundraising tour of Canada and America. In February 1918, the Church of Scotland Minister who had served for two years on the Western Front with the Gordon Highlanders and the Black Watch played at 200 meetings to raise over £25,000 for the Liberty War Loan.[33]

Civilian Musicians

In the summer of 1914, leading members of the theatre industry mobilised themselves in support of the war effort. The actress Ellaline Terriss said there was much to do: 'hospital work, matinées to be got up, for the less seriously wounded and the convalescent. There were bazaars to organise, working parties to be arranged, recruiting songs to sing – when asked – all very small affairs compared to the great struggle itself ... but still we felt they were part of the great machine'.[34] However, once war had been declared, many professional performers felt that they were expected to work for free.[35] Some of the biggest names in British music acted to rectify this situation. The celebrated contralto Clara Butt, for example, toured the United Kingdom with

Figure 2.3 IWM HU 51838: Harry Lauder with two pipers of the Scottish Field Ambulance. © Imperial War Museum.

small concert parties in aid of charities like the Red Cross, specifying that the performers were paid. By 1918, the *Daily Telegraph* estimated that Butt had raised £42,000 for the war effort, today's equivalent of just under £2.5 million.[36] After his offer of working as an interpreter for the War Office was refused, the composer and singer Isidore de Lara founded War Emergency Entertainments. Based at Claridge's Hotel in London, the WEE held 'tea matinées' at various hotels in the capital, and a number of concerts for civilians and soldiers. Like Butt, de Lara ensured that artists were paid a minimum fee of £1 for every concert. Approximately 1,300 concerts were organised by the WEE by the end of the war.[37]

The Music in Wartime Committee was founded in the autumn of 1914 by notable figures in the British musical establishment. Chaired by the composer Hubert Parry, the MWC included H. C. Colles – music critic at

The Times, W. W. Cobett – business and patron of chamber music and composition plus an amateur violinist, Ralph Vaughan Williams, Henry Walford Davies, A. H. Fox Strangways of *The Times*, and W. G. McNaught – editor of *The Musical Times*. The principle aims of the MWC were to counter the war's threat to musical activities, to give assistance to musical organisations, and to maintain a register of musicians looking for work. Henry Walford Davies toured military camps with a male voice choir under the aegis of the MWC to promote musical participation amongst servicemen. In early 1915, they joined with individuals working in this area Annette Hullah (musical entertainment for servicemen's families) and Mary Paget (fundraising for soldiers' music), also the Professional Classes War Relief Council. Committee became the PCWRC's musical section, which enabled the committee to extend its focus into helping musicians whose paid employment had been affected by the war. Auditions were held at the Royal College of Music. No men of military age or fitness were eligible, and only the very best performers were accepted. From the autumn of 1914, concerts were given in camps and military hospitals, social clubs for servicemen's wives, and lunchtime concerts for munitions workers. To assist their work, the PCWRC were given a subsidy by the British Red Cross in 1916. On winding up in 1920, 6,785 concerts had been given and artists had been paid tens of thousands of pounds.[38]

The Soldiers' Entertainment Fund was established in February 1915 by the writer and composer Lyell Johnston. The SEF concentrated at first on giving concerts in hospitals, and by May 1919, 750 artistes had performed 2,000 concert parties in London and the surrounding area. The SEF sponsored one excursion to a naval base in Malta in 1916, followed by a visit to a large hospital garrison for injured from Eastern Front.[39] Other bodies such as the United Services Welfare Committee sent comforts to troops in Egypt in the form of literature and gramophones. To raise money for the USWC they held a fundraising concert at the Sultanieh Opera House where the profits were split between the USWC and the YMCA's work with Lena Ashwell for 'Concerts at the Front'.[40]

Lena Ashwell (Figure 2.4) opened the Three Arts Club and the Three Arts Emergency Relief Fund for Women to assist 'Women Workers affected by the War' defined as 'those dependent on their livelihood on the Arts [who] are already suffering severely'.[41] Ashwell reflected that the moment war is declared 'artists are a useless burden on the community ... there is a vague feeling that, but for the brutality of the expedient, they would be better exterminated. There would be many unbelievers if anyone boldly asserted that music is as necessary to

Figure 2.4 NPG x85237L: Lena Ashwell in 1916. © National Portrait Gallery.

the human being as beef or boots'.[42] She explained that when she was a student at the Royal Academy of Music 'the common lot of the woman artist was filled with sordid discomfort, lack of food, and aimless wandering in the streets between lesson and class rehearsal and performance'. Ashwell recalled that the 'foolish waste of time, waste of energy, waste of creative power' made her determined to found 'some sort of [women's] club' in a central part of London.[43] The Committee worked with the Actors' Benevolent Fund, the Women's Emergency Corps, the Ladies' Theatrical Guild, and the Women's Employment Committee to liaise between those looking for employment and those who could offer paid work or training. Gifts of money or offers of employment or training were requested, and contributions could be 'earmarked for the benefit of any specified class of workers'.[44] They stated that 'distressing cases' had come to the notice of the Committee, and in spite of the efforts of all concerned to maintain the normal levels of employment, the resources were nearly exhausted. Ashwell's main intention was to prevent 'overlapping and waste of effort'. The Three Arts Club had, Ashwell maintained, 'the best possible facilities for making systematic investigation, and is the most practical centre for the organisation of relief of Women Artists'.[45]

Ashwell's work had a dual purpose: to enable professional performers to feature in servicemen's entertainments would be both useful and patriotic, but it would also provide paid employment in work for which they were well qualified, ensuring quality performances for the armed forces. In October 1914, Ashwell outlined her ideas in the national press. She proposed to the government a scheme which would provide 'every camp its own theatre' which would both 'brighten the lives of troops' while simultaneously 'alleviating the distress caused by the war among professional artists'. Ashwell contended that voluntary work was not desirable for two reasons; 'If ... the volunteer is an amateur – a vocalist or a reciter with a mission-room reputation at most as an artist – it is unfair to the troops. If the volunteer is a professional capable of the job it is unfair to the volunteer'. Ashwell proposed to create fifty companies, each playing three nights in one location before moving in circulation to around fifty venues in the United Kingdom. Each company would feature ten artists, both theatrical and musical. Some companies would specialise in plays and others variety entertainment. Ashwell estimated that each company would cost £50 10s. per week, with £40 for salaries and the remainder for rent of halls, lighting and travel. Soldiers would be charged between 2d. and 6d. per performance, and 500 tickets would be sold at each show.[46]

Ashwell maintained that this should be a government scheme: 'unless it is organised from the point of view of patriotism it would be difficult to get really good artists who have been in the habit of receiving £30 to £40 a week to play for £6 or thereabouts. It would be a pleasure for any artist to work for the Government in so good a cause'. Ashwell outlined that the logistics would be handled by established theatrical managers experienced in arranging and booking tours. The money, she suggested, might come from the Prince of Wales' Fund as many artists had donated to that scheme 'in the belief that the fund was for all those thrown out of work through the war' and secondly that 'the artists of this country deserve some recognition at this moment, since there has never been a cause of any kind ... to which artists have not most willingly given their services'. Finally, Ashwell underlined that employing 500–600 professional artists to perform for the troops would utilise the education and training of a highly specialised community which would otherwise be 'compelled to sink into grades of work unsuited to them, and already overcrowded'.[47]

Ashwell appeared in various high-profile charity performances, for example a matinée at the Mansion House in aid of the Belgian Refugees

Fund on 3 February 1915, organised by the Lady Mayoress.[48] Tickets for the event sold out in two and a half hours.[49] However, the government did not respond to Ashwell's suggestions to establish a camp in every theatre, and that professional performers should help boost servicemen's morale. In October 1914, she made every effort

to get the entertainment of troops put on national lines, and was interviewed several times on the scheme of 'every camp its own theatre', and the organising of work by professional actors, but there was little interest shown. This effort . . . was followed by the formation of a Representative Committee – which I invited to organise an appeal to the War Office – a gathering of noted musicians and actors, with representatives . . . of the Church as a guarantee of our respectability and good faith. An appeal was formulated and sent to the War Office that recreation should be organised, that the movement should be national, as national as the Red Cross, but our offer was refused.[50]

There were several reasons for the War Office's refusal to consider Ashwell's suggestions.

Firstly, they were busy with fighting the Imperial German forces, and the recruitment, training and deployment of men and material to the battlefronts was of course of greater importance. Secondly, hopes were high in the winter of 1914 that the war would be concluded in the near future so there would be no need to go to the trouble and expense of implementing Ashwell's suggestions. A third consideration must be that they were unaccustomed, if not extremely wary, of dealing with members of the entertainment industry, especially a woman like Lena Ashwell – a divorced, childless woman of means who was actively engaged in the suffragette movement. This, coupled with recent industrial unrest, for example the Music Hall strike of 1908, must have made the War Office nervous of dealing with what they may have perceived as an unpredictable and disparate number of individuals. Indeed, the investigations of places of entertainment by the National Committee of Public Morals may also have had a bearing on the government's reluctance to consider Ashwell's proposals. From the early 1890s, the London County Council's Theatres and Music Halls Committee had established a system of moral surveillance where inspectors would visit venues and file reports of their inspections. The Bishop of London, Arthur Winnington-Ingram, was a leading purity campaigner who chaired the London Council for the Promotion of Public Morality 'to purify and elevate the moral tone of London'.[51] They feared that places of amusement were being used by 'undesirable persons' and proposed measures to deal with a range of amusement facilities including 'closing private cinema boxes [and] the prohibition of undesirable films'.[52] The involvement of General Horace Smith-Dorrien in the campaign for moral purity in London, once he had been relieved of his command of the Second Army in May 1915, indicates that members of the British high command were not ignorant of the issues surrounding social and cultural life at home. Indeed, members of the military elite were practicing Christians and advocates of temperance. Puritanical leanings can be seen in Lord Kitchener's refusal to issue the BEF with prophylactics, preferring to advocate the safer (and cheaper) method of abstinence. Generals Sir Ian Hamilton and Sir Francis Lloyd were well-known temperance speakers.

For religious, purity and temperance groups, whose memberships featured many members of the upper classes, the war was 'a golden chance to correct the years of sensuality and licence since the death of Victoria'.[53] The Salvation Army had been waging war against social decay, degeneration and general Godlessness since the 1860s. Music was its principal weapon in fighting what it called the 'Salvation War' to save people's souls from sin and turn them to God. Salvation Army Bands were a fixture of British public life, playing at 'Open Air' services on the street, in bandstands, and in prisons. The Salvation Army was a key music provider. In September 1914, they asserted that the war was having some positive benefits. These included a 'growing sense of solidarity' among communities at home and throughout the Empire, that the war was 'a purifying and helpful influence' which encouraged people to help one another, and that everyone would have a chance to demonstrate heroism whether they were soldiers, sailors or stayed at home. In a characteristically martial tone *The Bandsman, Local Officer & Songster* asserted that war might be a 'terrible, horrible thing, but it has some wonderful and valuable compensations'. They suggested that conflict might be 'a great and powerful teacher ... as it stands there grim and formidable on its blood-spattered pedestal' and that its lessons 'will go a long way towards making war impossible'.[54]

Fundraising for Servicemen's Music

During the war, music was central to the multifaceted work of many charitable activities. Money donated to stage concerts 'produced benefits far more complex, valuable, and far reaching – in terms of both those employed to give the concerts and the effect on those who received them – than the merely exact value of the sums involved'.[55] At a wartime concert in the Albert Hall, the composer Sir Frederik Bridge sent round a hat to collect donations for mouth organs because '[m]usic the soldier must have, if only on a gramophone or concertina'.[56] Testimonies from entertainers who went out to entertain the troops were harnessed by those seeking to raise funds for musical instruments for servicemen. The publication *Musical News*, for example, ran a Mouth Organ Fund. In April 1915, one newspaper, in response to a dip in contributions, wrote that 'a good many people have not yet responded to our appeal. Perhaps they consider the mouth organ a despicable instrument, or perhaps they think that there is no real desire for it at the Front'. To encourage readers to donate, the paper published a letter from William V. Robinson who toured with one of the early YMCA Lena Ashwell parties to entertain 'the gallant fellows who are fighting Britain's battles – *your* battles, good reader – for the sake of the homes some of them will never see again'. Readers were assured that 'a mouth organ is productive of more pleasure than a box of cigarettes'.[57] Music was 'not so easily provided as may be thought'. Bands at that point were 'out of the question' and 'even instruments of a portable character like the violin, the flute etc, not only are few and far between, but require . . . a certain amount of musical education'. The 'humble harmonica . . . is dear to the heart of every soldier and sailor. It slips into his pocket, requires no tuning, is available in a moment, and can be played by one absolutely ignorant of the technicalities of music'.[58]

The Mouth Organ Fund was started by *Musical News* in January 1915 and in nine months had raised £50. After William Robinson's letter was published, it showed 'that the Fund, by heartening the soldiers, was doing more than a merely philanthropic work; it was really carrying out a national work, having definite military value, and the money soon began to come in'. In twelve weeks they had a further £300 in subscriptions and 250 instruments were donated. By August 1915, the Fund had sent out a total of 7,675 mouth organs: 5,675 to France, 1,000 to the Dardanelles, and 1000 to the Fleet. The instruments were German made (although some purported to be Swiss) and purchased before the war. There were anxieties about Tommy being offended by this but 'with his native sense of humour, he was rather tickled at the thought of making the enemy dance to a mouth organ manufactured in his own Fatherland'. As the stock of German instruments ran low, American mouth organs were ordered. Subscribers could request for mouth organs to be sent to specific units: this was only possible for a single donation of £9 11s which would enable them to send 200 mouth organs to a specified unit. School children were also encouraged to write a letter to a soldier to be sent with the mouth organ, to which the child would get a reply from the soldier. The mouth organs were said to be so gratefully received by the servicemen 'not only because they afford the means of much-desired relaxation from the stern business of war, but also because they demonstrate the kindly thought of those at home for the men who are risking life and limb for the peace and security of their native land . . . and are daily and hourly in our thoughts'.[59] The *Daily Express* also established a 'Cheery Fund' to raise money to send comforts such as footballs, gramophones and records, books, musical instruments and games to the troops.[60]

By the spring of 1915, Ashwell was working as the head of the Three Arts Women's Employment Fund (sometimes referred to as Bureau) based at the Three Arts Club. The organisation moved to new premises at 26 Somerset Street, London, loaned to them by Gordon Selfridge, owner of the eponymous department store. The Fund's move was to be celebrated by a 'house-warming' at which Ashwell would be a 'hostess' alongside other notable women performers acting as 'hostesses' including the singer Clara Butt.[61] By this time, the Three Arts Club was said to have around 1,000 members, and its president was Princess Marie Louise of Schleswig-Holstein. It was managed by Lena Ashwell's sister, Miss Hilda Pocock. The club was described as of 'industrial and professional character' which 'brings it within the radius of women workers of the better class to whom the boon of charming surroundings, excellent food at a moderate tariff, and admirable residential accommodation is at once apparent'.[62] The members of the club, it was underlined, 'were among the first to feel the pressure of circumstances' of the war and that 'a large number of women belonging to the stage and its sister arts of music and painting were thrown out of employment'.[63] Working in 'close co-operation' with the Actor's Benevolent Fund, *The Era* War Relief Fund, the Artists' Benevolent Funds and the Women's Emergency Corps, the Three Arts Women's Employment Bureau were actively arranging to send artists to entertain the troops. They specified that the minimum wage for women and girls employed by the Bureau was 12s. per week and two meals a day.[64] However, not everybody agreed that entertainments should continue at a time of war. Several weeks after the first concert party went to the Western Front, Ashwell published a vigorous defence of the entertainment industry's response to the war, harking back to romantic historical tropes when 'the old ballad-makers understood the alchemy of the primitive themes of life – love and death, war, and music'. Ashwell pointedly wrote that '[t]hey understood many things better in the Middle Ages' and quoted the following verse:

> When Captains Courageous whom could not daunt
> Did march to the siege of the city of Gaunt,
> Their leader (*a woman, incidentally*) cheered her soldiers, that foughten her life,
> With ancient and standard, with drum and with fife.[65]

Ashwell said that she had 'passed among hundreds of thousands of Captains Courageous in France in the most awful war the world has ever seen'. She underlined that she had returned 'filled with admiration for their endurance, and with a great desire to ensure that, until the War ends, they shall have the comfort, and inspiration, and happiness that beautiful music can bring to them'.[66] In the spring of 1916, Ashwell was touring the country with the play *Iris Intervenes*, but she also held fundraising meetings/concerts for the concert party fund. In advance of her appearances, as she did before performing in Nottingham at the Theatre Royal, she would often say in the press that she would be auditioning for performers for the concert parties.[67] By the summer of 1916, Ashwell continued her fundraising efforts:

Expenses are heavy in spite of the fact that many of us can go at our own charges. There must in any case be travelling and living expenses. There are now five parties working one at a time. Two pounds will pay for one concert, which may bring pleasure to any number of men, from 400 more or less in a hospital to 2,000 right up at the front. I want you to give me all you have got, and then more. What you have not got send on to me. My address is 36 Grosvenor Street. I want you to give me your new hat, your new carpet, your new teacups, everything you thought you were going to buy next week, and to give it to me for the sake of the boys at the front and the boys in the Navy.[68]

Lena Ashwell entertainers gave many concerts in Britain to raise funds for 'Concerts at the Front Fund'. In August 1916, a party led by Frederick Lake entertained an audience where they were invited 'to imagine they were men at the Front, who were listening to the entertainment'. Lake told them that 'he and his fellow Artistes would endeavor to give them just what they had to soldiers in France'. At this later stage in the war, each concert was reported to cost £2 to put on. The parties were not able to go into forward areas during the recent allied offensive but they were returning that month. Before their appearance at Southport, Lake's party had performed in Bury, Wigan and Birkenhead. A signed photograph of Miss Ashwell was sold by auction for £1, and the Southport audience donated a total of £21 17s 5d.[69] The flyer for the event stated that this was being given 'in response to numerous requests and by kind permission of Miss Lena Ashwell'. The lecture was followed by musical performances by Mrs Ernest N. Barstow (Soprano), Mr Harry Burley (Baritone) and Miss Nita Dinsdale (Solo Pianoforte). Williams' lecture notes refer to 'those good lads fighting for the freedom of the British Empire and so to protect every one of us from the rule of the Prussian Huns'.[70] Williams paid tribute to the work of the YMCA on the fighting fronts, singling out their care of the relatives visiting dangerously wounded soldiers who would not survive the journey home. As with Frederick Lake's fundraising lecture-concert, Williams and his fellow performers gave the audience a taste of what they had been performing for the soldiers at the front. The pieces included Williams' solos, and the classical selections he was soften asked to play, along with 'a number of popular melodies arranged by him ... in which the audiences joined most heartily'.[71] These arrangements included *Hello Hello Who's Your Ladyfriend*, *When Such Eyes are Smiling* and *The Sunshine of Your Smile*.[72] During the lecture element Williams underlined the need for concerts, specifically requested from the military authorities:

The plea for 'more Concerts' comes from all along the line, and Generals, Commanding Officers, Doctors and Chaplains of all denominations say that Concert Parties are accomplishing work of great military value. The war will be won by the spirit and nerve of our armies and it is the experience of the military and medical authorities that beautiful music happiness and laughter in the midst of so much pain and desolation, nerve racking [unreadable] and ugliness has a psychic and psychological value ... almost beyond the imagination of those who have not experienced the conditions of life at the Front.[73]

By underlining that the performers have experienced life at the front, certainly in comparison to the majority of those sitting in the audience, Williams is imbuing his words with authority and experience. He and his colleagues are presenting themselves as veterans of the front, asserting their moral authority over the audience at home to maximise their charitable donations to the cause of taking music to servicemen. Bandmasters at home would often be responsible for arranging and playing in concerts for wartime charities. In the Royal Marines, the band of HMS *Orion* raised £5 for the relatives of those who lost their lives in HMS *Monmouth* which was later supplemented by a further sum of £9 from the Commander-in-Chief's Band, Portsmouth.[74] The loss of the senior Bandmaster W. O. Edward Schofield and his band on HMS *Bulwark*, who were formerly at Whale Island,

has been deeply felt not only at the School of Music, but also by a greater number of the townspeople of Portsmouth who have had the pleasure of hearing them perform at the South Parade Pier, the Royal Sailors' Rest, and other places in the town, where their abilities individually and as a whole were highly appreciated. Band Sergeant Beabey and Lance-Corporal Barrell were especially well-known as talented soloists who will be missed by a large circle of musical friends. It is satisfactory to know that dependents left behind (a number of the Band being married men) will be well looked after in Portsmouth.[75]

Bandmaster Rogan made the arrangements for Guards' bands concerts, the majority of which aimed to raise money for various elements of the war effort. In May 1915, they played in the Royal Albert Hall at a concert organised by Clara Butt, in aid of the British Red Cross. As with many of the higher-profile charity concerts, the King and Queen attended. Two hundred and fifty professional musicians formed the choir, led by

Madame Albani and Edward Lloyd. The baritone Kennerley Rumford, the husband of Clara Butt who was serving in France with Red Cross Transport Section, was given permission to appear. The Coldstream Band accompanied most pieces, and raised over £8,000, equivalent to £422,000 today.[76] In May 1916, the Coldstream Band played in a concert in aid of the Prisoner of War Fund of the Household Brigade at the Albert Hall where nearly £5,000 was raised.[77] At a 'Grand Patriotic Celebration' in May 1918, the full band of Coldstream Guards with drums, fifes and the pipers of the Brigade of Guards played to 8,000 sons and daughters of fighting men. One thousand wounded officers and men were also present as guests of the K. K. Empire Association, and 'all joined in singing patriotic tunes'.[78] Rogan also helped arranged a military tattoo with 350 performers at the London Opera House, sponsored by the *Daily Telegraph* and *Daily News* to raise money for plum puddings for soldiers on Christmas day. When Louis Parker produced the spectacle *Follow the Drum* at the Coliseum for the Lord Kitchener Memorial Fund, Rogan arranged the music. The Coldstream Guards band appeared with the drums, fifes and pipers of the Brigade of Guards who played the tattoo.[79]

British military music was on several occasions employed to project power and inspire confidence among the Allies overseas. In Canada during October 1915, the Royal Marines band on board HMS *Donegal* were invited to play in a series of concerts in Ottawa, after 'a request from the officials ... to spend a week there to visit local hospitals and street fairs, in aid of the War Effort'. Ten days later they had a six-day tour of Toronto. Bandsman Reed recalled that the Canadians were 'warm and hospitable ... and appreciated our playing'.[80] Rogan recalled that music had helped 'warm up the impulses of men who ought to be recruits, and to herald the men who already were recruits in their marches through the town'. But there was 'yet another use for music – as war propaganda'. Rogan underlined that it was 'no exaggeration to say that every note played by any and every British military bandsman abroad helped in the great victory. Every note was a note of hope, confidence, and friendship'.[81] At the end of April 1916, after their first tour of the Western Front, Rogan and thirty-two members of the Coldstream Guards' Band departed Poperinghe on an early morning train to Paris. They were being sent on a public relations mission.

Rogan and the band appeared at the *Festival des Trois Gardes* at the Trocadero with the Garde Républicaine and the Royal *Carabinieri* playing alternately to an audience of approximately 7,000 people. The Coldstreams also played at French hospitals where the Parisians 'entertained us right well'.[82] The success of this venture led to more 'great musical propagandist journeys'. At the invitation of the French Government, the five Guards Bands travelled for a week's tour of Paris on 22 May 1917. The soprano Miss Carrie Tubb accompanied the bands.[83] The bands sailed from Folkestone to Boulogne with an escort of four destroyers, and Rogan recalled that 'thousands of civilians and military were waiting for us on the jetty; they gave us a great cheer as the strains of the "Marseillaise" and "God Save the King" reached them from the band, which I had assembled on deck'. At Amiens, the Coldstreams were joined by thirty-two bandsmen of the Grenadier Guards.[84] They arrived in Paris to crowds of 30,000 people where the bands of the Guarde Républicaine and the 237th Infantry Regiment played *God Save the King* and the *Marseillaise*. Rogan proceeds to order the five bands to play an impromptu performance of those anthems at the Arc de Triomphe which 'pleased the people very much and made a happy beginning in propaganda'.[85]

The bands were received by Poincaré and the President at the Grand Palais, where the Guards Bands played *Sambre et Meuse* after the anthems. Here Rogan met Sergeant André Caplet, a French composer and conductor serving in an infantry regiment, who had composed a special march and fanfare for the Guards to play at the Trocodero concert. Over 6,000 people attended, including officers of the Guards Division who were on leave in Paris. Sir Francis Lloyd, serving with the Grenadier Guards, wrote that the visit was 'an enormous success, both in terms of money and enthusiasm'.[86] The Guarde Républicaine had played *Salut à la Garde Britannique* specially composed by their conductor, Captain Balay, when the massed bands of the Guards walked on stage. Rogan underlined that 'the spectacle of 250 bandsmen of the Guards in their scarlet and gold uniforms and bearskin caps was exceedingly fine'.[87] The bandsmen had a tea reception in the garden of the British Embassy, and they went on to the opera house where a performance of *Samson & Delila* was underway. When they entered the auditorium, the performers paused while the audience cheered the British bandsmen.

The Guards' popularity continued when they made a visit to a Citrôen munitions factory where Rogan recalled that around 6,000 'girls made themselves our hostesses ... I have never seen anything to compare with the wholesale flirtation that ensued. As we went round the factory every bandsman had four or five charming girls for his very own escort'. This visit was filmed but the footage was not shown in England and does not survive today. Rogan thought this was best after he saw the film at a private view the next day as the bandsmen 'would agree that for sound reasons of a domestic character it were better not!'[88] On the

Sunday of their visit, the Guards played in the Place Vendôme then marched to the Tuileries where the massed bands played alternately with the Guarde Républicaine to 200,000 people at the gardens. They went on to play at various hospitals in the Paris region. At the Opéra Comique, the massed bands performed with Carrie Tubb. Rogan states that this was the first time military bands had accompanied a vocalist.[89] At the conclusion of their visit, four bands departed for London while the Coldstream Guards stayed on to join Guards Division for their second tour, for three months from 4 June 1917.[90]

Music was a universal language of diplomacy. Early in 1918, the massed bands of the Brigade of Guards were invited by the Italian government to go to Rome, Florence and Milan. Rogan recalled that the opinion of the authorities both in Italy and at home was that 'as the Paris programme had achieved such an emphatic triumph, a like result should follow in Italy, especially at that particular time, when the Allies, having at last under stress of dire events achieved something approaching military unity, were bracing themselves for the final tug of desperate war'.[91] This time, only those bandsmen who had served overseas were permitted to go to Italy. Rogan underlined that this order was 'for the benefit of certain individuals who had joined the bands for reasons best known to themselves'. He recalled that 'several of them did very little duty and were permitted to accept private engagements all over the country, while other men performed duties in London and at the Front'. Rogan emphasised that '[why] this should have been allowed was a puzzle to the other bandsmen and still remains a puzzle to most of us'.[92]

In Italy, 250 bandsmen of the of Guards met with 80 members of the band of the Guarde Républicaine, 35 bandsmen belonging to the 18th Regiment, American Expeditionary Force, and 70 Italian *Carabinieri*. Their first concert took place in the Augusteo Concert Hall. Rogan was determined that the Guards would make a good impression and ordered them to wear their full 'review order' uniform of best tunics and bearskin caps.[93] The bandmaster also realised the diplomatic power of a good choice of music and ensured that the Guards played the *Garibaldi Hymn* which 'Italian audiences loved'. Rogan was heartened that 'the Italians are a people readily moved by music' and 'the Guards' bands were now at the top of their form both disciplinary and musical'.[94]

As in Paris, the Guards had a very busy schedule of high-profile per-formances and receptions, for example, an open-air concert in aid of Red Cross societies at Villa Umberto – usually known as Villa Borghese – for an audience of 20,000.[95] Rogan describes this 'propaganda mission' as being 'a huge success'.[96] Indeed, the Italian tour was more successful than had been anticipated: 'it demonstrated once again the power of music to influence the minds of civilians, to stimulate ardour, energise resolution and fortify coherence'.[97] The British Ambassador in Rome wrote to the Foreign Secretary that 'the stature, precision and stately marching of the bands of the Guards Brigade gave an indescribable feeling of strength and security ... No better propaganda work had been done for the Allied cause, ... than the visit of the visit of the Guards bands to Rome'.[98] Indeed, the ability of military music to inspire courage and confidence was much needed in the British armed forces during the conflict. The next chapter will show that traditional music and musical instruments which had been part of military life for hundreds of years would once again be deployed on the fighting fronts of the Great War.

3   Instruments of War

In 1867, the year that Band Boy John Mackenzie Rogan joined the British Army, the rank of Bugler appeared in the Royal Marines. When the Marines were organised into Divisions in 1884, Buglers were trained at Chatham, Portsmouth and Plymouth, and with the RM Light Infantry at Forton Barracks.[1] However, Buglers in the Army and Navy were first and foremost drummers. All routine and tactical orders were passed by the beat of a drum, and three routine beatings still survive in the Officers' Mess Beatings, Retreat and Drummers' Call. Drummers provided an audible rallying point in close battle, second only to the colours as a visible embodiment of the honour of the regiment. Drummers were soldiers who were usually in the thick of the action, and they could transfer to the ranks and shoulder a musket as required. Bugle calls used in the British Army date from 1798 when the War Office commissioned the trumpeter and composer John Hyde to create the calls, published as *Sounds and Duty Exercise for Trumpet and Bugle*.[2] The calls became essential to organising armies in the field and the soldier's life in camp.[3] Buglers would also drum the beat for route marches, and the role was undertaken by young boys as an entry point into the army before they had reached the age of eighteen.[4] The secondary instrument of a drummer was a fife, a small wooden wind instrument similar to the piccolo. This was once called the 'Swiss flute' after the Swiss first used it at the battle of Marignano in 1515. It was introduced to England in 1557, and used with a drum for martial music by British Guards commanded by the Duke of Cumberland in 1747, then adopted by other infantry regiments including the Marines. Brass instruments, such as the key-bugle, began to replace fifes in 1817 but the fife did not disappear. In the British Army, all buglers had to be proficient in bugle, drum and fife into the 1940s.

In December 1914, Henry Newbolt invoked the nostalgic spirit of past military glory, where columns of troops would march to the beat and tune of drums and fifes when *The Times* published his poem 'The Toy Band: A Song of the Great Retreat'. This described how Dragoons at Mons were spurred on by penny whistles and a child's drum salvaged from a wrecked toyshop, exhorting the men to 'Fall in! Fall in! Follow the fife and drum!'[5] By the outbreak of the Great War, drums, fifes and bugles remained an essential part of service life. The routine of a military camp was run by signals from the bugle, from *Reveille* to the *Last Post*, and 'the army was ruled by [them]'.[6] George Butterworth, when he enlisted in August 1914, noted that route marches during training at Aldershot were led by a bugle band.[7] However, the conditions of industrial warfare raised a number of practical problems for buglers on the battlefield. As Bugler Charles Ditcham described, 'What I shall never understand is what I was supposed to do with a bugle in the front line during the battle'.[8] John Ford, fighting in the Gallipoli campaign, noted that the bugle was useless on the front as it '[gave] away your position'.[9] For various practical reasons, therefore, the bugle was generally replaced with an officer's whistle to signal an advance.[10] However, its use in army camps was held as a mainstay of army life, routine and the maintenance of soldiers' morale. Requests for buglers in the army continued throughout the war, despite the instrument's limited use in the field. Buglers were still highly valued in the Great War. This is evident in their rates of pay compared to an ordinary soldier in the ranks, particularly once they had qualified as a full Bugler. The average pay for a trainee boy Bugler was 4 pence a day, which rose greatly once qualified to 1 shilling and a penny a day as a full bugler, a 9 pence increase, around 10 pounds in today's money.[11] Bugler Alfred Hedges, stationed aboard HMS *Queen*, outlines they received 3 pence a day more than a regular infantry or artillery soldier.[12]

The issue of buglers in the expanding British Army caused some logistical difficulties in the War Office. In the 1914 orders to establish a reserve regiment for cavalry of the line, it is stipulated that two 'trumpeters' should be attached to each squadron, along with one Bandmaster who would be sent from a regular regiment.[13] On 20 October 1914, the Army Council outlined that the New Armies would not have any trumpeters, drummers or buglers. It decreed that the 'Sergeant drummer will be replaced by sergeants. Trumpeters will be replaced by mounted men who will carry out the duties of horseholders and orderlies normally performed by trumpeters'. Drummers and buglers were to be replaced by privates and were added to the establishment of rank and file in the unit. To sound 'such calls as are necessary, both in quarters at home and on service abroad, men should be selected . . . [and] trained and armed as soldiers'. While they were 'not be considered nor paid as buglers' once they are trained, they 'should be excused duty in the ranks'. This decision did not affect 'the sergeant-piper and 5 pipers of those battalions which have an authorised establishment of pipers'.[14] One month later, the Army

Council decided that 'drums and fifes should not be issued to units of the New Armies, in order that men should not be taken from their training as soldiers to practice music'. However, it went on to state that the provision of bands for the New Armies 'is recognized to be of importance, and proposals are under consideration for their formation outside the establishment of units'.[15] In December 1914, the Army Council changed its mind and issued orders for drums and fifes in new armies for trumpeters, drummers and buglers. Nevertheless, the Council strictly stated that it must be 'clearly understood that no establishment of sergeant drummers, buglers or drummer will be allowed and that men employed as such must not be taken away from their training as soldiers to be trained as musicians'. Soldiers employed as buglers or drummers should be 'selected from men who have had previous experience of the instrument they are to use, and any further training as musicians undergone by these men must be in addition to the training as soldiers given to them in common with all other fighting men in their battalions'.[16]

As experienced drummers in the regular units were posted to France, new recruits who displayed musical aptitude were encouraged to take up their instruments. One such solider was Tommy Keele, an NCO serving with the 11th Middlesex Regiment. He volunteered to become a regimental bugler shortly after enlistment, and after receiving training he was passed out by the sergeant to become a full regimental bugler.[17] The *Chronicle* of the Highland Light Infantry records the promotions of four soldiers – two boys, a private and a corporal – to the rank of Bugler in November 1914.[18] The 1st Cyclist Battalion of the Royal Fusiliers wanted to 'drive home to the recruits that by taking their places and helping to bring the drums up to their usual state, they are doing their bit'. The writer, 'Drummy', admitted that it was 'quite a nuisance having to learn anything ... but with constant practice and attention efficiency will follow'. Particular attention was drawn to the fact that the colonel was keen to see that the battalion maintained its pre-war standards and be 'top dog'.[19] Military bands and buglers were regarded as essential to military morale. Turville Kille, a British bugler with the East Kent regiment on the Western Front stated that the bands were hugely important and 'soldiers used to enjoy' being accompanied on route marches by the bugler drummer. He maintained that 'the band is the making of a soldier' marching on parade to music and singing.[20] When Chaplain Pat Leonard arrived at a chateau near St Omer in February 1916, a visit by Haig was suddenly announced. He wrote that he was 'startled by the guard turning out and the bugler playing the general salute'. He saw 'a dazzling cavalcade prancing & curvetting up the drive'. Leonard thought Haig 'looked very fine and soldierly and was followed by a Trooper carrying a Union jack on his lance, and five or six Generals resplendent in their red hats and brass fixings . . . It was quite an imposing sight, and was the first proof I had seen that the pomp and splendor of the Army is not yet departed'.[21]

The familiarity of the bugle calls and the tunes played by the bands acquired a 'greater authority' in periods of combat. Indeed, in 1916 HMV made a recording of *Bugle Calls of the British Army* with Rogan and the band of the Coldstream Guards. The bugle also provided continuity and stability in soldiers' lives.[22] The regularity of these calls, heard daily at designated times, reassured servicemen in times of unpredictability and strain. Each regiment had at least one of their own buglers who would play their own unique regimental call. Cecil Reginald King, a British NCO in the Royal Flying Corps, noted that the regimental calls were a 'signature tune' and were used as an identifier of 'regimental pride, leadership and discipline'.[23] However, not all soldiers were happy to hear some of the bugle calls, particularly *Reveille*, which acts as the army's alarm clock and instructs the soldiers to get up. An article in the *Manchester Guardian* from 1916 suggested a more negative image of the bugler and the soldiers' association with it. It notes that *Reveille* 'can never be a welcome sound to the soldier, whether it drags him from the mid-blanket stupor following a misspent evening', and that soldiers in hospitals could hear the reveille in the distance and were happy to ignore it.[24] As John Bourne has asserted, soldiering was fundamentally a form of work and the working class responses would therefore be much the same as they had been at home.[25]

In 1914, British soldiers learned many of the bugle calls by inventing their own lyrics to each sequence. This enabled the men to identify which call was being played, indicating which order was being given, which in turn allowed the soldiers to create their own – mostly humorous – libretti. Many of the words originated from army training manuals. Donald Hodge, a British private serving with the 7th Battalion Royal West Kent Regiment, explained that the first things new recruits had to learn were the calls of the bugle; they 'had to live the bugle call'.[26] Percy Snelling of the 7th Dragoon Guards spoke of army lectures to teach them men what each bugle call meant.[27] Many of these lyrics originated from conflicts before 1914. A bugler training manual from 1910 shows the clear imperial origins of the lyrics, unsurprising as the majority of the British Army in the pre-1914 period had served in India at some point.[28] The officers' mess call, for example, was accompanied by the words 'Officers wives get puddings and pies, and soldiers wives get skilly'.[29] This refers to officer's wives, who had moved out to the colonies with their husbands, being allowed to dine with them in the officer's mess. That these words were still being used 1914–18 speaks to the sense of tradition apparent in

army bugle calls. Indeed, women who lived in service married quarters would frequently become accustomed to various bugle calls and
their meanings. Sergeant Victor Shawyer, who was born into an
Army family, recalled hearing his mother singing this call in their
home near the barracks of the Rifle Brigade.[30] In recognition of the
need to teach new civilian-recruits the words to the various bugle
calls they would be expected to obey in camp, in 1915 the War
Office published *Trumpet and Bugle Sounds for the Army with Words
also Bugle Marches*. Some examples of the calls and words are as
follows:

Parade for Guard
Come and do your guard my boys! Come and do your guard! You've had fourteen
nights in bed, So it won't be hard.

Fatigue
I call'd them, I call'd them; they wouldn't come, they wouldn't come: I call'd
them, I call'd them, they wouldn't come at all!

Defaulters
Now throw all your cleaning traps down on your cots, And an'swer De-faulters,
my boys.

Sick
Come the sick, come the lame, All cures for your ills we've got, To free Tom-my
from pain.[31]

Soldiers' adaptions give illuminating insights into their attitudes to their
wartime experiences. Variations on the sick call included '64 94 won't go
sick anymore, the poor beggar's dead'.[32] Brophy and Partridge identified
the sick parade call as the most well-known bugle calls. Other calls take
a similar form, with the morning rouse accompanied by:

    'Get out of bed, get out of bed, you lazy dossers, I say beggar the orderly
man'.[33]

    Of the rouse it is noted that 'scarcely a hut or tent that had not a light
sleeper sufficiently awake to murmur the chant in time with the Bugler's
Brazen modulations'.[34] The words put to these calls, differing from the
War Office approved manuals, suggest a more personal attachment of the
soldier to the calls, indicating that the calls provided a continuity and
stability in servicemen's everyday routines, linking familiarity with the
bugler as a consistent and reliable presence in unpredictable times.[35] The
bugler was therefore seen as a traditional link with the past as well as
a source of regimental identity and comradeship.[36] Almost every rank in
the army was liable to be parodied at some point, and in July 1916, *The
Somme Times* announced its 'splendid new serial' *From Bugle Boy to*

Brigadier, or How Willie Prichard Rose from the Ranks. Even as Colonel in Command the *Blimp*-esque protagonist finds himself taking up a bugle to rouse his troops when they were suddenly surrounded by the enemy.[37] However, incidents like this did occur during the Great War. Drummer Ritchie of the Seaforth Highlanders stood on the parapet of an enemy trench during an attack, sounding the bugle call 'Charge', to rally the men who had lost contact with their units. The *Church Army Gazette* was so taken with this occurrence that they featured an illustration of Ritchie's actions, adopting his example to state to its readers that 'there is nothing more victorious than a POSITIVE PUSH'.[38]

Drums

Rudyard Kipling used the themes of drums and drummers in the British Army in several of his works; for example, two heroes in his short story *The Drums of the Fore and Aft* (1889), Jakin and Lew, are drummer boys, and the poem 'Tommy' (1890) showed how the sound of the drums can change people's attitudes towards the military:

> Then it's Tommy this, an' Tommy that, an' Tommy ow's yer soul?
> But it's 'Thin red line of 'eroes' when the drums begin to roll,
> The drums begin to roll, my boys, the drums begin to roll,
> O it's 'Thin red line of 'eroes', when the drums begin to roll.

Before 1914, a drummer who had attained a Second Class Certificate of education, and had joined an elite Guards regiment, would be paid 1 shilling and 2 pence per day, while a similar musician in the line would get 1 shilling and 1 penny per day.[39] Once the BEF mobilised in August 1914, the Royal Army Medical Corps aimed to have thirty-two stretcher-bearers for every thousand fighting men, bandsmen and drummers would add to this when their battalion was stationed on the battlefield.[40] A number of drummers from a range of regiments were awarded the Victoria Cross, for example Drummer William Kenny, 2nd Battalion the Gordon Highlanders. He was given the ultimate accolade for his actions on 23 October 1915, near Ypres for 'rescuing wounded men on five occasions under very heavy fire in the most fearless manner, and for twice previously saving heavy machine guns by carrying them out of action. On numerous occasions Drummer Kenny conveyed urgent messages under very dangerous circumstances over fire-swept ground'.[41]

The use of drums in action on the battlefield was stopped in the Great War for the same prosaic reasons as bugling. However, drummers would still escort troops on the march and military bands continued to use the drummer to 'drum up interest' to encourage men to enlist. However, during the first year of the war there was a noted lack of drumming on the Western Front. On 22 August 1915, as the 1st Battalion Coldstream Guards were marching from billets in Vermelles to billets in Annezin, 'just w[est] of Beuvry [the] drums met them & played them in to billets'. The war diary noted that this was 'the first time drums had played since the commencement of the retreat in 1914'.[42] For the elite regiments such as the Guards, orders were given that '[M]arch discipline cannot be too strict.... Officers should pay as much attention to discipline on a route march as on a ceremonial parade'.[43] The Drums were an essential element of keeping time and order on the march. On 23 August 1915, when the Black Watch sent their band and drums to play the Coldstreams out in front of Sir Henry Rawlinson, the war diary proudly records that 'The Bn marched very well'.[44] Wartime photographs show that drummers often accompanied columns of marching men. Drummers also had a central role in military ceremonies for VIPs. This was seen on numerous occasions on the Western Front; for example, the inspection of troops by the King and Queen of the Belgians just north of Curlu on 14 June 1917. The importance of getting the military choreography right for this ceremony is evident by the care taken to schedule in multiple rehearsals, as seen in the war diary of Headquarters, 2 Guards Brigade. A sketch of the parade plan is included in the diary, showing the location of the Band of the Grenadier Guards, with the massed drums and pipers drawn up in the rear.[45]

Pipes

In Scottish regiments, the pipes were deeply embedded in their unit's identity. The Pipes operated to reinforce cohesion at regimental and battalion levels through specific marches, tunes and calls. The impressive and rousing spectacle of the pipers of the London Scottish often featured in the British press; for example, as they mobilised and marched through the streets of London 'to the skirl of the bagpipes'.[46] The regiment had a poem, 'The Call', composed for them in 1915 which asked:

> For lives there a Scot who answers not
> When the pipers call and call?
> . . .
> As he swings his kilt to the mad'ning lilt
> Of the pipes that go before.[47]

At the level of the battalion, the pipes were routinely use for marching, parades, celebrations, funerals, acts of remembrance, send-offs, regulating the day and beating retreat in the evening. Below the battalion level, the pipes reinforced personal feelings of comradeship and thoughts of home.[48] The author and clergyman Lauchlan Maclean Watt, who served with the Gordon Highlanders, recalled the funeral of a comrade for which they secured the services of a nearby pipe-major. While 'a little group of bronzed and kilted men stood around the grave' the piper played 'the old wail of the sorrow of our people' *Lochaber No More.* Watt had last heard it when he 'stood in the rain beside my mother's grave; and there can be nothing more deeply moving for the Highland heart. The sigh of the waves along the Hebridean shores called to me there, among the graves in France'.[49] The Pipes were also played by Indian regiments, particularly the Pathans and the Dogras. This was of great interest to observers who witnessed 'turbaned tribesmen marching up and down the Grande Place between dense files of staring French folk'. The 'swart hillmen play the Marseillaise upon Scottish bagpipes, to the wonder of all'.[50]

The 15th Highland Light Infantry were just one battalion who used bagpipes to 'play them on'. Largely made up of men from the Glasgow tramways, it was said that the pipes 'have all along been an inspiration to Glasgow men. Coming down from the trenches, after a long and weary trek, the men are cheered wonderfully when they are met with a little music'. However, the practice of playing men into battle was discontinued as the 'cost is too heavy in musicians'.[51] In Highland regiments, an orderly piper formed part of the guard in addition to a bugler. Routine bugle calls would be followed by a piper, sometimes a pipe band playing specific tunes. After the bugling of *Reveille,* for example, the piper(s) would play *Hey, Johnnie Cope Are You Wauken Yet?* Fifteen minutes before the call for breakfast the piper(s) played *Come to the Cookhouse Door, Boys.* A call for later mealtimes might be followed by the tune of *Brose and Butter.* The melody of *Mackenzie Highlanders* would be heard before the advance was sounded, followed by the piping of *The Campbells Are Coming.* A route march would call for the playing of *Scotland, the Brave* and during a parade inspection, the pipers would play their regimental tune, *Highland Laddie.* As the day drew to a close, at the sounding of 'Retreat', the piper(s) would play *The Banks of Allan Water,* and shortly before the bugle call 'Last Post' the lilting melody of *Lochaber No More* would sound. At a funeral, *Flora Macdonald's Lament* would be played. Bugle Major Sergeant McCampbell declared that 'no instrument can describe the passions like the pipes'.[52]

In September 1915, at the Battle of Loos, the power of the pipes was showcased by the bravery of Piper Laidlaw of the King's Own Scottish Border Regiment. As his unit advanced, Laidlaw 'had the pipes going, and the lads gave a cheer as they started towards enemy lines.... they began to fall very fast, but they never wavered' as Laidlaw played 'the old air they all knew', *Blue Bonnets Over the Border.* Laidlaw described that he went forward with the men, 'piping for all I knew', before he was hit in the left leg and ankle by shrapnel near the German frontline trench. However, he said that he was 'too excited to feel the pain' and stumbled on, playing the *Braes o' Mar*. He thought it was 'a grand tune for charging on. I kept on piping and piping, and hobbling along after the lads until I could go on no more'.[53] Laidlaw was subsequently awarded the Victoria Cross. The Reverend Lauchlan MacLean Watt used the power of the pipes to great effect. Arriving in Le Havre on Christmas Eve 1914, Watt worked with the YMCA at various base camps, in 1916–17 as chaplain to the Gordon Highlanders on the Somme, and the Black Watch at Ypres. He became known for always carrying his bagpipes, on which he would play traditional Scottish tunes on marches and in camps.[54] Bagpipes were supplied by several specialist firms. Peter Henderson of 24 Renfrew Street, Glasgow, proclaimed in its adverts its status as an official supplier for military bands.[55] The firm R. G. Lawrie, also based in Glasgow, had offices in London and Edinburgh.[56] In Lahore, instruments including bagpipes could be obtained from Jenn & Ellerton who were dealers for David Glen's and Peter Henderson's pipes.[57]

However, the presence of pipes in close range was not always welcomed. To non-Scottish troops the bagpipes were often a target of parody, particularly in the fleet, where one newspaper pointed out that 'it took a war to force the bagpipes on the British Navy'.[58] One naval unit's journal published a satirical account of a naval battle in terms of a musical parody:

As the fleets engaged, she opened with a salvo from her ten 113.55" gramophones, all firing 'It's a Long, Long Way to Tipperary'. Two powerful piano batteries were also brought into action, using the same ammunition. All fired in different keys. The Germans, notoriously a musical nation, were badly shaken. But soon from a hundred accordeons [*sic*] belched forth 'De Wacht am Rhein'. The fate of the day hung in the balance. Then the secret of our fleet was revealed. A fateful pause – and suddenly from the foretop of the flagship rises a scream as of a million souls in torment. 'The bagpipes!' men whisper with blanched faces 'the Scottish bagpipes!' It is indeed that dreadful engine. One by one the German ships within hearing groaned, rolled up their eyes, and sank.[59]

On Burns Night, in January 1916, Chaplain Pat Leonard complained that as he was trying to write a letter home, the pipe band of the 1st Gordon Highlanders was practicing twenty yards from his hut. He enjoyed them as a band, 'especially when I can see the swirl of the kilt and the swagger of the Pipe Major'. However, 'sitting here unable to see them, I fairly hate them. Each piper is playing his own favourite lament regardless of the others, and the drums are practicing ragtime I think, so you must take that into consideration if my letter is more disconnected or futile than usual.'[60]

One month later, the Gordon Highlanders leave the camp, and Leonard records that it was 'quite a relief not to have their pipers practicing at my door'. Having spent the best part of a month living in close proximity to a pipe band he was fascinated by their manner:

I had never realized before what a strange race Scottish pipers are – a peculiarly self-contained introspective breed, placid volcanoes. They strut about detached from their surroundings, playing the mournful lament so dear to their hearts. Each evening they tear themselves away from the dream world in which they habitually live, and assemble in a wide circle to play tattoo. Even then, although they play in harmony with the others they still wear the vacant detached look of hermits. As a matter of fact the band is really first class, and the drums particularly are excellent. Such a swing and dash and precision about them. They are quite a treat to watch but it is the pipers who hold me spellbound. Each one beats time with his right foot, but not with the toe as ordinary mortals do, but with the heel![61]

Second Lieutenant Harper Seed, of the 17th Battalion Sherwood Forresters, noted that the battalion bands were usually left near the transport lines and spent their time rehearsing together or in private practice. A student at the Royal Academy of Music, Harper Seed often struggled with the music he heard: 'There is a bandsman making or murdering music on a euphonium in the neighbouring camp. All we need to drive us dotty is the addition of a bagpipe at close quarters.'[62] He wrote to his parents 'At each point of the compass there is a different tune going & the result is original if nothing else. All we want to complete the cacophony is the Black Watch Pipers.'[63]

Bands

Britain's armed forces had long been aware that music was the best means of 'exciting that passion which the most eloquent oration would fail to inspire'.[64] However, in many regular units of the British Army, on active operations, battalion bandsmen's primary role was switched to that of stretcher-bearers. As the war progressed and with the increase of 'Service' battalions, the role devolved to those with a modicum of basic first aid knowledge and the physical strength required for the arduous job of transporting wounded over difficult ground to safety and professional medical help. Nevertheless, this led to questions as to 'where are the regular Army bands? Far back, alas! Dispossessed and scattered.... Five thousand of our best bandsmen now act as stretcher-bearers at the Front, and come under fire as even the doctors do and the cooks, when the colonels bid them drop their pots and seize rifles or bombs in a hot corner.'[65] In the Territorial and New Army battalions, men who had worked as professional musicians, or those who had played in civilian ensembles or Salvation Army bands, formed their own groups with the support of their commanding officers. It was increasingly recognised that the continuation of a regimental band was regarded as a crucial component of morale playing the men to and from the trenches. The band was far more than an ornament or luxury item; it was part of the glue that held regiments together and kept men focused and engaged with the war effort.

By August 1914, the Royal Marines Band Service comprised of 1,450 men of all ranks, distributed in 53 bands serving in various parts of the world.[66] Royal Marines Bands were in constant use for both routine and ceremonial purposes; they would be used to mark the ship's daily routine that included the Morning Colours Ceremony, Divisions, Prayers, physical training and Evening colours, the latter being much more impressive to a ship's company when a band was on board.[67] There was also the frequent need for parades ashore and since many ships were flying the flag appearance was most important not only to those watching but also for the morale of the ships' crews. The Band was also used to give an impressive welcome to important official visitors aboard the ship. At all sporting occasions the Military Band was employed and frequent variety programmes were played on board to help relieve the monotony of long voyages and routine. As an orchestra, the musicians provided music for visitors dining on board, and orchestral and variety concerts for the ship's company were often held. The band would also play every Sunday at Church Service. Thus it was generally accepted that 'a band helped increase the efficiency of the ship, raised the morale of its crew and was very important to the daily business of showing the might of the British Navy to friend and potential foe alike'.[68] However, the absence of military music was keenly felt on the fighting fronts in the first year of the war. In September 1915, a correspondent to the *Daily Mail* complained that while 'some' of the Territorial units took their bands with them, he did 'not think there are more than three or four all told with our Army in the field'. He opined that 'all the Scottish regiments had their pipers and drummers; the Canadian Highlanders have their pipers, and so have some of the Indian regiments, notably the 40th Pathans'. He relayed that he often met the Scottish regiments on the road, 'trudging gaily along to the skirl of the pipes, and pity the English and Irish regiments that have to march to the tunes they whistle and sing themselves'.[69]

Bands in the RFC/RNAS were not of the traditional military marching band type. The earliest ensembles were closer to concert party groups who played for recreational occasions such as dances and mess dinners. In

1916, the Aircraft Park Orchestra of the Royal Flying Corps in Farnborough was conducted by Second Lieutenant A. R. Axford, and several of the musicians also appear in the photograph of No.1 Southern Aircraft Repair Depot Combined Bands at Farnborough in 1917.[70] The most well-known ensemble on active service on the Western Front was the fifteen-piece orchestra, or band, of 56 Squadron, conducted by Sergeant P. E. Gayer. It was established by Major Richard Graham Blomfeld, Commanding Officer of the squadron from February to October 1917.[71] There were three musical ensembles in the RNAS, all of which appear to have been located at the Royal Naval Air Station, Cranwell.[72] They were known as the 'Cranwell Orchestra' and the 'Cranwell Brass Band', conducted by Petty Officer Pond.[73] Yet music for airmen was always down to their own efforts and competition was rife. After a concert at a nearby airfield in September 1917, *The Fledgling* unit magazine asked of themselves that 'If a band, including piano, trombone, violin, flute, and 'cello can be formed in a camp of forty individuals what ought a Wing of over 1000 strong to produce? Yet, we are still without orchestra or band!'[74]

After an intense period of fighting in the trenches in October 1915, a Salvation Army bandsman wrote that 'a divisional band is being formed, and my name heads the list that has been taken from the "D" Company'.[75] Salvation Army bandsmen were also present and playing on ships such as HMS *Alcantara*. Music was ever-present on the fighting fronts, even in the trenches in action. On the third day of the Battle of Loos, when on 27 September 1915, Lance Corporal James Vickery of the 4th Battalion Seaforth Highlanders, carried out an act of bravery for which he was to be recommended for the Distinguished Conduct Medal for conspicuous gallantry. As his regiment was led into battle by a piper, risking their lives to inspire the troops, it is possible that their piper had been wounded, as 'At a critical moment L/Cpl Vickery and CQMS Beech steadied the men by getting up on the parapet and playing tunes on mouth organs, although exposed to a heavy fire.'[76] The mouth organ incident caused James to make the national press as, on Friday 24 June 1916, the *Daily Express* ran an article headlined

> Gold Mouth-Organ For A D.C.M.
> How Cheery Funders Will Honour
> Two Brave Men
> 'Despised Instrument'
> Seaforths Rallied at A Critical Time

The article went on to suggest the mouth organ James played was one sent by the newspaper noting with surprise that 'one of them would be the

direct means of steadying men at a critical moment and earning a D.C.
M. for the quick-witted gallant hero who played it'.[77] The writer
continued:

I went to our stock-room immediately and chose two of the very best-toned
mouth-organs from among the thousands we have. I removed the top and bottom
nickel plates. In their place I propose to have placed two real gold plates. These
will be inscribed with a short account of the heroic deed that inspired the gift, and
when they have been slipped into a lined morocco leather case, they will be sent to
C.Q.M.S. Beech and Lance-Corporal Vickery as a present from Cheery
Funders.[78]

James's gold mouth organ, suitably inscribed, is now in the possession of
The Seaforth Highlanders' Museum in Fort George, Inverness. The
Daily Express carried further articles on the 24, 26 and 28 June. 'Orion'
wished 'that Mr. Rudyard Kipling would immortalise this feat of mouth-
organry which has won the D.C.M. for Beech and mention for Vickery'.[79]
Money continued to be raised for the Mouth Organs and Orion argued
for an all-British mouth organ despite the manufacturing problems this
involved. Vickery achieved celebrity status. According to his School Log
Book, on 15 February 1917 whilst home on leave, he went to visit the
school, perhaps showing his medal to the pupils and possibly playing his
mouth organ.[80] Everyone could use a mouth organ. In 1915, Wesleyan
chaplain Reverend Herbert Butler Cowl was serving with the 69th Field
Ambulance ADS near Bois Grenier. His mess was a mile away in the
village inn, so Cowl and the doctor had to walk between the two locations
several times a day for their meals. Cowl recalled that 'the road by which
we passed to and fro was by no means a healthy place ... a goal for half-
spent bullets by German snipers; and without a shred of shelter beyond
a blade of grass'. He said that

there was nothing for it, but to find some salve for jumpy nerves. This took the
inglorious form of a mouth-organ: and how often he and I plodded back to our
cellar thro' the darkness to the enheartening strains of our one and only tune 'The
Cock of the North'. Imagine the scene when at the onset of the journey a sentry's
challenge was given, – 'Halt! Who are you?' the music ceases abruptly, and from
one to the other the reluctant confession is wrung – 'Doctor and Chaplain!' The
chuckle of the sentry was no matter of imagination!'[81]

Musical instruments were often in short supply on the fighting fronts.
A photograph of 'wounded soldiers, preceded by an impromptu band, on
their way to the doctors' published by *Birmingham Picture World* in
August 1915, shows six soldiers playing mouth-organs, tin whistles and
an accordion.[82] Where instruments were lost, damaged or otherwise
unavailable, servicemen improvised their own musical instruments from

the materials available to them. Serving in 25 squadron, 10th Wing RFC, Second Lieutenant Alfred Severs wrote that they had 'a marvelous mess orchestra consisting of all sorts of weird instruments a tin kettle drum, a pair cymbals (I should shay sho too), one string fiddles etc, and one or two tin whistles and flutes and such like'.[83] In mid-1917, Bandmaster Rogan states that the troops 'kept up their spirits in all sorts of grotesque ways. As an item in their sports the 3rd Battalion at Haut Schonbrouck had a mock band contest, each company entering a band of its own organisation, with weird instruments of its own manufacture.'[84] Lena Ashwell described how the British soldier 'needs music or some sort of cheerful noise'. She 'came across a "band" a lonely detachment of moto-drivers had improvised, with cardboard megaphones doing duty as trombones, and an empty petrol tin for a drum. ... the British army can stand anything except being bored'.[85] Ashwell performer Julius Harrison was particularly struck by a Red Cross motor driver called Barnes, from Ramsgate. He was 'the cheeriest soul I ever met, and his conducting of this wonderful orchestra (which consisted of two cornets, a petrol can, and various assorted gilded and card-board instruments looking like tubas, bassoons, clarinets, and euphoniums) was revelation to me'. Harrison was amazed that the man used his arms 'but his *feet* as well! ... "Signor Niffowiski" gave us a selection from the band's varied and cacophonous repertoire'.[86]

Musicians in Action

In August 1914, the Royal Naval Division deployed with the Royal Marine Brigade to the defence of Antwerp. Accompanying the 1st Naval Brigade were twenty-four musicians of a Royal Marine Band under the command of Bandmaster William Faithfull. The Band acted as a Red Cross Party at the siege of Antwerp and were captured (then released) when they accidentally landed in neutral Holland after the Brigade was forced to withdraw. Assumed to be non-combatants, the band were allowed to return to England and their instruments were replaced at Eastney. On their return from their brief captivity, the *Globe and Laurel* announced that 'Band Corporal Knowles and three musicians rejoined Headquarters after their enforced sojourn at Groningen, Holland, their only growl being that they were rather crowded for accommodation and their liberty somewhat curtailed.'[87] Bandsman Victor Shawyer, serving in the Rifle Brigade, first engaged with the enemy at Mons on 25 August 1914. The regiment lost over 350 men; many of the wounded had to be abandoned with the stretcher-bearers in the retreat. Shawyer wrote that the Band of the 1st Battalion 'got very roughly mauled'. Five bandsmen escaped capture at

Mons, but seventeen were taken prisoner, including Boy Bugler Lawson, who was seventeen years old.[88] When Johnson William Double of the Hampshire Regiment served in the trenches at Gallipoli he was wounded and sent to convalesce in Egypt in June 1915. As he returned to Gallipoli in September 1915, he 'renewed the acquaintance with 3 of my old chums in the Band'. However, he noted that 'They are on stretcher bearing duty, so I hope I shall not have to call upon them to attend to me.'[89] One bandsman was awarded the Victoria Cross – Thomas Edward Rendle of the 1st Duke of Cornwall's Light Infantry.[90] This was awarded 'For conspicuous bravery on 20th November, near Wulverghem, when he attended to the wounded under very heavy shell and rifle fire, and rescued men from the trenches in which they had been buried by the blowing in of the parapets by the fire of the enemy's heavy howitzers.'[91] In August 1915, Lance-Corporal Rendle was also awarded the Cross of the Order of St George, 3rd Class.[92] There were thousands of other men who performed similar actions to Lance-Corporal Rendle.

It was often the case that bandsmen serving as stretcher-bearers would be evacuating their former band colleagues. Shortly after their arrival in the trenches, Shawyer's band roommate Charlie Edwards was shot looking through firing loophole. He sustained a head wound and instead of waiting to be evacuated after dark, a request reached battalion HQ aid post that the 'semi-conscious ravings' of a 'a seriously injured N.C.O'. were having 'a bad effect on the men' who had to listen to him. Bandsmen Dan Liddiard 'took a stretcher bearing squad through some brisk enemy shelling and got a very bad jolt to find that the casualty was his own music desk-mate – they were both cornettists'. He redressed the bandages Edwards kept tearing off, and tied him to the stretcher. The shelling had increased in intensity so Liddiard went back to the first aid post alone. The doctor refused to go back with Liddiard but gave him enough morphine 'to still the ravings of the casualty'. Liddiard made his way back through the shelling 'to help his comrade of the Band. [He] sat beside the dying corporal Charlie Edwards through what was left of that autumn day, administering morphia at intervals till with the coming of early twilight, Edwards passed on, and Dan could do no more than leave the body where it lay, at peace, on the stretcher.' Shawyer recounted that 'so died one of the greatest characters I had so far met as a soldier'.[93] The Bandsmen of the Royal Marines suffered heavily. Sixteen bandsmen were killed when ammunition on board HMS *Bulwark* exploded off Sheerness in November 1914. Earlier that month, twenty-four musicians were killed on HMS *Monmouth* at the battle of Coronel.[94]

At Eastney Barracks, Marine Bandsman Reed and his colleagues 'practiced together every day, all the time waiting for the word "go". At last the great day arrived to join a ship.'[95] In September 1914, Reed was one of ten boys with a Band Corporal and three senior musicians plus a Bandmaster to join HMS *Donegal*, an armoured cruiser of 9,800 tons, 463 feet in length and with a crew of 742. They were issued with inflatable rubber lifebelts then on to a short course in Action Stations Fire Control. Reed recalled that they 'were under the Gunnery Officer at all times whilst the action lasted. One man to each gun casement, and one each in the fore and aft turret.'[96] The band shared the same living quarters as the other sailors, sleeping in hammocks and helping with coaling as Reed maintained that only the chaplain and surgeon were excused from that arduous duty.[97] Reed underlined that they did less music in wartime 'mostly in harbor, when not coaling; and at sea for the lower-deck ratings as they were called, usually between 12 and 12.30 pm, or after tea'. As young bandsmen, they were excused from night watches 'but at all "action stations" we were on duty round the guns'. In harbour they played for 'Colours', the hoisting of the Union Jack, and they also played the National Anthem of Britain's allies, which included 'France, Russia, Serbia, Montenegro, Japan, etc.'.[98] Three of the British battleships sunk at the Battle of Jutland carried Royal Marines Bands: forty-eight bandsmen were lost with HMS *Invincible*, HMS *Indefatigable* and HMS *Queen Mary*. More seagoing bands would be lost 1914–18, including those serving on HMS *Natal* and HMS *Vanguard*. From 1904, developments in gunnery required centralised fire control methods. Increasingly, musicians were employed in fire control teams as they were, by virtue of their musical training, to be 'better suited to the manipulation of delicate and complicated instruments than ordinary seamen'.[99] Greater demand for this type of skilled work on board may have contributed to the three-fold increase in recruitment into the Royal Marines music service between 1904 and 1912, as many more were required to work in ships' Transmitting Stations, the rooms where calculations relating to gunnery were worked, from which ranges and deflections were sent back to the gun crews.[100] H. P. K.Oram described how he served in the fire control crew of HMS *Orion* 'surrounded by Bandsmen acolytes', and Royal Marine bandsman George Moody was one of twenty-four musicians on Admiral Jellicoe's HMS *Iron Duke*.[101] Moody and most of the musicians were stationed in the bowels of the ship known as the 'Black Hole'. Moody recalled that they had to stay locked in for around three hours as the battle raged about them, knowing that they would not be released if the ship were to go down.[102]

The Royal Naval Music School continued to train and supply Marines Bandsmen for the needs of the fleet (Figure 3.1). Captain Franklin, Musical Director of the RNSM, held the usual half yearly examination

Figure 3.1 IWM Q 18673: A band composed of sailors and Royal Marines, playing aboard the light cruiser HMS *Concord*. © Imperial War Museum.

'which was entirely satisfactory, and, considering the large output of boys recently, and those under examination being consequently younger, was really above the average'.[103] Promotions continued and more bandsmen were enrolled at the school. In March 1915, the *Globe and Laurel* was pleased to say that 'It is satisfactory to know that these non-commissioned officers and also the other band ranks serving afloat in various parts of the world are fulfilling their not unimportant role in the fighting efficiency of His Majesty's ships in a commendable manner. ... This is a new departure for R. M. Band ranks and highly creditable.'[104] When the Royal Naval Division was reformed in 1915, a band was formed at HMS *Crystal Palace* as training establishment where it regularly led route marches and provided entertainments. Bandsmen were sent to the Mediterranean to take part in the Dardenelles campaign. Bandmaster Faithfull and his band once again went into action and served with great distinction with Drake Battalion on board the *Franconia* and sent to the Dardenelles, Cape Helles, as part of Mediterranean Expeditionary Force's first-aid party and stretcher-bearers. Three died of wounds or disease. The remaining bandsmen returned to Eastney at the end of January 1916. Bandsmen were fully occupied but the non-musical aspects of their work were emphasised: 'Bandmaster W. Faithfull and his band recently left with their battalion for a destination somewhere on the Continent' and that another band under Bandmaster George Devereux 'recently detailed for a ship . . . and are hard at work drilling at their new stations therein'.[105]

In early 1915, Sir John French was insistent that the BEF 'desperately needed bands, if morale in the ranks was to be maintained'. Kneller Hall dispatched instruments and music to the Western Front, although Kneller Hall's Commandant, Colonel T. C. F. Somerville, thought this was an opportunity to get rid of the older instruments which were returned and better stock requested.[106] The supply of instruments to fighting units was haphazard, and heavily reliant on charitable donations. This was also the case in the French Army where troops were supplied with instruments by the Ligue Francaise, the Ligue des Patriots and the Touring Club de France which provided flutes and violins, mandolines and guitars. Meanwhile, Bandmaster Rogan had made requests to take the full regimental Band over to the troops. However, permission was not granted until later in the autumn of 1915, when the War Office decided to send out bands of the Brigade of Guards in turn for spells of three months' duty with the Guards Division.[107] By 12 November 1915, the Band of the Grenadier Guards played to the Coldstreams in a concert at La Gorgue.[108] On 25 June 1916, 2 and 3 companies of the 1st Battalion Coldstream Guards enjoy a concert given by the Band of the Scots Guards.[109] Thirty-three members of the Coldstream band went out to France and Flanders on three tours (Figure 3.2). Two tours of fourteen weeks where undertaken January to May 1916 and also in 1917, and a longer visit of four and a half months took place in 1918 when the band accompanied the Guards Division from Berle-au-Bois to Lagnicourt, Cambrai, Mauberge, then on to Cologne where the band stayed for a month.[110] Rogan recalled that it was the highlight of his Army career as he felt that 'the fighting men, who had every kind of danger and discomfort to face – these too, so everyone felt, ought to have their own music'.[111]

The Guards bands were popular throughout the Army. On the first tour, Rogan and his musicians sailed from Southampton to Le Havre and marched five miles to the Guards' camp at Harfleur. They gave a concert in the camp that afternoon and stayed for five days to give numerous concerts to the men. They went on to join the Guards Division at La Gorgue. The bandsmen were billeted in two haylofts they named 'The Savoy' and 'The Cecil' hotels. Rogan was billeted in a house with refugees from La Bassée and Armentières. He was shocked by their accounts of their treatment by the Germans which 'was enough to make one's hair

Figure 3.2 Cartoon of John Mackenzie-Rogan and the Band of the Coldstream Guards playing on the Western Front: *The Gazette of the 3rd London General Hospital*, August 1916, p. 282.

stand on end with fury'.[112] The real work had begun. They played a concert at Divisional HQ in the morning, the square in the afternoon and in the cinema hall in the evening. The event was so popular men had to be turned away from the latter: 'At once we realised the great value of music to our sorely tried men.'[113] While he was at HQ, Rogan met the Prince of Wales who was serving in the Guards Division and who took great interest in the programmes. Rogan was invited to dinner at HQ and HRH visited Rogan in billets to discuss the music to be played at the concerts. Rogan underlined that the men knew of the prince's involvement and that they were grateful to their 'Royal comrade'.[114] However, Rogan spent a good deal of time in the field to ensure that the men were getting the music he had come to give them. Rogan obtained permission from his commanding officer, General Feilding, to play battalions going in and out of the line. This had not been done by any band before.[115] He recalled the first time the band went to meet a battalion coming out of the line:

We took them by surprise a couple of miles from La Gorgue and they happened to be our own 3rd Battalion, commanded by Colonel John Campbell.... They, good chaps, were tramping along, each man carrying his seventy or eighty pounds of kit, and many of them bent over with the weight of it. But, at the first tap of the big drum the difference in those self-same men was wonderful to see, and when the band began to play there were cheers you might have heard miles away. I saw tears trickling down Colonel Campbell's face. It was a wondrous and very affecting experience. We played them for five miles or so, then returned to La Gorgue.[116]

The Guards band played for every unit: 'On the way up we used to turn off at a given point, then play the battalion past with the quick-step of its own regiment.'[117] Rogan had many conversations about music with commanders in France and Flanders. He recalled that Brigadier-General John Ponsonby had a very keen interest in music and had many discussions with Rogan about 'music, music, *and more music*' for the troops.[118] Rogan arranged for ten to twelve bandsmen to play at smoking concerts organised by the sergeants. He appears to have found great satisfaction from getting out to the front, although in common with most officers, he strongly disliked having to censor the bandsmen's letters.[119] Nevertheless, the Coldstream Band had their own 'small experience of the real thing' during their performances which were often accompanied by 'earth-shaking shells exploding all the time a few hundred yards away from us and a big air fight proceeding simultaneously'.[120]

On their first visit, the Coldstream Guards band played at Merville, and at a YMCA hut in Laventie, assisted by a Welsh Choir. YMCA facilities were meeting places for the continuation of military music on less formal lines. The provision of a piano or a concert would draw in men who were musical and who were looking to keep up their practice, play music for sheer enjoyment or who thought they could do better than some of the performers they had listened to. Those who displayed a decent level of talent were picked up by the YMCA or the nearest Bandmaster, or both in the case of Corporal Johnson Double during his convalescence on Malta. Double was clearly regarded as a competent player of the piano and cornet. His diary records that he is playing with the band almost daily; playing music for drilling troops, concerts in the officers' and sergeants' messes, church parades, consecration of cemeteries and local ceremonial duties.[121] Double became a key figure for musical activities in his camp. After the bandmaster left the island with his band in March, he recorded that he was auditioning a few men for a concert to be held at a future date but they were '[a]bsolutely "rotten"'.[122] Nevertheless, membership of the band often conferred some privileges. After giving a concert in the officers' mess one evening, the band 'were all invited into the mess for refreshments, what ho!'[123] That Double's diary often mentions a 'thick head' in the mornings suggest that this was a reasonably regular occurrence. Increasing numbers were joining Double's band on Malta. By the end of October 1916, he recorded that the band occupied three tents.[124]

The presence of a unit's band was reported as a boost to the servicemen's spirits. In billets in late May/early June 1917, the presence of the Battalion Orchestra of the 2/6th (Rifle) Battalion 'The King's' (Liverpool Regiment) 'made itself felt, with excellent results'. Ten instruments were 'brought over for us by the Division' in 'regimental baggage'.[125] Chaplain Leonard sometimes found that 'it was impossible to realise that we were at war'. At a dinner for officers to celebrate their colonel's DSO in the King's birthday honours on 'a beautiful warm, scented night' the Divisional Band 'played selections from the musical comedies, inside choice wines and rare fruits circulated freely. The large French windows are thrown back and we could see and amid the flowering shrubs of the garden the flickering lights of the band, and the antics of the conductor.'[126] Certainly, the Guards' regimental band tours helped the men to feel that the army cared something for their well-being, and furthermore that bandsmen who largely stayed at home, as the Guards Division bandsmen did, were sharing in the dangers of the fighting areas. At an evening concert at a cinema hall close to the station at Poperinghe, the band was playing the music of *La Reine de Saba* when 'the building seemed to rock with the ferocity of the fire from the enemy and we could hear the splinters falling on the roof'. Rogan wrote that they finished the piece 'in record time'.[127] After a concert in the cinema hall at Poperinghe the night before their departure, Major-General Feilding said of the Coldstream Band that they had 'stood by us, has cheered us, and has generally made our lives bright. We see it go with much regret'. Three cheers were given for Rogan and the band. In his response, Rogan underlined that the band 'had only done our duty as soldiers belonging to a great regiment, one with imperishable traditions, which we all tried to live up to'.[128] He felt that his trips 'had told me much of the fine spirit of our men'.[129]

On his third visit to the Western Front in the summer of 1917, Rogan was suffering headaches and 'a general feeling of strain' but he was determined to stay on 'knowing how much the music meant to the troops'.[130] Rogan's sixty-fifth birthday on 5 February 1917 was the date on which he would have expected to leave army service, and the first request for Rogan's retirement was made in November 1916. However, the Duke of Connaught and the King instruct the War Office to extend Rogan's service, invoking Article 120 of the Royal Warrant which states that an officer may be retained beyond the normal age limit under special circumstances. In Rogan's case, the argument was made for his retention 'during the continuance of the emergency'. The matter of Rogan's successor appears to have caused some consternation among those waiting for the great bandmaster to retire. The first replacement to be suggested in November 1916 was Bandmaster Arthur Stretton of the Royal Artillery, Director of Music at Kneller Hall. This appointment would have been supported by Colonel Cameron Somerville, the Commandant of Kneller Hall. Somerville did not agree with the extension given to Rogan, and in January 1917 the War Office reassured Somerville that the retention of Rogan would make him 'supernumerary to the establishment' and would not block the promotion of another bandmaster. It was underlined that 'no injustice will be done' but that his disappointment was understandable that 'one of your waiting men will be prevented from getting the expected vacancy in the Coldstream Guards'.[131]

Rogan's work for the cause of military music was seen as essential to Britain's war effort. The bandmaster certainly believed that military music was a vital part of keeping men and money coming in to the war and maintaining the identity and morale of the men when they were on active service. The composer Henry Walford Davies would have been in whole-hearted agreement. Having worked with the YMCA to encourage choral singing, in April 1918, Henry Walford Davies was appointed Organizing Director of Music for the RAF.[132] Many people thought there was no need for another military school of music, but he continued with his quest to put music in the RAF on the same footing as the Navy and the Army. He immediately requested from the Air Ministry approximately 100 bandsmen to establish the first official RAF bands, planning for four regional bands with a fifth 'central' band based in London. This was at first approved but the Director of Manpower reduced number to fifty musicians. Walford Davies then asked for fifty instructors, each to lead one voluntary band, which was granted. After discussions at the War Office that mooted the idea of basing the RAF Music School with that of the Army at Kneller Hall, it was decided that there was insufficient room for the RAF musicians, and they were granted the use of a house at No.1 Fitzjohn's Avenue, Hampstead, NW3.[133] The RAF music school opened on 2 July 1918, and its first Commanding Officer was Captain Claude Powell. The first regional band was established at Blandford, Powell taking twenty-five musicians from there to France.[134] Thanks to Walford Davies' work to establish the RAF Music School, by the closing months of the war Britain's armed forces had three military music schools from which they could train and deploy their own musicians. Music in the form of military bands had continued to prove essential to servicemen's morale and identity, and it is the ways in which servicemen maintained their espirit de corps through song to which we will turn in the following chapter.

4   Songs, Identity and Morale

Songs have often been linked to certain periods of warfare. At the fall of Sevastopol, the song of the day was said to have been Henry Russell's *Cheer, Boys, Cheer!* At the Relief of Lucknow, it was *The Campbells are Coming*, and in the Boer campaign *Soldiers of the Queen* was often sung.[1] There were a number of publications that sought to provide appropriate songs to be sung by members of the British armed forces. Composer Charles Purday had edited *The Royal Naval Song Book* in 1867. Two examples from the 1890s include Chief Bandmaster G. W. Bishop's *Royal Naval Song Book* (1890), a collection of fifty national songs using the tonic sol-fa method, and George Farmer's *Scarlett & Blue: Songs for Soldiers and Sailors* (1896) which contained a selection of one hundred 'stirring' songs to be sung by servicemen, including *The British Grenadiers* and *Ye Mariners of England*.[2] The Naval and Military Musical Union also produced their own collections of songs to encourage part-singing and participation in their annual competition for the George Farmer Cup which was first contested in 1912.[3]

These collections had two main objectives. Firstly, they ensured that the traditional songs of the Army and Navy were preserved as essential parts of each services' identity and heritage, to encapsulate their sense of espirit de corps and to be passed on to newly enlisted men. Secondly, they acted as a barrier to protect the musical traditions of the forces from being affected by 'popular Music Hall effusions'.[4] *Marching Songs and Tommy's Tunes: A Handbook for Our Soldiers* was published shortly after the declaration of war. The object of the volume was 'to lighten the long monotonous tramps which belong to the training of recruits, whether for the front or the Territorials'. The book was intended to act as prompt for 'the tired soldier' who may not be able 'to call [the songs] to mind on the spur of the moment'. Explaining the way singing on the march worked, the book states that 'some musical spirit strikes up a familiar song which goes with a swing; others join in, and success is established'. However, music hall numbers were not included because the editors said they had 'lost their freshness' and 'for this reason we have not included in the present collection any songs of that class'. Instead, they selected 'the sterling, undying National Melodies of England, Scotland, Ireland and Wales' because they are 'melodies which bring with them memories of home. There is not a solider in the British army whose heart is not quickened, and whose nerve is not steeled by thoughts of those for whom he is fighting.'[5]

The volume starts with the songs *John Peel*, *Killarney*, *Britannia the Pride of the Ocean* and *The Campbells are Coming*. The marching songs include *Oh, Dem German Rippers*, *The Distracted Kaiser*, *The German Bounder* and *The Muddled Kaiser*. In 1914, Lord Wolseley's *Soldiers' Song-Book* stated that troops who sing on the march 'will not only reach their destination more quickly, and in better fighting condition, than those that march in silence, but inspired by the music and words of national songs, will feel that self-confidence which is the mother of victory'. The German Army was known to regularly use music on the march. The Salvation Army, firm believers in the power of song, claimed that the song *Wacht am Rhein* had been 'chanted along every road in the east of France [and] superadded to the Germans a fighting value of the moral kind equivalent to at least a couple of army Corps'.[6] Indeed, the National Service League's *Songs for Our Soldiers* is introduced by Field Marshal Roberts who wrote that he hoped 'the words of favourite songs that have shortened many a weary mile may increase that melody on the line of march, which is the expression of the buoyant spirits for which the British soldier has always been famous'. The NSL's collection opens with *The Old Brigade* and includes *Tipperary* and *Marching Through Georgia.*[7]

In 1915, Henry Walford Davies' *Songs Old and New: For Use in Wartime* featured a mixture of patriotic and folk tunes. A year later, the composer released *The Aldershot Song Book for Regimental Choirs: Thirty-Eight Songs for Camp Concerts.*[8] Some regiments produced their own collections of song. For example, the Artists' Rifles published *Songs for Marching and Camp* for 'private circulation'. The opening number is the unit's 'regimental chorus', *Cum Marte Minerva*, which outlines that 'Ready at England's call are we;/The arts of peace themselves shall aid us,/We fight for King and liberty.' The collection contains some recognisably folk-based ditties such as *Mowed Meadow*, but it also includes Farmer's Harrovian anthem *Forty Years On*, and finishes with *They All Love Jack*, the regimental march.[9] It should be underlined that servicemen may have read some of these collections, but they did not necessarily use them as the editors intended. Arthur Ainger's *Marching Songs for Soldiers* (1914), for example, contained a number of patriotic songs.[10] However, the lyrics provided by the retired Eton schoolmaster did not appear to sit comfortably with some of the men he expected to sing them. A correspondent serving in the Army identified only as 'H. L.' wrote to *The Times* to point out the unlikeliness of his colleagues using some of the high language featured in Ainger's collection. Instead, he helpfully offered the lyrics to 'the latest popular marching song from Aldershot':

> Send out the Army and the Navy,
> Send out the rank and file.   (Have a banana!)
>
> Send out the brave Territorials,
> They can easily run a mile.   (I don't think)
>
> Send out the boys of the girls' brigade,
> They will keep old England free;
> Send out my mother, my sister and my brother,
> But for goodness' [Gawd's] sake don't send me.'[11]

Every unit had a few men who had a repertoire of popular tunes and could sing well, songs such as *The Lost Chord, Trumpeter, What Are You Sounding Now* and *Sweet and Low*. Some songs were inherited from the professional Army and Navy pre-1914 and many derived from an oral tradition reaching back to the press gangs and prisons of the eighteenth century. Not all soldiers' songs are bawdy. The soothing lilt of lullabies and ballads were popular at nightfall, especially those with domestic themes that reminded the young men of their homes and families.[12] Certain songs were popular at specific periods in the war. The most common themes found in the songs of the war are morale boosting, looking forward to better times ahead and the dream of home. The songs would also mock the Germans and take a sardonic view of authority, and at least 20 per cent of soldiers' songs are humorous in content.[13] Soldiers sang on the march, for exercise or to move quarters, after the commands of 'March at Ease' and 'March Easy'. The Army encouraged singing as they thought it was good for morale: destinations were not widely shared or correct so distances were generally unknown. In August 1914, it was reported that the Buckinghamshire Territorials had taken to singing as 'an aid to energy'. It was 'found that the music relieves the weariness of long route marches'.[14] There were 'a very few things that helped to alleviate the lot of those who toiled and fought through the anxious years of 1914–18' and among them were the songs men sung on active service. There were hundreds of songs that were sung across the services, and for veterans 'the idle humming of a bar' could 'bring the war vividly back into memory'. Only smell was thought to be 'so powerfully evocative of the past as a tune. Most of the smells, mercifully, do not come back, but the tunes do, bringing pleasanter memories with them.'[15] The majority of songs were never meant to be taken too seriously. The *Airmen's Songbook* fondly insists that the majority of songs are 'mere doggerel', that they had 'no pretensions for lyric quality' and warning that once they are deprived of their spontaneity 'you take away their fun and spirit'.[16]

Musical tastes remained highly subjective. One newspaper opined that 'the Boer War was a picnic to that obtaining now, yet no one has come forward with a real tearaway Tommy song'.[17] There was a difference between the songs servicemen liked to sing and those the civilians thought they ought to be singing. The prime example of this musical disconnect between the home and fighting fronts is the song *Tipperary*, written by Jack Judge and Harry Williams in 1912. It was one of the most popular anthems sung by soldiers on the Western Front during the early stages of the war in the autumn of 1914 because George Curnock, a newspaper war correspondent for the *Daily Mail*, had heard a band play the song for one of the first ships of British soldiers to disembark in Boulogne in August 1914. He made a great deal of the song in his dispatches, and within a few days a great number of newspapers had printed the lyrics and they were shown on the screens in cinemas.[18] It was quickly taken up by the music halls and thousands of performances followed, particularly after references to the song were made in relation to the Army's retreat from Mons. Described by one journalist as 'the majestic epic of endurance ... when the artillery of five German army corps ... were turned upon Smith-Dorrien's exhausted men, one of our Engineers struck up "Tipperary" ... Our fellows were dropping by the roadside an falling asleep in their tracks ... the old tune revived them.'[19] By the end of 1914, some 2 million copies of the sheet music had been sold.[20] To hum or sing the song became the patriotic thing to do, but ubiquity soon bred contempt. By the winter of 1914, although civilians retained their affection for the song, the soldiers were sick of it, and attempts to sing *Tipperary* were 'often howled and whistled down'.[21] Chaplain Tiplady of the London Territorials wrote that by 1918 he had only heard it sung once in France, and that was by 'a little French boy on the tail of a cart'.[22] NCO Percy Harris recalled that he and his comrades on the 15th Battalion King's Liverpool Regiment 'didn't think much of *Tipperary*' which they believed had been 'fathered on the British troops by a newspaper correspondent'.[23] American tunes were popular, but Harris also underlined that on the move his unit liked to sing their own version of the regimental march, *Here's to a Maiden of the Bashful Fifteen*:

> What did you join the Terriers for?
> Why didn't you join the Army?

What did you join the Terriers for?
You must have been bloody well barmy!
Skilly and duff, skilly and duff,
Blummy good stuff but you don't get enough,
Skilly and duff, skilly and duff,
Blummy good stuff but you don't get enough. [*sic*][24]

The popular music publishing industry saw an opportunity to combine patriotism and profit. When Britain declared war on Germany, the search for a new hit started, and by 1915 a competition for new wartime songs was run by Francis and Day publishers. For a total prize fund of 100 guineas, the search was on for the best examples of ballads, chorus songs and marching songs. The judges were music hall star Harry Lauder, theatrical director Albert de Courville and the publisher Fred Day. In August 1915, *The Era* newspaper announced that the song *Pack Up Your Troubles in Your Old Kit Bag* by Felix Powell and George Asaf had won first prize for a marching song, with Tony Lloyd and Bert Lee gaining second prize with *Taffy's Got His Jenny in Glamorgan.*[25] By January 1916, *Pack Up Your Troubles* had 'won for itself a front place in the affections of the public. The chorus is conceived in the spirit of melodious optimism and possesses the infectious quality so essential in a song if it is to stand any chance of becoming a great popular favourite.'[26] *Pack Up Your Troubles* was regularly performed in concert parties and music halls on the home front, and was translated into several different languages. However, in August 1917, *The Spectator* asserted that a 'visitor from Mars would make no correct conception of the British Army by the study of its songs. ... English soldiers sing as children sing – for the pleasure of shouting'.[27]

Informal singing had always taken place on board the ships of the Royal Navy. When Bandmaster Rogan sailed to South Africa in July 1867 on the troop ship *Malabar,* there was no band on board but 'whenever the evening was fine bluejackets and troops would assemble on the fo'c'sle and sing popular songs and sea chanties [sic].'[28] In September 1914, an article in *The Fleet*, the weekly naval paper, sought to define 'The Spirit of the Navy': 'In warfare, whether by land or sea, ... the thing that matters most to us in this immense conflict, the thing that is infinitely more to us than our supremacy in ships and guns, is the spirit of our men.'[29] *The Fleet* claimed that this spirit stemmed from a 'tradition of success', and that 'Jack Tar', 'The Man Behind the Gun', was even impervious to the praise he received in the form of popular music:

I've seen my tally mentioned in the pages of the Press;
I've 'eard my praises sung in music 'alls;

I've 'eard a lot of gushin', light an' foolish more or less,
An' what I dares to do w'en duty calls.[30]

The strong tradition and inheritance of naval music can be seen in the
feature 'Sea Songs Old and New', printed over three pages of *The Fleet* in
December 1914. They included *Neptune to England, Fair Sally Lov'd
a Bonny Sailor* and *The Hero of the Steam*.[31] Certainly, Gunner Jakeman
of the Royal Marine Artillery wrote in March 1915 that it was 'wonderful
to see the high spirit our men fight in – every man happy and singing on
going into battle'.[32] Spontaneous singing was a natural group activity
among excited – and nervous – young men. Shortly after enlistment,
George Butterworth enjoyed the train journey from Paddington to the
regimental depot at Bodmin saying that it was 'a hilarious one – beer and
singing *ad. Lib*'.[33] In 1915, it was noted that British soldiers 'are happiest
in sing-songs of their own devising, whether in grim war-zone towns, in
the ruined village "Place" or in Allied company round the camp fire by the
ghostly wood's edge'.[34] Private E. Todd recalled that

There'd be times when you would sit around on the fire-step. The lads would
sit and talk and sing. Coming towards evening they would get sentimental
talking about their homes. We had one chap who was a very, very good singer
and he used to indulge in his singing and lead us in the choruses and he was
always inclined to get a bit sentimental. But we had to shut him up for obvious
reasons, as we couldn't stand too much of that.... We would have mouth
organs of course and well, there was nothing else to do but talk, reminisce
and sing.[35]

Echoing Bruce Bairnsfather's cartoon, 'The Conscientious Exhilarator'
(Figure 4.1), one young soldier wrote to his parents that the day before he
had 'felt in despair, and the others were just as bad. Then I caught sight of
a box lying on the ground in the middle of the camp, and some impulse
made me jump on it and begin singing, "There's a land, a dear land."
Everyone gathered round and cheered at the end. *After that we all felt
better*.'[36] When the surviving sailors from the torpedoed ship *Laurentic*
were rescued and taken to the nearest on-shore camp, the local mayor
relayed that the first thing a 17-year-old sailor did on entering the recreation hut was to sit down at the piano and play *Pack Up Your Troubles*.
A group of his comrades gathered around the piano to sing along. The
mayor wrote that he found himself 'in the presence of what I can only call
the unconquerable spirit of the British Navy'.[37] Indeed, the therapeutic
benefits of singing en masse were recognised during the war. The composer Henry Walford Davies dedicated himself to teaching soldiers to sing
in participatory concerts with a broad repertoire of folk tunes, homely
ditties, rounds and sea shanties.[38] Davies underlined that

The Conscientious Exhilarator

" Every encouragement should be given for singing and whistling."—(Extract from a " Military Manual.")

That painstaking fellow, Lieut. Orpheus, does his best, but finds it uphill work at times

Figure 4.1 Bruce Bairnsfather, 'The Conscientious Exhilarator', *The Bystander*, 1917. © 2019 The Estate of Barbara Bruce Littlejohn. All Rights Reserved.

A brass band is all very well in its way, but it does not come near the male voice choir in the production of the best music.... Get the men to do something together and you have started an *esprit de corps* among them which will have a tremendous influence for good, and will do more than any of us imagine to make life in camp, in barrack, or billet, or in the outpost more tolerable.[39]

From December 1915, Ivor Novello's *Keep the Home Fires Burning* was popular with both civilians and servicemen. While it was not used as a marching song it was seen as 'a cheerful song ... calculated to keep up the spirits of both listener and singer'.[40] However, many of the servicemen's favourite songs were not designed to be marching tunes. Written in 1913 by American composer Alonzo Elliott, *There's A Long, Long Trail* was turned down by all the major American publishers before the outbreak of war. Elliott is reported to have had in mind Napoleon's retreat from Moscow when he composed the song, and it was not until Elliott moved from Yale to Cambridge University in 1914 that the song was taken up by a British publisher. Out to buy a new piano for his room in Cambridge, Elliott happened to play *There's A Long, Long Trail* to test each instrument, and piano dealer was so impressed by the song he put the composer in touch with a music publisher. The song was soon taken up by Canadian troops – 620,000 of whom fought for Britain in the Great War – who were heard singing it while sailing down the Thames, and it was also keenly taken up by American troops who started to arrive on the Western Front when the United States entered the war in April 1917. The song proved to be commercially successful with 4 million copies sold over the course of the conflict. Another example is *Gilbert the Filbert, 'The Knut with a K'*, performed by Basil Hallam, was a popular tune before anyone thought of it as a marching song. Columns of men, 'many of them approximating to the type which the song satirized, swung along in the newly-learned march-step' and sang the song in the early months of the war. Another of the best-liked, *Yip-i-addy-i-ay*, 'might never have been heard had not George Grossmith insisted on singing it at the Gaiety, against the judgement of George Edwardes'.[41] Another was:

> Hullo! Hullo! Who's your lady friend,
> Who's the little girlie by your side?
> . . .
> It's not the girl I saw you with at Brighton!
> Who – who – who's your lady friend?

The three 'whos' in the last line produced an enormous effect when they were roared out by a company of young men going along in the easy rhythm of the route march. So did the climax of *Hold Your Hand Out, Naughty Boy*.[42] Different companies and battalions within the Army would have a preferred repertoire of songs and they would often customise the words. The voice of the soldier is preferred to that of the establishment. Soldier-composed songs were often based on existing popular songs or hymns and were collectively or anonymously composed usually existing in many variants, for example *Mademoiselle d'Armentières*. This was the song that Bandsman Shawyer remembered the most, recalling that it swept through the ranks 'like a dry grass fire'. To his mind 'it was a foregone conclusion that such a song would one day arrive, and when it did, it was bawled with gusto, and many variations of the words, along the cobblestone roads, the tree-lined unending country roads, and in billets where the B.E.F. happened to be'.[43]

Some sources have also attributed *Mademoiselle d'Armentières* to Lieutenant Gitz Ingraham Rice. Rice studied at the Conservatory of Music, McGill University, before joining the Canadian Expeditionary Force, enlisting in what became the First Canadian Contingent, the day after Britain declared war against Germany. He served on the Western Front as a gunnery officer with the 5th Battery, 2nd Brigade, Canadian Field Artillery. Rice joined Princess Patricia's Canadian Light Infantry Comedy Company as a piano player. According to one version of events, Rice wrote his own lyrics to this tune, while in a café in Armentières in 1915. The lyrics are said to have been inspired by a barmaid he observed serving drinks to soldiers. Some days afterwards, he sang his new lyrics for the Canadian troops of the Fifth Battery, Montréal, stationed nearby. However, Rice is most closely associated with the patriotic songs he wrote during the First World War, and with the concert parties that became a big part of building the morale of Canadian troops. Rice epitomises the close connection between soldier and professionally composed songs. Many of his songs were patriotic or sentimental such as the hugely popular *Dear Old Pal of Mine*, especially in the version sung by John McCormack. But he was also responsible for *The Conscientious Objector's Lament*, often titled *For Gawd's Sake Don't Send Me* in its 'trench' version. This was composed with Davy Burnaby for the musical revue *Round the Map* in which it was sung by one of the music hall's biggest stars, Alfred Lester.

It was said that the year 1917 would be characterised by 'Tommy and Jack, the high-spirited men who comprise 66 per cent of the audience at any house of entertainment, no matter what type of production. Our fighting lads are fully entitled to say what they want.' The song *The Conscientious Objector's Lament* was listed as 'a laughter number' and the lyrics of the chorus were printed to whet the audience's appetite.[44] Despite the success and popularity of *The Conscientious Objector's Lament*, Rice was best known for songs he composed during the Battle of Ypres in 1915; *I Want to Go Home* and *Dear Old Pal of Mine*. The latter was his most popular song, in which a soldier laments his absence from his girlfriend. The first line states 'All my life is empty, since I went away' and the refrain affirms the soldier's loneliness: 'Oh, how I want you, dear old pal.'[45] Along with *Pack Up Your Troubles* and *Colonel Bogey* Arthur Boynton*'s Are we downhearted?* was a popular song sung by British troops on the march. In August 1915, this song formed part of the Reverend Noel Mellish's attempts to describe his auditory experiences of the Western Front to his parishioners at home. Among the sounds of motors, trams and horses, he wrote that it was the marching songs of British soldiers that stood out:

Here they come, drafts of different regiments for the front, a compact body of hard, bronzed fighting men. Each man carries a heavy load – pack, ammunition, entrenching tool, and rifle. His ration-bag is tied at the back, and swings backwards and forwards with his stride. His hat is pushed back on his head, he is sweating under heavy load and a three-mile march from camp . . . and what is the song he sings? Its constantly repeated refrain is, 'We are not downhearted yet'.[46]

Chaplain Pat Leonard was similarly taken with soldiers' songs. He wrote that his unit had been on the move for twenty-four hours, with nothing to eat 'but a drink of tea made on the field', as the men marched to billets 'the whole country side [sic] was awakened by [their] full throated craving to return to Dixie land or Michigan or some other uncouth place in Ragtime land, or [their] vociferous protestation that [they were] or would be true to some lady unknown, but masquerading under a galaxy of *noms d'amour*'.[47] In 1916, a YMCA hut leader described how

Soldiers sing even when they must have for accompaniment the unceasing growl of the guns on the way to and from the trenches. . . . Often I have stood almost reverently fascinated as there passed along the road to 'the salient' companies of war-tired soldiers, singing as they went to take their place behind the sand-bagged parapet . . . lightening that heavy pack and making light their own spirits as well, singing in resounding unison some cheery, rollicking songs . . . many of them topical and original. Mr Thomas Atkins is past-master in the art of improvisation, and so it is not surprising that he often adapts words of his own to some familiar tune.[48]

There were some occasions when song was used to indicate the feelings of the men to their commanding officers. Frederick Nettleingham asserted that he had heard of the song *Grousing* – sung to the tune of *Holy, Holy, Holy* – 'being sternly suppressed by company commanders, where men have spent long hours on the march, as being detrimental to good discipline'. It contains the verse:

Marching, marching, marching,
Always ruddy well marching,
Marching all the morning,

> And marching all the night.
> Marching, marching, marching,
> Always ruddy well marching,
> Roll on 'till my time is up,
> Then I shall march no more.[49]

Some British soldiers were fascinated by the music of the men in the opposing trenches. In December 1914, an English officer described the German soldier saying that 'He isn't the downhearted kind of man that everybody tries to believe. Night upon night we hear them singing their patriotic Kaiser Bill kind of songs in their trenches.' The officer added that 'they even join in the chorus of that "Tipperary" thing when our soldiers sing it in the trenches, which I think shows they are not as blue as people like to believe'. Furthermore, the Germans have 'a brass band somewhere behind their trenches, which sometimes plays in the evening'.[50]

George Butterworth relayed that the Durham miners under his command had taught him a number of good folk tunes.[51] Before the outbreak of war, Butterworth was a founder member of the English Folk Dance and Song Society, founded by Cecil Sharp in 1911. Sharp was leading the revival of British Folk music in the early 1900s, and Butterworth had been a member of Sharp's Morris Dancing demonstration group. The drive to collect and preserve the songs of rural England was a primary aim of Sharp and the members of EFDSS.[52] The anthropological significance of songs sung by communities is in evidence during the Great War. However, the desire to preserve the songs of servicemen was not a peculiarly British pursuit. In 1917, American Air Force pilot John J. Niles began to collect the wartime songs sung by the black soldiers of the AEF. Niles had been inspired after seeing a copy of Théodore Botrel's *Les Chants du Bivouac* in Paris. Singer-songwriter Botrel had been commissioned by the French Ministry of War to sing and recite patriotic songs and poems to French servicemen, to whom he was known as *Chansonnier des Armées*. Niles soon found that the 'white boys' tended to sing not from their imaginations but from Broadway shows, so he decided to study the songs of black soldiers because they had 'their own kind of folk music' which they 'brought up to date and adapted according to the wartime conditions'.[53] Another example comes from Private Sam Naishtad of the South African Infantry Brigade. He published fifty-five songs in *The Great War Parodies of the East, Central African and Flanders Campaigns,* which he claimed 'explain in merit the life of soldiers on the fields of battle and in the base camps'.[54]

During his thirteen months of service with the RFC from July 1916, in October 1917, Second Lieutenant Frederick Thomas Nettleingham[55] underlined that 'the great aim of this work is to present and perpetuate the original and unwritten tunes and rhymes' of the British servicemen at war.[56] *Tommy's Tunes* and its sequel are fascinating primary sources which tell us a great deal about servicemen's attitudes to various aspects of their wartime experiences. Nettleingham warned that 'woe betide any foreigner who dares to opine we're not what we think we are. The spirit really evinced by these songs, in spite of their oft-time derogatory purport, is that of a lofty cynicism and a confirmed fatalism, but real, thick, unadulterated sarcasm – never.'[57] Reviews of the first collection in publications such as *The Spectator, New Statesman* and the *Musical Herald* were rather condescending.[58] Not that Nettleingham cared as he had already stated that they 'should be reviewed by none other than men with Army experience'.[59] The songs belonged exclusively to servicemen, a sign of membership and belonging which excluded those who had not served.

As the servicemen's self-appointed musical spokesperson, Nettleingham stated that men liked 'the latest music-hall ditties' but 'the enthusiasm soon wears off'.[60] Songs were customised to the needs and wants of the men in each service, and their tastes would alter over time. As most RFC men transferred from Army, there was a fluidity between the services in regard to their songs. Different versions of songs would be adapted as required, for example *I Don't Want to Join the Army* became *I Don't Want to Join the Air Force.* Just like the Army, the men of the RFC found relief in singing 'When this war is over/You can have your R.F.C.'[61] The mocking of military authority is another theme found in many songs, and as it was often the NCOs, particularly the sergeants, who were the subject of some ribbing from the ranks. The men of the RFC were by no means immune to grumbling about the sergeants. The RFC adapted *Never Mind.* in place of the words 'If the sergeant steals your rum, never mind', the RFC sang about a sergeant 'who went to fetch rations in a side car, the light tender usually employed for this purpose being otherwise engaged. Not being able to get it all in, he tied the bread round the side and back. When he arrived at the unit, not unnaturally the bread was "napoo".' Nettleingham said this was usually performed at lunchtimes:

> If the Sergeant's lost your bread – never mind.
> If he sticks it round a side car – never mind.
> And even if it's messed – he did it for the best.
> For he's the sergeant – dontcherknow – so never mind.[62]

Chaplain Thomas Tiplady, who served with the London Territorials on the Western Front, said that there was 'no real difference' between the songs sung by officers and men. His main observation was that, in eighteen months he spent in the fighting lines, with the exception of the national anthem on formal occasions, he never once heard a patriotic song sung by British troops. Tiplady explained that the reason was simple: the soldiers' patriotism 'calls for no expression in song' as they were 'expressing it night and day . . . in the risking of their lives'. The men's hearts 'were satisfied with their deeds' and that 'songs of such a character were superfluous'.[63] Nevertheless, music had always been used as one of the mechanisms for servicemen to indicate their level of satisfaction with their officers. In the Navy, this was particularly audible at Christmas where the singing and playing of certain songs, or in the worst cases – silence, indicated the mood of a ship's crew. Lionel Yexley, editor of *The Fleet* weekly newspaper with a large circulation among the ranks of the lower decks, outlined that the real relationship between the officers and men of a man-at-war could always be gauged on Christmas Day:

It is the custom . . . just before noon, the captain, followed by all the officers, and headed by the band playing the 'Roast Beef of Old England', make a tour of the mess decks, accepting pieces of pudding, cake, and various other things offered by the cooks of the messes. Should there be any little grievance affecting the men generally, suggestive mottoes are hung up where the captain cannot fail to see them, and these, in ships where the captain takes an interest in the men, generally have the desired result.... After dinner it was the invariable custom . . . to 'chair' the officers from the command down, and carry them round the decks to the strains of 'For he's a jolly good fellow.' In ships where a good feeling does *not* exist the mess decks are left bare . . . as . . . an open declaration of resentment by them at their general treatment.[64]

Servicemen used music and song in their everyday routines on the fighting fronts. Percy Harris, a British NCO with 15th Battalion King's Liverpool Regiment, is a great example of the soldiers' adoption of tunes and music as outlets to parody their pay, conditions and routine. Harris recalled that they 'did not suffer in silence . . . we referred to our pay in song, the particular favourite in my mob . . . being':

> He's a ragtime soldier, a ragtime soldier
> Rarely on parade every morning,
> Standing to attention with his rifle in his hand,
> He's a ragtime soldier,
> Happy as the flowers in May, gawd blimey,
> He's fighting for his King and his country,
> For a lousy old tanner a day.[65]

They would also sing:

> Kitchener's Army, working all day,
> But what do they give you?

A tanner a day,
If you don't like it old Bogey will say,
Put him in the guard room,
Stop all his pay.[66]

Using a well-known hymn tune Harris' unit also sang:

We are but little soldiers meek,
We only get three bob a week,
The more we do the more we may
It makes no difference to our pay.[67]

As a new force, the RFC was beginning to develop its own musical culture.[68] The earliest squadron song is *The Bold Aviator*, sometimes referred to as *The Dying Airman*, which dates from 1912 when the RFC was formed from the Air Battalion of the Royal Engineers. Sung to the tune of *The Tarpaulin Jacket*, the chorus directs that:

Two valve springs you'll find in my stomach,
Three spark plugs are safe in my lung (my lung),
The prop is in splinters inside me,
To my fingers the joystick has clung.[69]

The narrator then proceeds to describe his funeral and the alcoholic beverages his comrades should drink to remember him. RFC pilot Sholto Douglas first encountered the song when he enlisted in the RFC in 1915, with 2 Squadron at Merville. He underlined that it was sung throughout the war by all ranks at every occasion when 'vigorously we would bawl' the chorus.[70] The words were customised by different squadrons as desired. James Gascoyne, who served with 3, 9 and 92 Squadrons on the Western Front, recalled that 3 Squadron would often sing their own version of this song in their mess.[71] Douglas refers to *The Dying Airman* as 'the perfect example of the humour that was developing' in the RFC in the early period of the war.[72] Indeed, in all of the armed forces, humour was utilised as 'a coping mechanism to deal with loss and trauma, hopelessness and dread'.[73] As Sigmund Freud's essays on 'The Joke and Its Relation to Unconsciousness' (1905) and 'Wit' (1916) outlined, humour allows topics which may be taboo to be openly articulated and expressed. This means that it was of significant use for flyers in both world wars who operated 'a veto on [the] verbal acknowledgement of fear'.[74] On a visit to the Western Front with the YMCA in 1917, the composer Percy Scholes was told by a Colonel that he hated to hear his men singing before action, but liked to hear them swearing:

'Why?' I asked.
'When men are swearing it shows they are forgetting their danger', he said.

'And when they start singing they are remembering it?'
'That's why they sing' was the reply, 'They do it to keep their
    courage up.'
'And does it do so?'
'It does.'
'Then song is the very thing we want?'[75]

Lena Ashwell wrote that while the British are 'a tongue-tied breed' it was
through music that 'we can voice our feelings without shyness or
shame'.[76] In September 1915, at Suvla Bay, Corporal Johnson William
Double of the Hampshire Regiment was preparing to disembark from the
steamer, *Prince Albas*. He wrote that the men were packed in tightly, 'like
sardines in a tin', but 'the 10th seem to be making the best of it, they are
down in one of the holds singing all sorts of songs, I expect some of that
will be taken out of them when they get into the firing line'. Double was an
experienced territorial soldier who had fought in the Boer War, and he felt
that there would be 'enough music from the shells and bullets, without
a lot of rubbishy modern songs'.[77] Singing to stave off fear was common.
In November 1916, Private H. Molsom was with the South Staffordshire
Regiment also sailing to Salonika. He wrote to his wife that they were
having a very rough voyage, and while he was staying up on deck during
a violent thunderstorm, he 'could hear the fellows singing down below'.[78]
As Francis has underlined, the RAF's hierarchy 'approached fear as
a collective problem, a challenge to military morale, discipline and fighting effectiveness which could spread like a virus through a whole fighting
unit'.[79] This was a virus that could not be allowed to infect its frontline
fighters, and methods were sought by airmen to ameliorate feelings of fear
and terror through diversions such as sport and music, superstitions,
alcohol and drugs.[80] In the First World War, as in the Second, we can
see that the fear of being killed 'was less acute than the fear of being
thought a coward by one's comrades, and with all the consequent ostra-
cism that might follow'.[81] When in 1918, an airman serving in Egypt was
overheard saying that after a raid on the aerodrome he 'had the wind up',
many of his colleagues were aghast:

What an example for the young pupils, to hear an Active Service Pilot admitting
that he 'HAD THE WIND UP'. I thought . . . that it is shocking bad taste to admit
the bare possibility of 'having the wind up' – besides, from a psychological point of
view, entirely the wrong atmosphere to create. . . . 'What a rank outsider that chap
is! We don't talk like that – damn it, it just isn't done!'[82]

The concept of 'having the wind up' could however be shared in
a humorous way via the medium of song. These kinds of tunes were
born out of mess parties of pilots and other aircrew while on operations.

The song *Omer Drome*, sung to the tune of *My Old Kentucky Home*, not only satirises the fact that aerial combat is conducive to 'having the wind up', it also makes a feature of No. 1 Aircraft Depot, St Omer. This was the base through which all machines and newly enlisted airmen had to pass on their way to their designated squadrons: 'I've got a windy feeling round my heart/And it's time that we went home/I've got a great big longing to depart/Somewhere back to Omer Drome.'[83] However, the airmen's experience has been reduced to romantic notions of RFC pilots as the 'cavalry of the clouds'. This encouraged the view that the airmen were the last vestige of chivalry, the sheer embodiment of valour and athleticism. It has led to them being perceived as supermen, possessing 'nerves of steel' and superiority of body and mind.[84] The flyers of the elite fighter squadrons, such as 56, may have been 'duelling' with their German counterparts, but they were still fighting over a modern battlefield, dominated by long distance killing by means of heavy ordnance or the machine gun, 'a domain in which the enemy was invisible and the weaponry of war highly impersonal'.[85] Nervous cases were widespread in the RFC. At least 3,149 personnel received treatment for nervous disorders, representing 13 per cent of all RFC casualties seen by medical boards. However, only 2.5 per cent were categorised as 'shell shocked'.[86] In the midst of combat, flyers were known to sing. Maurice Baring recorded that 5 Squadron named anti-aircraft fire 'Archies' from the song *Archibald! Certainly Not!*, a music hall number written in 1909 by John L. St John, and pilot James McCudden recalled that pilots would sing the refrain as they flew: 'Archibald – certainly not. Get back to work, sir, like a shot/ When single you could waste time spooning/But lose work now for honeymooning/ Archibald – certainly not!'[87]

On the ground, Douglas recalled that one of his strongest first impressions of life in the mess in the RFC 'was the way in which there was always this cheerful readiness to gather around and give voice to songs about flying'. He noted that it was 'another of the aspects of the laying down of the tradition, and our songs became an interesting and often amusing expression of our way of life'. He underlined that the key person in every squadron was the Recording Officer, equivalent to Adjutant in the Army, and that in 43 Squadron one of the best features of their popular RO, Tom Purdey, was that he was an accomplished pianist.[88] Singing was an everyday activity in the mess. Music in various forms was an important part of everyday life for all the servicemen of the RFC, and there is also strong link between the consumption of alcohol and squadron songs. RFC airmen had a reputation for heavy drinking which sometimes resulted in the smashing up of a mess or a local café.[89] In the 1970s, Alan Clark may have overstated the stereotypical RFC/RFC 'binge', which 'would begin at dusk and continue often until those taking part were insensible', but there is plenty of evidence to support the assertion that many airmen became heavy drinkers.[90]

Reverend Pat Leonard, who in November 1917 was attached as a chaplain to the RFC on the Western Front, wrote that '[m]y parish consists of four squadrons, two here and two about 3 miles away ... everybody has been perfectly charming and cheery ... tho' many of the younger ones drink more than is good for them'.[91] This facet of service life was parodied in their songs, and Arthur Gould Lee, who served with the fighting 46 Squadron on the Western Front, recalled that their usual after-dinner routine would involve the singing of songs such as '"When this ruddy war is over" ... and "The green grass grew all round" and some less delicate ones such as [Skiboo] ... which becomes more and more blue'. As for Skiboo, Lee admitted that he had 'no idea what it means, but it's very good for yelling at the top of your voice when you're ginned'.[92] The Army was also fond of a drink. Royal Fusilier Charles Quinnell recalled that their sing-songs would often occur out of the line 'when the wine used to flow – in other words the beer – some of the songs were most profane ... after you'd had half a dozen beers, the world was quite a good place'.[93] Indeed, it was while men were more relaxed in the safety of the mess that they could confront the prospect of their deaths. Sung in many RFC messes in France, *An RFC Toast* recalls an older song from the nineteenth century and was sung to the tune of Arthur Sullivan's *The Last Chord*:

> We meet 'neath the sounding rafters,
> The walls all around us are bare;
> They echo the peals of laughter;
> It seems that the dead are there.
> So, stand by your glasses steady,
> The world is a world of lies.
> Here's a toast to the dead already;
> Here's to the next man who dies.[94]

There was a suitable piece of music for every occasion. On St Patrick's Day 1916, Colonel McCalmont of the Irish Guards asked Bandmaster Rogan for the band of the Coldstream Guards to play to his men at Poperinghe. They went straight to the Irishmen and found a football match in progress. The Coldstreams 'struck up their regimental march' to attract their attention and a crowd gathered for an impromptu concert. Later that day the Irish Guards moved off to the trenches. Rogan and the Coldstream band took them a few miles on the way before wheeling off and playing them past to the tune of *St Patrick's Day*. When the Coldstreams performed for the 49th Canadians (Edmonton) in the middle of a ploughed field, Rogan said that they had loved *The Maple Leaf* and *O Canada*. He told them 'if they could sing as well as they could fight they had nothing to fear. How they let the choruses go after that!'[95]

Musical Memorials

Soldiers also used music to remember and commemorate their comrades. To the Royal Engineers who were killed in action at Soissons Bridge in September 1914, a musical memorial was composed two months later. *In Memoriam* is a piece of piano and solo voice, which encourages the listener to: 'Oh! Weep not for the gallant dead/By Soissons Bridge who proudly fell/'Twas for old England's name they bled/And they have served their country well.'[96] *Carry On! A Ballad of the Somme* was written by Norman Wrighton, a well-known Shakespearean actor and an ex-sergeant of the Third County of London Yeomanry. Wrighton had written and appeared in the play *Kultur*, which was often used by military recruiters.[97] In December 1915, he appeared in the press when he gave a recruiting speech, possibly from *Kultur*, on the Charing Cross Road in full medieval armour.[98] *Carry On!* was published in *The Era* and dedicated to his friend, Lieutenant Nelson Ellis.

> Somewhere down along the Somme,
> Way out there along the West,
> There's two magic words that tell,
> Even 'midst that worst of Hell.
> They are neither very long,
> But they make that grim, sweet song.
> That echoes by the Somme –
>   Carry on![99]

After the 3rd Battalion of the Guards Division return to Herzeele, Rogan was saddened that the casualties included some of his friends, including 'that dear, charming gentleman' Lieutenant the Hon. Esmund Elliot of the Scots Guards, who was General Feilding's junior ADC.[100] Rogan had dined with Elliot the night before he went into the line and he had promised that he would write a march and call it *Michael*.[101] Rogan does not appear to have composed such a piece, but he did write and record the military march, *The Bond of Friendship*, in 1925. This may relate in some way to the deaths of his colleagues during the Great War. Other songs were composed to commemorate happier elements of the conflict. An RAF Chaplain wrote *A Song of Stunting* in 1918, the refrain of which is 'Sing a song of stunting on a frosty day!' The text is inscribed 'with happy memories of the old avro [sic]'.[102]

While some like Nettleingham believed that the soldiers' songs should survive long after the war, there were others who did not. In 1918, Chaplain Thomas Tiplady believed that none of the wartime songs would survive 'on their own merits'. He equated them to daisies who will 'have their day and pass away to make room for others. It is best so.' Tiplady assures the reader that 'We tire of the eternal.... The transient songs I have quoted here have been meat and drink to our soldiers in the most terrible war ever raged. They may be poor stuff in comparison to our classic songs but ... For the purpose in hand they have been better than the classics, otherwise they would not have been chosen.'[103] What we do know, however, is that for servicemen fighting in an industrialised war in which personal agency was greatly reduced, their songs are evidence of their robust rejection of victimhood and an emphasis on perseverance, articulately expressed through humour, which became the new ideal of courage.[104] Servicemen's abilities to maintain composure in the face of fear and adversity would be sorely tested if they found themselves prisoners of the enemy. For those who were captured and interned in prisoners of war camps, musical activities would prove to be useful and effective ways that enabled servicemen to best manage their time in captivity. It is to the military camps to which we turn in the following chapter.

5 Captivity

The Geneva Conventions agreed in 1864 and 1906 focused on the provision for sick and wounded on the battlefield; it was not until the fourth Geneva Convention in 1949 that it was specified that prisoners of war should be provided with means of recreation.[1] Therefore, during the Great War, there were no official sanctions on the treatment of prisoners of war, military or civilian. Approximately 6.5 million people, including civilian men, women and children, were interned by the combatant countries of the Great War.[2] A total of 185,329 British servicemen, including 7,776 officers, were captured and imprisoned in Germany alone.[3] British military personnel from all services would also be found in prisoner of war camps in Turkey, Hungary and Bulgaria. The experience of being taken captive differed between officers and other ranks, the unit in which the prisoner served, the period of the war in which they were taken, and the nationality of the men who captured them. There are varying reports of treatment and conditions by prisoners, and as the BRC pointed out in the summer of 1918 'conditions vary in the different German Army Corps Commands in which the prisons are situated'.[4] Camp Commandants were responsible only to Corps Commander then the Kaiser – not to any government department. The camps therefore differed 'according to the character of the Commandant, and particularly according to the Corps Commander in whose Division the camp is'.[5] In the opinion of one British prisoner of war, who experienced life in seven German prison camps between 1916 and 1918, the three worst camps in Germany were Schwarstedt, Strohen and Holzminden. They were all in the Hanover District of the 10th Army Corps commanded by 'Von H., who simply loathed the British . . . it was said because he had got into disgrace on the Somme by losing them two German divisions'.[6] Some men were not taken prisoner at all but killed by the enemy shortly after capture.[7] Non-commissioned officers and men in the ranks who were fit enough to do so were generally formed into working 'commandos' by their captors. Due to the nature of aerial warfare, a high proportion of fliers from the

RFC/RAF were taken prisoner when they were shot down over enemy territory. These officer-prisoners were not put to work, but enforced idleness presented its own challenges to young, fit men who had been suddenly removed from the battlefield.[8]

Musical activities took place in the majority of prisoner of war camps where the upkeep of morale and discipline, and plain survival, was paramount. Prisoners had to find a variety of ways of dealing with the enforced idleness and monotony of prison life. Sports were popular and the production of concerts and plays particularly so. Musical entertainments such as concert parties were, like sport and the cinema, part of prisoners' lives, and a much-needed lifeline and link with home. At a basic level, concerts in a camp 'passes a couple of hours away'.[9] In Crossen PoW camp, where many British servicemen were held, 'there is an orchestra numbering twenty-one which gives concerts daily'.[10] Certainly, escaping from enemy hands was a primary occupation, and it was 'the duty of all soldiers to escape' where possible.[11] As in every theatre of war, the upkeep of men's morale was of the greatest importance. The biggest challenge was to avoid getting 'mouldy'. This referred to 'the mould which germinates in the minds of men who are prisoners of war . . . upon whom shadow of captivity has fallen with all its devitalising darkness of mind and atrophy of sense: a state comparable to premature burial'.[12] In 1919, the Swiss physician Dr Adolf Lukas Vischer identified this as a psychiatric syndrome among prisoners of war, the 'barbed-wire disease' that follows a long-term incarceration, with symptoms including boredom, confusion, clouding of consciousness and amnesia.[13] Perceived idleness while the war continued to be fought by their friends, family and colleagues was felt as a form of torture. One officer recalled that he believed that those in the ranks, who were forced to work, were better off because he saw 'many a man driven morbid and mad by this terrible inactivity'.[14] Whatever conditions British servicemen prisoners found in the camps in which they were held, their duty was to keep functioning as representatives of their country, not least His Majesty's armed forces. In January 1918, the British BRC published a letter from a PoW in Russian Poland telling the organisation that he and his fellow prisoners had invented a motto for themselves: 'B.B.K.S'. Translated into words, it signified 'Be British, Keep Smiling'.[15] Music was an important part of this, as a form of resistance against their enemy-captors. One officer wrote that '[n]othing has the power of music to lift one out of one's surroundings; and to none more poignantly than to prisoners-of-war does Music bring her valiant reminder of things "outside," the refreshing comfort of a world of realities transcending human chance'.[16]

Supplying the Camps

By 1916, the principal efforts on behalf of British prisoners of war were coordinated by the Joint War Committee of the British Red Cross (BRC) and the Order of St John of Jerusalem. This 'working arrangement' had been agreed between the two organisations in October 1914, at the behest of the Army Council, 'with a view to efficiency and economy'.[17] A Central Prisoners of War Committee was created and entrusted by the government for care of naval, military and civilian PoWs. Based at 4 Thurloe Place, London, the Committee aimed to send three parcels of food and thirteen pounds of bread to every PoW in Europe once a fortnight. From January 1918, they also published a journal, *The British Prisoner of War*, to act as a focus of efforts for and news and ideas about the welfare of British PoWs.[18] It was an enormous task. In two years of operations, the total expenditure of the Central Prisoners of War Committee on supplies for prisoners, including all Care Committees, Local Associations and Regimental Committees up to 11 November 1918 was £6.5 million [£383,449,300 today]. One third of this funding came from the General Fund of the Joint Societies of the BRC and the Order of St John, and two thirds from public donations. Administrative expenses were covered by a direct grant from the War Office. The Committee and its departments sourced, packed and dispatched 9 million food parcels and 800,000 clothing parcels to British prisoners wherever they were held. They received a total of 1,160 million items of correspondence, an average of 250 per day, from prisoners and their families. This work was done by approximately 700 workers, 300 of whom were volunteers.[19]

Prisoners would write to the Committee to ask them to send additional items, and the more unusual orders tell us a great deal about camp activities. In the autumn of 1917, the Prisoners of War Department officially requested the Committee to supply 'a stock of theatrical properties, numbering hundreds of articles, for the use of prisoners at Ruhleben … smart blouses, strong corsets, and Lisle thread stockings, greasepaint, haresfeet, crape hair, beards and moustaches. We have interested the theatrical world in this consignment, and hope to collect all the articles asked for, and to forward them to the camp as soon as they arrive.' The journal included that it may also interest their subscribers to know that 'lately we have presented a ventriloquist's dummy to one of the prisoners' camps in Germany'.[20] Another request was received 'from the working commando at Altendorf (under Chemnitz) for a Cornet, Clarionet [sic] and Accordion. It is just possible that one of our readers may care to present these musical instruments to the prisoners in this place.'[21] In the next issue was a further appeal for gramophone and instruments: 'we have gratefully to acknowledge one gramophone, one clarionette, and one concertina. These instruments are being promptly dispatched to the camps, where we expect they will give great pleasure.' The article goes on to state that a prisoner at Sprottau 'has just written to ask us for a "banjo-mandoline." Can any reader spare such a thing?'[22]

In addition to sending food parcels and clothing to military and civilian prisoners in Germany, Bulgaria, and Turkey, in August 1918 the BRC were requested to send to prisoners fifty 'Rosaries', fifty 'Gardens of the Soul' hymns and prayer books, pens, ink, a stage curtain, ladies' wigs, grease paint, Indian clubs, music, a billiard table cloth, billiard balls, punch balls, boxing-gloves, base-ball outfits, and stationery. They underlined that they 'take a good deal of trouble to meet the wants of any prisoner who writes to us, and as far as the exigencies of the censorship admit objects which are asked for are invariably dispatched with the least possible delay'.[23] These shipments included forty dozen tennis balls per week in the summer, and fifteen footballs per week to Germany in the autumn/winter. From early 1917, the BRC had sent games to 1,520 men.[24] The sending of sports equipment became more problematic after 1917, as the British government prohibited the export of leather and rubber goods to enemy countries. However, the War Office permitted the BRC to send one football per 100 men, one pair of boxing gloves and six tennis balls per man. These items had to be purchased from an authorised shop or ordered through the Committee's Special Department. This was also the section which dispatched gramophone records and 'musical instruments of all kinds ranging from mouth-organs to bagpipes!'[25]

Requests to the BRC were normally made by individual prisoners or through the Care Committee of each camp, the prisoner's former employers, or his family. Of these committees, the BRC themselves reported that '[f]oreigners are apt to laugh at us and say wherever a few Englishman are gathered together they form themselves into a Committee. It is an admirable habit, at any rate in a prison camp, and deserves every encouragement.'[26] Different types of committee could be found in most camps, mainly the Care Committee in addition to those for Concerts, Theatricals, Football and Escapes. Committees were normally run in a continuance of the military hierarchy. In a similar way to public schools, men of higher rank who had been in the camp for the longest time would take the lead. Captain F. W. Harvey, of the Gloucestershire Regiment, was captured raiding a German trench on the Western Front in August 1916. He described his earliest days as a 'new boy' in Gütersloh camp:

A polite but icy demeanour was generally acknowledged to be the bearing proper towards new prisoners . . . 'What use are you to this camp?' That was the unasked question which had to be answered by every new arrival. It was hard, rank Socialism, but very successful. You lived for the State, not yourself. Could you write? There were two camp papers needing contributors. Could you sing? There were concerts. Could you play games? The inter-barrack matches would give you the opportunity. Could you act? Could you drink? There was the canteen, and those birthday evenings, something you *must* do to keep the life of the camp alight. *Something* you must do, or be damned.[27]

Camp Concerts

Harvey wrote that it was his knowledge of 'Chesteron's drinking songs set to homely tunes' which enabled him 'to gain admittance into society'. He continued to play an active role in camp life by writing poems, essays and reviews, in addition to playing hockey, giving lectures and attending 'cheery evenings with consistent regularity'.[28] At Limburg camp, British PoWs had formed committees for Concerts and Football. John D. McIlroy, who was taken prisoner in October 1914, was the President of the British Concert Committee. In a letter dated 1 June 1918, he explained that they had sought permission from the Camp Commandant to hold concerts every third Sunday. These events took place in the wash-house as it was 'the only place adaptable to such under-takings as Concerts'. McIlroy relayed that everyone attended the perfor-mances, 'which are of necessity of a variety nature, which [is] . . . the best form of entertainment in such a situation as this'. It was particularly important, he wrote, that the concerts gave a 'bright impression and example [that] carries great weight with the new-comers, who come in week by week'. He underlined that '[t]he completeness with which the singers, artistes and musicians perform, and the businesslike manner in which the Committee and Stewards conduct the performances, never fail to drive home to the new men how useless it is to be otherwise than cheerful, and the concerts are generally the sole cause of the recovery of men from melancholia and pessimism'. Since 1915, the British Concert Committee at Limburg had presented *Passing Show*, *Dollar Princess*, *Patience*, *Iolanthe* and several other light pieces. However, McIlroy asked the BRC to send them the sheet music for 'some lively marches, two-steps or waltzes, either in an orchestral form or in a dance album', specifying the musical publishing companies Feldman's and Francis, Day and Hunter's, as they would be 'a boon and blessing to all'.[29]

The performances, along with the football league, were seen as essen-tial elements of camp life. British footballers played matches against their Belgian and French counterparts, 'promoting comic and burlesque matches'. These attempts to see the lighter, more humorous side of life were evidenced in 'the remarkably clean bill of health of the British prisoners in the Stammlager'. McIlroy maintained that the Concerts and Football Committees at Limburg 'keeps men in touch with one another' and 'fosters *espirit-de-corps*'. By their continuous efforts, the two Committees felt that they were responsible for the mental and physical condition and state of the Camp. McIlroy was writing from Limburg in what was the final stages of the German Spring Offensive. From the start of Operation Michael on 21 March 1918, tens of thousands of British soldiers were taken captive and transported to Germany until the Allies began to fight back five months later. McIlroy concluded his report and request to the BRC by saying, 'I will leave it to you to estimate the grand influence, example and steadying effect on the morale of our men which the Concert and Football Committees are responsible for.'[30] Evenings in the camps could be long. However, soldiers, sailors and airmen by necessity were particularly good at creating their own entertainments, which they continued as far as they could in captivity. This generally involved an impromptu sing-song, and a typical 'celebration' evening is thus described by an officer at Gütersloh in 1917:

Imagine a room tightly packed with people who are sitting on beds, on chairs, and on the floor. A large kettle of punch is brewing on a spirit-lamp. The punch is composed of bad German wine, tinned fruit, and smuggled cognac, raisins, cloves, cinnamon, and a spot or two of Worcester sauce – for bite. Each guest has brought his own mug along (for that is the prison custom) ... By general request 'Boats' is singing, for perhaps the 109th time in captivity, an old sea-song concerning

> 'A girl called Mary
> Who lived in Drury Lane,
> Whose master was unkind to her
> Whose mistress was the same.'

After this a Frenchman ... recites with gusto a poem by Olivier Basselin ... Then perhaps the Canadians give us some potted stories from Scripture, and everyone joins in the somewhat mysterious chorus ... apparently designed to pass away the long winter in snowed-up shacks, wherein fishermen were huddled around the stoves ... for at this point a burst of well-judged applause invariably stopped the singer.... Between the songs scraps of tales are overheard out of the babble of voices ... A Canadian is heard complaining that someone has 'a point of view about as broad as a hen's face', and is abjured by his countrymen to 'cut out the rough stuff'. Then an Australian officer obliges the company with a song called 'Waltzing Mathilda'.... Sooner or later in the evening comes 'The Old Bold Mate,' the most frequently sung song in *gefangenenschaft*.

The sentry appears, shouting: 'Lichts aus!' He refuses to sing the Hymn of Hate. We give him three glasses to drive him home, and chant the tune [*Drive Him*

Home] till he goes. In five minutes he will reappear with a guard. Then we shall disperse to our rooms ... Silence will creep over the barrack. The P.T. [name given to Tunneling Party] (still on night shifts) will recommence work.[31]

The Old Bold Mate, a tune by Harvey's friend Ivor Gurney, with words by John Masefield, 'echoed through a dozen prison *lagers* in various parts of Germany'.[32] Indeed, when Harvey was reunited with some of his prisoner friends after the Armistice, at Scheveningen in Holland, they immediately boke into singing *The Old Bold Mate*.[33] What Harvey said he 'missed most at the front' and 'what most I craved in captivity was good music'.[34] He maintained in his 1920 memoir, *Comrades in Captivity*, that '[t]o suppose that the British are unmusical is wrong. I have never been in a prison camp where there was not made an attempt, generally successful, to form an orchestra and perform good music. Nor was this interest in music the work of a few enthusiasts.'[35] At Freiburg the officers had established the Freiburg Amateur Dramatic Society. The genesis of this group began with impromptu 'smoker' concerts after the evening meal in the dining room at least once a week. During these gatherings '[o]ur talented pianist, F. M. Duff' of the 54th Battalion Australian Imperial Force accompanied men who were willing to sing for their colleagues. Among these, Captain William Robinson, V.C., was among the leading vocalists.[36] At that point, they did not have any sheet music apart from a few opera scores, so 'repetition was the rule rather than the exception'. They progressed to performing skits and monologues, for example, 'The art of song writing' and 'Water Scenes', also North Country Yarns from F. E. Hill[s][37] (RFC), but 'the paucity of material and the readiness with which the camp appreciated any efforts to entertain them, is afforded by the volley of cheers which used to greet J. M. O'Byrne's contribution "The Green Eye of the Yellow God."'[38] This varied programme 'with a liberal allowance of cheap wine enabled us to pass many pleasant evenings'. As more PoWs arrived they moved to larger premises:

This seemed our opportunity: we at once had visions of a stage and a 'pukka' concert party. The authorities were approached on the moot question of costumes and wigs. They did not however receive the suggestion very enthusiastically. Nothing could be permitted they said that would be likely to assist escape. Owing to our inexperience this seemed to us final ... and in consequence the theatrical party was indefinitely postponed.

They continued to hold the weekly 'smokers', and more men with musical leanings arrived. Lieutenant B. M. Greenhill, of the Household Battalion, was described as 'a talented violinist' who was sent to Freiburg after his capture in 1917.[39] They did not have a stage, merely 'a narrow platform and the pulpit were where the cinema box now stands'. With increasing talent from British and French newcomers they were permitted to install lighting effects which were obtained 'from the present gas brackets by the aid of reflectors consisting of toilet mirrors'. An orchestra was formed under J. W. Shaw (RFC). This ensemble 'proved more humourous than talented. The instrumentalists were armed with anything from a penny tin-whistle or mouth-organ to a bass viol or drum.' It was said that their principal item was 'a scarcely elevating refrain popular in those days. This and other pieces were unceasingly practiced to the discomfort of officers seated in the yard.' By November 1917, the Freiburg Amateur Dramatic Society was officially set up under two RFC officers, C. Clifford[40] and R. E. Martin[41], and their first performance was a Pierrot show given on 24 November. In April 1918, Lieutenant-Commander Wybrants Olphert[42] of the Royal Naval Reserve took over management of FADS and performances had to run over two consecutive nights to fit everyone in. A booking office opened for advance tickets. Sketches included *Captain Jones Gets Home* and *Lessons in Lager Etiquette*. F. M. Duff 'developed a first-class orchestra – operative concerts despite difficulties in men being sent to Holland etc'.[43]

The Freiburg Amateur Dramatic Society had two principal ladies – Cissie Airth and Gertie Andrew – who appeared in every production. These characters were the source of great excitement, as 'on the eve of each production, great is the interest of the front rows to guess what new costumes these two Circes will have chosen with which to dazzle the eyes of the "gefangener" officers'.[44] However, the prisoners were sometimes very taken with the 'ladies' as well. Harvey recalled that his fellow prisoner, known as 'Fluffy', was 'a fine little sport, and the chief female impersonator in our plays and sketches at Holzminden, though I don't think he much liked the job. Still, somebody had to do it, and he did it well.'[45] Harvey provides an interesting analysis of prison psychology via an extract from another female impersonator PoW:

The attitude of officers towards other officers dressed as women in plays, etc., was very peculiar . . . in a large mixed camp, I was in female attire, representing Egypt in an Empire tableau, and noticed with surprise how attentive officers were in keeping me supplied with refreshments . . . their manners completely changed when speaking to me. . . . They were most careful in avoiding the usual camp language. . . . They insisted on giving up their seats for me. . . . I had to pull them back into reality by swearing vigorously, and so far had they fallen under the illusion of my femininity that I fear I shocked them by doing so.[46]

Upholding the tradition of a Christmas pantomime performance was widespread in military prisoner of war camps. At Trier, in December 1917, the interned officers put on four evening performances of *Aladdin* after three weeks of morning and evening rehearsals. The script

Figure 5.1 The orchestra at Holzminden PoW camp, December 1918.
© Liddle Collection.

was written by Lieutenant V. B. Shott, British and French officers painted
scenery and both nationalities made up 'a special augmented orchestra'
under the direction of Lieutenant C. Rigby. Lieutenant V. C. Coombs
was at the piano playing the arrangements he had written with Lieutenant
B. P. Luscombe, and '[m]any of the latest songs have been worked into
the production and dances'. The cast and crew list are considerable. The
production had a business manager, stage manager, and properties master; an advert in *The Barb* detailed that tickets would be made available at
the theatre's box office between 10 am and 12 noon on the day of each
performance.[47] While he was interned at Trier, Coombs as a keen amateur pianist was taught to play the double bass and trombone by Bernard
Luscombe who played several instruments. At Holzminden (Figure 5.1),
Coombs continued to be very active in various musical productions,
including a comedy called *Parcels: If You Don't Want the Goods Don't
Mess 'em About!*[48]

A letter from the wife of an officer held at Afion-Kara-Hissar, Turkey,
describes the activities in the camp in which her husband was being held.
The majority of these prisoners had been taken at Gallipoli two and half
years before. Much of their music was provided by Captain Dyson[49] who
held services every Sunday with music from an 'American organ':

[S]ome do wool-work, carpentering, painting and drawing; some make jam and wine; others write books, and plays which are performed from time to time. There is a lively debating society, and a dancing class in winter. Besides the American organ there are three mandolines [sic] in the camp, and Russians sometimes come over and sing. Chess and bridge of course are played, also badminton, cricket and football, and boxing and gymnastics help fill up the time. These things all sound very fine, but the reality is a very different thing. The badminton ball is an old sock, the organ is almost falling to pieces, and there is only room for three couples to dance at a time.[50]

The correspondent also added that '[t]hey have a fairly large collection of books, both novels and educational works, and they have particularly asked not to be sent any more American novels by sentimental women authors'. Nevertheless, despite these hardships, when the Swiss Commission visited the camp in 1916, it pronounced them 'the cheeriest lot of men they had seen'.[51] Voluntary-aid organisations were sometimes permitted to establish huts inside or in the vicinity of prisoner of war camps. Support and attitude of the Commandant was key to how much the prisoners could do. For example, there were five prison camps in Bulgaria, the largest at Philippopolis: eight huts each housing 250 men. At Christmas 1917, there were 590 men and 36 British officers on the camp roll. Colonel Nicoloff at Philippopolis was said to be very supportive of the men's reading.[52] Therefore, in the spring of 1917, the YMCA were permitted to set up a recreation hut for British and French soldiers. It had a library, a piano, and other musical instruments for the men's use. A Committee was formed to organise religious services, books, education, theatricals and concerts. This Committee was led by officers, NCOs and men from various units interned in the camp, first by Lieutenant Gilliland of the Norfolk Regiment. They would also receive and distribute money and supplies and look after the general welfare of the men.[53]

Songs about Captivity

PoWs would, as they had in their fighting units, make up songs to reflect their everyday experiences, or to make their views on recent events known. Sergeant Joe Fitzpatrick, of the 2/6th Battalion (Manchester Regiment) was held in Soltau after his capture in 1918. While the prisoners were on route marches outside the camp during the German Spring Offensive, they would pass a shop which displayed in the window a map of the German army's advance. In response the British PoWs would sing:

> One, two, three, the Kaiser's after me,
> Four, five, six, we're in a right bloody fix,
> Seven, eight, nine, there's a Heinrich on the line,
> We'll be in Soltau, in Soltau, tonight.[54]

In October 1917, Canadian prisoner Leslie Norman[55] was among 100 soldiers who were sent by the German authorities to Constance for medical examinations to determine if they would be sent to neutral Switzerland, 'Chateau Freedom', for the remainder of the war. Norman detailed that they were all reluctant to leave their camps as they would lose touch with their colleagues, not to mention their letters and parcels via the BRC, but the thought of sitting out the war in a Swiss hotel-spa was a tempting prospect. The medical inspections were much tougher than expected, and over half of the PoWs were dispersed to a number of German camps, not neutral Switzerland. In response to these events, Norman chanelled his disappointment by writing his own version of *Tipperary* – *It's a Long Way to Chateau Freedom*:

> They sent us off to Constance much against our earnest wish,
> Clapped us on the back and said 'Goodbye, you're off to Swiss,'
> Smile, and reassured us that we'd very soon be free,
> But Switzerland's a long way off, just take the tip from me.

Chorus:

> It's a long way to Chateau Freedom,
> It's a long way to go;
> We are still in the land of boredom –
> For how long we do not know.
> If they send us back to Lager we won't sit down and fret;
> It's a long way to Chateau Freedom but we're not downhearted yet.
> [Verse 2, Chorus]
> We linger here week after week, uncertain of our fate;
> It's enough to make a man get up and sing the song of hate.
> But keep your hearts up, sonny boys, do not swear and cuss,
> It's a clean walk-over next time and we'll pass without a fuss.

Chorus

> I heard last night that we shall be inspected on the first;
> Let's hope the date is right, for then we'll know the blooming worst.
> Whatever be our prospects, we have had a darned good rest,
> So keep you heads erect and grin, and hope on for the best.[56]

At Holzminden, a song was composed and performed to mark the unsuccessful escape attempt of Second Lieutenant Robert Stanley Capon[57] (RFC) who had worked at Greenwich Observatory and had recently given his fellow PoWs a lecture on astronomy. Capon had removed a number of wooden planks from the dining rooms and tried to use these as runners from second-story window over the head of the sentry and over the wire to the nearby road.

'Capon swore a feud
'Gainst the fierce Niemeyer
… how sadly all his brave plans fell with his planks to the ground
None could keep them back,
Though strong men did tug hard,
So the blooming show
Was absolutely done in.
…
The frightened guard
Shrilly blew his whistle,
Then the great Niemeyer
Bravely waved his pistol,
And he did resolve
To extirpate the vipers,
All the men of Mons,
All the boys of Wipers.
… [since planks had all been extracted from the dining-rooms]
'Fat is dis dey do?
Dare dey cock der beavers!
I ill teach dem – zo,
Fat is good behaviours.
I a sight will have
For mein gaze to gloat on:
I will notice give
Dining-room's VERBOTEN'.[58]

In mid-August 1918, F. W. Harvey was sent to Stralsund, an island camp in the Baltic. He found it very 'mouldy' there and decided to use music as a means of protest. Only once during his stay there 'did I come out of my shell to sing at a camp concert, and then I narrowly escaped being sent to prison about a song I had made up about the condition of the bed-linen in one of the huts. It went to the tune of 'Cockles and Mussels.'[59] Harvey was particularly interested in the music of other nationalities. He stated that it was the Russians who were the acknowledged musicians of the camp: 'all of them sang, and nearly all played an instrument, if only the balalaika. It was inspiring to hear an excited crowd of them after some mad escape marching round the camp, singing national songs, several hundred voices blended together in "Volga, Volga."' Harvey recalled that this traditional song was sung by the Russians 'twenty times for every one time they sang their national hymn'. He stated that it was 'their equivalent of our 'Old Bold Mate' – whom I hold to have been a much pleasanter fellow'.[60] Harvey wrote a floridly poetic review of a Russian concert where he felt he was transported to 'a rich great garden' where 'bird-song was in the air' and he could hear 'the plash of playing fountains'.[61] Quoting Dr Johnson's quote of music being 'the least objectionable of noises' to

Harvey 'it is not less than a passion. If the gods were moved by such human prayer I should certainly be a musician . . . But not, thank Heaven! appreciation [sic] From a Queen's Hall concert or such an evening as this last, I come away literally crammed with *new experiences* – richer by so much *life*.[62] Large mixed camps like Gütersloh and Crefeld were able to form orchestras which were regarded as 'very good'.[63] Harvey wrote that he could remember the music and the effect it had on him well: 'I do not need the old programme now before me to remind myself of the burst of sweetness and light which fell upon me at the hearing of four 'cellos playing together very softly that aria of Bach for strings; and the strange, sudden sense of exultation over circumstance called up by Schubert's "Unfinished Symphony"'.[64]

Instruments

Musical instruments were in great demand. In some camps, it was said that the German government had an agreement with the British that PoWs in Germany could receive some of their pay in order to purchase certain goods. Coombs described how the money was 'converted very unfavourably into camp money' to buy items such as musical instruments locally.[65] However, this sort of arrangement did not hold for many PoW camps and the men had to improvise. A British prisoner held at Kedos, Turkey, described how PoWs resorted to making their own instruments. He said that it was 'quite marvelous the things some fellows have turned out here . . . G– is making a violin, and I am making a banjo out of walnut, and intend to inlay the back, but it is no light work, as our tools are not the best'.[66] In some German camps, prisoners were allowed to buy or hire musical instruments. Harvey spoke kindly of the commandant who permitted prisoners 'to hire a piano on which Chopin could be played . . . The folk-songs of France and of Russia, and that divine prelude and fugue of Bach in E Major (surely the talking of angels overheard), was a joy hard to overrate.'[67] 'A piano was out of the question at Schwarmstedt, so the dulcitone was used for all concerts, and was a godsend both there and at Holzminden, until in the latter camp it was possible to hire a piano from Hanover.'[68]At Doeberitz, a small orchestra was established mainly owing to the efforts of Mr Williams, the civilian British chaplain at Berlin, who visits the camp on alternate Sundays to conduct service. This gentleman procured various instruments 'by the help of English ladies resident in Berlin'.[69]

Holzminden was said to have been 'a thoroughly bad camp . . . the Commandant, Niemeyer, was the evil spirit of it . . . a cad, a boaster, and a bully of the worst type. He had lived in America, and was commonly known as "Milwaukee Bill".[70] Had it not been for Niemeyer, Holzminden may have been a good camp. Decent buildings, not leaky huts, rooms clean and pleasant and beautiful surrounding countryside – although parole to walk out was not given for 6 months.[71] Niemeyer also forbade field games and 'he disallowed our little entertainments . . . which we gave in the dining-rooms, where planks of trestles did for a stage and the dulcitone replaced a piano – . . . because he felt annoyed that somebody had got away'.[72] At Doeberitz, the Commandant, Colonel Alberti, was sympathetic with the men's need for amusements. From March 1915, PoWs were permitted to use an old marquee to serve as a chapel on Sunday and as a theatre during the week. It was in this tent that the original Doeberitz Empire was established. One of the organisers of music at Doeberitz was C. S. M. Francis of the 1st Cheshires. Prominent among the artists was Able Seaman Cecil A. Tooke of the Royal Naval Division.[73] An established and well-known artist, Tooke was taken prisoner at Antwerp in 1914, and was the main force in organising small concerts and sports. Tooke and Jack Bygrave, also RNVR and who were captured at the same time, were responsible for painting the scenery of the Doeberitz Theatre. In September 1917, they were granted the use of a large wooden building fitted with electric light. They decorated the stage with the Doeberitz motto – *Don vivivus vivamus* – 'while I live, let me live'. Costumes were made by the men and all designed by Tooke. The BRC featured a photograph of a Doeberitz cast in *The British Prisoner of War*:

we are told that among the most successful of the 'gets up' was the man in the third row, representing half a soldier and a half a sailor, another man, also in the third row, dressed in a coat made entirely of cigarette cards, the King and Queen of Hearts in the centre, and Little Red Riding Hood (a drummer in the Suffolk Regiment) next to a lady in a yashmak. This lady's wig was made of rope, unraveled and plaited again.[74]

By the summer of 1918, Tooke had a number of jobs in the camp, including 'Theatre Manager, Director of the Fire Brigade, and Chief Librarian'. The BRC also featured a drawing by Tooke, entitled *'Ope,* of which they said 'artists and British prisoners are not the prey of circumstances; they mould them to their will. If the base on which the figure stands typifies the affection and effort of those from whom our prisoners are separated it will prove solid enough, we are sure, to support them to the moment of realization.'[75] At Gütersloh, the British Amateur Dramatic Society, 'having pressed into service as scene-painters such artists (professional and amateur) as the camp possessed, and as manager of lights, stage carpenter, dresser, prompter, etc., such other gentlemen especially fitted for such tasks, decided to give a really magnificent production of "You Never Can Tell"'.[76]

Artists, particularly painters, where as highly prized as musicians in PoW camps. Second Lieutenant John Chapman[77] was shot down over Douai in July 1917, and held at Heidelberg, Holzminden and Schweidnitz camps. Chapman was an artist and painted several theatrical sets.[78] His diary written in captivity describes many of the concerts he attended, and the satirical names which indicate the high proportion of RFC men in the camps. One week At Heidelberg, Chapman records that there was a sketch 'called "The Red Streak", introducing Percy "Sopwith" from "Joystick", Mrs "Rumpity", Henry "Martinsyde" and Nelly "Newport". There were three numbers only and the whole thing was splendidly staged.' At Holzminden, Chapman records that on 4 November there was a performance of *The Magic Flute*. Two days later Chapman attended a lecture on music. By December, when Chapman had been moved to the more comfortable Schweidnitz camp, he headed up a small team of PoWs to design, draw and paint the backdrop for the camp stage. However, he complained that his 'scheme of work had not been adhered to owing to stage scenery' and then a few days later the 'stage [was] growing but not nearly ready – rehearsal in the evening did considerable damage'. After their Christmas meal, they sang songs in the dining room with a piano accompaniment with various PoWs taking turns to play. On Boxing Day, the dress rehearsal was successful, and on 27 December the show was put on and 'all the turns went well ... the making up in the wings was a continual amusement to me'.[79]

This full theatrical production, complete with stage, set and costumes, was advertised in the October 1918 edition of Schneidnitz PoW camp magazine, *The Barb*. The magazine was written by British officers, and began in Trèves where there was a significant number of men from the RFC/RAF. Rennbahn, one of the four PoW camps at Münster, had a number of camp publications. The *Rennbahn Review* featured a diary column 'Peeps from the Past' giving humourous notes from camp life; the *Church Times* was produced by Drummer Victor Champion; and the third paper was *Echo du Camp*, featuring poetry, amusing illustrations and articles such as 'the Song and Rhythm of the Mussulman Tartars' and news of concerts and parcels.[80] Of Rennbahn, returned prisoners told the BRC that the church is usually packed and 'the Theatre is a fine one, some people going so far as to tell us that it comes up to some of the best in England'.[81] The cinema was also an important mode of entertainment. As we can see on the fighting fronts, cinema shows would often share the same space and billing with musical entertainments. At Trèves, *The Barb* reported that the Commandant's permission had been obtained for a machine to be purchased by a syndicate of British officers, and that

arrangements are progressing to secure feature films, install the electric connections, etc. . . . the *Barb* is assured that highly interesting and amusing subjects will be procurable. It is even possible that we may be able to refresh our recollections of the one and only Charlie Chaplin as he playfully slaps a fat policeman in the face with a currant pie. Or, again, we may voyage to darkest Africa with Teddy Roosevelt to see him shoot the festive lion. Who can tell? Perchance the film reels will unfold for us a tale of Cleo and Mark, or of Nero fiddling while the insurance companies went bust.[82]

At Freiburg the Dramatic Society specialised in 'Cinema Plays' – skits of the German films they had been watching by arrangement with a local cinema to give 2 showings a week for PoWs:

Elemental Comedy and Phantasmagorical Drama usually make up the night's programme. Strange to say that the comical film generally evokes little or no laughter, whilst often every phrase of the three or four reels, which make up a self-respecting tragic film drama are received with rapturous shouts of laughter.

The camp playwright, R. E. Martin, produced several of these cinema plays, the first one carried the title *Purplepazionheit*.[83]

Escape Attempts

Concert Committees were also joined by Escape Committees, and in some cases the two existed together. Captain Thomas Mapplebeck was a British officer served as an observer flying with 5 Squadron on the Western Front, 1915–16. He was shot down during an attack on a German balloon in the La Bassée sector on 9 November 1916. He spent periods of time in Douai, Cologne, Osnabruk, Clausthal and Shweidnitz PoW camps. Mapplebeck was involved in several escape attempts, and at one point was head of an escape committee at Cologne. Mapplebeck described one instance of how musical activities often provided a cover for escape attempts. In late 1916, Mapplebeck was one of the many British prisoners sent to Clausthal. He recalled that they were held in 'a lovely hotel, extended. We had two tennis courts there and a small, miniature golf course. But of course, I had to get busy, so I sent to the Army and Navy Stores for a copy of their catalogue . . . I used to order escape materials, compasses and all the rest of it, in from them'. Mapplebeck ran the escape committee, much against wishes of his senior officer, Major-General Ravenshaw, who ordered Mapplebeck to stop his attempts because everyone would be punished as a result. Nevertheless,

Figure 5.2 IWM HU 58478: The 'Freigefangenenburger' Orchestra, formed by Lieutenant Shaw as a cover for an escape attempt from Freiburg prisoner-of-war camp, 1917. © Imperial War Museum.

Mapplebeck continued despite being sentenced to repeated periods of solitary confinement. At Clausthal, the hotel had a very large dining room which also had a stage:

Underneath the stage we were digging a tunnel. While we were digging we had to make sure that the noise from the tunnel didn't leak out, so we decided to start a military band. I had to get all the instruments. Only one of us had ever played a trombone or something before ... we bought the instruments ... they said 'It's all very well Tom but what are you going to play?' I said 'Please, aren't I doing enough?' I was running a projector, hand-driven, and translating as the films came on [German feature films] ... They said 'You've got to come in with the orchestra' well, I said 'I can't read music' ... they said, well 'the Tuba was a perfectly simple thing to blow, and you can see the note we will write the number of the stop you have to use, and you play the tuba.' So I had to learn to play the tuba.[84]

Mapplebeck's service record testifies that he was mentioned in a report 'for valuable service in captivity'.[85] He nearly escaped from Schneidnitz, but his main achievement was that the materials he had obtained during his stay at Clausthal were taken by twenty-two men when they were transferred to Holzminden and used in the most well-known escape of the Great War.[86] Lieutenant Jack Shaw,[87] of the Oxfordshire and Buckinghamshire Light Infantry, had been taken prisoner at Messines in 1917 and held at Freiburg (Figure 5.2). As conductor of the Freiburg prison camp orchestra Lieutenant Shaw feigned an injured foot during a comedy sketch, while giving a concert in the Germans' dining room. He tried to escape from his dressing room window, but he was intercepted and sent to Holzminden. Lieutenant James Whale[88] of the Worcestershire Regiment, an actor, director and set-designer, was already at Holzminden when Shaw arrived. Shaw and Whale were then involved in the construction of the famous 'Holzminden Tunnel'. Using many of the escape items sourced by Mapplebeck, twenty-nine officers escaped on the night of 23 July 1918. Shaw was the thirty-first in the queue and the tunnel subsided and collapsed on the man in front and the attempt was abandoned. Of the twenty-nine who did escape, ten succeeded in making their way to the Netherlands, and home to Britain.

Coming Home

When PoWs did return to home soil they were greeted by BRC Reception Committees who were generally accompanied by one of the Guards' bands to welcome them home with popular tunes (Figure 5.3). Prisoners' Reception Committees would meet servicemen off the trains in London:

Figure 5.3 Bandmaster Rogan (far right) with the Band of the Coldstream Guards marching with British soldiers at a London station. Courtesy of the Coldstream Guards.

on the evening of Saturday 23rd February 1918, 25 officers, 3 civilians and 225 men arrived at St Pancras station: 'the G.O.C. London District gave permission for the Guards' band to play on the platform, a concession that pleased everyone hugely.... The first train arrived at .20, and was welcomed by the usual motor horns and sirens and cheers, and when this din had subsided, the strains of the band were to be heard playing patriotic tunes and familiar airs, like 'Home Sweet Home'.[89]

Another reception committee, but the biggest since permission to publicise arrivals was granted in May 1918:

a very large crowd thronged the entrances of St Pancras Station on Whit Sunday evening. The Band of the Coldstream Guards was on the platform, and Major Rogan also came to meet the trains. A trolley load of flowers bought by the different ladies of the Reception Committee made the grey station platform look very gay; there were red tulips, lilac, narcissus and masses of lilies of the valley. The first train had 70 cot cases on board, and very pathetic these wrecks of humanity looked lying there in their bunks receiving the King's card of welcome and the bunches of flowers that were given to them. Some of them smiled and some of them wept, and some of them sang as the band played the old tune, 'Soldiers of the Queen'; one or two of them bravely said 'It is worth all our sufferings to come home and be met like this'. The second train contained all the walking cases, and they cheered and cried out 'Are we downhearted? No!' ... By the time the ambulances and motor-cars began to roll away from the station an avenue of human beings stretched from St. Pancras Station to the Tottenham Court Road.[90]

Two train loads of prisoners repatriated from Switzerland arrived on 14 June at Waterloo. The BRC Reception Committee 'met the trains and presented the King's card of welcome and flowers to the home comers. The band of the Welsh Guards was on the platform and the cheerful welcoming music they made was greatly appreciated by everyone.'[91] Indeed, in December 1918, the BRC reported that 'we are getting our men back as quickly as trains and boats can bring them. The warmest and most enthusiastic welcome awaits them at Hull and Leith and Dover.' From those ports they are transported to dispersal camps near Ripon, Canterbury, and Dover, where 'they are entertained and given the largest amount of liberty that is compatible with the object of the authorities, which is to get them ... dispatched to their own homes in the shortest possible time'.[92] The men were returning to homes they may not have seen for four years. During that time, for men still at the fighting fronts, it was the aim of chaplains and various religious voluntary-aid organisations to provide servicemen with 'a home from home', and it is to the huts and tents of these agencies to which we now turn.

6   Religion and Pastoral Care

Music was an essential part of religious worship and pastoral care on the fighting fronts. It played an important role in the work of the chaplains, particularly in the form of hymns during church parades, and created emotional and aural links with home. This is illustrated at Talbot House in Poperinghe, where the piano remains in the dining room. Known by servicemen as 'Toc H', Talbot House was founded as an 'everyman's club' in 1915 by arguably the most well-known chaplain of the Great War, the Reverend Philip 'Tubby' Clayton. Hymns would be sung, accompanied by a harmonium during services on the upper floor while more recreational music was played on the piano downstairs. In this way, music and hymn-singing were central components of the work of various religious organisations who provided physical comforts, spiritual and moral guidance, education and entertainments for servicemen, such as the YMCA, the Salvation Army and the Church Army. These agencies, along with many other smaller groups, recognised that the war was a great opportunity, and at the outbreak of war they helped to provide essential services for the troops fighting for Britain and the Empire.[1]

Music and Chaplaincy

Approximately 5,000 chaplains of various denominations served with the British armed forces in the Great War.[2] While they wore the uniforms of officers, they were non-combatants who were unarmed and ordered to stay away from the front lines. However, many chaplains accompanied their units to provide comfort, support and solace to the men in forward positions. While they buried the dead, liaised with servicemen's relatives and acted as a 'prisoner's friend', the wartime experiences of many chaplains indicate that formal and informal musical activities were important, if not vital, elements of their work during the conflict. All British servicemen on land and sea would sing hymns every week during Sunday church parade. While the practice of organised religious worship was in decline during the late nineteenth century, hymns were an established feature of life in the Edwardian period. By 1914, around 40 per cent of the adult population worshipped at least once a month, and at least 80 per cent had attended Sunday School during childhood. This meant that while many men were 'deeply ignorant of Christian doctrine' they were 'remarkably well versed in Christian hymnody'.[3] For Anglican clergy, the selection of hymns was chosen by their bishops. Hymns were often chosen in response to wartime events, and on both the home and fighting fronts *Oh God Our Help in Ages Past* was regularly sung. The war also inspired the writing of new hymns, many of which asserted the righteousness of Britain's divine cause.[4] Several diaries record the communal singing of hymns as part of an organised service, but they were also sung spontaneously. Every military band would have a number of hymns in their repertoire. Captain Rowland Fielding, who served on the Western Front, recorded that the hymn *Abide with Me* would be played at the change of guard when the unit was out of the line. Wartime clergy were not immune to the popular music of the period. In January 1916, a journalist for *The Era* reported his astonishment when he heard a sermon in which the preacher quoted the lyrics of *Pack Up Your Troubles*, saying that they 'contained much more healthy and helpful teaching than any sermon he could preach'.[5]

Church parades were generally led by the unit's chaplain and, where available, accompanied by their own band. At sea, Marine Bandsman Reed recalled that they were 'lucky enough to have our Chaplain, who conducted morning service mostly on the Aft deck, to which the band played a hymn ... followed by a double round decks'.[6] A typical Sunday morning on board the HMS *Iron Duke* was described thus:

At 9 o'clock, the shrill notes of the bosn's whistle were heard screeching throughout the ship ... each man answered to his name and was handed a card, upon which was a number of hymns. The ships' bell then sounded for Church Service. On the command 'Roman Catholics fall out', men of that faith broke ranks. The ship's band ... struck up 'Onward Christian Soldiers', ... two deep, the men marched to the quarter deck. The padre ... takes up his position with the officers. The order 'off caps' is given ... then another hymn accompanied by the band, then a reading and 'on caps' before marching back along the deck.[7]

At end of the service, the order 'off jerseys' was given: 'the ship's band struck up a march and ... the ship's crew swung along each side of the deck ... the music quickened to 'Ragtime' and the men moved at the double ... The music slowed into a march once more, and ... at the sound of a bugle, a welcome halt was called.' William Allen, of the canteen ship SS *Borodino*, wrote on hearing the sailors sing 'those grand old hymns' that

[c]old indeed must be the heart that is unmoved ... by the rich melody of music their singing affords ... and hear borne across the waters from one giant battleship the strains of 'O, Day of Rest and Gladness' while from another floated the words of 'Rock of Ages' and from other ships afar off came faint whisperings of other of those grand old hymns which have taught our forbears how to live, and in honoured old age, have faltered lovingly upon their lips in death.[8]

In the RFC/RAF church parades were not compulsory. Chaplain Leonard found that '[t]here doesn't appear to be such a need or scope for a Padre [in the RFC] as in the infantry'. He found it 'harder to get in touch with the men. They are always busy and being specialists are a good deal scattered plying their various trades. Unfortunately there are no trenches to wander around, where men are only too ready to have a crack to fill up a slack half hour.'[9] The lack of a church bell or bugler meant that 'the only way to ensure having a congregation is to go round the huts and wake up all those who signified their intention of coming. . . . This I generally achieve by lighting a lamp or switching on their torchlight so that it shines in their eyes.'[10] The airmen appear to be less keen on any form of religious music, as seen at a Sunday concert in Bernaville, the largest aerodrome in France near the Headquarters of the 7th Army. A 'tremendous crowd' was gathered and 'although the great audience showed little enthusiasm over the singing of the solos from the Messiah, they seemed to enjoy them, though not too enthusiastic'. In the second half of the programme, which was secular, 'the rafters fairly shook'.[11] However, in the Army Bandmaster Rogan saw that 'beneath that manful cheeriness lay a vein of serious thought'. While the Coldstream Guards band was playing at a service in Poperinghe, conducted by Bishop Gwynne, Rogan was impressed that the soldier congregation 'listened intently and about two hundred officers and men stayed for Holy Communion' because in his long years of experience 'soldiers generally are inclined to fight shy of the Sacrament'. Indeed, Rogan noted that 'many of these communicants went into the line that night' and he 'wondered how many brave fellows would return'.[12]

Many chaplains worked hard to get around the various units in their vicinity (Figure 6.1). A typical Sunday schedule for Chaplain Leonard in 1916 featured three celebrations with seventy-four communicants, two church parades, and voluntary Evensong and sermon in the evening. Leonard found that the services 'are not so tiring in themselves ... it is the unpacking and packing of my communion bag & robes, the long rides between each service, and above all the constant strain of trying to keep up to time and avoiding or counteracting the unexpected, which is always a very present menace on active service'.[13] The areas behind the lines were not always the most peaceful places to hold services. At one church

Figure 6.1 IWM Q12109: A chaplain conducting church service from
the nacelle of a Royal Aircraft Factory F.E.2b night bomber at No. 2
Aeroplane Supply Depot, 1 September 1918. © Imperial War Museum,
pending.

parade, Leonard admitted it was difficult to concentrate on the service,
for they were 'surrounded by three Battalion camps, with bands playing
continually and horses and cookers and a game of football as it were
inundating us with distractions and noises'.[14] Wesleyan Chaplain
Reverend Herbert Cowl, serving with the Durham Light Infantry, wrote
that his 'open-air parades follow just the same order of service as an
indoor service and singing a foremost part and goes well'.[15] Of one of
his earliest services on the Western Front, he described that some were
conducted in an old theatre, and others were held in more makeshift
surroundings. On one such occasion church parade took place in

a great rambling loft in an old deserted farm, just out of the fire-zone. In a broken
chair ... the padre seated ... Round him were about 20 armed men, singing too
for all they are worth. On two jutting beam ends are stuck three guttering candles –
all the light we can muster, and we have covered the glass-less windows and gaps
in the roof, lest any of this excessive radiance should attract the eye of a watchful

German gunner. You would have heard the old favourite hymns as they have seldom been sung and would have felt the warming of those hearts as we prayed for you at home. As I write they are marching by in the cold darkness to retake their places in the trenches.[16]

Some chaplains found that the soldiers made a far more rewarding congregation. Chaplain Thomas Tiplady recalled that at home, preaching to the owners of 'stolid features' who have 'come out of habit rather than need', was very different to ministering to soldiers at the front because 'how the eyes of the soldiers in France glow and burn; how their features speak, and make the Preacher speak in reply!'[17] Reverend David Ffyfe, writing to the YMCA on his return from the Western Front, said that despite his twenty-five years of ministry, 'in seven weeks near the firing line [he] had more intimate touch with individual souls than in as many years of the past'.[18] Certainly, Tiplady felt that the Western Front was one of the 'kindest' places he had ever been for the atmosphere of brotherhood between British servicemen, and that the war had found 'warm fellowship between men of differing creeds and varying religious communions'.[19] An Anglican chaplain serving on a hospital ship in the Mediterranean spoke of the need 'to adapt oneself to one's congregation ... even a bit of Presbyterian to Presbyterians'.[20]

Many churchmen were found in the BRC ambulance convoys, including members of pacifist religions such as the Quakers who opted to serve the war effort in non-combatant roles.[21] Furthermore, chaplains and padres would base themselves in and around medical establishments to be on hand to help the wounded.[22] The ambulance units therefore housed a number of religious beliefs. However, despite evidence of tensions between religious groups in the fighting areas,[23] the ambulance convoys were proud of 'the harmony which prevailed between members of different religious bodies'. In the early weeks of the war, a member of Jewish faith suggested a service for all ambulance personnel. In this 'he was cordially supported' by a member of the Roman Catholic Church, and the service was conducted by a Salvation Army Section Leader. Among the congregation were clergymen of the Church of England, who were there as voluntary drivers, and 'all joined in the service and hymns'.[24]

Voluntary-Aid Organisations

While some memoirs might be seen to overstate the atmosphere of brotherliness between denominations, much of the kindnesses Tiplady described are evident in the work of the voluntary-aid

organisations throughout the war. Despite their ideological differences and methods, the Church Army, Salvation Army and YMCA
believed in expressing their Christian philanthropy via the provision
of pastoral care to nurture men's minds, bodies and spirits. These
organisations had been established in the nineteenth century to help
the poor through social reform and education. All were pro-
temperance, sharing the belief that alcohol was the root cause of
Britain's social problems amongst the lower classes. Their canteens
in tents and huts on home soil and near combat zones were often the
first point of contact that their workers would have with British
servicemen. Canteens were an established feature of service life
which helped soldiers' pay go further and acted to keep the men
nearby and under control. Canteens would sell tobacco, beer, soft
drinks, books, newspapers, candles, tinned food, biscuits and choco-
lates. The military reforms of the early 1900s had made changes to
the ways in which divisional canteens were run, and in the pre-war
period many units' canteen services were contracted out to civilian
suppliers and organisations, which included the Church Army,
YMCA and Salvation Army.[25] Nevertheless, the wartime situation
regarding the relationships between the agencies and the military
authorities, not to mention between the organisations themselves,
was often fraught with tensions and difficulties. As Jeffrey Reznick
has underlined, these organisations were in many ways competing on
traditional religious grounds to care for war-weary souls. They were
also embracing 'a new economic competitiveness' which affected
their relationship with military authorities. Although the War Office
and Admiralty were forced to rely on these groups because of the
scale of the war effort, the military continued to defend 'its traditional right to regulate the provision of comforts to resting soldiers
and claim profits that were reinvested into services provided'.[26] By
1917, the voluntary agencies were generally working under the
Assistant Chaplain General.

The YMCA was established in London in 1844 by George Williams.
Working in the drapery trade, Williams was concerned about the welfare
of his fellow workers, so he founded a prayer and bible study group to
keep the apprentices away from the dreadful delights of the metropolis.
By the early 1900s, the YMCA had established branches in many countries all over the world, including Africa and India. The YMCA was an
interdenominational yet Anglican-based organisation which stressed the
value of self-help and encouraged both physical and moral fitness. Its
membership was drawn primarily from the middle-classes. His Majesty
King George was the President, Countess Dorothy Haig was a committee

member and Princess Helena Victoria headed the Ladies Auxiliary Committee. Gwendoline Jellicoe was involved in appeals for comforts for the fleet.[27] Lady Jellicoe worked with 'a band of ladies' at her house in Sussex Square which she had turned into the Junior Army and Navy Stores offices in London.[28] The comforts and supplies they collected were sent on to the Junior Army and Navy Stores Ship, the SS *Borodino*, in Scapa Flow. This was a vessel fitted with a 'Grocery and Provisions Shop, a Laundry, and also a Hairdressing Saloon' and was attached as an auxiliary to the Grand Fleet. Its role was to go alongside battleships in the North Sea and act as a floating canteen. On land, the Sailors' Rests were the established canteens of the Royal Navy. The first of these were opened in the 1870s by Agnes Weston at Portsmouth, Devonport and Keyham.[29] The Rests were designed along the lines of a canteen, providing refreshments and meals, and they were run along strict temperance lines. Weston published *Ashore and Afloat*, a journal given free to naval servicemen, also available to civilians on subscription, which had a circulation of over 652,000 in 1910.[30] The work of the Sailors' Rests continued throughout the war. Marine Bandsman Reed recalls their open houses on Sunday afternoons when they offered tea and cake after singing, Bible stories and prayers in a small hall in Albert Road, Eastney.[31]

The Salvation Army was already active in many servicemen's communities, but they were particularly successful in naval towns as well as running missions across the world. It was established in May 1878 by William Booth, a London minister who took his ministry into the streets where it would reach the poor, homeless, hungry and destitute. Its leaders and members were working-class men and women who believed in moral purity and self-restraint to establish a right relationship with God. Highly evangelical, they saw themselves as fighting the Salvation War via military rhetoric, ranks, uniforms, flags, parades and bands. The Church Army developed a similarly martial character with ranks, uniforms and parades (Figure 6.2). It was founded in 1882 by Wilson Carlile, a curate working in the slums of Westminster. The Church Army developed a programme of social reform using military rhetoric, seeking to train working-class men and women to be lay evangelists. In addition to their work among the poor in the slums they also ran prison missions, took horse-drawn carriage missions around the country, and established 'Fresh Air Homes' for city dwellers in poor health. In the pre-war period they assisted those affected by high levels of unemployment, established their own printing press and made effective use of the cinematograph to publicise their work.

Figure 6.2 Interior of a Church Army hut on the Western Front. Courtesy of the Church Army.

Supporting the War Effort

Within ten days of the declaration of war, more than 250 YMCA centres had opened in Britain. By October 1914, some 400 marquees had been erected to assist Britain's armed forces with the hundreds of thousands of new recruits flooding into the training camps. In the first week of September, the Salvation Army declared that for the Salisbury Mission, 'being situated near the military camps at Bulford and Tidworth' that the Sunday night open-air service 'has become very martial like, and it is not unusual for the market-place, the scene of our evening's service, to resemble a miniature scene of Church parade at camp'.[32] In St Albans, thousands of Territorials, including the London Scottish and London Irish, were attending Salvation Army services, with some meetings held in a cinema.[33] Among the Church Army's first facilities for servicemen were opened Bedford, Luton and Newhaven, and two of its Missioners worked with 16,000 men at camps in Shorncliffe and Colchester.[34]

However, as with many international organisations at this time, the outbreak of war against Germany caused a great deal of moral discomfort. The Salvation Army, for example, had only recently held their international meeting, the Congress of the Nations during the summer of 1914. One of its first actions was to dispatch a small Army expedition to accompany the troops departing for the Continent. The expedition was under the care of the 'Army veteran' Brigadier Mary Murray. Brigadier Murray was in 1914 the head of the Salvation Army's Naval and Military League. She had served with the Salvation Army in the South African War, and she was closely related to many high-ranking military families. She held the South African medal and a letter of recommendation from the War Office referring to her work in South Africa. Together with senior bandsman Staff Captain John Aspinall and Ensign Mary Whittaker, Murray went to Belgium and France in August 1914 to assist the men of the British Expeditionary force, hoping that the authorities would give permission for them 'to be present in the field hospitals'.[35]

The first weeks after mobilisation were challenging for the agencies' services in Britain. Civilian recruits like George Butterworth found the army's facilities at Aldershot to be 'very unsatisfactory' and 'insufficiently equipped'. He complained that there was nowhere comfortable to sit out of the wind, and the YMCA tents were too crowded.[36] Worse, in Butterworth's opinion, was that the beer was 'simply not worth fighting for'. Food was also an issue. Butterworth relayed that with his friends he had 'formed a habit of going into Farnborough every evening and getting a proper supper', but as he admitted, 'there are not many who can afford that regularly'.[37] All the agencies moved quickly to increase the accommodation for recruits by erecting marquees and huts which could hold hundreds of soldiers. Most facilities run by the Salvation Army, Church Army and YMCA were open to all servicemen of any rank, with a handful of locations reserved for officers. The tents and huts quickly became known as places which would provide servicemen with hot drinks, food and a quiet place to rest. In addition to a quiet place to read, write home, pray, chat or take refreshment, these huts provided a space for soldiers to listen to musical talks and recitals, as well as for their own music-making such as informal sing-songs around one of the YMCA's pianos which was provided for exactly that purpose. The organisation also distributed 20,000 copies of a selection of popular songs for in-house entertainment.[38]

By November 1914, the Salvation Army, Church Army and YMCA were all establishing facilities for servicemen in France and Belgium along the Lines of Communication. They began by establishing themselves in the port of Le Havre, expanding into further centres down to Marseilles and across the Mediterranean. The Salvation Army were particularly pleased to report that the military authorities generally 'are appreciative of The Army's efforts on behalf of the men, and the testimonials received from Commanding Officers and Chaplains are most encouraging'.[39] Their facilities grew rapidly. When the Bishop of London visited the Western Front in 1915, he wrote that 'to enter the Base Depots [at Rouen and Le Havre] is to enter a perfectly organised small town. There is to be found a Military Church, with the bell sounding for an evening service; there is the great cinema ... there are the Church Army Hut and the Y.M.C.A. hut ... line after line of hut as we have grown accustomed to seeing rapidly erected in England.'[40] Indeed, Chaplain Mellish in July 1915, described a camp at Rouen which had 'YMCA huts at each end, Church Army hut in the middle'.[41] As the conflict continued into 1915, the War Office saw that the rapid expansion of troops to the fighting areas necessitated a more coherent – and profitable – canteens service. In February 1915, the Army Council formally agreed to provide a forces-wide canteen service, and voted £27,000 from profits made from canteens in the Boer War to help establish the service. In France, Lieutenant Colonel E. C. Wright pioneered the Expeditionary Forces Canteens (EFC) service, which was amalgamated with the Army Service Corps on 7 July 1915, designated as the Expeditionary Forces Canteens Section (ASC). The EFC was staffed and administered by the ASC and helped to reduce the War Office's reliance on the help of the voluntary-aid organisations. By the end of the war, there were 577 canteens in France alone, with many more in the Middle East which were staffed by approximately 500 ASC personnel with staff from QMAAC. The EFC also managed officers' rest houses and messes, leave billets, mineral water factories and bakeries.[42]

Music was a large component of the work of the voluntary-aid organisations. On the fighting fronts, music of all kinds helped them to reach large bodies of men who they might not otherwise have contacted in times of peace. The YMCA believed that the outbreak of war was an opportunity to rehabilitate their pre-war image as 'effeminate and namby-pamby' and 'a somewhat milk-and-waterish organisation run by elderly men, to preach to youth'.[43] Similarly, the Salvation Army was keen to work to its strengths and experience. It had already established a tradition of vocal and instrumental excellence as a primary weapon in the Salvation War. One month into the conflict, the organisation looked to its musical comrades who should 'seek to do all their power in bring cheer and relief to wounded hearts' as 'behind their music they have the mighty lever of prayer'.[44] At home the same thing can be seen. The Church Army and the Salvation Army were very active in caring for the thousands of Belgian refugees arriving in Britain. The Salvation Army's Deputy Bandmaster in Folkestone, for example, transported men, women and children from the harbour, 'his pony and trap busy going to and fro with their belongings ... while behind a straggling little procession followed the refugees'.[45]

Salvation Army officers would often step in to help with military funerals at home and abroad. In the first week of the war, before many chaplains reached the men, Salvation Army members were sometimes asked to pray over the bodies of fallen comrades in place of a priest.[46] At home in November 1914, military authorities requested a Salvation Army band in Cardiff to play for the funeral of a soldier who died of wounds received on the Western Front. The senior officer 'warmly thanked the Band for its attendance, and it was commandeered by the YMCA for a return visit to the camp'.[47] In Coventry, at another funeral, and despite the rain 'the crowds lined the principal thoroughfares of the city as the Band played the Dead March in "Saul". After the "Last Post" had been sounded, the Band and the local Territorials lined up and marched to the Headquarters to the lively strains of "Conqueror", "Veteran", and "Citadel".'[48] The structure of this music, of playing more stirring, patriotic tunes after the music of mourning, was a hallmark of Salvation Army worship. When a Salvation Army band played at memorial services for one of their own officers, for example, Assistant Young-People's Sergeant-Major Potter, a gunner on HMS *Cressy,* his Bible and uniform were placed on a Union Jack, the service began with the National Anthem, and the band played *Never Quit the Field.*[49]

On the fighting fronts it was difficult to observe the level of funeral ceremony that would have been taken for granted in peacetime. In Egypt, at a hospital treating the wounded from the Dardanelles, Corporal Johnson Double noted that '[t]here were 3 bodies taken from here this morning for burial ... covered with the U.J. No band however'.[50] In France and Belgium, Salvation Army officers attended servicemen's funerals as representatives of the nation but also the men's families. In January 1915, when Ensign Mary Whittaker heard of the death of a reservist Guardsman in a hospital in Paris she 'walked behind the coffin five miles in the rain – the only English people who followed that soldier to his grave. We would gladly have walked fifty miles had it been necessary ... He had left a wife and two children; had faced the enemy, got seriously wounded, and died amongst a strange people in a strange land.'[51] However, members of all the voluntary-aid agencies often found themselves in the range of fire. Indeed, by July 1916, the Church Army described their workers as 'Trench Churchmen'.[52] Brigadier Murray found herself in the midst of the battle of the Aisne in September 1914, reporting that she was 'watching the shells as they fall. They are pretty enough, as long as you are not underneath them.' Finding that musical metaphors helped to describe the action, she wrote that 'the appalling noise makes us deaf. Shells are not the instruments I shall choose to play on ... the harmonies are not good enough.' She states that she has 'been slightly burnt by a shell', but that the sights she had seen 'will ever live in my heart and vision'. By 1915, Murray's Salvation Army workers had erected marquees, huts and rest rooms in 75 camps and centres, used by over 110,000 soldiers every week, with 195 officers and employees engaged in the work.[53] All three agencies were present in, or rather under, the ruined buildings of Ypres. Both the YMCA and Church Army ran facilities in the city, and of the latter it was relayed that it had a piano, gramophone and games, and that 'the nightly sing-song and Family Prayer renew nerve force and spiritual power'.[54]

The Salvation Army maintained its strong tradition of hymn singing. Brigadier Murray supplied thousands of hymn sheets for use in huts and tents, and one Salvationist wrote they were 'more than ever convinced that the power of The Army is in its wonderful singing ... it is astonishing how these men love to sing those grand old hymns ... the wonderful power of song ... above any denomination'.[55] In addition to hymn sheets, lanterns and slides were sometimes used to project hymns lyrics to congregations. By 1915, the Church Army's Lantern and Slide Department had over 1,000 slides available which included the words to hymns and prayers as well as pictures of various wartime scenes and 'Celebrities of the War'. Their Lantern Intercession Series was given to naval chaplains free of charge. They were also sent a set of Evening Prayer slides and others featuring the lyrics of twelve hymns for use with the Fleet. Similar slides were also used in some Church Army huts and hospitals where they were a popular feature.[56] The YMCA also deployed lantern slides to encourage the mass singing of hymns. In India, Scottish regiments had 'lantern song evenings' which were 'held in the open-air ... the only things visible among the deep Indian darkness were the hymn words on the lighted screen'. The congregation were said to have sung 'many, many hymns as though they wanted to continue singing'.[57]

Hymns were sung spontaneously on the fighting fronts. General Booth wrote in October 1914 that he had heard 'of Army lads singing our songs in the trenches, which have been taken up by their comrades around and passed along the lines. Think of the wonderful triumphs of our songs! Sing on!'[58] A correspondent to the Church Army reported that he had seen the 'most pitiful' sight of a small party of men returning from trenches singing *Onward Christian Soldiers*, which he thought was 'beautiful to hear' until he noticed that 'each were carrying three or more rifles' belonging to men who had been killed. He believed that the men were marching back, 'worn out and thoroughly done for, yet happy in finding comfort from the word of God'.[59] The quality of the music and its religious meaning were not always seen as important. One officer called hymns 'meaningless modulations' in that 'they meandered fitfully round the walls of the old church', but it was this sense of meditation that meant he 'would not have exchanged them for all the ordered wealth of Bach or Palestrina'. He found that they 'did their job, lying lightly on our soldier-spirit and bringing us to serious mood'.[60] Chaplain Leonard wrote that 'to be able to sing a psalm instead of a hymn is a great pleasure' but that he was 'beginning to get hymn-singing indigestion. I get altogether too much of the few well-known hymns to which we are confined.'[61] Chaplains like Leonard often recruited and trained choirs, and in January 1916, while in Flanders with the Kings Own, Leonard held choir practice for the Suffolks as he wanted them 'to sing the responses and the chants on the Church Parade next Sunday'. He felt that this was 'rather ambitious at an open-air service, but the Welsh Fusiliers sing the whole service regularly, and beautifully they do it too'.[62] Leonard was delighted to find an RFC observer who until his enlistment had been leading boy chorister in Lincoln Cathedral. His voice was still unbroken and Leonard describes that it was 'a perfect joy to listen to him'. However, on hearing the lad's 'sweet voice warbling away', a Colonel thought 'there must be a lady in camp, and refused to believe otherwise until the fellow was produced and made to sing in his presence'.[63]

The musical accompaniment of hymns was a consideration for Chaplains. In 1916, the church parade for the Kings Own was 'held in a most delightful and shady orchard with the drums and fifes to play the hymns'.[64] When Chaplain Leonard was serving with 7 Squadron, RFC, an Intelligence Officer from a neighbouring squadron played the hymns and chants on Leonard's 'wheezy little portable harmonium'.[65] Pianos were sometimes used as altars. At a service in a YMCA hut near the front lines in May 1916, 'the top of the piano was retable with Cross and flowers upon it'.[66] Reverend Mellish noted that on Sundays when his Battalion was out of the line they held their services wherever they could. At Reninghelst, services were held in the YMCA hut and in the Cinema at Poperinghe, both of which contained pianos. Mellish's favourite location, however, was 'the beautiful chapel in Toc.H'.[67] The communal aspect of group singing brought the men together both physically and figuratively. While he was joining the singing of 'our dear old "hopping" hymn, *God be with you till we meet again*', in one of the YMCA huts, Mellish found he was standing next to several men from his Deptford parish who were serving in the Buffs.[68] Whatever music was used during services, *God Save the King* would always be sung, as dictated in any prayer book authorised by the Chaplain-General.[69]

The sound of servicemen singing hymns was said to have been different from the sound of their singing other types of songs. During a service led by the Bishop of London during his visit to the Western Front in May 1915, the Church Army reported that the unaccompanied singing of the hymn *When*

I Survey the Wondrous Cross was 'not singing as the soldiers sing "Tipperary," ... there was a notable softening'. It was noted that the Bishop 'stood listening with his head tilted back, as if to him the music was sweet indeed'.[70] Chaplain Thomas Tiplady, who served with the London Territorials, described the hymn as 'a song of the inner life'. He said that soldiers were 'extremely fond' of hymns, with the two most popular being *Abide With Me* and *When I Survey the Wondrous Cross*. Tiplady said that there was 'nothing written by the hand of man that could compete with these two in the blessing and strength which they have brought to our soldiers, especially during an offensive when Death has cast his shadow over the hearts of all'. He recalled that his unit sung the latter hymn during every service in the 'bitterest' weeks of the Somme offensive, saying that with 'its assurance of redemption it gave comfort in the face of death'. Other popular hymns on the Western Front included *Rock of Ages, Jesus Lover of My Soul, Fight the Good Fight, There Is a Green Hill, At Even ere the Sun Was Set, O God Our Help in Ages Past* and *Eternal Father Strong to Save*.[71] The Church Army underlined that the lyrics of hymns soldiers sung as children were still 'ringing' in their heads: 'how full of comfort and meaning they now sound'.[72] However, religious music was not always welcomed. In September 1914 at Aldershot, after the Salvation Army's weekly open-air service, the Salvation Army Band 'and a few of the local Soldiery ... were attentively listened to by a fine congregation of men belonging to Scottish regiments'. As the Band marched off to the tune of *Jesus is My Saviour*, 'something like fifty of these brawny Highland laddies formed fours and followed behind' singing *Tipperary* in an attempt to drown them out. However, 'the five or six gallant Bandsmen proved equal to the occasion and completely drowned every attempt at secularity'.[73]

The Church Army believed that despite his 'rollicking fun and careless good-humour', Jack Tar was 'a thoughtful chap' who, on 'the wide inimitable ocean, comes nearer to God'. They underlined that Sir John Jellicoe held frequent Holy Communions on his flagship, and like Lord Kitchener, was a regular churchgoer.[74] In the Soldiers' Homes of the Church Army, hymns were sung every day at 8 pm.[75] However, the Church Army were concerned that servicemen, particularly those in the BEF, did not have adequate time for silent prayer and reflection. In February 1915, they began to raise funds for 'Huts of Silence'. The organisations were by then opening fifty recreation huts in the largest military camps in England, France and Egypt, in addition to increasing their considerable work with the destitute at home.[76] By March 1916, the Church Army was running a 'floating hut' on 'a large barge' on the canals of Flanders which could follow the men and 'be at their behest at any moment'.[77]

A Point of Contact

Chaplains found that hymns were their best point of contact to get in touch with the men, particularly in dire circumstances. British Army chaplains had a crucial role in the delivery of a death sentence, mostly as 'prisoner's friend'. However, only a small proportion of British Army chaplains were called to attend a military execution as they were a very rare occurrence; the 306 British soldiers who were executed represent 0.005 per cent of the 5.7 million men who fought for Britain 1914–18. Only two Chaplains attended two executions, Reverend Julian Bickersteth of the 56th (1st London) and Reverend Leonard Martin Andrews of the 3rd Division.[78] In July 1917, Bickersteth was serving as an Anglican Army Chaplain with the 1/12th Battalion, London Regiment. The unit was at that time in the front lines at Wancourt on 1–3 July 1917, approximately four miles south east of Arras.[79] Bickersteth was informed by his Colonel that a man who had deserted four times in the preceding six months, who was already under a suspended death sentence, had deserted again during the Battle of Arras. Bickersteth had been attending the man in the Guard Room every day and was now called upon to assist with the arrangements for the sentence to be carried out. The prisoner had twelve hours left to live. Bickersteth recalled that many of the man's comrades 'said he was mad or at least that there was something wrong with his brain, but our doctor had been unable to certify that he was in any way not responsible for his actions, and certainly he was quite intelligent in a good many ways. He could read and write well.' The description of the man's final hours is a detailed and moving account. Bickersteth wrote that the man was unresponsive, and the chaplain did know how he could reach him until he produced an Army Prayer Book, which contained about 130 hymns. Bickersteth handed him the book and asked him to find a hymn he knew. The prisoner found *Rock of Ages* and asked if they could sing it. Bickersteth admitted that

The idea of our solemnly singing hymns together while the two sentries eye us coldly from the other side of the room seems to me so incongruous that I put him off with the promise of a hymn to be sung before he goes to sleep, but he is not satisfied and he returns to the suggestion again. . . . we sat there and sang hymns together for three hours or more.

Bickersteth is amazed that the prisoner 'takes command of the proceedings. He chooses the hymns. He will not sing any one over twice. He starts the hymn on the right note, he knows the tunes and pitches them all perfectly.' The chaplain admitted that the man 'knew more tunes than

I did'. After exhausting the Army Prayer Book, Bickersteth brought him a YMCA hymnbook that contained several more hymns, including *Throw Out the Life-Line* and *What a Friend We Have in Jesus*. At 10:30 pm the stock of hymns was nearly exhausted 'as he would never sing the same hymn twice over'. The men agreed to stop singing after they had sung one of the hymns he had already sung. The man chose *God be With us till We Meet Again*, which he sang 'utterly unmoved'. The prisoner then insisted that they sung *God save the King*, which finished all military concerts and services. The two Military Police, who had replaced the ordinary guards, 'had to get up and stand rigidly to attention while the prisoner and I sang lustily three verses of the National Anthem. A few seconds later the prisoner was asleep.' Bickersteth felt that to the prisoner, hymn singing was synonymous with religion, and that no other aspect of religion had ever touched him. Now that he was facing death, the man 'found real consolation in singing hymns learnt in childhood – he had been to Sunday school up to twelve or thirteen'. That was the point of contact Bickersteth needed. As the man faced the firing party and was bound to a stake, Bickersteth whispered in his ear the title of the hymn, *Safe in the Arms of Jesus*: he repeated it quite clearly, 'Safe in the arms of Jesus.'[80] At the end of December 1917, the 1/9th Battalion, London Regiment (Queen Victoria's Rifles) were in the front-line trenches at Gavrelle, four miles due east of Roclincourt.[81] Bickersteth was once again called upon to attend a soldier who had been condemned to death. Again, the most effective way of reaching out to the prisoner was by the use of a hymn 'which will for ever now have a new meaning to me, and which was in every line and every word appropriate. "Just as I am without one plea!" As they bound him, I held his right arm tight to reassure him – words were useless at such a moment.'[82]

Hymn Parodies

Popular music and hymns were not mutually exclusive, and religious leaders were quick to recognise that '[s]ongs and tunes will live when sermons are long forgotten'.[83] Hymns would often be sung at the end of concert parties where Chaplains chaired the concerts, although Lena Ashwell believed the changes in musical mood 'from gaiety to gravity' occurred with a swiftness that was 'disconcerting' to the churchmen.[84] Hymns were a regular feature of band repertoire and would always be sung by troops at Sunday church parade. Therefore, as with much of the music in Britain's armed forces, it was used for the purposes of comedy and parody. The ASC, for example, had their own satirical take on hymns according to their daily schedules:

5.30 am, Reveille, 'Christians awake, salute the happy morn'

. . .

6.30 am, Breakfast, 'Meekly await and murmur not'

7.00 am, Arrive at Depots, 'Here we suffer grief and pain'

1.00 pm, Dinner, 'Come ye thankful people come'

. . .

6.30 pm (if lucky) Dismiss, 'Praise God from whom all blessing'

. . .

10.00 pm, Last Post, 'All are safely gathered in'

10.15 pm, Lights Out, 'Peace, perfect peace'[85]

A very similar example of using the hymn form to parody routine can also be found in hospitals. In a VAD medical facility the same hymns are used for *Reveille* and *Lights Out,* with some additional events noted by the nursing staff such as:

8.15 am, Coy. Officer's parade, 'When he cometh'

2.15 pm, Rifle Drill, 'Go labour on'

3.15 pm, Lecture by Officer, 'Tell me the old story'

. . .

6.00 pm, Free for the night, 'Oh Lord, how happy we shall be'

10.30 pm, Inspection of wards, 'Sleep on beloved'[86]

Many servicemen's songs adopted hymn tunes to which they would set their own lyrics. For example, all services had a version of *When This Ruddy War is Over* which was sung to the tune of *What a Friend We Have in Jesus.* Another prime example is the setting of the hymn tune *The Church's One Foundation.* This was adopted and personalised by many units during the Great War. The Royal Engineers sang *Fred Karno's Army,* the Motor Transport (ASC) had *Kitchener's Army,* and the Artists' OTC, the RFC, the ANZACs and the RNAS all sang *Ragtime Army,* all to the same tune.[87] The use of a hymn, which would have been known and sung by the majority of soldiers, was an easy way to create and share a song of their own making. The RFC/RAF were also particularly fond of adopting religious texts for their songs. Appearing around 1916, *The Pilot's Psalm* was a parody of the 23rd Psalm of David:

The B.E.2c is my bus; therefore I shall want.
He maketh me come down in green pastures.
He leadeth me where I will not go.
He maketh me to be sick; he leadeth me astray on all cross-
country flights . . .[88]

Servicemen who were active members of the religious organisations liked to compose their own versions of popular songs. One serviceman sent into the Church Army his own version of *Pack Up Your Troubles in Your Old Kit*

Bag, and the *Church Army Gazette* instructed its readers to 'sing it until you believe and mean it, then you can face all troubles with the same brave spirit'.

> Pour out your troubles unto Christ our Lord,
> For He does care,
> His heart is overflowing with great love,
> That all mankind can share.
> Where's the need for worrying,
> Since He will make us free?
> So bring all your troubles unto Christ in prayer.
> He will bless thee.[89]

There was also a Church Army version of *My Little Grey Home in the West* entitled *At the Church Army Hut in the West.*[90] In October 1914, the Salvation Army' 'Song of the moment' was *On the Ocean of Love and Mercy* which was sung to the tune of *Tipperary.*[91] This came after Salvation Army Sergeant-Major James, a sergeant in City of Westminster National Reserve, marched off with the men singing 'the popular ditty' in September 1914. Sergeant James 'was not at all satisfied as to the suitability of the words for a Sunday'. James 'suddenly recollected that his good wife had . . . handed him some words which went well to the melody . . . and commenced to sing:

> On the ocean of Love and Mercy,
> To the Homeland I go,
> I'm determined to trust the journey,
> In the safest Hands I know;
> Good-bye sin and folly,
> Farewell worldly care,
> For the path of glory is before me,
> And my Home is there'.

The Salvation Army relates that the new lyrics apparently soon spread through the column and 'were lustily singing them'. The captain 'noticed that certain of his men were singing "religion", so he beckoned to Sergeant James. "What's this the men are singing . . . Just give me the exact words, will you sergeant?"' By the time the regiment passed Buckingham Palace it was reported that 90 per cent of James' company, including the officers, were singing *On the Ocean of Love and Mercy.*[92]

Music and 'Hut Culture'

The tent and hut facilities provided by the Church Army, Salvation Army and YMCA became central points for musical activities for all servicemen.[93] The band of HMS *Queen Elizabeth*, for example, landed for regular orchestral practice at the YMCA in Rosyth with the well-known composer and conductor Hamilton Harty who was then on the Admiral's Staff.[94] On Malta in January 1916, Corporal Johnson Double of the Hampshire Regiment found that Sundays were his busiest day. His diary notes that on average he played for two church parades each week, but he would often be called to play the piano for additional events. On one Sunday in March 1916, Double played for two church parades, a service in the YMCA and then a sacred concert organised by one of the officers. Double noted that he was at the piano from 5.30 pm to 9.15 pm without a break.[95] After being 'collared for piano' by the YMCA once again, he was thinking of adding 'OTHMF' to his name: 'Organist to His Majesty's Forces'.[96] In October 1916, three concerts took place simultaneously in the Church Army, YMCA and in Headquarters tent.[97] Double and the other members of the band were called to play at various ceremonies and events on the island. On Sunday 27 February 1917, for example, they 'were taken to Valletta in the afternoon and played for a consecration service in the cemetery and gave a concert in the gymnasium in the evening. Arrived back in camp about 11.30 pm.' On 2 November, they played at the memorial service 'for the souls of men fallen in the war'.[98] Double mentions a few specific hymns that were performed regularly on Malta. *Fight the Good Fight* was sung in the YMCA, and he often sang the solo *I Will Arise* at evening services.[99] Double spent the rest of his time on Malta in the camp's band and playing for the YMCA almost daily. In March 1916, Double and his band colleagues gave a concert in the YMCA tent as a farewell to 900 men leaving for active service the following day.[100] In April 1916, the band begin practicing Handel's *Alleluia Chorus*, of which Double reports that it is 'not difficult but wants plenty of wind'.[101] In April he '[g]ave another programme in the YMCA tent … was thoroughly enjoyed by nurses, officers and men alike. The place was crowded, and the applause spoke well for the efforts of the artists. All, of course, men from the camp.'[102]

The organisations promoted the work of their more well-known members and associates who would become familiar names to servicemen. The YMCA worked with the evangelist Gipsy Smith, a man whose hymns-singing and rousing sermons saw 'thousands upon thousands of boys turn their hearts to God during the years of the war'.[103] Smith 'did not sing a hymn of hate for the enemy', nor did he present a 'fiery denunciation of sin'.[104] He generally began with a few well-known and popular hymns, and servicemen would go to see him in order to hear something that would remind them of home.[105] Salvation Army Brigadier Tom Plant, over the course of two years from 1915, regularly visited servicemen at Salvation Army huts on the Western Front. He was there principally to play music and help conduct Meetings, but he was often said to roll up his sleeves and help when there was a rush on for tea. Plant was renowned for playing a range of instruments, including the banjo. In 1917, it was said that Plant had played Salvation music 'to men who have been drawn up ready to set off for the trenches. So great was the crush at one camp gathering that all the seats were taken out of the hut and the men stood in a solid block for an hour and a half. Up in the rafters and on the window-sills too, were men, while outside the crowd heard the music and its message from the open doors and windows.' The Salvation Army emphasised that the 'influence of the gatherings counts for good and the officers are as grateful as the men'.[106]

Plant's work on the Western Front and Salvation Army bands' appearances at home encouraged the organisation to claim that public appreciation of their music 'is today everywhere manifest. The old order of outward repugnance to our methods, resistance to our message, and opposition to our aggressive tactics, have disappeared.'[107] In a similar way, the leader of a YMCA hut in Havre felt that 'thousands of men hold a different view of Christianity and the YMCA as a result of [our] work'.[108] At a hut in Calais, it was reported that 'an increasing number of men use our hut for the social and educational facilities provided.... The games' department is one of our very busiest and provides the men with a desirable counter-attraction to the more insidious pleasures which the town, close at hand, affords.'[109] Indeed, this reference to the facilities available to soldiers in nearby towns reflects the fact that local *estaminets* were popular with the troops. At best, the local hostelries charged high prices, but they were also often linked to brothels which was a problem when 32 out of every 1000 British/Dominion soldiers were admitted to hospital for venereal disease.[110] The desire to provide facilities which would act as attractive 'counter-attractions' to less wholesome venues is evident in the efforts the YMCA made to provide decent entertainments. In 1915 they produced a handbook, written for YMCA leaders in battle zones in Europe, which included tips on how to conduct a sing-song and how best to set up concert parties and dressing rooms. On 12 April 1915, the YMCA announced that it was starting to provide cinematograph entertainments for men at the front. Three buildings had been secured. At Havre, a cinema hut seating 1,200 people was opened by a concert given by a YMCA-Lena Ashwell party. It was said that 'no form of entertainment is so popular with the rank and file as the cinematograph; the pictures cover a variety of subjects, and already the YMCA has 200,000ft of film ready to be displayed. English and American firms have given their best films free of charge.'[111]

The military value of the agencies' work in terms of morale and discipline was highly valued by the British High Command. Drunkenness was an issue across all of the British armed forces. Instances are not difficult to find; for example, on 22 September 1916, Driver G. Plunkitt (ASC) was conveying convalescents from Noyelles station to the Depot when he crashed into a café at St Valery. He was arrested for drunkenness and subsequently disciplined.[112] Major-General Chichester of the Second Army wrote to the head of the YMCA in France on behalf of Plumer that 'he wishes me to express to you his high appreciation of the good work being done by your Society. The entertainments and comforts provided are greatly enjoyed and have had a good effect in decreasing the cases of drunkenness especially in Bailleul and consequently improving the efficiency and discipline of the men generally.'[113] This goes some way to explain why music for entertainment and educative purposes was an integral component of the YMCA's wartime work and why the organisation spent £166,672 [£7.2 million] on free concerts and entertainments.[114] Musical activities were encouraged in canteens and huts in the fighting areas, with pianos available for any serviceman to play. Chaplain Mellish relayed that in the Church Army hut 'we have a piano which is serving its country well; a notice on it pleads with the intending performer "Don't hit me hard; I'm really quite tame."'[115] In another Church Army hut on the Western Front, it was said that the 'excellent piano' was 'going almost all day', and that evening concerts were attended by an average of 400 men a night.[116] Percy Scholes wrote that in some huts 'the piano is hardly ever silent. I remember a Rest Camp in France where it was going from six in the morning till half-past nine at night, unless it might be at meal times; and even then it was not silent long, for some boy would hurry over the meal so as to be first back and get the piano whilst it was free.' Scholes noted the wide spectrum of players. He heard 'boys who could merely pick out the notes of the airs of a song-book, extemporising a left-hand part that did not fit, boys with wonderful natural "ear", who without having had a lesson in their lives or knowing the name of a note could rattle out rag-time by the hour, and boys who played Beethoven and Chopin in a way which must have made our poor little French piano feel ashamed that it could not do these great composers greater justice'. Scholes was adamant that 'the piano and the gramophone have done great service to *morale* in this war'.[117]

The YMCA Music Department

In the autumn of 1914, the YMCA established its own Music Department which carried the motto 'Whatever Cheers the Warrior

Helps to Win the War'.[118] This was led by the composer Percy
Scholes and it was very well resourced. Among its activities was the
ability to organise speakers for talks on composers and on subject
such as 'how to form an orchestra'; providing a list of musicians,
lecturers and entertainers available; maintaining a music library; and
the sale of instruments at reduced prices through deals with suppliers.
Musical competitions were also held on the Western Front. After
a visit to the Western Front in 1917, Scholes provided his own answer
to the question 'Will music help us to beat the Boche?' He reported
that, as a University Extension lecturer was just beginning his talk on
'The Story of British Music', that question was 'hurled' at him by
a British soldier:

[the lecturer] looked round the crowd of men squatting around on the floor of the
marquee, men just out of the trenches the day before, and replied: '. . . gramophones in their thousands, Miss Ashwell's concert parties, visits to the front of
crack Army bands, and now University Extension lectures on Music. Are these
things helping you "to beat the Boche"?' And every man shouted 'Yes'.[119]

Those involved with the work of the YMCA Music Department identified
a 'tremendous awakening of interest . . . in music . . . both from the point
of view of performance and appreciation'.[120] Copies of 'good' music were
often requested in the press. In October 1918, the Church Army appealed
for the music of Mendelssohn to be sent to one of their huts in Italy as part
of 'a widespread general plea for the best classical printed music of all
sorts for men using these centres, who ask for good music'.[121]
    The 'cellist Helen Mott was one of many musicians who went to the
Western Front with the YMCA Music Department. Mott relayed that she
expected it to be 'uphill work'. She pointed out that the men were
accustomed to listening to in music 'not always from their choice', but
they had 'proved themselves to be the finest audience in the world for an
historical or scientific lecture on an understandable subject'. Mott and
her colleagues' faith in the men's musical capabilities 'was fully borne out
by the keen interest and thorough appreciation which they always gave
sincerely and spontaneously . . . they used to come up afterwards and ask
questions – or tell us that they liked so-and-so (usually Beethoven),
because their mothers or sisters used to play it'. She recalled that servicemen regularly 'spoke of the *peace* and *rest* it gave them to hear good music,
and those who were not quite so accustomed to it evidently found plenty
of interest and enjoy [sic], for they came more than once, and our
audiences grew rapidly'.[122] The musical content of the lecture-recital
was pitched to inform as well as educate. Each session was timed to last
one hour, and the performers would each provide an introduction and

a commentary on the pieces played, taking it in turn to play solo and together. The programme was divided into three sections: 'Past and Present', 'Old Dances' and 'Great Masters', and included the music of Handel, Beethoven, Schumann, Schubert, Rachmaninov and Grieg. Mott explained that she liked to keep the lecture element of the recital to a minimum so the music 'served as a relaxation . . . aiming more to give an idea of the period in question, the character and human aspects of the composer, and . . . where all this could be traced in the particular piece of music'.[123]

The YMCA at Ciro's

The expansion of the YMCA's services, particularly concerning music and entertainment, was seen as something of a surprise to some during the war. In December 1916, one writer marvelled that

Various prophets foresaw the Great War and foretold its advent with more or less accuracy; writers of sensational fiction foretold some of its more lurid surprises – Zeppelin raids, for instance, even tanks; but nobody, not even H. G. Wells, ever conceived so improbable and fantastically sensible a notion that the vast armies camped in France should be officially accompanied and chaperoned by an elaborate extension of the Young Men's Christian Association, and that a Ladies' Auxiliary Committee of that peaceful and estimable organization would be called upon to supply a clamouring army of some millions of men with concerts . . . the incredulity of both Army and the YMCA would probably have been crushing.[124]

The prospect of the YMCA taking over a nightclub in Soho was even more unlikely.[125] In March 1915, Lena Ashwell had recommended that 'anxious parents who . . . write to newspapers that they do not approve of night clubs . . . might set to work to organize an alternative scheme of entertainment'. She recommended the provision of 'good surroundings where good young people could dance, and where the advantages of a good cook and the good cellar are not ignored'.[126] Two years later, a solution presented itself. In the spring of 1917, the management of Ciro's restaurant offered their premises in Orange Street, Central London, to the YMCA, free of rent until the end of the war. It was felt that the concert parties on Salisbury Plain had been so successful the work should be extended further, and the YMCA'S Emergency War Committee awarded £350 for equipment at Ciro's.[127]

In May 1917, the YMCA announced its tenancy of the club. It was reported that the premises would open its doors to servicemen so that 'a man can take his mother, his wife, or his sweetheart to these luxurious reception rooms for recreation and refreshment. He can meet his friends of either sex and enjoy with them a cup of tea while listening to music under the most ideal conditions.' A soldier back for a few days' leave from the trenches may no longer 'wander forlornly round the town' because at Ciro's he could have the chance of 'happy friendly intercourse with the class he would like to meet'.[128] Entertainments were held every afternoon and evening under the direction of Lena Ashwell. However, the YMCA was anxious about running a London club and kept a close watch on proceedings at Ciro's during the summer of 1917.[129] However, the venture proved to be a huge success. It was reported in June 1917 that 1,780 men and 300 women had used the premises in just twelve days.[130] Many of the composers and performers who worked with the YMCA appeared at Ciro's. This included Henry Walford Davies, Gustav Holst and John Foulds.[131] Foulds was deemed unfit for military service so he served as the Musical Director of the YMCA in London from May 1917. Like Foulds, Gustav Holst had been rejected as unfit for military service so in 1918 he went with the YMCA to organise musical entertainment and education to British and Imperial troops awaiting demobilisations on the Eastern Front. Performers on their way to the Western Front with a Lena Ashwell-YMCA concert party often played at Ciro's on their way through London before catching the train down to Folkestone.[132]

Folk Dancing

The YMCA also encouraged folk dancing. This was an established form of recreation and exercise in the pre-war years, and the English Folk Dance Society was invited to contribute to the wartime entertainments schedule. Daisy Daking, an established folk dancer, teacher, and active member of the EFDS, was asked to go to France by a senior member of the YMCA in March 1918. Daking's journal details that she arrived in France and made herself known to the YMCA headquarters in Le Havre. She recalled that 'It took four months to get up a show. . . . You found an old granary and bullied permission to rent it and you and your five soldier friends set to and scrubbed it. . . . You collected a few YMCA typist girls and made them learn some country dances and you had your five soldier friends to tea every Sunday . . . and you stole a piano.'[133] Daking had a significant impact as she eventually led a team of seventeen full-time dance teachers who worked at the convalescent camps at Trouville, as well as Boulogne and Étaples in the spring of 1917.[134] Daking was called upon to entertain hundreds of soldiers at very little notice, usually when a concert party or lecture-recital performers were running late. To attract the men's attention in a large camp like Havre, she 'stood on a table in the canteen hut *between* the times of lecture or concert, blew [her] whistle and said that there would be country dancing in the concert hall'. Daking recalled that the men would follow her in, describing 'the shuffle of feet, the slight coughing, the wet smell of khaki', and they would 'all sit down passive and good'. She would then 'persuade about 30 of them to stand up and would teach for about an hour and they and all those watching would enjoy themselves'. She recommended that any instructor should 'always remember to dig out the Australians first as they are always ready for anything and they are not shy: pair them off with any Scots as these are born dancers and cannot stay still in front of a tune'. Daking relayed that 'the quiet English will unobtrusively join in a little later on'.[135]

Work for Indian and Chinese Servicemen

The YMCA also worked closely with non-British soldiers and labourers serving with the British Army. The organisation spent £45,000 [£1.95 million] supporting work for Indians in France, £75,696 [£3.3 million] for Indian men in India and Mesopotamia, and £65,000 for work with Chinese men in England and France.[136] By the end of the war, India had deployed over one million men overseas in both combat and supporting roles; 657,000 men served in Mesopotamia, 144,000 in Egypt and Palestine, and 140,000 on the Western Front of which 90,000 served in the infantry and cavalry, 50,000 as non-combatant labourers. Smaller numbers were sent to Aden, East Africa, Gallipoli and Salonika. In August 1914, there were three YMCA centres in India, and by January 1915 there were ten.[137] On the Western Front, the YMCA provided one centre for every Indian cavalry brigade, sent workers to visit Indians in hospitals, ran a leave hostel for Indian officers in Paris, and provided various entertainments and services to labourers including language lessons, letter writing and barbering.[138] By 1918, there were fifteen YMCA establishments for Indian soldiers in France, thirteen in India, thirty-five in Mesopotamia, nine in Egypt and four in East Africa.[139] The YMCA was particularly keen to get among these men as they believed they were in the most need of education. The organisation took care to encourage soldiers to play their native instruments wherever they served. On the banks of the Tigris at Amarah, outside a YMCA hut made of palm trees, 'Indian Regiments of various creeds enjoy their evenings in their own fashion. Here they have their tamashas, tom-toms and reed musical instruments, being supplied by the YMCA who cater for all tastes.'[140] For the Indian Labour companies, the YMCA imported Indian harmoniums and gramophones were provided with records 'from Calcutta and Rangoon, giving Indian and Burmese music, so weird to European ears, but which has sent [them] into ecstasies of delight'.[141]

In the YMCA huts on the Western Front it was said that 'instruction, education and moral elevation take pride of place'. Where the Indian cavalrymen were generally content, labourers required more guidance and reassurance to feel comfortable among 'local habits and customs'.[142] Of the Assamese it was said that 'the simple hillmen of Assam are very musical' and Indian soldiery overall was said to 'love music'.[143] The YMCA observed that 'a good singer in a regiment is a very proud person, and sometimes commands more respect than an officer'. If a singer is not present, 'the Gramophone takes his place, and a hypnotized audience sits around it, with softened faces and a sad, far-off look in his eyes'. This was believed to be because '[g]ood Indian music is sad and plaintive'. In addition, most regiments had a poet and they sometimes held 'tribal dances'.[144] After a performance of Indian music and dance in Marseilles, the YMCA commented that 'the Indians are by nature and by tradition lovers of music', that wherever they go 'melodies follow them'. The hut was said to have been 'packed' to hear the performances of a 'syce' (groom) Syalkoti and 'a young soldier-boy' called Budloo, who 'kept the audience spell-bound' with the song 'O, stranger, stranger in a strange land'.[145]

By the last stages of the war, there were 195 Chinese Labour Corps of approximately 95,500 men working on the Western Front.[146] The YMCA provided facilities for the Chinese Labour Corps across 124 huts along the Western Front (Figure 6.3). This work was done 'at the discreet request of the authorities, and was a means to keep the men happy and contented'. Approximately 16,000 Chinese Labourers were enrolled in English classes at the YMCA in the Vlamertinge area. After the armistice, YMCA workers visited 156 'isolated' detachments which included Chinese and Indian labourers working with the Exhumation Labour Companies and Graves Registration Units. The services supplied included canteens, concerts, lantern and cinema showings, games, lectures and letter writing.[147] Of the gramophones used for labourers, it was said that 'it interests them enormously'. It was said that many 'looked inside to see who was producing the sound, and will sit round in a circle listening to it for hours'. Those men who were literate made good use of the YMCA's free writing paper, and it was also said that '[q]uartettes are sung by Karen and Chinese Christians'.[148]

The Great War brought together a wide variety of musical cultures. In October 1915, a British soldier on the Western Front described seeing, for the first time, a group of Indian soldiers who met regularly at sundown to pray. He relayed that after half an hour of prayer led by one of their

Figure 6.3 YMCA/K/1/23/8: Members of the Chinese Labour Corps with their instruments at a YMCA facility on the Western Front. © YMCA England and the Cadbury Research Library.

number, 'they ... sat round and sang, I suppose, their hymns'. He commented that 'the same thing went on in the trenches as far as duties would permit'.[149] Percy Scholes was fascinated when he passed through Dieppe in 1917. He saw 'an Algerian, sitting at an open window of one of the big hotels, now used as a hospital, and playing on a flute the same little phrase over and over again'. The composer did not think it was 'much of a tune' but he saw that it 'brought to the windows all the brother Algerians, who stood or sat, quietly listening so long as the playing continued'. Also in Dieppe, Scholes witnessed a group of Senegalese 'walking through the streets to the sound of a one-stringed instrument with a parchment body and a plectrum consisting of the tooth of some animal fastened to the finger of the performer on a leather loop'. Scholes describes how he stopped them, asked to examine the instrument, and considered buying it. He decided that 'it would have been cruel to deprive these men, so far from their home, of the tones and tunes that remind them of it, and took them in memory back to their inland swamps or the silver sands of their Atlantic shore'. Of the Chinese labourers, Scholes watched them 'work to music about the docks at Dieppe, with their blue costumes and their little round brown caps. The foreman gives the order by a little phrase and the coolies respond by rhythmic movements, in lifting or pulling, or whatever the task may be, singing as they do so.'[150]

Lena Ashwell made sure to underline that her YMCA concert parties 'play to all sorts of conditions of men . . . – men from the uttermost ends of the empire – all classes, all creeds, all branches of the army'.[151] Indeed, as a result of the injuries inflicted during the conflict, many of these concerts would take place in hospitals and convalescent camps, to which we will turn in the next chapter.

7   Medicine and Therapy

Throughout the war, music was recognised for its ability to enhance servicemen's well-being. This was of prime importance when the physical and mental discomfort of staying in a military hospital, convalescent camp or isolation unit could lead servicemen to experience a range of feelings from frustration to boredom, anger to despair. Music and musical activities were highly valued by all of the organisations involved in the welfare of British troops. In 1915, it was reported that 'the effect of the music on soldiers who for many months have heard nothing but the ravaging sound of warfare is most marked'. An Army doctor stated that 'one concert did the wounded men more good than a month's nursing'.[1] In 1917, Bruce Porter, Colonel Commanding the 3rd London General Hospital, wrote to the Music in Wartime Committee that he hoped that 'nothing will stop your concert parties coming here while the war is on. As I live among my patients, I can speak with some authority as to the effect of these concerts on the sick and wounded.' Porter maintained that 'the good done to patients by getting away from the atmosphere of the ward is an actual value in the saving of patients'. He underlined that it was the opinion of the staff that entertainments such as those provided by performers with the MWC reduced the period of illness by an average of five days. If, as Porter estimated, the duration of a patient's stay averaged thirty days, 'the concert-room entertainments are equal in value to 300 beds in a large hospital like this'. Porter emphasised that in the past 'no provision was made for this form of treatment' but it was his opinion that music 'is actual medical treatment'.[2]

The primary role of the British Red Cross (BRC) during the war was to assist the Army Medical Service for equipment, staff, accommodation and transport of wounded. As the war continued this would include the supply of comforts, 'in the nature of what may be called luxuries ... to be more generous than might have been possible otherwise'.[3] Money to fund the BRC work was boosted by *Our Day* campaigns and the support of Lord Northcliffe's *Times* Fund. The latter raised £16,510,023 6s. 5d. [£973,962,597.75 today]. The sales of Northcliffe's *At the War* (1916), which was dedicated to BRC staff, went to the organisation to support its wartime work.[4] Other schemes were 'initiated on private responsibility' and 'appealed to particular sympathies and tastes'; for example, the Cinematograph Trade Ambulance Fund and the Butt-Rumford Fund, founded by Clara Butt and her husband, the baritone Kennerley Rumford, who was serving with the BRC on the Western Front. In this way, Dame Clara Butt arranged concerts around the United Kingdom, one of which in the Albert Hall in 1915 raised £7,500.[5] These fundraising activities were much needed. The British BRC spent £127,032 13s. 1d. [£7,493,935.74] on recreations and amusements, and stocking the War Hospital Library cost them £63,061 16s. 5d. [£3,720,155.55].[6] The BRC Joint Stores Department, based in Pall Mall, was 'asked to supply a very varied and large assortment of everything that could be required for the comfort and amusement of the men'. This included playing cards, chewing gum, musical instruments, theatrical accessories, footballs and skates, and in some cases they were given only 48 hours to get the supplies on to a ship already preparing to leave.[7]

In a similar way to the YMCA, the arrangements for entertainments in BRC establishments were generally led by committees of aristocratic women. After the outbreak of war, Georgina, Lady Dudley, resumed her work with the Department for the Assistance of Convalescent Officers as she had done during the South African war. The BRC eventually took over from Lady Dudley in June 1915 when the workload became too great.[8] The BRC Compassionate Fund was established by the Marchioness of Ripon. This was modelled on regimental funds and supplied items such as cigarettes, tobacco and matches 'to ensure that patients should have the small extra comforts which are not provided by a military institution'.[9] The concerts and entertainments at the King George Hospital, close to Waterloo Station, and its Affiliated Hospitals were under the charge of Lady Tree. In the hospital's concert hall 'the best performances of every kind, from classical instrumental concerts to variety entertainments, were given to the patients'. In addition, the resident Chaplain 'arranged on one evening each week, a lecture on some subject of general interest . . . by men of note and illustrated with lantern pictures'.[10] From November 1915, Frognal House, Sidcup, was purchased as a permanent specialist Maxillo-Facial hospital, and here entertainments were run by a ladies' sub-committee which collected a special fund to pay for the recreation rooms, theatre, billiard room, writing room and a canteen.[11]

In February 1917, the BRC established a Convalescent Camps Department to provide comforts provided for hospitals, camps and depots. Items supplied included furniture, clothing, amusements and games (indoor and outdoor), pianos (mostly by grants towards purchase), bagatelle boards and tables, billiard balls, roller skates, gymnasium apparatus, gramophones and records, band instruments, music (orchestral), pipes, tobacco, cigarettes, stationery, cooking utensils, and medical and garden requisites.[12] The demand was enormous. In France and Belgium, by 20 October 1918, the BRC had eighty units serving with Army formations. They were running 1,484 motor ambulances, three ambulance trains, ten BRC hospitals, eight convalescent homes, five hostels for relatives of wounded officers, six railway rest stations and seven recreation huts where lectures, entertainments and games were provided daily for men in the convalescent depots. The total expenditure in France and Belgium for four years ending 20 October 1918 was £2,022,426 1s. 9d. [£119,307,393.74].[13]

To continue their work with the forces, the BRC, like the other voluntary-aid organisations, had to liaise with numerous government departments during the war. They recognised that these 'formalities and delays' were 'irksome', but they appreciated 'the paramount importance of preventing spies from getting through [the] organisation, a danger which was constantly before the various authorities charged with the control of passports'.[14] Furthermore, once the Military Service Act was passed in 1916, no passport could be granted to anyone eligible for the Fighting Forces and the BRC had to submit weekly returns listing the details of new staff.[15] The name of every BRC worker had to be submitted to the Intelligence Department of the War Office. Passports then had to be stamped by the Military Permit Office and the Passport Department of the Foreign Office, the latter having to re-stamp the passports of personnel on leave. Visas from both the civil and military sections of the French Consulate had to be stamped on every passport, and every BRC worker had to apply for a pass from the Army's General Headquarters in France. It appears that the BRC received priority treatment as they acknowledged they were 'granted facilities which were denied to others in respect of Passport business'.[16]

In 1915, the BRC began to improve the appearance of the wards of casualty clearing stations by supplying red blankets for beds and linoleum for the floors. By 1916, '[c]oloured curtains hung on the windows, whilst periodicals lay on the occasional tables; here and there stood a wicker chair, and somewhere in the ward a patient would be supplying the motive power to the inevitable gramophone'.[17] Divisional Rest Stations were opened from the summer of 1915 by the Army Medical Services with the support of the BRC. At these places, men with minor ailments or injuries requiring rest for seven to ten days could be accommodated and enjoy what one RAMC officer described as 'colour, cooking and music'.[18]

The task of the BRC stores was mainly to provide the first and last of these components for men's rest and recuperation. Music in this context was another way of providing a distraction for the men, and articles provided for servicemen's amusements included indoor games (chess, draughts, dartboards) and outdoor sports equipment, 'as well as gramophones, mouth organs and penny whistles'.[19] Comforts were also supplied to hospital barges on the Somme and the canals in Northern France, in addition to the hospital ships travelling between France and England. From the summer of 1915, three Officers' Rest Stations 'within the sound of the guns' were established and kitted out by BRC Stores. At Mont Noir ORS, located in a chateau, Advanced Stores at St Omer had converted it into 'a charming home' for thirty officer patients.[20]

Hospital Recreation Huts

In 1916, the BRC Building and Construction Department was established from the Stores Department. Two full-time BRC workers with construction industry experience designed new huts and supervised construction, which was contracted out to English firms by tender. During the war, this department constructed ten 'club room' recreation huts for convalescent camps and hospitals and eight 'concert halls' for convalescent camps and hospitals. Four carpenters and six painters were employed full-time for maintenance and repairs.[21] The BRC felt that no branch of their work 'came home more to the rank and file of the Army than that undertaken in connection with Convalescent Camps, especially the Recreation Huts established 1916–17 at the request of the Military Authorities at the various Convalescent Depots'.[22] Each of these depots accommodated several thousand men, and their prime focus was to get them back to fitness for their units. The BRC recognised that 'healthy recreation was an indispensable part of the treatment, and it may safely be said that no effort was spared to provide it in every possible variety'.[23] Sports kits for outdoor recreation of 'almost every known game' were provided. In addition, instruments for drum and fife bands were sourced 'in order to relieve the monotony of the route marches, which were part of the process of getting the convalescents fit'. Indeed, many camps 'had full brass bands or complete orchestras for the amusement of the men'.[24] Recreation huts would provide indoor activities such as reading, writing and playing games, and 'most Depots also had a Concert Hall where concerts and other entertainments were given regularly. In some Halls complete cinema outfits were provided'.[25]

Most convalescent camps run by the BRC had two types of recreation hut: a 'Club-room' and a 'Concert Hall'. Both were supplied and built by the BRC Stores Department. A 'Club-room' was a hut 130 feet long and 30 feet wide. It was divided into three rooms: Recreation, Reading and Billiards. The Recreation Room was 80 feet long, with a small stage at one end. It was furnished with tables, chairs and a piano, and an assortment of indoor games would be provided. A Reading Room was 25 x 20 feet, soundproofed by double walls packed with sawdust. The Billiard Room featured two three-quarter billiard tables with seats on a narrow platform at the sides for onlookers.[26] The 'Concert Hall' had the same dimensions as a 'Club-room' (130 feet long x 30 feet wide) but was one single hall with a 'roomy' stage at one end with three dressing rooms behind. There was an orchestra pit in front of the stage which could be covered over, and the audience benches were graduated in height to ensure a clear view of the stage. Each Concert Hall could comfortably accommodate 1,000 men.[27] They were also used for the drilling of convalescents, who were 'thus able to go through their physical drill irrespective of the weather'.[28] In four of the Recreation Huts in convalescent camps there were full 'Cinema Outfits'. These consisted of 'a petrol-drive generating plant and a projector', which were housed in a special fire-proofed continuation of the Hall. Films sufficient for a two-hour programme were supplied and changed twice a week. The films were hired by the BRC from the Expeditionary Force Canteens and the cinemas were operated by patients in the camps, 'amongst whom could always be found a motor mechanic and a cinematograph operator'.[29]

Each Recreation Hut was under the management of a VAD Superintendent. They were assisted by VAD members and orderlies who also distributed free writing paper and organised the entertainments, concerts, competitions and classes. The staff were constantly busy. Statistics for all ten of the BRC's Recreation Huts on the Western Front were not retained, but we can see that the Hut attached to the 54th General Hospital (Wimereux) was used by 224,083 men from 1 November 1917 to 1 May 1919. A total of 425 entertainments were given, and 18,667 games of billiards were played on the two tables.[30] 'The stage scenery and Proscenium were all made and painted by patients.'[31] The BRC report underlined that 'the huts were always full, there was always something going on, and their usefulness is beyond question'. The BRC believed that 'a large part of their success is due to the spirit in which they were run. ... the staff succeeded not only in giving the huts a thoroughly home-like appearance, but what is far more difficult is that they managed to create a real atmosphere of home among these numbers of men whom chance had brought together'.[32]

Recreation Hut at No.7 Convalescent Camp (Boulogne) was opened in January 1917. It was staffed by six VAD members and a team of orderlies led by a corporal. The staff reported that the shortage of food meant the canteen became very popular, and that 'a canteen is a definite factor in promoting sociability in a hut'.[33] They also identified that having a canteen lessened servicemen's temptation to 'break camp', and a daily programme was drawn up so that on every evening without exception there was some event to interest the men and keep them close by. This normally featured games, whist and bridge-drives, dancing or songs, and on Sundays a hymn sing-song, followed sometimes by a short talk from the chaplain.[34] Dances, aided by the camp band, 'became quite a feature of the camp life'. It was said, 'The dancers were all men, and really good dancing was the rule and not the exception.'[35] Needlework became very popular. Embroidery classes were led by a VAD, and the sewing of the men's regimental badges was commonplace, especially among long-term patients. The artwork was supplied by VADs then men did embroidery, making frames out of woodbine cases. They held three exhibitions and pieces were sold to generate money for materials. Furthermore, finding that 'the Military exigencies of the situation demanded the frequent transferring of men from their own regiments to other regiments of which they had no knowledge and in which they therefore took no interest, the V.A.D. Officer in charge of the Hut began "talks" in the hut on regimental histories and the significance of regimental badges, the embroidered badges and the badge-drawing serving as excellent texts'.[36]

The BRC reported that when 90 per cent of the men who stayed in one of their camps returned to the line 'they felt their stay . . . was like an oasis in the desert'.[37] The presence of women was also a boon to men's spirits, not least because it reminded them of their girlfriends or families at home. The Recreation Hut at No.6 Convalescent Camp, Étaples, which was opened in March 1917, instituted weekly dances 'at which the men came in large numbers'. When the Women's Army Auxiliary Corps (WAAC) was formed in spring, 1917, with the approval and consent of G.H.Q., weekly dances for the men and WAACs took place. Approximately seventy couples attended each dance.[38] Depot bands would play at these dances, and one or two evenings a week there would be a concert party from one of the various parties in the different regiments, who would also give performances in other Depots.[39] They were, however, still within firing range. On 31 May, 1918, 'the hut was badly bombed [but we] carried on just the same, and the day after had a Concert Party, but many men had to be sent away suffering from bad nerve shock'.[40]

The Recreation Hut at No.10 Convalescent Camp (Ecault), opened 14 July 1917, was used by around 2,000 men at a time. The piano was provided by BRC Stores and it was officially opened by the Camp Concert Party. This facility was so popular it was often very crowded, the report stating that men often sat on the floor. Despite this, the Hut at Ecault was so popular that the men greatly missed the hut and would write back to the staff once they were back with their units. The Recreation Hut, No.11 Convalescent Camp (Buchy) was opened in August 1917, but had to be extended as 'After a short time the dimensions of the Hut were found to be quite inadequate.' One thousand men would attend at a time, and the stage was improved and widened and fitted with nine sets of scenery painted by the men and proper stage lighting. The orchestra 'well' was built 'and the band of 25 performers greatly added to the popularity of the hall'.[41] A cinema was then installed and quickly became 'the most popular entertainment in the Camp'. The hut, like many others, boasted a very excellent concert party, which gave two shows a week, including Revues, Plays, Pantomimes and Variety performances. At one point, when there were 5,000 men in the camp, staff had to institute two showings/sittings for performances and whist drives.[42] A typical schedule for BRC Recreation Huts was as follows:

> Mondays – Games
> Tuesdays – Dancing, WAAC members present once a fortnight
> Wednesdays – Bridge Tournaments
> Thursdays – Concert by Depot Concert Party
> Fridays – Chorus Sing Song
> Saturdays – Whist Drive
> Sundays – Chorus Sing Song[43]

Patients in Egypt and Palestine 'perhaps needed more than on any other Front Recreation Rooms where they could amuse themselves, or to be amused, in order to get over the long and weary days of illness or convalescence'.[44] The building and equipping of Recreation Rooms in the Middle East 'did not come under the scope of the Army Medical Service and the Societies were called upon to undertake this most essential work'.[45] The BRC had to build them, and provide marquees in forward areas. They also had to provide large quantities of furniture, games, writing materials and books. Orderlies were appointed, and where possible 'local ladies were put in charge . . . in order to organise games, concerts, whist drives, etc'. Concert stages were erected and many grants were made to concert parties which were formed for the express purpose of providing entertainment for the patients.[46] Special entertainments and teas were frequently provided in the local theatres, where men had 'an opportunity of enjoying under comfortable conditions, a concert, play, or a cinema show'.[47] The BRC also coordinated patient outings to the pyramids, the Zoological Gardens and the Delta Barrage, as well as motorboat trips on the River Nile. Approximately 565,000 men went on

BRC outings.[48] On 18 June, Private Double writes that he '[v]isited the zoo again this evening and listed to the Band [sic] the native music sounded to me more like the wailing sound of a soul in agony than anything else I can describe. However, some European music was played with great Eclat and on the whole I enjoyed it.'[49] On 1 July, a conjuring evening was preceded by 'selections of Arabic music. Conjuring was splendid but music was more like people crying than ever. Never heard such a row, worse than African Kaffirs.' The next day, his last before being shipped home to England, Double spent the morning 'playing billiards and getting names for concert tonight. Went to the zoo for an hour in the evening . . . had cinematograph entertainment . . . played piano for pictures and accompaniments for songs, everything voted a great success.'[50] The main hospital bases for sick and wounded from the Dardanelles were at Mudros (on the island of Lemnos), Egypt, and Malta.[51] There were a large number of hospitals on Mudros set up by Army Medical Services, and several convalescent depots on the island of Imbros. These premises were also 'of great value for the reception of men from the trenches who needed rest or slight medical treatment'. As these were 'sparsely inhabited' islands it 'was considered important that the BRC should equip the marquees which had been placed at our disposal by the authorities as Recreation Rooms and Concert Halls'.[52] On a visit to Macedonia, the Chief Commissioner reported to the RC Joint War Committee that the pianos in the recreation rooms 'have given a great deal of pleasure, and several times on a hospital ship I have seen the delight with which patients who are carried up on deck listen to entertainments which are provided with the help of a BRC piano'.[53]

The BRC transport vehicles were a vital part of the war on the fighting fronts. On the Western Front, it had seven one-ton lorries and seven two-to-three ton lorries, and in the northern section, a fleet of twenty to twenty-five 'touring cars' that were used by BRC staff and relatives of the seriously wounded. These transports were also used to help move civilian entertainers around for their performances.[54] The BRC played a vital role in providing transport. While the BRC led the way in ambulance services, they worked with other groups to evacuate wounded men from the battlefield. For example, the Boulogne Convoy of ambulances comprised seven sections. One of these was the Salvation Army section, manned entirely by Salvation Army officers who worked as ambulance drivers. It was this group of Salvation Army officers, predominantly bandsmen, who were responsible for the formation of 'an excellent Band' which became well-known in the region. The BRC reported that, in addition to providing a high standard of performance, the influence of these Salvation Army bandsmen 'had a marked effect on the general tone

Figure 7.1 The Salvation Army Motor Ambulance Band. © Salvation Army International Heritage Centre.

of the personnel attached to the Garage'.[55] The bandsmen were working under the auspices of the Salvation Army's Naval and Military League, led by Brigadier Mary Murray. With the British BRC, they established their own ambulance unit under Bandmaster Captain Bramwell Taylor (Figure 7.1). He wrote in February 1915 that his team had been dubbed 'The White Brigade':

due to our abstinence in the matter of strong drink, loose talk, gambling, smoking, and other things we need not mention. The hard work we do is a 'sermon' the men can understand, and they respect and appreciate us. At night, when we go to our shake-down, more and more of the men and lads bring their straw near ours way from the 'hot' talk, improper song, and questionable yarn. When we get a chance, before we 'drop off' we start an old song with memories in it, and in the darkness it is surprising how many join in; and afterwards all is quiet, and every man jack of us falls asleep feeling mighty good. The fellows like music, and it is here that we are getting a grip of them.[56]

Concert Parties in Hospitals

As it will be seen on the fighting fronts, servicemen's concert parties liked to parody the situations in which they found themselves. At an isolation

camp in Britain, for example, it was said that 'Microbes, daily fumiga-
tions, and bi-weekly swabbings did not appear to damp the ardour of the
unfortunates who were segregated. Drill parades and lectures continued
as usual, and occasional concerts helped to make evenings enjoyable.'
A concert on 21 August 1917 was opened with a chorus performed by
'The Microbes' and featured 'sentimental and comic songs, parodies and
monologues, the most popular of which was performed by Sergeant
Friend titled 'How I marched to Kandahar and lost my kilts at
Waterloo".[57]

The first professional concert party for wounded men, led by the well-
known actors Seymour Hicks and Ellaline Terriss, took place at the end of
December 1914.[58] One of Terriss' most difficult moments came when
she was told that there was a young soldier who was dying and who had
been unable to be carried into the main hall for the entertainment:

He had asked to speak to me. I went to a bed in the dark shadows behind a screen.
I felt a hand grope for mine and then take it – and I saw that the soldier was little
more than a boy. As I bent over him he actually thanked me for coming. Taking
a firm grip on myself, I asked if there was anything I could do for him, and he
whispered, 'I should like to hear you sing "The Honeysuckle and the Bee" – just
once again.' Somehow I did it . . . I sang to him very quietly, leaning over him and
almost whispering it right into his ear. . . . I sang it right through – and he smiled.
His eyes closed and he was still smiling as I went very softly away into the
darkness.[59]

Between February and September 1915, approximately 2,000 concerts
were given by the YMCA-sponsored Lena Ashwell performers, the
majority in hospitals and convalescent camps.[60] Sister Blair, serving
with the QARANC, recalled that in March 1915, the second Ashwell
concert party played in her hospital in Etratat. Blair recalled that the
concert party leader 'was careful to say, in a little introductory
speech . . . that all male members of the party had volunteered for the
front and been rejected'.[61] Ashwell explained that the 'least-afflicted'
patients would be assembled in the 'great ward', then they would proceed
'to visit other wards, and play gently to the more severely wounded'.[62]
Sister Blair recalled that two ladies, a singer and a violinist, readily agreed
to play for men who could not attend the main concert. Their 'special
little show' featured three songs, including *Here We Are, Here We Are,
Here We Are Again,* to which Blair recalls 'one boy, 19yrs, with a shattered
knee, trying to join in the chorus with proper gusto'. The nurse remembered that 'he was suffering great pain and a couple of days later he was
dead'.[63] All the performers found their performances in military hospitals
to be the most difficult. On seeing wounded in hospitals, it was 'terrible to
see some of them. Some without limbs, some still gasping with gas fumes,

some whose eyes have looked into hell and will never forget it. Even our sweetest music and merriest jokes have failed to raise a smile.'[64] In the hospitals, Ashwell relayed that 'sometimes the great burly patients are moved to tears, and the girls themselves find the experience often painful'.[65] Ashwell performer Julius Harrison recalled that at a hospital before a concert 'we had been told beforehand to brace ourselves up ... for we found out very soon brave and cheerful faces were absolutely essential to success. We simply *had* to appear light-hearted, whatever our feelings might have been. The first concert was a dreadful ordeal.'[66] Ashwell herself described 'an atmosphere so impregnated with concentrated pain that at first we are almost afraid to begin, so strong is the impression of suffering'.[67]

The emotional and physical strains felt by the performers are evident. One of Edward Pierpoint's colleagues, C. W. James, wrote to him after their return from the Western Front expressing her thanks 'for all your help and your kindness during the Tour. You were a tower of strength to me, and made my work very much easier by your sound and ever ready advice and suggestions.' James said that Pierpoint had 'set such an example to us all of willingness to do what was best for each occasion'.[68] William Brereton also spoke of the emotional strain of performing to large audiences of soldiers. He referred to 'their tense silence during the music, give one a lump in the throat. We often felt that we could hardly go on'. Brereton said that 'it required more self-restraint to keep one's self control in the hospitals. To see a wounded man try to smile when we were doing our comic bits was often more than we could bear.' In wards where soldiers were too ill to be moved, the performers 'would go to them and sing just one or two songs, and their pleasure and gratitude are things we shall never forget'.[69] The young violinist, Gwendolyn Teagle, was one of a Lena Ashwell group who travelled in ambulances to play to the wounded after the battle of Neuve Chapelle in March 1915. On one day alone, she witnessed thirty funerals. Teagle later recounted one occasion where a badly wounded soldier requested she play him Mascagni's *Cavalieria Rusticana*: the man died before she had finished playing. When she visited the wards of seriously wounded men she would use the mute on her instrument, and in some cases this soft playing helped the men to sleep.[70]

In January 1917, Harry Lauder conducted a tour of military hospitals in the Boulogne area where he would sing and tell stories to the men. Unlike many of the other civilian performers who visited the fronts, Lauder was not paid for his concerts. He stated that '[h]ere was an audience that had paid to hear me in the dearest coin in all the world – their legs and arms, their health and happiness. Oh they had paid!'[71] On seeing the results of modern industrial warfare, specifically gas, Harrison raged about 'this diabolical weapon of *murder* – I cannot say *war*. There, for once, we felt our music to be of no avail. I cannot describe in any words the sight of scores of men grasping for their very life-breath, some of them blue in the face with the agony of drowning ... and we all came away unable to say a word. It was a sight I will never forget.'[72] The memory of one particular injured soldier stayed with Ashwell. His face was:

grey and tense with pain, his shoulder was in a surgical bath, all nerves exposed ... I went and sat beside him, and put my hand on his head ... as the strain relaxed, he began to cry – why shouldn't a man cry? The men turned away not to see his weakness, and I crept away while his sobs broke the silence of the ward. When I went back to that ward one of the concert parties was singing a chorus song ... the boy was singing louder than the rest. The tension gone, he was able to forget the pain a little while in music.[73]

During their first tour the Coldstream Guards band plays at No.2 Clearing Hospital. They had just begun the song *I Hear You Calling Me* as cornet solo when the coffin of a young officer who had died in one of the wards was carried across the yard to the mortuary. Rogan recalled that the cornet soloist 'gave such a beautiful and pathetic rendering of the song I have seldom if ever heard, before or since'.[74] When Guards moved from La Gorgue to Hazebrouck Rogan arranged with the town mayor for the band to give concerts every day in the *Grand Place* and at the British and French hospitals. After the concerts for the wounded, Rogan would sometimes walk through the hospital wards. He said that there was 'never a murmur from the men, terrible though their injuries often were. What a noble example!'[75] The Coldstreams also played at a large French military hospital, and the bandsmen were very moved by civilians, including children, who had been wounded at Armentières.[76]

The performers felt that having been to the fighting fronts and experienced elements of what the armed forces were living with, they were well placed to both understand and to help salve the servicemen's discomfort. It was emphasised that it was 'impossible for those who have not heard the screeching of heavy shells, the roar of the cannon, and the whistle of bullets to realise the nerve-shattering ordeal through which the men in the trenches have to pass'.[77] For readers at home, however, performers would relay their experiences of seeing the wounded in terms of patriotic pride. Lauder maintained that despite the 'dour sights, dreadful sights in those hospitals ... overall there was a spirit that never lagged or faltered ... it was the spirit of the British soldier triumphant over suffering and cruel disfigurement'.[78] On returning from one of her visits to France, Ashwell wished she 'could make the laggards at home see ... something of what

I have seen! How quickly they would fly to the colours – the courage . . . the cheerfulness . . . [the] tremendous endurance in suffering . . . Tommy would put his last effort into a smile.'[79] At one hospital camp concert in July 1917, Williams' party performed to a large number of men who had been gassed. He recalled that it was 'very sad to see them altering their eye bandage to have a hurried glance and then quickly put them back'.[80] Robinson wrote in the *Musical News* of a concert given to 'about 1,000 wounded' in the grand stand of Rouen racecourse. At every concert he offered his mouth-organ to the best player. On this occasion, instead of the usual scramble:

a number of voices shouted out . . . I could not catch the name they gave, but handed the little box to a man, and it quickly disappeared . . . one of the doctor's said to me 'Do you know who got your mouth-organ? . . . That poor chap at the back with the bandaged eyes . . . he has been shot across both eyes and will never see again. Go over and speak to him'. I . . . found a lad of twenty-years sitting with [the] mouth-organ in his hands. A wounded 'Tommy' sat each side . . . trying to cheer him up . . . We had a little chat . . . he could play it when he thought of his home in England, and it would make him feel happy . . . I am trying to convey to you the wonderful thoughtfulness of all those other wounded lads. They had time to think of the one whose burden was the heaviest among them. These are the men who are keeping the old flag afloat.[81]

A memo sent by the Director of Medical Services to the Governor of Malta, Lord Methuen, outlined that 60,300 patients had been treated in their hospitals since May 1915. In total, the Malta medical establishments had been able to accommodate up to 25,000 beds within the first few months of their arrival. The work of various philanthropic organisations was praised, particularly the BRC. Methuen attributed the orderly con-duct of the patients 'in a great measure to the concerts and other amuse-ments so admirably organized in the different hospitals and camps'.[82] As the work of the BRC on Malta expanded, concert parties began 'as circumstances permitted'. The medical and nursing staffs were said to have been particularly interested in this branch of the work 'as they readily recognized the good results which the entertainments brought in relieving the monotony of a patient's life in hospital'. Indeed, the RAMC and the Army Mechanical Transport 'contained many professional artists, who provided really first class amusement'. Two BRC Concert parties came out from England. The difficulty was to give the number of entertain-ments that were demanded, 'and even when as many as fifteen Concert parties were enrolled under our auspices this number was not sufficient to meet all calls'.[83] Chevalier de Lancellotti, of the Grand Opera on Malta, gave many concerts for thousands of sick and wounded men at the Grand Opera House. Lancellotti also permitted many of his artists to perform in

BRC hospitals which were normally followed by 'a substantial tea' provided by the BRC. Unpaid performances were given by Malta's leading
opera singers including 'Madame Marta de Sac, Madame Pavoni, Signor
Salvati and many others'.[84] The Grand Opera House was also used as
a venue for several concerts to raise money in aid of the BRC with the
assistance and permission of Lord Methuen, who was also said to have
performed in most of them. In total, on Malta the BRC sponsored
3,241 concerts, and its two cinema outfits gave 846 cinema showings, to
an estimated audience of 1,824,925 service personnel.[85]

By 1916, every single BRC hospital and camp on the island of Malta
had a recreation room or club. The largest club establishments were
found at the Australian Hall, the Valletta Club and the Ghaien Tuffieha
Club. The Australian Hall had been erected by the New South Wales
branch of the Red Cross at a cost of £3,000. It was a large building
capable of seating 2,000 men. It also had six billiard tables, one hundred
tea tables, and rooms for reading, writing and games. The BRC Service
Club at Valletta featured a restaurant, kitchen, and a room for entertainments where the island's BRC orchestra played twice a day. It also had
two billiard rooms each containing three tables, a library, hairdresser's
and lace department, with further rooms for games and music rooms on
the second floor.[86] In close proximity to a BRC convalescent camp
housing 5,000 men at a time, the Ghaien Tuffieha Club was
a 'handsome stone building' with rooms for recreational games, reading,
writing, billiards, music and a restaurant with a verandah offering a fine
sea view. From the spring of 1915, the hospitals and convalescent depots
established on the islands of Malta and Gozo dealt with over 135,000 sick
and wounded, chiefly from the campaigns in Gallipoli and Salonika,
although increased submarine activity in the Mediterranean meant that
fewer hospital ships were sent to the island from May 1917.

Music featured with increasing frequency in Private Double's diary
entries in Malta, particularly after he was transferred to a convalescent
camp near Mtarfa. In addition to ad hoc entertainments in camp,
Double played with a band in town squares and hospitals on the
island. They usually had motor transport but often had to march up
to twelve miles a day, a significant distance, particularly for those in
convalescence. On 27 March, Double and the band gave two concerts, one at Floriana and the other at St Elmo Hospitals in Valletta.
'They seemed to be very much appreciated by the patients who turned
out in force. The walking cases naturally. Cot cases could not come to
the squares in which we played but all windows were kept open for
them to enjoy the music.'[87] The next day they marched to a hospital
at Imtarfa [Mtarfa] to give a programme. The band were becoming so

established by this point that Double hoped 'that we shall visit England as a band and play at hospitals, convalescent camps and seaside bandstands during the summer season'. However, on the march to Mtarfa Double had to drop out of the ranks as his leg 'gave way owing to the old knee wound ... I could get along allright at my own pace.[sic]'[88] Nevertheless, even at the convalescent camp, the Bandmaster had Double and the rest of the band doing drill 6.30 am 'as some of the Officers think we are getting too easy a time and are getting out of condition'.[89] This concern on behalf of the officers may have been due to the band members being treated to tea and refreshments at most of their playing engagements. On 4 April, Double happily notes these occasions, for example, at a concert at St David's Hospital that afternoon 'the authorities gave us a jolly good spread for tea after which we gave the programme while the doctors and nurses were having a cricket match'.[90] A few weeks later, the band gave an evening programme in the Palace Square, Valletta. Afterwards they were entertained by 'The Kings Own Band' of Malta in the Chief Guest Chamber of the Club Buildings. Double proudly relates that he enjoyed the spectacle:

The members of the Kings Own had their flags and we marched in procession with flags flying and our own band playing a march called *Argandab*. The crowds were that dense that we had some difficulty in keeping together. I think the reasons of such excitement was that we were advertised in the *Malta Chronicle* as a band consisting entirely of 'Convalescent Heroes' they called us, who have received wounds or succumbed to illness through the hardships we had experienced in Gallipoli. Valletta had turned out to give us a rousing welcome. Rich and poor alike were represented amongst the crowds ... and although it rained ... we still played on and the ardour of the crowds did not seem to be in the least damped by the downpour. The rendering of our bandmasters arrangement of the Allies National Anthems was received with such applause and cheers that it was almost deafening to us standing in the centre. We finished up the evening with the gratifying honour of every member of our band being officially inaugurated as Honorary Members of 'The Kings Own Band', the highest compliment that it was possible for their members to pay us. I may mention here that the patrons of this institution include all the best inhabitants of the Island, and our honour entitles us entry to the Club and all privileges of members whenever we choose to visit Valletta in the future'.[91]

On 23 May, Double played in a concert at the YMCA hut. The orchestra played selections and a comedy sketch was performed by 'the sisters of [Mtarfa] ... which caused roars of laughter to everyone as it was a skit on hospital life'.[92] By August 1916, Double and the band were giving concerts outside headquarters to crowds of approximately 2,000 troops. They were having two practice sessions every day except Saturday, two church parades plus extra on Sunday, and concerts most days of the week. Double's diary records that his health is deteriorating. He is still officially classed as a convalescent, but he is constantly working with the band, orchestra, YMCA and Church Army, plus private engagements for officers. In the spring of 1917, however, Double was discharged from the convalescent camp on Malta. He was transferred to the Oxfordshire and Buckinghamshire Light Infantry and deployed to the Western Front.[93]

From May 1915, hospitals for Indian troops serving with the British Army were established in Cairo, Alexandria, Kantara and Suez. They were also fitted out with recreation rooms and suitable reading material was provided.[94] Sick and wounded servicemen from the Dardanelles would be evacuated to hospitals in Egypt and Palestine. The BRC ran a hospital at Gaza Schools from May 1915 until July 1918 to which 13,551 patients were admitted. Fifteen convalescent homes were established and over 2,500 officers and men admitted in three and a half years.[95] In August 1915, Sultan Hussein offered the ex-Khedive's palace at Montazah to the BRC. This became known as Convalescent Home No.7 (Montazah). It stood in 600 acres of land, 12 miles from Alexandria with a station on the Alexandria-Aboukir line. It had a large acreage of pine woods, orchards and gardens running down to the Mediterranean. It opened with 500 beds, but after eight new wards were built at a cost of £5000, this BRC establishment expanded to a capacity of 2,000 beds.[96] Every effort was made to provide for the comfort and amusement of the patients; 'there were countless attractions in the form of boating, fishing, football, tennis, crickets, bowls, billiards, libraries, concerts, cinematograph shows, etc. … as well as a Canteen … at a cost very much below market prices'.[97] The catering was done by 'a well known firm of Hotel Proprietors' and there was a dental section which treated 12,651 patients.[98] In three and a half years Convalescent Home No.7 at Montazah admitted 72,290 patients.[99] The BRC believed that the success of this work in Egypt was due to 'the keen desire of the Joint War Committee that the patients should be well fed and cared for and amused to the fullest possible extent consistent with good discipline'.[100] The Sultan also placed the Walda Palace at the disposal of the BRC which was used as a convalescent home with 100 beds for NCOs and men.[101] A total of 99,625 patients passed through RC hospitals and convalescent homes in Egypt, with many officers also accommodated in private houses.[102]

Music and Therapy

By August 1915, it was recorded at No.5 Convalescent Depot, Wimereaux, that a Recreation Tent 'for the use of Patients at the Depot has been opened under the auspices of the Chaplain' and that the men 'seem to take the utmost advantage of the opportunities and facilities extended to them through such a medium'.[103] A few weeks later, the Commanding Officer of the Depot recorded the following in the War Diary: 'I have observed that much pleasure is derived by the Convalescents in this Depot from the various concerts which are provided. The men are brighter in spirit for them, and I look upon them as being of distinct assistance towards the Convalescents' ultimate fitness.'[104] However, not everybody was happy about entertainments. Reverend Noel Mellish, Chaplain to the Royal Welch Fusiliers, wrote of an infantry depot in Rouen that the Commandant of the Camp 'was an old Colonel and a more incompetent officer to have charge of such a Camp it would have been hard to find. His chief idea in life seemed to be to give entertainment to travelling theatrical parties who came to provide edification for troops at the base.' The Colonel's entertainment, which included champagne and liquors, was paid for by the Officer's Mess, and that '[t]he unfortunate subalterns, who passed through in great numbers at this time ... paid for it largely by heavy mess subscriptions'.[105] Meanwhile, the patients themselves were being encouraged to stage their own entertainments. These were said to 'show a distinct tendency towards assisting the early convalescence of the men, and the nature of the functions makes for a brighter and healthier disposition becoming apparent among the men'.[106] By January 1917, the YMCA provided Wimereaux with a cinema for the enjoyment of approximately 3,000 patients being treated in the Depot.[107]

Music was also used for exercise. At Trouville Convalescent Depot, military bands were used for drills and 'P.E. [Physical Exercise] Parades'. In August 1917, the P.E. Parades 'commenced as a very humble affair' with a group of convalescent men being marched down to Trouville beach accompanied by a small band of tin whistles. While they were on the beach they would play 'the usual P. E. games' under the direction of a Divisional Commander and a Supervisor of Physical Training. This gradually developed into '120 bandsmen, Full Brass Band, Pipe Band, Drum and Fife' and became 'an organised and well conducted affair'. The Depot War Diary credits this to Captain A. Arrigonie, 'the Supervisor' as 'the Parade depended entirely on his personality'.[108] The Parade was seen to have been 'the most important item in the day'. It is recorded that the event was 'continually under open criticism by all officers' and that a number of 'conferences' were held 'to get a definite scheme laid down'. With the permission of the Divisional Commander, Captain Arrigonie devised the following schedule:

1. 09:00 hrs. Marched off.
2. Arrived at beach ½ hour later.
3. Coats removed and work commenced.
4. 3 or 4 Competitive Games indulged in – duration 15 minutes.
5. Parade formed up into Hollow square facing inwards with the Band in centre – instructors in front of squads.
6. Preliminary Positions and Rehearsal of Controlled Exercises.
7. Same exercises to music.
8. Repetition.
9. Singing.
10. Marching – formation of Maze.
11. Fall in and march back to Camp.
12. March past 11.30 hours.[109]

The singing was said to have 'constituted a rest'. This was to ensure that 'no slovenly attitude might creep in' as the men stood at ease and 'held themselves upright'. Four or five 'popular choruses' were deemed to have been sufficient which was observed to have formed 'a happy diversion' after the exercises. The marching section combined sequences of slow, quick and marching at the double for which the Band 'was trained to increase and slacken the speed as required'. In addition to the physical benefits, the Parade was said to have exerted significant positive mental effects on the men. The process of marching to the beach and the playing of games on arrival acted to divert the men's attention away from the exercise as work and fostered 'a good sense of freedom and comradeship'. Laughing and joking were permitted so 'his state of mind is thoroughly contented' before the more serious work begins. Then 'almost before he is aware' the men found themselves rehearsing exercises previously learned on parade, although they were doing it to music:

The first moment the Band starts he is off working hard and doing his best . . . until as the time changes he finds he must go quicker to keep up . . . The Band suddenly stops and he is left breathless – laughing and ready for anything. Steady him at this moment, remember you are working with the slowest man. Give them therefore a cooling off and resting exercise, what better than singing and whistling. He loses himself again . . . Up to the Camp, the Band playing . . . the rest of the Camp turns out to see him – good – he must just do the last lap down the straight at attention as the Officer in charge . . . is going to see him come past. [He] immediately falls in for dinner. The morning has gone and he is well content.[110]

The Divisional Commander in charge of the Parade would observe, 'carefully noticing any who were backward or . . . unable to join in the more vigorous movements'. Generally, they would be more interested in the men of their own Division and would use the Parade to form 'a very useful impression of the men who would eventually come forward for evacuation'.[111] The War Diary account proudly states that 'B men', who initially were excused the exercises on the beach, in many cases requested to take part in the full Parade before they were ordered to do so, and that on leaving the Depot the average man 'stated that he had never felt so fit in his life'.[112] From August 1917, the Convalescent Depot Trouville treated a total of 66,798 servicemen, returning 47,903 as fit for duty.[113] The War Diary states unequivocally: 'RESULTS TELL'.[114]

Trooper Michael Kearns, of the Guards Machine Gun Regiment, was a patient at Trouville.[115] He spoke at length that the instructors at the Depot were 'not Militarists, but Sportsmen', and that as he marched behind the Band to the seaside, he 'became imbued with a feeling of buoyancy, and was conscious of that happy thrill which the swing of the Military Band inspires'. Kearns spoke of the 'novelty' of doing physical drills to music on the beach, and related that the motto of their leader [Captain Arrigonie] was 'Life is what you make it, let's make it worth living.'[116] Kearns and his fellow convalescents at Trouville were encouraged to play sports in the afternoons, and at the end of each day they were 'tired physically but mentally acute'. In the evenings, concerts were used to 'keep the men out of the town' which prevented them from 'getting into mischief'.[117] The camp authorities were well aware that the amusements needed to be of high quality, and they record that two concert parties ran simultaneously, accompanied by 'a very fair string band'. The dining hall at Trouville was used for concerts, and around 3,000 men would see a performance of some kind on most evenings. The hall would normally be 'heaving with merriment' and the men would join in the choruses. However, 'the silence following a dud turn made it very clear to the performer he was not up to standard and his services would no longer be required'.[118]

No.13 Convalescent Depot at Trouville appears to have been the flagship establishment. The War Diary states that on 10 November 1918, a series of films and still photographs were taken by the Cinema Representative of the Ministry of Information, *How Our Wounded Are Made Happy*. The scenes are said to have included the P. E. Parade and the concert parties. However, it is unclear as to how many other similar medical establishments followed the Trouville method. What we do know is that it was widely held by the majority of all those involved that music of all kinds could be used to heal the psychological and physiological damage caused by the war. Ashwell said she feels professional entertainers 'bring a positive electric current, a mysterious magnetism to make the atmosphere vibrate to memories of happiness, love and joy'.[119] Theosophy was an alternative spiritualist movement popular with a number of prominent English intellectuals and artists in the late Victorian era, and Theosophists believed that of all the arts it was music that could be most effectively used to connect mankind with the natural workings and divine inspiration of the universe. This belief system continued to be popular into the interwar era as a means of dealing with the emotional turmoil caused by the Great War.[120] While Theosophy may appear to be a rather esoteric system of beliefs, the religion had a broad following in the intellectual life of Britain in the early twentieth century, particularly in the musical field. Musical Theosophists of the Great War period include John Foulds, Gustav Holst, Peter Warlock and Cyril Scott. For composers who were influenced by Theosophy, music was more than a means of artistic expression: it was 'an objective physical phenomenon with an active occult agency in social, psychological, and spiritual life'.[121] In the postwar period, writers influenced by Theosophy were concerned that British soldiers returning from the trenches were coming home to the 'jarring sounds of motor-horns, whistles, grinding brakes and so forth' which would 'exercise a cumulative and deleterious effect upon the entire organism'. They believed that 'certain composers will be used to evolve a type of music calculated to heal where these discordant noises have destroyed'.[122] Ashwell wrote that in the hospitals music was found 'to be of enormous benefit to the wounded and convalescent. It makes the men forget their suffering, and it takes their minds away from the awful memories of modern battles' which she underlined was 'from the physician's point of view a most desirable consummation, difficult to achieve'. Music, Ashwell said, has 'a wonderful psychological effect; it succeeds in relaxing the terrible nervous strain from which the men almost invariably suffer, and the doctors ... Even to the dying, music brings comfort and happiness.'[123] Civilian performers who entertained the troops were keen to give a number of examples of occasions when their music had almost miraculous results. Lena Ashwell performer Kenneth Ellis (Bass) said of Ernest Groome's performance of *Mother Machree* at a base hospital in France:

Among the audience was a soldier who had been through severe fighting, and had received such bad injuries that his mind was a complete blank. He had no memory whatever of his past, and his words were a meaningless babble ... the man caught the word 'mother' in the song ... when the singer was finished he still repeated the word 'Mother! Mother!' ... till its constant repetition proved the key to his memory, and unlocked the whole of his previous existence.[124]

In October 1916, John Galsworthy contacted the BRC to suggest they use the model of the California House for Wounded Belgian Soldiers, which was providing training and rehabilitation classes for wounded men.[125] He offered his home, 8 Cambridge Gate in Regent's Park, as the first premises of what became known as the Kitchener House Clubs for Wounded

Soldiers and Sailors. Opened on 6 February 1917, it was a club for wounded men in hospital 'where they may come and go as freely as hospital regulations permit, where discipline may be relaxed, where entertainments can be arranged for their benefit, and where they may find a cheerful, comfortable refuge from the street'. The principle aim was to provide wounded men with 'occupations' to 'relieve the monotony of their lives, stimulate their minds, and ultimately point the way to a possible livelihood after their discharge'. It was thought particularly important 'to protect them from the demoralising effects of enforced idleness extended over a long period of time'.[126] The club was open between 10 am and 6 pm, with classes held in the afternoons. These included 'business training, languages, various arts and crafts, painting, basket and soft toy making, metal work, knitting on machines and music'. The teaching in music is reported to have appealed to many of the men, even among the seriously disabled. In one instance 'two friends from one hospital, who possessed a single pair of hands between them, showed the greatest industry in learning to play the piano together'.[127] The BRC estimated that 40 per cent of men arrived at the club to enrol in classes immediately while 'others yielded gradually to the influence of work going on around them'.[128]

Between February 1918 and February 1919, eighty men received music lessons at the club, while classes in commerce, languages and small arts and crafts were most popular. A second Kitchener House Club for Wounded Soldiers and Sailors opened at Upper Heath, Hampstead, in a house lent by Lord Leverhulme, which was close to a number of military hospitals. A third Kitchener House Club opened in 1918 at 34 Grosvenor Place, run by its own committee (with BRC representatives) directed by Lady Barker, and financed by Vickers and Co., the machine gun manufacturer.[129] However, where developing technology by firms such as Vickers had changed the nature of warfare, it had also produced the gramophone – a piece of equipment which had provided music, amusement, relaxation, education and an ultimate link with home to millions of servicemen during the war. We will now turn our attention to the gramophone's wartime service.

8   The Gramophone

By November 1918, gramophones were ubiquitous on the fighting fronts. As we have seen in the previous chapter, organisations like the British Red Cross worked hard to ensure that hundreds of them were sent abroad to PoW camps and hospitals, and few messes, dugouts and canteen huts would have been without their own gramophone. Discs were purchased at home and taken back or posted to the fighting fronts. Classical music was popular, in addition to dance music, ragtime, comedy sketches and numbers from London's West End shows. There was also a growing appetite for jazz and blues, particularly after more American servicemen arrived on the Western Front in the winter of 1917. In 1914, the gramophone was a relatively luxurious item. However, developing communications technology meant that it was not a requirement to even be in the same room as a gramophone in order to hear music. In January 1915, the *Talking Machine News and Journal of Amusements* relayed that 'some of the refinements of active service to which we are being introduced' meant that 'men in certain front-line trenches have been regaling themselves by listening on the telephone to a gramophone concert eight miles away'.[1] This was not uncommon. Another correspondent wrote of one quiet day on the Western Front when his telephone operator summoned him to '"Take up the receiver" I was told, "and listen". I did, and was deliciously held by "Keep the Home Fires Burning" rendered by mandoline at brigade headquarters, some miles behind the firing line.'[2]

The phonograph, a device for the playing and recording of sound, had been invented in 1877 by American businessman Thomas Edison. Modifications to it were made by Alexander Graham Bell's Volta Laboratory, and this version was trademarked as a gramophone by the Gramophone Company in 1887. The generic term gramophone was commonly used in Britain from 1910, by which time the machines figured prominently in British culture. It has been estimated that the British public owned 3 million 'talking machines' and were buying 4 million recordings a year.[3] The Gramophone Company Ltd, of Hayes, Middlesex, had been producing records in London since August 1898.

By August 1914, companies such as Colombia, Zonophone, J.E.Hough Ltd. and His Master's Voice were established manufacturers and suppliers of gramophones and records, with branches and factories worldwide. These companies would publish seasonal catalogues detailing the specifications and prices of the latest gramophones and comprehensive listings of records. There was an established trade press with titles such as the *Talking Machine News* and *Journal of Amusements*. Top professional artists and entertainers were engaged under exclusive contracts; for example, leading tenors Enrico Caruso and John McCormack, who recorded a broad range of music from folk songs to opera. Caruso, it was said, earned over £16,000 a year in UK royalties alone.[4] The popularity of the foxtrot, a dance which started in 1914, boosted sales, along with the new American 'ragtime'. After the outbreak of war, the gramophone and recording industries in Britain were quick to underline that it was Britons' patriotic duty to keep buying records and gramophones. One trade paper commented that 'this healthy state of the trade is one which we feel to be a subject for the self-congratulations of all those engaged in it'.[5] At the Edison Bell factory, two days before Christmas 1914, there was a continuous demand for records, particularly the 'Winner' from all over the UK, and '[d]ealers were frantically crowding in the waiting room'.

[D]uring this period of national stress ... it is only necessary to carry one's mind back to the first week in August to recollect the shock which thrilled the whole country ... There was an immediate paralysis of all trades, and gloomy forebodings reigned supreme. The talking machine trade set itself up manfully to stem the torrent, and by the issue of records of encouragement and patriotism managed to keep 'business as usual' ... by the issue of gramophone records which have relieved the mental strain in many households, provided amusement during the dark evenings, stimulated patriotism and encouraged the people to hold on strenuously towards the goal of victory.[6]

This sense of patriotism can be seen across the range of records available. 'Opera in English' was launched by HMV in 1915 and proved to be highly successful, and the company also produced lots of Elgar. A wartime records catalogue, *His Master's Voice Records of Patriotic Songs: National Anthems of the Allies, Military and Naval Airs, Songs about Tommy Atkins and Jack* – includes numerous recordings by the Coldstream Guards, conducted by Captain J. Mackenzie Rogan, who also accompanied Clara Butt's recordings of *God Save the King* and *Land of Hope and Glory*. Other performers featured include Harry Lauder singing *Ta-ta, My Bonnie Maggie Darling*, the Black Diamonds band, the Pipers and Drummers of H.M. Scots Guards and six speeches by Field Marshal Lord Roberts.[7] Other types of recordings were made for sale. The 1914

Lord Mayor's procession in London discarded the usual mythological themes and took the form of a military display. Sections were recorded, including 'the comments of the crowd, the cries of hawkers . . . the various marches of the military sections' and available in the 'patriotic list' of the Winner Company.[8]

Comedy voice recordings, sometimes referred to as 'laughing records', were also very popular. In January 1915, it was reported that the comedians Billy Whitlock and Chas. Penrose had joined the forces, 'and as a proof of their originality and versatility have produced for several of the leading record manufacturers a splendid series of topical numbers. Incidents of the war have been depicted with dramatic force or treated in a spirit of burlesque with gratifying results and equal success.'[9] Charles Penrose & Co. also recorded *The V.C.* and *The Spy* for distribution by Favorite Records, and Billy Whitlock and party produced skits on 'our German foes and their methods of conducting the war, together with some wonderful imaginary experiences in Krupp's works, in Zeppelins and so on, [that] are very funny'. Increasing numbers of military records were produced. The Black Diamonds Band and the Royal Military Band feature in many listings.[10] The Coldstream Guards band has a long list of recordings in the HMV catalogue of September 1916, as did the Colonial Cavalry Band, the Metropolitan Military Band, the Pipers and Drummers of H.M. Scots Guards, as well as Basil Hallam '(the late)', who had died on the Somme earlier that year.[11] The Zonophone Company's recordings of the most popular pantomime hits included the songs *Sandy Boy*, *My Soldier Laddie* and *Sister Susie's Sewing Shirts for Soldiers*.[12] Meanwhile, on the Regal label's list, Bernard Dudley's renditions of *Hearts of Oak*, *British Grenadiers* and *Come on Boys Sign On*, was joined by *The Bugler's Dream* by Sergeant Leggett and orchestra on the other side.[13]

Gramophones and Fundraising

Manufacturers such as Columbia Co., J.E.Hough Ltd. and His Master's Voice Company were all reported as regular donors to the various charitable organisations in gifts of goods or money. By January 1915, Colombia had given £1,000 cash to the Prince of Wales' Fund, and J.E.Hough Ltd. had 'responded to the demand for records and machines – and needles – for the Fleet'. The company sent 28,000 titles, 100 machines [gramophones] and 70,000 needles to the Navy which 'will without doubt reinforce our gallant bluejackets, and so fortify the heroes who are now fighting for the independence of our Empire and the freedom of the civilized world'.[14] Indeed, a Bluejacket on board HMS

Conqueror underlined that '[t]he merriment on board still continues. There is always some skylarking about, the same singing and wrestling, and the gramophones and cinematograph, worked by the chaplain or doctor.'[15] Indeed, old gramophone records were among items requested by a private appeal for comforts for sailors on HMS *Iron Duke*.[16] Many artists' music was used to raise money for wartime charities. For example, Mark Sheridan's *Belgium Put the Khibosh on the Kaiser* and *Here We Are Again* were available on Colombia-Rena's war records listing which informed customers that by purchasing these records they would also be contributing to the National Relief Fund.[17]

In August 1915, *The Sketch* emphasised that music 'hath charms to soothe a soldier's breast; our men at the front, if they cannot have it any other way, do so by mouth-organs. What they really love, in their time of leisure, is a gramophone. It gets their thoughts right off the war they are in the midst of, and gives them rest and relaxation.'[18] By June 1916, it was said that '[w]herever the British soldier goes a gramophone goes along, somehow, *anyhow* – but it goes! To Mesopotamia, to darkest Africa, to the shores of Greece, or the trenches of Flanders – there, with his complicated kit and his grubby photograph of his best girl, Tommy Atkins lugs a gramophone.'[19] Gramophone records were seen to be playing 'a large part in the history of this war. It's a well-known fact that music and warfare have always marched together. But this is the first war in history wherein the gramophone has taken a big share in keeping up the spirits and cheeriness of our fighting men. In the trenches or on the sea, wherever the fighting man betakes himself and his belongings, the gramophone goes along!'[20] Gramophones were essential to the enjoyment of most men in the fighting zones. The officers of the Machine Gun Corps emphasised that the essential ingredient of a mess was 'a few sheets of corrugated iron, a quantity of sandbags *pro rata*, with your terms of friendship with the C.R.E, a packet of Kirchner postcards and a gramophone'.[21] They were adamant that 'the traditional uniformity of the British Army asserts itself . . . in, on or by the mess gramophone'.[22] While they admitted that tee-total messes did exist, it might be possible 'to find an officers' mess without a syphon, but never without a gramophone'.[23] They explained the gramophone's unique abilities in that they 'baffle bores and break up bridge; they soothe the sentimental and madden the musical. They inspire the impressionable and ordinarily offer relaxation to overworked Orderly Officers at odd hours. They are helping to win the war. A popular love ballad has set many a boy out to deeds of fame and valour, when all he wanted was a "Blighty."'[24] Gramophones and their music had a broad appeal. A gently satirical portrait of 'Johnny Gurkha' in *The Bystander* reported that the Nepalese soldiers were 'the almost perfect type of

soldier, always cheery, extraordinarily well disciplined, of perfect beha-
vior in billets, the most easily amused person in the world, and the least
easily moved'.[25] The Gurkha, they said, 'seldom ... indulges in song, but
he has a passion for a gramophone, and if presented with one will only
cease working it when there is a breakdown in the machinery'.[26]

The outbreak of war significantly increased the demand for gramophones. *The Graphic* reported that they were 'urgently needed by that
great B.E.F. – wherever it may be. They are wanted by controllers of
Y.M.C.A. huts, by mess presidents, by matrons of countless hospitals.
For the wounded, the blind, the maimed, when genuine players
cannot come to cheer them, a gramophone provides a splendid
substitute.'[27] Even as early as January 1915, *The Bystander*, a journal
which was very popular with servicemen, published a tongue-in-cheek
letter: 'To a Fellow at the Front, by an envious stay-at-home at the
back':

My Dear Old Chap,
    You, in your luxurious trench, know little of the horrors of war ... snugly
ensconced in quarters replete with every comfort, from gramophones upwards ...
showered upon you free gratis for nothing by a grateful public ... It's good
business to you ... Nobody supplies *us* with gramophones, and if we try to buy
one we are told that the price has gone up double on account of the demand for
gramophones 'at the front.' ... All my socks are wearing out, but I simply daren't
go and ask for some new ones. 'Very sorry sir, great demand for socks at the
Front'.... It's rapidly coming to this, old man, you chaps at the Front will have to
play the game and send us back some of those socks and gramophones and things
you've collared – otherwise, we shall have to come out and fetch 'em.[28]

By the time the 1915–16 catalogue was released by Edison Bell
Discaphones, the recorded music industry was showing signs of strain.
The company admitted that the catalogue had been compiled with 'much
difficulty owing to the national crisis through which we are passing. Many
of our staff, especially in the manufacturing departments, have responded
to the wider call of patriotism and are serving their country on the field of
battle.' This was 'coupled with the fact that a large part of our Factory is
now being used for the manufacture of Munitions of War' which had
'enormously increased the difficulties of manufacture, while the steadily
increasing price of materials has added to the commercial anxieties of the
situation'.[29] Meanwhile, the wartime period sees rapid rise in demand for
gramophones. In December 1915, *The Sketch* declares that there was
a 'boom' in gramophones:

Belgravia and Bermondsey, the trenches and remote Tooting are all fired with one
ambition – to become a possessor of a gramophone and an immense number of
records.... Who would have imagined that one effect of German 'frightfulness'

would be to stimulate interest in gramophones and raise that instrument to heights of popularity never yet achieved in its successful career?[30]

In the 1915–16 Edison Bell catalogue, the cheapest gramophone is the 'Arthur' model priced at £1 15 0, and the most expensive, the 'Ante', cost £10 0 0.[31] *The Sketch* column 'Woman about town' published advice to women who were looking to buy gramophones for men at the front: 'send the one that is easily portable, that is perfectly simple, powerful in tone, with musical qualities equal to those of the most expensive gramophone-cabinets, and that will play any size and make of needle-records'. The recommended model was by Decca, weighing 13lbs. It 'closes up like a bag and needs no cover'. This, and similar models the article suggests, could be bought at Army and Navy Stores, Harrods, and music dealers everywhere.[32] The gramophone was seen as 'all things to all men'.[33] However, buyers had to ensure the best sound quality, and by December 1915, *The Sketch* were recommending models by His Master's Voice. The production and sale of gramophone records can also help indicate the cultural and musical mood of wartime audiences. By the end of 1915, for example, on the home front, the sort of music people wished to listen to in private shifted away from overtly patriotic music towards gentler, reassuring songs:

> Popular songs, like women's clothes, go out of fashion . . . one might as well try to feel fashionable in a last year's frock than as to attempt to thrill an audience with *démodé* sentiments. Since last year there has been a revolution in popular taste . . . twelve months ago the song that was full of raging, tearing, if light-hearted patriotism carried all before it. This year, we are inclined to homely sentiment, and are inflamed with a passionate desire to 'keep the home fires burning' while our men are fighting away. . . . what is a patriotic song when the millions are not there to join in the chorus?[34]

It was felt to be '[n]o wonder that the heart of the pleasure-seeker turns with warmth to the gramophone, which will provide him with songs, grave or gay, according to his mood, and whose generosity in the matter of encores is tempered by no selfish considerations'.[35]

Criticisms of 'Mechanical Music'

However, the gramophone had its critics years before the outbreak of the war.[36] In 1911, J. Swinburne outlined his strong distaste of gramophone technology in *The Musical Standard*, saying that the gramophone 'has been vulgarized by the lovers of the music hall and the pet solo singer. The singer record gives a tremendous volume of singer . . . then a mere tinkling of accompaniment. You thus get a roar of voice, generally with a vibrato that makes you want to shoot somebody.' He also indicated his dislike of music hall songs which 'are frankly vulgar, but not as vulgar as the adoration of star singers'.[37] Indeed, the popular stars of the day were 'making tinned music for Tommy' which meant they 'have "sung" under shellfire'. Clarice Mayne received a letter from an unknown officer, telling her that 'she had calmly continued to inform she was "A Good Little Girl" ... during a heavy and unexpected bombardment'.[38] Florence Smithson had a similar communication which informed her that 'while she was singing the "Pipes of Pan" in a dig-out somewhere in Flanders, a stray piece of shrapnel had the bad taste to descend on the record – plunk! – splitting it in half, to the great distress of the owners'. The soldiers wrote to Miss Smithson for a new record 'which reached them as soon as the post could carry it'.[39] George Robey received numerous letters from soldiers and sailors, 'describing the weird adventures of his "records," and the narrow escapes undergone by records and audience, who are apt to forget there's a war on ... while he announces that "what *was* there was good!"'[40] *The Graphic* quoted 'a hefty warrior' as saying: 'Real concerts we has, out here, all the tiptop stars, I give you my word, on the gramophone – and it ain't half a scream to hear some good old comic chortling his latest howler, with Jack Johnsons and coal-boxes banging away – makes you think of The Strand on a Saturday night!'[41]

Gramophones were described as 'these carriers of West End London right to the heart of the war zone'.[42] Describing at length how records are recorded and made, *The Graphic* underlined that '[o]nce the "negative" is ready, printing records is rapid work; and the result of the Bing Boys and Emma's exertions, that summer day, may be heard in the trenches to-night – and on a hundred nights to come'.[43] Indeed, at the start of the *Bing Boys* run, George Robey and Alfred Lester received a letter requesting some records of the songs be sent to a battalion as some of its members were shortly going on leave 'and wanted to know the songs before they saw the show, so they could join in the choruses!'[44] Civilian concert parties would often feature recording artists. In a description of a concert in a YMCA hut on Salisbury Plain led by Courtice Pounds, an officer in the ASC underlined that the singers were 'heroes of a thousand gramophone triumphs'.[45] Nevertheless, *The Sketch* agreed that if one could not attend a musical comedy in person, 'the next best thing is to shut your eyes and try to imagine ... that you are listening to Mr George Grossmith or Caruso'.[46] That is exactly what many servicemen did. After a die-hard dinner party of Army rations, including 'Whizz-Bang Soup', 'Lobster Salad á la Dugout' and 'Jam Sandbags' for dessert, Lieutenant Jack Wood of 15th Middlesex Regiment, with his colleagues 'sneaked' a gramophone belonging to the officers of a nearby artillery position. Thrilled with their acquisition, Wood relays that this meant they 'had an orchestra during dinner!' Afterwards they

> decided to go to a theatre . . . & imagined we were dining at the Savoy. As we could not go to a theatre afterwards, we had the gramophone & imagined ourselves in the stalls with the orchestra playing during the intervals.... We thought of the audience chattering away, chocolate-boxes being passed round, & all the sort of flutter that goes on during the interval.[47]

In the summer of 1917, Arthur Hemsley, an officer with the 12th Battalion East Surrey Regiment, was made the forward lines officer. He recalls that while he was stationed alone in a dugout during the preparations for the Passchendaele offensive (Third Ypres):

> there was a particularly nice major in the [Australian] Army signals. At night time he always felt that I must be lonely, which I might easily have been, but he would ring me up and say 'one of us has just been to England . . . to see *Chu Chin Chow*, and we'd like you to hear some of the music'. He'd then start this gramophone record and he'd put the receiver beside it, and I'd sit back there listening to all this lovely music I hadn't heard before. He did that for some weeks, in intervals, calling me at night.[48]

At a battery in Wancourt, signaller Private George Cole with the 3rd Northumbrian Brigade, Royal Field Artillery, was on night duty, routinely checking the telephone lines with Headquarters every fifteen minutes. After exchanging the usual call signs and code names with Headquarters and establishing the routine 'Ok the lines', the officer at Headquarters told Cole to 'hold the line . . . I've got something important for you . . . Now listen carefully.' Thinking the battery was about to be informed of something important about the war:

> all of a sudden we hear the music. It was the tune . . . *Yakadola heykidola* . . . some people at Headquarters had fetched a gramophone and put this record on. And all the battery was listening, it was quiet, nothing was stirring, and that was all we could hear, *Yakadola heykidola!* We burst out laughing and asked them if they could put one or two more records on.[49]

An Edison Bell advert in *The Sphere* in December 1916, lists a number of records for sale. A significant number of the songs are music from the theatre shows including *Chu Chin Chow* and *Bing Boys*, *High Jinks* and *Razzle-Dazzle*. The advertisers also promise that they would pay 'Special and prompt attention to B.E.F. orders.'[50] Indeed, the existence of gramophones on the fighting fronts, and the records that were played on them, give us the closest snapshot of what sort of music servicemen wanted to listen to. However, extensive details of music played on servicemen's gramophones are rare. But there are some clues; for example, the war diaries of Lieutenant R. P. E. Roberts, Royal Field Artillery, which contains lists of a large number of gramophone record titles. This indicates that Roberts, and junior officers like him in his regiment, had access to a number of records in the various officers' mess they attended. Of the forty tracks or selections which are listed, seven are classical, eight are dance tracks such as waltzes and foxtrots, seven originate from four different musicals/revues, and eighteen are popular songs.[51] This indicates, in the Army at least, a realistic mix of musical tastes found among servicemen in the fighting areas. Despite the evident popularity of the gramophone among the majority of servicemen, criticisms remained:

Do people nowadays realise the beauty of which the musical instrument in capable: beauty of colour and voice, and grace of form? Or have the piano-playing machines beloved of the moneyed Philistine and gramophone of yet more undiscerning vulgarity demoralized our taste until it is past praying for? Their synthetic eructations and blarings, ground out by sewing machine pedals or electricity, or wound up by springs or hand-turned cranks, answer to the snow-white linen spats and white slips to waistcoats that are the outward signs of self-satisfied success.[52]

The Saturday Review maintained that good taste 'can only spring from Knowledge, Judgement and Sensibility, and all justly blended. Few people possess even two of the three qualifications.'[53] It emphasised that music 'is the voice of love and food and exaltation – the expression of self, the solace of the soul. We want no archaistic revival ... but a movement from the parlour, from the drawing-room, from the people, to drive out "ragtime" ballads and music (!)-hall inanities, and to give us music in their place'.[54] However, this view did not hold water with many men serving in the forces. Captain James Agate, an officer in the Army Service Corps, hoped that 'if we can't persuade the great arts to unbend, we can obtain for the little ones a trifle more courteous recognition'. Taking popular music as his theme, he means 'the songs the solider likes to hear sung' and not 'the unsingable stuff that ought to be popular, the chanteys, the folk-songs, and other erudite nonsense, but the rowdy chorus and plaintive anthem with which we are all made genuinely jolly and pleasantly sad'. Adding to the debates about tensions between elite and popular music, he underlined that

For the first time in the history of this country our aesthetes and intellectuals have had to do a little mental slumming, have been brought into actual contact with vulgar intelligence and popular feeling; and the intellectual mind has discovered that you cannot grub out of a common dixie, wash at a common tap, pig in a common tent, and ignore common discomforts without sharing the simple emotions and ways of expressing them that are common to the crowd.[55]

He has, he claims, seen an audience of the New Army, 'clever and simple together, held in ecstasy as whole-souled as any amazement of the expert for the latest bloom of a Delius or a Stravinsky'.[56] Surely, he continued, it should have been recognised that music 'possessing so great a power over the emotions of so vast a number must be the concern of sympathetic not supercilious criticism'.[57] Even if the writer displayed little objection to popular music in general, the fact that music could be produced by any-one at any time meant that they had the potential to be irksome among neighbours. A journalist from *Answers* described the gramophone as a 'suburban peril'. He quipped that '[s]ome people keep gramophones as a hobby; some do it on purpose ... What did Edison want to invent such things for? One of these days I shall write him a jolly stiff note about it.' The effect on his work led him to ask the reader what they would do if they were trying to write an article 'to be greeted with the information that it is still a considerable distance to Tipperary'.[58] Similar sentiments were expressed on the fighting fronts. However, Enid Bagnold, who served as a nurse during the war, had no such qualms.[59] A short story she penned in 1918 for the hospital journal *Reveille*, described how, on a quiet summer's evening, 'thin, glamourous tones break into a song and sing without hesitation. The Flying Corps Mess next door have turned on their gramophone.'[60] The story, 'Outside the Hospital', is a love letter to the talking machine: 'Little gramophone, dispersing the silence; little box of tricks evoking the flowers of our civilization – the cinema, the music hall, the footlights ... oh, little gramophone with the heart of steel, full of pluck and tune, and thin, glorious defiance ... what a part you have played for us, and for Them!'[61] In response to those who have spoken out against the technology, she pointed out that was 'of no use for musicians to sigh and stop their ears and complain' because, she tells the gramophone, 'over the people, the Army, you wave a wand, you make the heart swell and beat, you are romance, you are pleasure, you are London!'[62] Bagnold mar-velled at the ability of the gramophone to take music right into the fighting zones. She wrote that 'I can see them in little Messes along the line, men who sit in an earthen hole by a table spread with a newspaper, until one of them rises and, crossing over to you, sets you at your tricks afresh, fixes your needle, winds your handle.'[63] The admiration continues:

You mix yourself up with death – you are the light, treble accompaniment of everlasting guns, the memory in the ear of that deafened man who has no other memory – you are sometimes glamour, sometimes romance. You are love. It is strange to think that man should carry such a thing back into the caves and holes of the ground to which war has sent him; that the voice of his almost-forgotten glorious and monstrous cities should beat against the walls of earth and clay, under the open sky, where he lives now; that the little box of screws, threads, wheels, disc and needle should tell such a story of man's invention, his dingy jokes, his gaiety, his whirling mind, his incomprehensible speech, to such surroundings.[64]

Plenty of odes to the gramophone were written during the war (Figure 8.1). In April 1918, the journal of the 7th Canadian Infantry described the gramophone as 'a souvenir of the old days of stationary trench warfare'.[65] Furthermore, echoing Bagnold, the machinery was referred to as a female being. Despite their gramophone's advanced age – 'it's speech was halting and uncertain, its high notes were sheer torture to all but the hardened soldiery who sat round it and gazed lovingly on its ancient, time-battered carcase [sic] – the Canadian infantrymen maintained that 'the chief engineer knew and loved all its whims, and was invariably able, given time, to coax it back to articulation'.[66] They had three records: *Only One Way*, *If You Were the Only Girl* and *The Broken Doll* who were 'like old friends'.[67] However, it was not so much the playing of the gramophone 'which brought solace, and cheer, and pictures in the fire to the warriors grouped around it', but that their machine was so worn out 'it made one enjoy the silence so much better after it had stopped'.[68] The female qualities of the gramophone were recognised in tandem with the tradition of naming donated items after the donor. As the

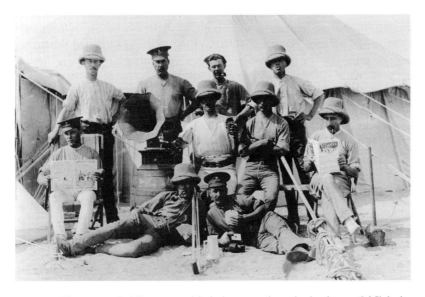

Figure 8.1 Soldiers pose with their gramophone in the desert. © Nicholas Hiley.

YMCA named their huts after the people, companies or organisations which funded them, servicemen named their tanks and equipment, and civilian concert performers named their portable pianos, gramophones were given their own monikers. At the Guards Division at Renescure, in the mess of 3rd Battalion, Bandmaster Rogan was shown the gramophone one of his daughters had sent out. The soldiers called it 'Miss Rogan' in compliment, but Rogan found that 'it was a little disconcerting to hear a Tommy say, some time after, "Put Miss Rogan up on this d—d wagon and let her give us a song!"'[69]

Gramophones were obtained by various means. The officers of the Machine Gun Corps outlined, in typically ironic fashion, three of the best strategies in acquiring a machine. First, they reported that in their mess there is 'a sustained and sporting interest in sending home for one, the idea being to see how many of the original subscribers are still in mess when the machine arrives'.[70] Second, an opportune visit to a salvage dump 'has been known to offer a wide selection in talking machines'.[71] Their final suggestion was 'the method followed by most P.M.C.'s is to send two subalterns to the nearest French town with a draft on the Field Cashier and instructions to order a few things for the mess. They will forget the fish and leave the lime juice, but they will certainly bring a gramophone.'[72] Captain H. B. Viney, serving in Egypt with the ASC, asked the staff of his family's firm for a gramophone and some books to be sent to relieve 'the monotony of their desert life'.[73] The money 'was quickly raised by friends in the office, and the Kirby Street Soldier's Fund added a parcel of records'. Captain Viney's reply outlined his thanks, and that the gramophone 'was in use the first evening it arrived in the men's mess hut'. When he explained to his men how it had come to be sent, he relates that 'they were very touched. It is in nightly use.... Besides the actual enjoyment, I am sure that they are all delighted to think that people at home are grateful to them for doing their bit. A great many of my drivers are men aged thirty-five to forty, or even older, who have really given up good positions at home . . . to come out.'[74] The Red Cross received requests for gramophones and records from five commando working parties attached to parent camp at Chemnitz: 'If any generous person feels disposed to present a gramophone to any of these working commandos it will be received with great gratitude. We must remind readers that records can only be ordered on permit from an authorized shop, but that we would be glad to receive subscriptions for the same.'[75] Chaplain Pat Leonard had also suggested that family friends might send him a gramophone. In place of securing and arranging live performers for his men, a gramophone would allow him to provide music whenever and however it was required. Leonard thought 'what a blessing one would be to wile away a tedious hour when our boys are resting out of the trenches and this is the result; so whenever I can I will take it round to the men's huts and have little impromptu concerts in the evenings'.[76] Leonard was particularly glad that once a soldier's sing-song was in full swing, the gramophone could take the strain. When he 'couldn't stand any more caterwauling about the dear old home, I turned on the gramophone which was a welcome change'.[77]

Records

In February 1916, Lieutenant Richard Noble, serving with the Royal Artillery in France, requested that his wife send him some records, instructing her to send them with the bill. He wrote that they 'should like some rag time [sic] songs such as Lee White's songs and one or two fox trots and things'.[78] Ten days later Noble wrote to his wife that the gramophone records had just arrived – they had taken 10 days to reach his unit. He told her that out of this consignment they already had one of them, so he would wait for the second batch and send any repeats back to her. He was also appreciative that his wife did not send the bill that she 'must have spent a fortune on us'.[79] According to the HMV catalogues, in 1916, a twelve-inch double-sided gramophone record cost an average of 4/- and a ten-inch was 2/6, making them reasonably affordable.[80] The officers of the Machine Gun Corps described their own system of acquiring records:

A supply of records is maintained by a rule which insists that each member of the mess, returning from leave, shall bring a certain number of records back with him.... By this means one certainly obtains variety, sometimes to the exclusion of everything else. The fellow who brought back six songs by My Harry Tophole – the Vocal Vickers – illustrates my point ... his transfer came through together with another subaltern, who as 'O.C.Records' ... forgot to change the needle before putting on the Commanding Officer's favourite Hawaiian harangue.[81]

That there was a junior officer given the rank of 'O.C.Records' is telling. The same tradition was upheld in military prisoner of war camps, such as Trier, Germany. In December 1917, the camp journal, *The Barb*, reported that their gramophone was being fitted 'with an attachment for playing Pathé records'. The machine could be borrowed by applying to Lieutenant H. Kirby, Room 75, acting as 'O.C.Gramophones'. This was possible, the journal says, because of an arrangement with YMCA in Berlin that the records would be sent once a month on exchange. The article also stated that there were a large number of needles in the camp library which could be borrowed.[82] The gramophone was also an essential, if rarer, piece of kit for military prisoners of war. Second Lieutenant John Chapman's PoW diary records that they had many good evenings listening to a gramophone, and that, when permitted, the gramophone was 'going almost all day'.[83] The British Red Cross dispatched a number of gramophones to various British military hospitals: there are no such statistics for Prisoner of War camps. However, we can see from other sources that gramophones were provided by the commander of the camp as a special privilege which could be withdrawn as a penalty for escape attempts or other incidences of indiscipline. The Prisoner of War Committee of the British Red Cross and the Order of St John of Jerusalem received a number of requests for gramophones and records. In June 1918, the care committee representing five commando working parties attached to Chemnitz camp asked the Red Cross to send them a gramophone. The BRC Committee asked the readers of their *British Prisoner of War* magazine[84] for donations as the BRC negotiated special deals with certain suppliers, although the list of companies who agreed to this undertaking has not survived.

Hospitals

Gramophones were much prized in hospitals. Servicemen in want or need of music would gravitate towards the gramophone in wards, recreation rooms and huts, generally provided by the British Red Cross or the YMCA. At a hospital on the island of Malta in January 1916, Corporal Johnson Double wrote that he had 'spent most of my time in the recreation room listening to a gramophone which had records of 2 of my songs, "Nirvana" and "My Dreams"'. Johnson underlined that they lacked a piano 'except in the Sergeant's Mess and that is of course "Holy of Holies" as regards us'.[85] The BRC reported that for gramophones, 'the issue was only limited by the number obtainable from England, as every hospital unit in France and Belgium, from Field Ambulances to General Hospitals clamoured for them'.[86] To keep up with the demand for gramophone machines, the BRC unit for salvage and repairs to equipment had to attend to '[h]undreds of gramophones' as well as 'deck-chairs, camp-stools and lamps of all descriptions' which were repaired and reissued 'to the value of several thousands of pounds'.[87] Gramophones appear in the majority of lists of 'principal items' which the BRC sent to military medical establishments in Egypt, Palestine and Syria. In addition to 640,000 gift bags, which included stationery, a pencil, soap, cigarettes, matches and sweets, the BRC sent 1,700 gramophones, 56,000 gramophone

records, and 3,400,000 gramophone needles. To these areas they also
sent 200,000 packs of playing cards, 313,000 pipes and 39,500 bottles
of *eau de cologne*.[88] In Egypt, the BRC had depots at Alexandria and
Cairo with offices at Port Said, Ismailia and Suez. Medical supplies and
comforts were dispatched from London, India and Japan.[89]

The BRC Store at each Base Hospital was presided over by 'local
ladies' who would oversee the distribution of comforts and supplies.
On a visit to Macedonia, the Chief Commissioner reported to the RC
Joint War Committee that 'it was very nice to see how deeply our
work is appreciated by medical officers and patients alike ... The
wards were well supplied with games, books, newspapers, stationery,
bed pockets, gramophones, and the various little articles that mean so
much to a sick man ... that cannot be well supplied by a Government
department'.[90] The inspector also noted that he 'went into a hospital
for Indians and found some of the patients sitting round
a gramophone entranced at hearing from real Indian records, while
others were dressing their hair with native combs and oil which the
Red Cross had specially sent from Bombay'.[91] To military medical
establishments in Mesopotamia, items supplied by RC Stores in
Basrah from 1 March 1917 to 1 March 1919, not including items
which were purchased locally, included 1,080 gramophones,
1,898,666 gramophone needles, and 865 gramophone springs.
Additional items sent to Basrah included:

   Badminton sets – 151
   Billiard tables – 21
   Champagne – 130 bottles
   Chocolate – 4,266 lbs
   Cigarettes – 20,208,179
   Claret – 729 cases
   Cricket balls – 1,417
   Eau de Cologne – 7,168 bottles
   Footballs – 1,412
   Harmoniums – 46
   Ice cream machines – 47
   Music books – 320
   Pianos – 45
   Playing cards – 29,609[92]

A further forty-four gramophones, sixty-two footballs and one piano were
included in the items sent from Baghdad RC Stores from 1 October 1918 to
1 December 1919.[93] In October 1916, *The Silver Lining or Sister's Smiles:
A Journal for the Patients of the 42nd Casualty Clearing Station* agreed that the
gramophone was indeed 'an asset':

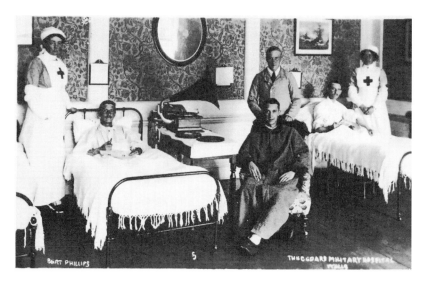

Figure 8.2 Patients and nurses at the Cedars Military Hospital, in the ward with their gramophone. © Nicholas Hiley.

It's rather a pity there aren't more of them available. The fellows forget their little troubles when the Gramophone is in full swing – when Vesta Tilley lauds 'the lass who loves a soldier', and Lauder brings tears of laughter to our eyes. And those band selections – fine and fiery harbingers of happy times in the near future! No wonder the good work of the Gramophone has been placed *on record*.[94]

However, there were of course times when the nursing staff experienced some irritation with the use of gramophones in their wards (Figure 8.2). One nurse endured so many repetitions of the song *Bumblebee,* with soldiers singing the chorus 'poor old bumble-*bee'* so much she 'banished the gramophone for the rest of the day'.[95] Another nurse recalled that while a gramophone was playing in the ward 'a mouth organ was started in opposition, until I put my foot down'.

'One or the other, but not both at once'. Finally I forbade either. Check. Silence reigned for a space, then another patient blew in from the corridor. 'Let's have a tune', quoth he. He was consigned with the gramophone to the outer darkness of the side ward. Comparative peace for a time, when we heard the strains of the mouth organ playing 'As pants the heart'. 'Now who on earth is that?' I asked. 'It's Mills, Sister!' 'I'll have his life.' Chorus: 'You can't, Sister, he's in the bath', and so he was. Checkmate.[96]

A nurse of the 3rd London General Hospital, Wandsworth, was subject to her charges' gramophone pranks:

One evening the spirit of mischief induced them to hide the gramophone on the rafters of the ward. A record had been put on and a string tied to the switch. In the small hours Night Sister was startled by hearing 'Dixie, all aboard the boat for Dixie', etc. The wretched gramophone couldn't be found anywhere. The strains made night hideous. And the Night Sister due on her round! Imagine the scene! Not a giggle from the naughty boys and the frantic nurse.[97]

Also at the 3rd London General Hospital, the satirical Do's and Don'ts for patients included the advice 'DON'T put "Tonight's the Night" on the gramophone when Nurse is cross. (Her evening off has probably been postponed till Friday.)' This was followed by the warning that '[e]ven if you are fond of music, DON'T put "Salut d'Amour" on the gramophone *more* than four times in succession. If you do, some other silly idiot, whose brain does not soar above ragtime, will develop a headache and Sister will ban the gramophone for the rest of the day.'[98]

Gramophone Concerts

Captain John Mackenzie Rogan, Bandmaster of the Coldstream Guards band, established a trend for large-scale gramophone concerts. He was concerned that the troops might have had too much popular material, and that they would 'heartily welcome a change to some better class music'. He mentioned his idea to the Prince of Wales who was keen enough to lend Rogan his car to go to Laventie and get a good gramophone, borrowed from the YMCA. This machine 'enabled songs by Melba, Caruso, Clara Butt and others to be heard all over the Hall'.[99] The idea was that the band played a live accompaniment to the singer on the gramophone. They could obtain just three that were suitable for band accompaniment – by Melba, Clara Butt and Caruso – so band also played the *Peer Gynt Suite*, *Cassenoisette*, *1812 Overture* and two light selections 'of the Sullivan type'. Rogan recalled that the troops were enthusiastic:

This decided me to go on with my scheme for getting out from home a large-size gramophone with a number of good records that the band could accompany. The Gramophone Company, when they heard of our need, generously sent out to the Guards Division, free of all cost, a beautiful machine and about forty records of the best singers. There are people who think that Tommy Atkins only wants music of a light kind, but my experience shows that if he is given music of a good standard and if it is explained to him – I always did so when playing indoors – there is no better listener and none more appreciative.[100]

Men were invited to sing choruses and patriotic songs. The atmosphere was informal and relaxed; 'Officers and men smoked to their heart's content, the Prince with his pipe leading the way; he not only started the smoking but the singing as well. It frequently happened that we could scarcely see the audience for tobacco smoke; still, we carried on and enjoyed every moment of it.'[101] Officers would lend their gramophones for concerts in their units. Lieutenant Morris of the 2/7 Manchester Regiment, for example, was widely thanked for loaning his gramophone to concerts held in the mess tents for A, B and C companies.[102] Gramophones also provided the music for intimate gatherings. Chaplain Pat Leonard wrote that he was able to enjoy a hot bath – 'in my little hut in front of a nice red charcoal fire. It was priceless. As I bathed I had the gramophone playing all the latest waltz and gaiety music. Quite a sybarite.'[103] During an evening as the guest of the 2nd Suffolks, and 'after a sumptuous seven course dinner [including oysters] we adjourned to the kitchen and danced to the music of a gramophone until our shirts were wet and the hours small'.[104] Chaplain Leonard recalled that

Ladies being less easily procured out here than oysters we had perforce to dance with each other. It was great fun. The stone-flagged floor, unseen in the dim religious light cast by a single candle, beaten and caressed by the feet of a dozen young men tunic less & heated, hugging each other & performing the latest steps from London. Foxtrots & Turtle Run etc.[105]

Music on the Forecastle of H.M.S. Duncan.

Figure 8.3 Sailors listening to the gramophone on HMS *Duncan.* © Nicholas Hiley.

In the RFC/RAF, Cecil Lewis recalled that pilots on duty had to stand by dressed in flying kit and wait for the hooter. He said 'there was nothing to do but play poker, put on the gramophone, and drink ... The Mess was strangely quiet on such nights. The voices of the pilots calling their hands, Kreisler's *Caprice Viennois,* the chink of bets dropping into the saucer on the table.'[106] Indeed, gramophone music would feature in many men's wartime memories (Figure 8.3). A special correspondent from the *Daily Mail* recalled that one of his lasting impressions of this war was 'a scene in an old Flemish farm, where a field ambulance was established, with German shells bursting noisily in the near distance and Miss Elsie Janis singing (on the gramophone) "Florrie was a Flapper" to a rapt audience of sunburnt and admiring young men'.[107] Even the sounds of war themselves would be recorded for posterity. On 9 October 1918, a recording was made by the Royal Garrison Artillery at a farmhouse near Lille which was under attack from shelling, preserving the only authentic sounds of the conflict.[108] However, for the servicemen of the Great War, the gramophone helped them forget the noise of artillery fire. For many of those who served in the conflict, the only thing better than the gramophone was the live performances of concert parties, so it is the work of professional civilian performers on the fighting fronts which will be discussed in the following chapter.

9   Civilian Concert Parties

There were a number of groups in Britain who worked to send professional civilian performers to sing, play and dance for British servicemen at home and abroad. The majority of those who coordinated the performances for servicemen did so with four key aims in mind; to do their patriotic duty by contributing to the war effort, to maintain professional standards of performance, to ensure appropriate moral and educational content of the entertainments, and to provide paid work for performers whose livelihoods were compromised by the war. Numerous civilian concert parties were formed by various groups and committees, in many cases led by leading composers, such as the Music in Wartime Committee and the Soldiers' Entertainment Fund. Others were inspired by leading theatrical managers who joined forces with non-voluntary organisations like the British Red Cross and YMCA, such as Lena Ashwell and Basil Dean.[1] Commercial firms also acted to provide concert parties for servicemen. For example, the John Broadwood piano company sponsored the Broadwood Camp Concerts, a scheme funded by subscription through the pages of the *Daily Mail* to provide concerts for soldiers in training camps 'in outlying parts of the country where there was not either a Hall or a Cinema'. Starting on 17 November 1914, 236 concerts were given at a total cost of £4988; £4624 had been raised by public donations through the *Daily Mail*. They paid numerous visits to Harwich to play for sailors and submariners as 'the Navy rarely got the opportunities of enjoyment afforded to the Army'. The programmes generally consisted of a baritone and soprano, a conjurer, an entertainer at the piano 'and some artists who could sing all the chorus songs which were so popular at the time'.[2]

Ellaline Terriss and Seymour Hicks

In August 1914, the actor Seymour Hicks joined the queues of men waiting to enlist in the British Army. However, at forty-five years of age he was 'laughed at' by recruiters and told to 'get on with his own job'.[3]

MR. & MRS. SEYMOUR HICKS.

MISS ELLALINE TERRISS   ROTARY PHOTO. E.C. 3405

Figure 9.1 Seymour Hicks and Ellaline Terriss. © Lucia Stuart and the Seymour Hicks Museum.

This he did, and like many others in the British theatrical industry, both Hicks and his wife, the actress Ellaline Terriss (Figure 9.1), 'plunged right into the job of trying to enlighten the lives of those who carried on the war'.[4] The idea of taking performers to the troops in France was reported to have come from a wounded soldier who had listened to Ellaline Terriss performing in a military hospital in Britain.[5] Hicks 'leapt at the idea like a trout at a fly'.[6] Terriss stated that '[w]ar might be the business of the generals, but entertainment was our business, and we thought we knew our business as well as they knew theirs'.[7] However, the couple were concerned that '[t]o put such a proposal before the authorities without great influence seemed almost an impossibility. Song and dance didn't seem to fit in with the mighty difficulties of men and guns, and casting about in our minds for someone powerful enough to open the doors of the War Office.' That person was Lord Burnham, an 'old friend' of Terriss's late father.[8] Burnham owned the *Daily Telegraph* and had connections in the government. At Hicks's request, Burnham provided a letter of support addressed to Lord Kitchener, and he offered to pay half the cost of the enterprise.[9] Lord Kitchener was apparently 'very skeptical'. When Hicks and Terriss informed him that they wanted to start the performances on Christmas Eve he enquired if they thought the British Army was going to stop fighting on Christmas Day 'and make a holiday of it'.[10]

Hicks and Terriss persisted until the War Office 'were satisfied in their minds that entertainment for battle-weary and nerve-strained men could not be other than good'.[11] Sir John French emphasised that 'owing to the constant and unremitting attention necessitated by operations' he could not permit them to visit troops at the Front, but that it would however 'be a great boon to those in hospitals and camps on the lines of communication at such places as Havre, Rouen, Abbeville, Boulogne'.[12] French sent a telegram telling Hicks and Terriss that if 'a lull in the operations' should give him the opportunity of attending a performance he would 'not fail to do so'.[13] However, the military authorities would take no responsibility for transport or supplies. Terriss underlined that they 'did not care [because we had] permission to go to the Front and that was enough for us'.[14] The couple formed a small group of performers they felt would be popular with the troops (Figure 9.2). The actress Gladys Cooper was already appearing with Hicks in the West End, and Terriss was delighted that they had 'the most beautiful girl in England – not to mention her talent – for the soldiers to see at Christmas'.[15] The Scottish performer, Willie Frame, was nearly seventy years old, but Hicks and Terriss 'wanted variety and somebody the soldiers knew well'.[16] Some 'really good low comedy' was provided by Will van Allen who was billed as 'The Musical Tramp'.[17] The comedic actress Ivy St Helier, the Welsh tenor Ben Davies, and Eli and Olga Hudson made up the group. All the artists were released by their managements, including Oswald Stoll, the Variety Controlling Theatres and Moss' Empress Limited.[18] A portable cinematograph was supplied by Pathé.[19] The highly experienced W. H. 'Billy' Boardman, of the Hippodrome in Brighton, was the tour manager. Such was the novelty of the expedition that two journalists accompanied the party: Robert McGuire of the *Daily Telegraph* and Jimmy Waters from the *Daily Mail*.[20]

On 22 December 1914, *The Times* announced that the concert party would be leaving 'on Sunday morning next, with permission of the military authorities, to play for a week amongst our soldiers in France'. It was underlined that the entertainment 'will be of a kind suitable to the very special circumstances in which the company have the privilege to find themselves'. It was underlined that Sir John French had approved the scheme. The full party consisted of twenty-two people who would be transported in ten motor-cars, and that arrangements for food and accommodation had been arranged to have a minimal impact on the local authorities.[21] The party's 'bill matter' was published ahead of their departure, with a heading of all the allied flags and the headline 'THE NATIONAL THEATRE AT "THE FRONT"', and it was underlined that the party would perform anywhere be it 'A Tent, A Roadside, A Hospital, Anywhere'.

Figure 9.2 Cartoon of the Hicks-Terriss concert party, December 1914.
© Lucia Stuart and the Seymour Hicks Museum.

> We, your brothers and sisters, have come over from
> England to try to entertain and amuse you during
> New Year's Week and to bring you
> *A Message from Home*
> You have only to command us and we shall be proud to give
> you the best entertainment in our Power
> . . .
> It's a long way to Tipperary
> but not too far for us
> Bless You!

Soldiers were urged to attend as many performances as they liked, and the invitation was extended to 'the angels in disguise, the brave ladies who nurse you, ask them to honour us with their presence also'.[22] The party departed from London Victoria station on the morning of 27 December 1914.[23] The station was crowded 'as a large number of officers and men, after their brief Christmas holiday, were returning to the seat of war by the same train, amid the mingled cheers and tearful farewells of relatives and friends'.[24] After a rough Channel crossing, the party arrived in Boulogne Harbour at dusk. As news of the party's arrival spread, the docks were 'absolutely thronged with soldiers' who sang *For He's a Jolly Good Fellow* when Hicks appeared on the gangway. There was no scenery or costumes, and the party proceeded by car to Wimereaux. Within an hour of their arrival they were giving the first concert in the Casino Hospital, Boulogne, where they performed in the Baccarat Salon to an audience of 2,000 soldiers who had been wounded at Mons (Figure 9.3).[25] Terriss performed her most famous song, *A Little Bit of String*, which contains the verse:

> Just a little khaki string,
> Just a tiny little thing,
> Tied as tightly as a string could be,
> Oh, it still is holding strong,
> And it's growing twice as long,
> It's a string of British lads, you see.

The press reported that the entertainment 'was greatly appreciated by the men' although they refrained from joining in the choruses, including *Tipperary*. But at the end of it, all those who could stand stood up and joined in singing *Auld Lang Syne* and *God Save the King*.[26] A special part of each performance was Terriss reciting 'A Message from Home' which had been specially written by Arthur Wimperis for her to perform to the servicemen, to convey to the soldiers 'the regard and affection of those for whom they are fighting'.[27] Terriss recalled that she found this very difficult when she could see the faces of the

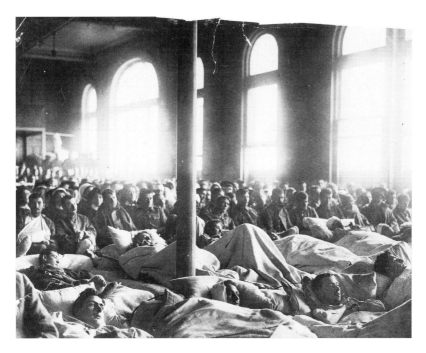

Figure 9.3 Injured soldiers watch the Hicks-Terriss concert party in the
Baccarat Salon of Boulogne Casino, December 1914. © Lucia Stuart
and the Seymour Hicks Museum.

men.[28] Indeed, performing to wounded men, and those who were soon
to march into combat, was hard for all concerned. In one of the
hospitals, Terriss sang *Tipperary*, 'giving the chorus softly, and the
patients joined in, just a low murmur, all the men singing together ...
I had to leave the song unfinished'.[29] At the Fish Market in Boulogne,
Terriss recalled that

It was not the hardship, the bad conditions for working, the almost complete
darkness ... and the very strong smell of fish ... It was the strain of our emotions at
the sight of our men – we could feel rather than see them in the darkness – we
could see the gleam in their eyes ... we knew little of war then and to us these men
were complete heroes, like the knights of old, fighting for us, giving their health,
and their lives – each one of them a St. George sworn, on our behalf, to kill the
Kaiser-Dragon. It was one of the most moving things in which I have ever
partaken.[30]

The party gave three performances in one day at Lady Sarah Wilson's
hospital in Boulogne, then four the day after that. On Monday,

30 December, the party performed at the general hospital in Wimereaux, and the Christol Hospital, Boulogne. The audiences averaged 1,000 soldiers at a time.[31] After Wimereaux, Hicks, Davies, Frame and Eli Hudson returned to the Fish Market in Boulogne to entertain the Royal Welsh Regiment. As the soldiers prepared to march out of the concert, Ben Davies sang *Land of My Fathers*. There was

A sharp command and the men halted. A momentary pause and then his magnificent voice rang out ... He sang it in Welsh, his tongue and theirs. And hardly as the first refrain ended then all those men sang it again; they who had learnt this anthem at their mothers' knees, and had sung it so often in their lovely peaceful country, now sang it again when they were going to face Death. ... the singing coming right from the heart – and then – silence. One knew their thoughts were back home, in their valleys, on their hills, where their loved ones were thinking of them and maybe singing that song too. It was not only that which was in their voices as they sang. As if they made a solemn vow to fight to the end for their Motherland.[32]

Their commander, Colonel [Lord] Ninian Crichton-Stuart, said 'Men of Wales, three cheers for your countryman, Mr Ben Davies'. Davies was moved to tears. He bowed and moved away, and the men marched on.[33] At the Boulogne Fruit Market, the party performed for 1,500 men of the garrison. Only half of the vast hall was available as the other half was stacked with fruit baskets and crates, or occupied by beds in which soldiers slept. It was a wet stormy night and 'a high wind howled in the rooftop'. When Ivy St Helier sang *Are We Downhearted?* the whole audience joined in shouting a resounding and emphatic 'No'. As an encore she sang *The Sunshine of Your Smile*, but as she began the second verse the electric lights went out and the hall was left in darkness. While lights were procured St Helier sat at the piano and played popular airs that the audience joined in singing, and at the special request of the men, she sang *The Rosary*.[34] Motor car lamps, acetylene lamps and candles were brought in, and Terriss proceeded to sing the first verse of *Sister Susie's Sewing Shirts for Soldiers*. The words of the chorus were projected onto the wall at the back of the stage 'and all the men were invited to join in singing them ... And so the evening ended in great good humour.'[35]

The next day the party made a twenty-three-hour train journey to Rouen to give concerts at a Rest Camp based at the racecourse. They gave three concerts to just over 2,000 men at each one. During a five-hour stop outside Amiens, the performers gave the men an open-air show.[36] In many cases the performances were on makeshift stages with little lighting, and in very muddy conditions. Terriss recalled that, 'in some places ... soldiers tossed up for the privilege of carrying the girls of the party across it'. They enjoyed two 'normal' performances when the Mayor of Le

Havre gave them the Grand Theatre, which could seat 1,800 at a time. Furthermore, the British commander at Le Havre insisted that tickets to both showings should be split equally between British and French soldiers.[37]

Terriss returned to the West End stage before the end of the tour as she was contracted to appear in *The Earl and the Girl*. On her homecoming, she told reporters that 'Boulogne is a city of hospitals. The ordinary life of the town is completely changed and the streets are filled with Red Cross ambulance cars. We saw the wounded being brought back from the front.... The whole visit was a most moving experience.'[38] *The Times* reported that '[t]he recruiting staff have received an unofficial addition to their number' in Terriss, who said that she 'went away an actress' and she 'returned a recruiting sergeant. People in England can't realise what the conditions are in France. We who have been to Boulogne know it is the duty of every man in England who is free from responsibilities to go and help our brave fellows on the Continent.'[39] However, the tour took its toll on the party. Several performers, including Hicks, fell ill at the end of the tour with double-pneumonia. He crossed the channel four times on the *Asturias* hospital ship among cot-cases from front-line as he was too ill to be landed.[40] It would also later transpire that Gladys Cooper was pregnant with her first child, a son who was born in 1915. However, the performers' war work continued. Terriss played to the men of the Royal Navy at Rosyth just before the battle of Jutland, and with Hicks she continued to put on concerts in London with programmes which contained a similar message of welcome to servicemen as had been used for the first concert party.

Harry Lauder

The Scottish performer Harry Lauder had also attempted to enlist in 1914. However, at the age of forty-six and in poor health, he was told that 'there was more and better work for me to do at [home] in Britain, spurring others on, cheering them when they came back maimed and broken; getting the country to put its shoulder to the wheel when it came to subscribing to the war loans and all the rest of it'. However, Lauder was 'not content'. He felt that 'it was no time for a man to be playing and to be giving so much of his time to making others gay', but he believed that he was doing 'some good at least, and giving cheer to some puir laddies who needed it sorely. But ... it was no what I wanted to be doing when my country was fighting for her life! [sic]'[41] Lauder was impassioned in his support for the war. He led successful fundraising efforts for war charities, and he organised a tour of music halls in 1915 to aid recruitment. His pro-war stance was strengthened with the death of his only son, John, a Captain in the 8th Argyll and Sutherland Highlanders, on 28 December 1916 at Pozières. In the wake of John's death, Lauder continued to press for permission to perform to servicemen on the Western Front. Lauder maintained that he was getting a significant volume of letters 'from laddies whom I'd helped to make up their minds' to enlist in the forces. The men told Lauder that 'they felt they knew me because they'd seen me on the stage; or because their phonograph, maybe, played some of my records; and because they'd read that my boy had shared their dangers and given his life, as they were ready, one and all, to do'.[42] Most of these letters, Lauder recalled, asked Lauder to perform for them at the front. The War Office eventually agreed, on the condition that Lauder's performances took place at British bases. However, Lauder maintained that it was 'the real front' he was eager to reach:

> I wanted to be where my boy had been, and to see his grave. I wanted to sing for the laddies who were bearing the brunt of the big job over there . . . I wanted to go up to the battle lines themselves and to sing for the boys who were in the thick of the struggle . . . I wanted to give a concert in a front-line trench where the Huns could hear me . . . I wanted them to learn once more the lesson . . . of the spirit of the British Army, that could go into battle with a laugh on its lips.[43]

Once it became known that Lauder was to travel to the Front, a London piano manufacturer built a small and light-weight five-octave piano that could be transported by car. Lauder gave the instrument the moniker 'Tinkle Tom'. Lauder was also joined by James Hogge, Member of Parliament for East Edinburgh, who was campaigning to improve the pensions of injured servicemen and their dependents.[44] Lauder's party also included his friend, the Reverend George Adam, then a secretary to the Minister of Munitions. Lauder recalled that as soon as the soldiers heard of the combination the tour was named 'The Reverend Harry Lauder, M.P., Tour'. They travelled to the Western Front in the spring of 1917, under the care of a Captain Godfrey. Despite the lack of official publicity, Lauder recalled that their arrival 'was like that of a circus, coming to a country town for a long heralded and advertised engagement. Yet all the puffing that we got was by word of mouth.'[45] Before his performance, there was a talk about the war and its progress and the things supporting the war effort in Britain. Then Lauder performed with 'Tinkle Tom'. The party performed in convalescent camps and YMCA huts in the Boulogne area to around 2,000 men in one night. They also played in rest billets behind the lines, often at various chateaux, giving up to seven concerts in one day. British NCO Lendon Payne attended one of the many wartime concerts given by Lauder:

[H]is stage was an orange box and there was a small piano they brought with them and he sang for about, oh, over an hour all his various songs. And the troops nearly blew the roofs of the buildings around about down with the noise they were making. I remember that very well [Lauder] was only a little man but he had a fine voice and he was a very fine comedian and great humourist. The troops were absolutely delighted at it.[46]

William James Reynolds, serving in the Nelson Battalion of the Royal Naval Division, attended the first concert of Lauder's tour. Reynolds recalled that Lauder 'sang several of his best songs and told some good yarns and at the finish made a short speech. He is a fine speaker. With him was Mr Hogge the M.P. who is trying to get us pensions. Both speakers were fine and they touched lightly on the war. They spoke more of the time after it was finished.'[47] Like all other civilian performers, Lauder recalled that playing to servicemen on active service was a difficult experience. Lauder felt that 'tears come into my eyes and my heart is sore and heavy within me when I think that mine was the last voice many of them ever heard lifted up in song'.[48] Lauder felt that he was better serving the war effort while he was under fire at Arras, performing with shells and planes overhead while the men would 'roar out' the choruses of his songs. He described the tour as 'a labour of love'. He believed that 'I sang a little better on that tour then I have ever sang before or ever shall again, and I am sure too that Hogge and Dr Adam spoke more eloquently to their soldier hearers than they ever did in parliament or church.'[49]

Lena Ashwell

Lena Ashwell said of the British Army that it was 'the most wonderful organisation in the world . . . but there are three things which our wonderful machine does not supply . . . some sort of garden, some sort (any sort!) of dog, and some sort of music'.[50] While the gardens and the dogs were beyond her influence, arranging for performers to entertain the troops was entirely within her means through the agency of The Three Arts Club. Ashwell believed that the need for entertainments was particularly acute for newly enlisted soldiers whose divisions had yet to organise their own ensembles. However, without the personal connections of Terriss and Hicks, and the popular celebrity of Harry Lauder, the War Office was unresponsive to Ashwell's offer, so she continued her work with the Women's Emergency Corps and the Three Arts Club Employment Bureau. Then, 'on one never-to-be-forgotten day, when I had quite lost hope of the drama and music of the country being regarded as anything but useless, Lady Rodney called on behalf of the Women's Auxiliary Committee of the YMCA. She had returned from France, and came from Her Highness Princess Helena Victoria, Committee Chairman, to ask if it was possible for a concert party to go to Le Havre.'[51]

These royal connections helped smooth the way with the War Office, and Ashwell arranged to cover the expenses privately. It was argued that 'owing to the very suffering state of men at Base Camps who had passed through a very difficult period of fighting, and were to be at Base for rest and further training, this experiment of sending recreation should be made'.[52] Those involved understood this to be a one-off arrangement. Conditions were put in place that there should be no advertising and that the performers would not use the event to increase their professional popularity. A further stipulation was that all members of the concert party had to be known to Ashwell and become known to Her Highness as the latter was to be responsible for their persons and conduct. The Three Arts Club therefore selected and put forward performers for concert parties which 'are arranged for us by the YMCA to whose magnificent organisation the Army and the whole nation is greatly indebted'.[53] The YMCA made the billeting arrangements in France, and the places and times for the concerts. However, Ashwell recalled that there were 'grave doubts' on behalf of the YMCA about working with members of the theatrical profession: 'To them we are a class of terribly wicked people who drink champagne all day long, and lie on sofas, receiving bouquets from rows of admirers ... I think some expected us to land in France in tights, with peroxide hair ... a difficult thing for a religious organisation to camouflage.'[54]

The early Concert Parties set the pattern for the concerts which would follow throughout the war with a soprano, contralto, tenor, baritone/bass, instrumentalist and entertainer. The first performance was held at No.15 Camp, Harfleur Valley, on 18 February 1915. It was led by the pianist Theodore Flint, with William Furness (tenor), Frederic Hudson (baritone), Grace Ivell, Alice Lilliez (soprano), Kathleen Thomas (violin), and Bret Hayden (humourist).[55] This group also gave a high profile fundraising concert at the Folies-Bergère in Rouen which was enthusiastically reviewed in the French press.[56] Ashwell asked Flint to let her know how each member of the party had fared in France, and he replied that all members 'are all so excellent in their way, and are all so obliging and charming, and don't mind a bit how much they sing or what they do'. Flint outlined that the YMCA had asked to extend their visit but that finding accommodation was problematic. On another practical point, Flint writes that 'the high boots have been an enormous success; I don't know what they would have done without them, as the mud has been too awful'.[57] Frederick Hudson also wrote to Ashwell to relay that:

I am afraid it made me awfully nervous, first to drive through the camp and see what discomforts those splendid fellows must have had to put up with – thick clay, mud, wet and cold – in tents! Think how cheerless it must be. Really it brought the nearness of the War home to anyone who saw it. During the second concert we could hear the rain beating down on the roof of the hut. The officers ... took us to their mess to dinner and supper, and fed, 'wined', 'liquered' and 'cigared' us to great extent![58]

Once the six members of the first Concert Party returned home, having given thirty-nine concerts in fifteen days, another party started a tour of Boulogne and Dieppe. The aim was to give performances at two camps and one hospital every day.[59] The YMCA were evidently delighted that the concerts were 'a tremendous help to us in every way' by helping to raise their profile among the servicemen.[60] However, at the end of February 1915, Ashwell continued to persuade the YMCA and Princess Helena's Auxiliary Committee of the value of continuing to put on entertainments to the troops as had been done so successfully the month before. Ashwell arranged a matinée performance to raise funds for soldiers' concerts with the help of Mr Oswald Stoll, owner of the Coliseum Theatre.[61] Queen Mary agreed to attend, and it was reported that boxes for the concert would be priced at 25 guineas each, 'so that a purchaser ... will, in addition to getting his own entertainment, be providing the means for a week's entertainment for our soldiers on the front'. Ticket sales were so successful that day before the event Ashwell declared that there 'was now enough money to let us send to France as many concert parties as the military authorities will permit'.[62]

Buoyed by the success of the first concert party, and the successful fundraising concert, the YMCA agreed to facilitate further missions. A young singer from Wales, Ivor Novello, joined the second Lena Ashwell concert party, appearing in a series of what were billed as 'YMCA Grand Concerts' on the Western Front, 22–27 March 1915. Novello is listed as a tenor alongside Alice de la Bennadiere (soprano), Paola Rivers (contralto), Gwendolyne Teagle (violinist), Sergeant G. Rowland Morfitt RAMC (bass-baritone), W. Robinson (entertainer) and Theodore Flint (accompanist).[63] By spring 1916, there were four Permanent Parties based in Calais, Abbeville, Havre and Rouen; three Visiting Concert Parties performed in Dunkirk to Étaples sector, Étaples to Dieppe and the third from Dieppe to south of the River Somme. From the spring of 1916, Mediterranean Concert Parties were based in Malta, Alexandria, Cairo, Suez and Sinai, with three along the River Nile and one in the Libyan Desert.[64] However, Ashwell wanted 'to go right up to the Front to be able to give concerts when the men come out of the trenches, and though we have been very near we have not yet been able to obtain permission to go nearer'. She maintained that the performers 'would gladly risk what the RAMC risk, and die if we could help those who are dying for us'.[65] The performer's schedules were intensive. Miss Ada Ward, a performer from Bradford with an early Lena Ashwell concert party wrote home that 'it is no rest cure we are having, it is downright hard work'. She outlined her schedule, along the Lines of Communication on the Western Front in the summer of 1915 as follows:

2.30 motor fetches artists from hotel
3.00 concert in hospital
4.30 tea with matron, nurses and doctors
5.15 motor to another camp
5.30 concert in tent or hut
7.15 motor to another location
7.30 concert in tent or hut
9.30 supper with officers

Ward cheerfully related that their evenings with the officers 'always [featured] a jolly menu, for we can let ourselves go after our last concert, and the officers seem so glad to entertain us!'[66] This aspect was not popular with everyone. At General Headquarters in Montreuil it was claimed that 'after 1914, except for nurses and Q.M.A.A.C.s, it was very rare for a woman to enter British Army areas. Those few who did come had very definite business and were expected to attend very strictly to that business and then to move off.'[67] This was not always the case. Shortly after his arrival at a camp in Rouen, Chaplain Noel Mellish was dismayed to find that the Commandant of the Camp had made it his 'chief idea in life . . . to give entertainment to travelling theatrical parties who came to provide edification for troops at the base'. This 'of course included champagne and liquers'. Mellish's sympathy was for the 'unfortunate subalterns who paid for it largely by heavy mess subscriptions'.[68] Nevertheless, the social aspects of these informal evenings were of mutual benefit. Both the servicemen and the performers as the concert party artists were deeply affected by the sights they saw in the battle areas, and a social mixing of the sexes would have provided welcome reminders of their pre-war social lives (Figure 9.4).

From January 1916, nine 'firing line' parties were sent closer to the forward areas of the Western Front. No more than two parties went out at any time, and they were each made up of four male performers 'who are either over military age or have been medically rejected by the Army'.[69] They began in the northern part of France and Belgium in the vicinities of Ballieul, Poperinghe and Locre. By the middle of February, they were with the Second Army Corps. The parties shared two small portable

Figure 9.4 YMCA/K/1/1/95: 'Miss Lena Ashwell's Concert Party, play in the open-air'. © YMCA England and the Cadbury Research Library.

pianos, five-octave pianettes which they named 'Little Peter' and 'Wee Donal', and were transported by car. The first party of this type featured Harrison Hill, Ernest Groom, Noel Fleming and Sidney Brookes, accompanied by 'Peter'. With the help of the YMCA Ashwell said that 'the concert party and Peter travelled to places where no concert party has been before … in many places that are euphemistically called "unhealthy"'.[70] It was reported that the concerts were often given in the open, 'punctuated by 9'2 guns, with one or two aeroplanes coming over the platform' which was two packing cases of unequal height. Guns 'were firing directly over the concert, so the party were literally performing under fire'.[71]

The schedule of one Lena Ashwell 'Firing Line' tour in January–February 1916 shows both the number of performances and the range of venues. At the end of January, the party were touring the Peuplingues area. On 29 January, they performed at a Casino (2.30 pm), Convalescent Hospital (4 pm), Mercer's Hut (6.30 pm) and a Hospital Ship (Brighton, 8.15 pm). On 8 February, at a concert at a casualty clearing station 'near

Flying Ground' at Locre, it was 'rather a muddle' and they had 'very little audience'. Later that day, however, at Caisse d'Espagne, the house was packed: 'men had marched in with rifles and smoke helmets, ready to start for trenches at a moment's notice if necessary'. On 10 February at a second casualty clearing station, the 'guns [were] going all the time – windows rattling – audience greatly amused by our surprised faces'. On 15 February, they gave a concert in the 'old Cinema Hall' at Dieppe. On the way there it was noticed that the walls were 'plastered with bills within a mile of the trenches' and they 'went home in an ambulance'. On 16 February, they played to the Cheshires at the Caisse d'Espagne and gave a short concert at Armentieres. The guns were very active at Renninghelst the day afterwards, and at Poperingue on 18 February. On 19 February, at Canada Huts, there was 'very heavy firing' and there were Taubes over Bailleul.[72]

Transport arrangements were 'many and varied'. Performer Julius Harrison wrote that they travelled in 'everything from a Rolls-Royce to a dirty old wagon, very seldom on a train. Our most hated enemy was a Ford, which had been converted into a covered-in van. For all the world it looked like a meat-safe on wheels.'[73] One typical concert was given in a barn by the roadside. To reach it, the artists, with 'Peter', travelled twenty-five miles in a motor lorry transport wagon. The barn was dark as it was 'unhealthy' to show lights so near the enemy line: 'The platform was lit by two acetylene lamps, and in the straw in the darkness was crowded the audience ... lines and lines of faces looming out of the dim light, on the floor and up in the eaves.[74] Each of the artists were provided with a gas helmet, 'a fearful head-dress, rather like a diver's helmet, but even more like a medieval doctor's plague-mask when it is on'. The performer's proximity to 'the real thing' was brought home to them early in their tour by one of the YMCA leaders at a hut where a concert was to be given who told them that 'There may not be a very large audience today ... we had a shell through the roof yesterday.'[75] It was underlined that the Firing Line parties were right at the heart of the action with the soldiers. The *Daily Chronicle* reported that the British soldier 'can enjoy a 'cello solo or a song while shells are whistling overhead and our own artillery are replying in impromptu accompaniment'. They added that 'it is only fair to record that the nerves of the performers seem to have been as equal to the occasion as those of the more experienced audiences. Only at the first terrific crash were the performers visibly startled, much to the joy of the noise-hardened audience.' However, 'the men's brains are weary of the roar of the guns and the scream of the shells' which is why 'the concert parties are such an immense boon'.[76]

Figure 9.5 YMCA/K/1/1/91: Lena Ashwell-YMCA concert party in Egypt. © YMCA England and the Cadbury Research Library.

The YMCA concert party tour of Malta, coordinated by Ashwell, began on 23 February 1916. The party was very popular, particularly with the YMCA representatives who 'have had the joy of knowing that everything the party did was done in the most perfect taste and to the honour of the ideals for which the YMCA stands'.[77] By early May, ninety-nine concerts had been performed in convalescent camps, hospitals, hospital ships and small outlying forts (Figure 9.5). It was reported that the concerts were 'a real mission of mercy'. In the early days of the tour, 'the party had the privilege of singing to men broken in health by arduous months on the Gallipoli Peninsula. No one, except those who have themselves gone through the experience, can fully appreciate what such concerts mean to men who heard little music save the sounds of the guns during these months of hardship and suffering.'[78] Indeed, the positive reception and effect on the soldiers in Malta led the YMCA to suggest that concert parties be put on the troop transport ships which passed the island. Several concerts were arranged to great effect and 'the reader's imagination can perhaps realise the unique circumstances of a concert given on thronged decks to men for whom, after a rough passage in an over-crowded boat, a good entertainment was a veritable God-send'.[79] In September 1916, a Lena Ashwell concert party performed on board HMS *Agamemnon*. A naval officer of the ship described them as:

> most awfully good and certainly the best concert I have seen on board. Two ladies who sang, a lady with cello, one man with a ripping baritone voice, and another conjurer and ventriloquist fellow, who was marvellous, and very funny. Both the ladies had simply topping voices, and especially a contralto, they sang very pretty songs. 'No John, No John, No' was the best I thought, but they were all awfully good and sang so clearly. Many officers from other ships came over. The acting sub lieutenants sat together and led the choruses, and tried to bowl out the conjurer without success. We had a big supper afterwards, and the band played on deck until midnight.[80]

The reception the Navy gave to the concert parties led the YMCA to suggest further entertainments should be provided on board, helped by Lady Limpus, the wife of the Admiral Superintendent, who was a principal YMCA contact in Malta. Thursdays were devoted to concerts in the naval hospitals or the large naval canteen for men serving on war-ships or the Merchant Navy. Concert parties were also given for the survivors of torpedoed or mined vessels, including the *Simla,* the *Minneapolis,* and later HMS *Russell.* These were for the performers 'happy and sad events – sad because thoughts of the men who had lost their lives inevitably came to their minds'.[81] Fuelling some inter-service rivalry, the *YM* asked which of the two services supplied the most enthu-siastic audiences: 'The body of opinion favours the Navy ... not that the men of the Navy are of higher musical taste that the Army, but that so much less is done by way of entertaining them.'[82]

Men evacuated from the Dardanelles campaign were generally sent for treatment on the island of Malta. Corporal Johnson William Double, in a convalescent camp on Malta, acted as a warm-up act before the profes-sional performers arrived. On 6 March 1916, Double records that he played 'a few popular airs' before the Lena Ashwell party appeared. He thought that '[t]he party who entertained were excellent and I thoroughly enjoyed the programme and I think by the vociferous applause accorded to the performance, that all the rest of the Tommies were of the mind as myself [sic]. A cello solo stood out in my mind above everything, but there was not an indifferent item ... and the pianist was excellent.'[83] The pianist was Theodore Flint, and the 'cellist was Adelina Leon. Their Lena Ashwell party appeared at Spinola on 9 March, and the *Daily Malta Chronicle* rightly pointed out that 'Tommy Atkins is a great critic'.[84] Double's diary shows that he was very honest in his reviews, but he certainly appeared to have enjoyed this professional concert party.

On 14 April 1916, Double and his colleagues were delighted that the performers returned, although there was some awkwardness regarding the etiquette of handing over the platform. Double was

amusing the fellows with mandoline and piano for about ½ an hour before the concert and … the party came in while we were finishing a piece. We were immediately pounced on by the leader of the party and made to give another piece for them … they insisted we played them 'Rastus on Parade' a ragtime selection and they cheered us to the echo. Whether it was meant for sarcasm I could not say as their pianist is one of the best in London and their Cellist one of the leading lights in the musical profession. … the situation seemed to tickle everybody in the tent.[85]

The professional singer Edward Bantock Pierpoint led two Lena Ashwell concert parties on the Western Front, in April and December 1916.[86] Pierpoint and his colleagues visited many hospitals. On Tuesday 18 April, he wrote: 'Convoy of wounded came in during concert. Saw them brought in to receiving room … Very pathetic sight.'[87] They performed at Wimereaux, Calais and Peuplingues after which they dined with the Colonel and officers at the Remount Depot where a Major Aitken 'promises to do his best to get me some momentoes of the fighting'.[88] On 25 April, they gave one concert to the men of the Somersets and another to the King's Liverpool Regiment. The next day the party performed at the YMCA's Keswick Hut and then on to a nearby Cinema Hut in the evening where there was an audience of 1,200 men. Pierpoint's party returned home on 30 April 1916. He received several letters of thanks from the YMCA leaders who facilitated his party's tour. From Calais, one leader, E. A. Pleasance, wrote that 'The enthusiasm of the men has I feel shown how much they have enjoyed the musical treat you have given them and how much they have been cheered and bucked up by the splendid efforts of all the party. Personally I can't tell you how much we appreciate your help in assisting us in our work out here.'[89] It is often mentioned by the YMCA that the concerts 'have always been of the highest possible tone and the enthusiasms of the men have shewn [sic] how they enjoy good music as you have given them'.[90]

Pierpoint returned to the Western Front on 20 December 1916, staying for two weeks at the Hotel De Commerce in Lillers. On arrival, he had no concerts fixed, nor any rehearsals, so he gave 'a short trial show at the YMCA hut' and 'sang for a lot of officers' in the evening after dinner. He travelled ten miles to sing at 33rd Clearing Hospital which had been shelled two weeks previously, then a YMCA hut in Bethune where he wrote that the concert went well 'but carols were not good.' On 22 December, he performed at the 2nd London Clearing Hospital where there was a 'very good audience, chiefly orderlies and men, with few nurses and the Drs'. That evening the hut was 'crammed and noisy'. The men were 'half from trenches, others men just up' but the 'concerts were going better'.[91] Pierpoint talked about the members of the party being forced to cram into one motor car, and having to return to their billet in an ambulance. He enjoyed dinners with officers where he often had a 'lively time afterwards, singing etc'. On Christmas Day, Pierpoint's party put on an evening concert where a Colonel 'told us that we ought to have gas masks & should always have them'. By this point Pierpoint's chest was suffering from the damp weather, and he was admitted to that hospital on 29 December.[92] Two annotated Army Field Medical Cards show that in the first week of January 1917, Pierpoint stayed in No.24 General Stationary Hospital in Etaples with bronchitis. His regiment was noted as 'Lena Ashwell's Concert Party'.[93]

Travelling to France was not undertaken lightly. Arthur Walker, a 42-year-old instrumentalist who was professionally known as Gordon Williams, took two tours to entertain the troops along the lines of communication in France in July–August and December 1917. Williams' diaries provide a detailed insight to how the concerts were organised. On 6 July 1917, Williams arrived in London and went to the 'office for Concerts at the front', where he met the other members of his party. After spending several hours at the 'Military Permit and Foreign Office' he was introduced to Lady Besborough 'who takes a very keen interest in all the Artistes who go to the front'. While in London, he played at Ciro's, Lena Ashwell also appearing on the programme. The morning afterwards, Saturday 7 July, at Holborn, Williams got his first taste of warfare earlier than he expected when he was caught in a large air raid over London. Nevertheless, he played at another concert [at Ciro's] on Saturday night 'and scored another success although I was in anything but good form after my experiences earlier in the day'.[94] On 9 July 1917, Williams and the other members of his Lena Ashwell concert party left London Charing Cross station, arriving in Folkstone for the 11 am crossing. As with all passengers who journeyed across the Channel, the tickets included in red writing a stark reminder of the dangers involved during the war 'the Managing Committee are not be held liable for pecuniary or other responsibility for injury or accident, whether fatal or otherwise, … due to the acts of the King's enemies'.[95] The journey was 'rough' and the vessel was escorted by five cruisers, arriving in Boulogne just after Williams enjoyed 'the excellent lunch on board' despite having to wear his lifebelt for the duration of the voyage. They were accommodated at 'headquarters' for an early departure by train to Abbeville the next morning. The party was collected by a Red Cross transport which took them the final thirty miles to their billets, and a rehearsal was arranged for the following afternoon.

It was inevitable that performers touring the battle zones found themselves confronted by the effects of death and destruction. Williams was moved by his first sight of the war's fatalities; and of a British cemetery, he wrote that '[a]ll the little wooden crosses neatly fixed looked in the sunshine like crosses of gold, and although it was in close proximity to scenes of great activity everything there was peaceful.' He noted that each cross 'bore a brass plate with the name of each gallant hero who had laid down his life for King and Country'. His transport was then halted 'for coming towards us was a little procession and in the centre was a hero covered with the union jack and slowly the hero's comrades take their chum to his last resting-place'.[96] Williams' diary records that they 'passed miles of ammunition dumps and saw other interesting materials all in connection with the great raging war'.[97] As civilians with no prior knowledge or experience of war, other than what they may have read in newspapers at home, the reality of the fighting fronts challenged performers' nerves. However, they were accorded the status of minor celebrities, and they identified as being 'on active service'. Many of them were well known in their local areas, and the men would greatly value the link from home that the performers represented. Williams' first concert 'was a great success and afterwards several Harrogate boys came to see me. One boy, obviously anxious to know if I would tell his relations where he was stationed, asked if I would do so and was very disappointed when I told him that I was on active service and that my letters, like his, were censored. So he said, "Well, tell mother I am quite happy won't you."'[98] The performers were civilian-visitors who were placed under military protection and authority for the period of their tour. They were often treated as inspectors, their civilian status as serving with the YMCA and Red Cross conferring upon them elements of moral authority, to bear witness and act as truth-tellers at home of the sights they had seen. Williams' party came face to face with the enemy when they visited a German Prisoners' Compound: '[t]he Major in charge showed us over. The men were paraded for Roll Call and we could move freely amongst them.... Before moving to our next show we witnessed 2 teams from the audience playing football their other spectators being the rest of the boys and the German prisoners. This scene certainly had its pathos.'[99]

The performers' accommodation and schedules were coordinated by voluntary workers with the YMCA. Rose Venn Brown, who arrived in Le Havre in the spring of 1915, was by November 1917 in charge of coordinating entertainments for the YMCA around the Havre region.

This area contained thirty-five different camps, each one had to have 'nightly a concert, play, cinema, lecture and Sunday a service this means arranging for about 240 per week'. Brown was also 'Lena Ashwell's representative' so she hosted 'Lena Ashwell's parties, regimental shows, lecturers sent out by the War office, and local lecturers for the above entertainments'. Brown appears to have spent many hours in the service of the Red Cross and the YMCA and was so effective at her work that in January 1918, Ashwell asked Brown to work with her directly as 'organising Secretary for her in France, with Headquarters in Paris'.[100] Brown declined Ashwell's offer as she was reluctant to leave her friends in Le Havre. By the later stages of the war, in the course of her work, Brown had met and socialised with a large number of celebrities, writers, authors and entertainers of their time, including 'George Birmingham the author, John Drinkwater the famous actor ... John Lancaster the writer, Gipsy Smith, Canon Savage, Hugh McNeil, Professor Holland Rose, Professor Ramsay Muir, Martin Harvey the actor, Dr Kelvin the famous Scottish Divine ... George Morley the writer, Carrie Tubb, Margaret Yarde, Penelope Wheeler, Leslie Banks and several others all known on the London stage.'[101]

By the summer of 1917, Williams' diary confirms that the numbers of men attending the concerts were considerable. 'We gave the next concert in the open and there must have been 2000 in this field, which had a hill slope. Here the boys planted themselves and were awaiting us. After a great preliminary reception we gave them a special show and moved on about 15 miles where another enormous crowd was waiting.'[102] News of a touring concert party would often be spread by word of mouth, and between YMCA facilities. Williams records that 'The fame of the concert party spread like magic all along the line and special calls to distances 40 miles away became an everyday event.'[103] The visit of a concert party clearly meant a great deal to the men. Williams was touched that the men 'had rigged up a little stage profusely decorated with wild flowers and shrubs ... The piano was a wretched instrument several keys missing but our excellent pianist seemed to make light of these defects.' He admired 'what care the lads will take of a temporary platform. They will rig up in some cases wings and a curtain and a scene to give it the real touch & even footlights shaded with old tin cans.'[104] On one of her visits to the Western Front in 1916, Ashwell recalled that 'We gave "The School for Scandal" in a wood ... "Macbeth" in a great hangar, with army blankets for the walls of the banqueting hall and a sugar-box for the throne.'[105] In one new hut, the acetylene light went out as the performers arrived. Determined not to miss their concert, the men 'promptly collected every candle they could find, 36 for footlights and others arranged round the enormous hut:

and as the candles smoked and the audience of 1,500 smoked as hard as the candles the concert began in a dark fog. We weren't sorry when the light suddenly came right.'[106]

By 20 July 1917, Williams' party was on the Somme. While they were arranging to move to new quarters they 'could not get away for 5 hours in consequence of a large army of wounded men coming down the line. We were all cheery enough however – we travelled by a Red Cross van to a place about 30 miles passing many ruined villages on the way. Here we had billets on the banks of the Somme the river running within a few yards of our quarter [sic].'[107] Here on one Sunday, Williams watched a number of Tommies fishing in the Somme, but the peace was short-lived as soon 'The guns were barking away day and night. Aeroplanes in great numbers all over the place.'[108] Williams' diary records that on Sunday 29 July, 'A great battle has just commenced in the northern section. The boom of the guns sounds heavy and at night there is the sound of Antiaircraft guns and the familiar sound of aeroplanes. I was awakened at 2 o'clock with the terrific noise. It was a very difficult thing to get any rest.'[109] Finding themselves rather nearer the action than they had anticipated, Williams and his colleagues 'had to travel with great caution here being stopped at every point by French Sentries. We gave these lads a great time and distributed 1000 cigarettes.'[110]

As military orders to go into action were often made at short notice, commanding officers made last-minute requests for the presence of a concert party to cheer the men before they left. Williams described how one Major called upon the party 'to give a show at 10.15 pm to a great crowd of men just going into action. The Male members only of the party attend and we have them a great time.'[111] The female performers were excused as they had already retired for the night, but perhaps a more likely reason was that without the presence of women the men would be able to provide a rather more raucous entertainment for men marching off to possible death and injury than they were otherwise authorised to do by Ashwell and the YMCA. Something similar occurred again, at the end of July in the Somme region when they had '[a]nother call to a late concert to 500 R.F.C. men under orders for the line'. The concert did not commence until 10.45 pm and they had already given three performances earlier that day. However, the party 'gave the men 1000 cigarettes and the applause during and at the end of the Concert was simply deafening'. As the men fell in, Williams and his colleagues were amused to see '[t]heir famous mascot a large monkey in khaki marched along with them holding his master's hand. We were told he had been the battalion pet for 2 years and had been through several battles with them. It was really funny to see the monkey salute.'[112] By early August 1917,

Williams' party were still performing to troops fighting in the Somme region. They were being required to travel considerable distances over difficult terrain, but the satisfaction of playing to such large audiences gave them the impetus to continue. At one camp the first concert of the day was attended by 'quite 2000 and the second in the evening probably not less than 5000'. Williams wrote that it was 'almost impossible to describe the sea of faces. After a tremendous reception for "Stars & Stripes" march I played the well known "Policeman's Holiday" and the whole audience take up the refrain.'[113] When Williams and his colleagues transferred to new quarters sixty miles away, they 'passed a convoy of wounded men from the front line. These brave men actually cheered. Knowing who we were. Surely this is the greatest admiration of all.'[114]

The popularity of the shows meant that overcrowding was a regular occurrence. Williams stated that even the largest huts in the district 'are not nearly large enough to accommodate the lads and it is rally pitiful to see hundreds outside in a pouring rain [sic.] straining their ears to catch some of the items. Men sitting on the rafters of the hut and in spite of all this great anxiety and the crush, the greatest respect is paid to every artist.'[115] Of the audiences Williams said that they were 'getting more enthusiastic (if possible) than ever double encores which are really forbidden have to be given'.[116] Williams was not unusual in his expressions of patriotism. He was on the Western Front on 4 August 1917, the third anniversary of the start of the conflict. On returning to billets they saw 'a very large convoy of wounded – the Hospital vans just crawling along with their precious brave heroes just from the battlefield dressing station, all mud bespattered & still cheerful'. He noted that 'today is the beginning of the 4th year of the war. Here we find ourselves in the midst of awe inspiring scenes but our work is to cheer so ... we throw off as much as possible, the despondent creepy feeling which is bound to come over one, and cheer these brave lads as they move slowly on to the field hospital'.[117] Williams' party was invited one night to witness 'a rehearsal of battle'. They saw 'lines of trenches and lads on the parapet' when 'A Great yell is heard & the charge is made. The noise is deafening. Volumes of smoke roll on being the simulation of a gas attack. It is a weird sight ... as though it was an actual battle.' Williams notes it was 'a real privilege to witness this important event'.[118] Shortly afterwards, Williams writes that 'The big push is at its height and in consequence Concert Parties are absolutely forbidden in the shelled area. Several huts have been blown to smithereens and road torn up by enemy shells so we have to keep at a safe distance.'[119] By the time their tour was completed, the Lena Ashwell concert party, of which Gordon Williams was a member, during July and August 1917, gave a total of 74 concerts to audiences of between 250 and

5,000 around the Somme region. Williams played at every single concert and he estimated that he personally performed over 300 selections.[120]

Gordon Williams returned to the Western Front in December 1917. His second tour began in dramatic style when the performers' car was shelled. William and his colleagues 'only suffered shock' and were able to walk two miles to the camp where they were due to perform. The professional performers continued to provide links with home. In December 1917, a local Harrogate newspaper published a letter Williams sent from the Front. In it he stated that the performers 'can instinctively feel that these brave lads are enjoying themselves, and so we give of our best'. While they are 'often bothered with the lights being suddenly turned out' and 'one has to wrap up well, [to] keep fit for the heavy work' they were arranging 'special Christmas programmes' where they are expected 'in at least six different places during Christmas Day'.[121] A Harrogate newspaper also published a letter from Bernard Hollins, a soldier from Harrogate known to Williams, serving on the Western Front, to ask for second-hand music stands for a friend 'who has scraped a small orchestra together to keep us as lively as possible in this quiet seaside village. . . . They visit from one hospital to another, and are very short of stands.'[122]

Concert parties were also used as opportunities to distribute instruments such as mouth organs supplied by charity campaigns led by sections of the British press. In March 1915, Ashwell performer William Robinson described how at concerts in the Rouen area he was giving out the mouth organs funded by the *Musical News*. He relayed that when he finished his act he informed the men his instruments were funded by the readers of the *Musical News,* and he presented the one he has just used 'to the best player in the hut or ward, as the case may be, provided he promises to write to you as per the request in each instrument box'. This was a popular occasion and Robinson describes that he 'could give away fifty or a hundred at each performance'. As he left the concerts 'the men crowd about me and beg for an organ. . . . So I wish to thank you for helping me to amuse the bravest, kindest, and most cheerful lads in the whole wide world . . . Every little mouth-organ you or your readers have sent has furnished a heap of fun to crowds of our "Tommies".'[123] That the performers were representatives of home was of great importance to Ashwell who spoke of 'bringing some brief hours of enjoyment with happy memories to thousands of men, many of whom have been out at the front from the beginning of the war and have had nothing in the way of relaxation'. She said that 'the feeling that this is done by the people at home for the men, without them having to pay, is a fine one. They are the honoured guests and the feeling does good.' Ashwell underlined that the concerts were 'a work of civilisation on the borders of life and death' and 'must not be allowed to lapse'.[124]

Ashwell's concert parties tried to reach as many units as possible. On a visit to 'Cinder City', described as 'a piece of marshland reclaimed from the sea and filled with cinders', Ashwell experienced performing to thousands of transport workers. The monotonous and heavy, industrial nature of this work meant that they were in just as much need of good quality music as those servicemen in closer proximity to the enemy. Ashwell described the men of the Army Service Corps as 'all the men behind the line who are the mainstay of the forces in the field, the shaft of the spear'. She emphasised that many of these men had been in the trenches and have been invalided down from the firing line, though they are not ill enough to go home. Here they had 'splendidly happy concerts … it's the violin what the men like most. Handel's *Largo*, Schubert, dances representing national fetes and folk-songs, and the big simple airs, are more appreciated than any chorus-song.'[125] While most of the servicemen were said to enjoy the entertainer's jokes and stories, and 'a stirring song in a big bass voice', their deepest approval 'is reserved for the young pretty girl who sings their old familiar songs with a sentimental appeal, and they are doubly grateful if she leads them in a swinging chorus'.[126] Describing the music and the involvement of servicemen in this way enabled Ashwell to give an aural impression for the reader, to those who would never see the trenches, but who would be very familiar with these melodies. By using the music pieces as the touchstones of home, the readers of Ashwell's words may have imagined that they were being drawn closer to the war and their loved ones at the fighting fronts. For the YMCA, the Ashwell performers were a desirable counter-attraction.[127] They were praised for providing 'a great piece of Christian service' by diverting the men away from less salubrious pursuits, and 'by maintaining a splendidly high tone in every programme that they rendered, thus exerting a strong and noble influence over the thought and life of the men'.[128]

For servicemen, civilian performers were an important link with home which satiated what one officer called their 'Blighty hunger', their 'longing for the gaiety and sentiment of life'.[129] However, in the next chapter it will be seen that many servicemen were not only keen, but incredibly adept at putting on their own entertainments. By forming concert parties, bands and orchestras, and showcasing the variety of talent in their units, servicemen used the music hall-style template they enjoyed at home, adapting it to parody aspects of their wartime experiences.

10   Servicemen's Concert Parties

Servicemen's concert parties performed the same vital functions as sports; they bought all ranks together in a spirit of community, gave rest from autonomy and obedience, and helped displace anxiety. That they acted as a safety valve is well known, in that servicemen's entertainments helped dispel any tensions within a unit, often by making light of recent events or parodying less favourable aspects of military life.[1] Furthermore, military concert parties, like a unit's band, were often regarded as mascots. The exchange of concert party performances became a regular occurrence, allowing the men to see other combinations with different songs and skits to those performed by their own troupe, often with a hint of competitive spirit. In the latter stages of the war, other nationalities within the Allies would tour around other units, meaning that British servicemen had a wide range of musical experiences, from 'a truly authentic American jazz band' to an ensemble of musicians from the Chinese Labour Corps. The use of pantomimes also had a strong propaganda element. The traditional 'baddies' were often recast as Germans or Turks, storylines were adapted to wartime settings such as Flanders or Mesopotamia, and the moral of the story supported the Allied cause for war in a comedic but nonetheless serious way.

However, the recreational needs of Tommy and Jack were not among the principal concerns of the War Office or Admiralty in the early stages of the war. As the conflict drew on, increasing numbers of civilians entered into the armed forces which created a large audience of men whose discipline and morale needed to hold fast. After food, equipment, transport and medical services, men needed to be entertained. While British servicemen were appreciative of the efforts made by civilian concert parties like those hosted by the YMCA, soldiers, sailors and airmen were adept at organising their own entertainments, and many relished doing so. Concert parties were found in every military context; in Army camps, aerodromes and ships, British servicemen were making their own musical entertainments. The expansion of Britain's armed forces brought into the services many professional and keen amateur musicians who continued to use their talents to cheer their comrades and maintain a link with their pre-war lives. John Barbirolli, for example, who in 1918 enlisted in the ranks of the Suffolk Regiment, performed 'cello solos and conducted a small orchestra during his stay at a military camp on the Isle of Grain.[2] Furthermore, entertainments given by and for servicemen gave aspiring performers opportunities to entertain that they may not have had as civilians. For some, this encouragement led to them working as professional performers after demobilisation. Servicemen typically experienced impromptu sing-songs in their evenings out of the lines. One such occasion, in a YMCA hut, was described thus:

> On a narrow platform at one end of the hall is a piano. A pianist has taken possession of it. He has been selected by no one in authority, elected by no committee. He has occurred, emerged from the mass of men ... has made good his position in front of the instrument. He flogs the keys, and above the babel [sic] of talk sounds some ragtime melody ... Here or there a voice takes up the tune and sings or chants it. The audience begins to catch the spirit of the entertainment. Someone calls the name of Corporal Smith. A man struggles from his seat and leaps up onto the platform. He is greeted with applauding cheers. There is a short consultation between him and the pianist. A tentative chord is struck. Corporal Smith nods his approval and turns to the audience. His song begins. If it is the kind of song with a chorus, the audience shouts it, and Corporal Smith conducts the singing with wavings of his arm.[3]

A range of concert parties developed across the services during the conflict. Some were formed by small groups of servicemen drawn to sing-songs around the piano in their local YMCA, Salvation Army or Church Army hut, and others were run by professional performers. The performances owed a large debt to music hall with a combination of singing, reciting, conjuring, comedy, ventriloquism and ensemble sketches. Crudely written skits that ribbed authority were most popular, and female impersonators, bawdy songs and jokes were staple features. Entry was generally free of charge, if not admission charges were cheap and rarely exceeded a couple of francs. The events were very well attended. The news of a forthcoming concert was sometimes announced via posters, but information was generally spread by word of mouth and announced at morning parades. A year into the war, evening entertainments could feature a range of attractions and would often dovetail with sporting fixtures. The finals of boxing in the Third Division, for example, was 'a strange show, a medley of boxing, wrestling, a funny man and a glee party' comprised of subalterns from the Gordons.[4] By the end of 1916, most divisions had an official concert party and by the end of 1917, they were universal. All four Scottish Divisions and the single Ulster Division each supported one troupe. Both Welsh divisions and two of the Southern Irish, the New Zealand and the Canadian division also had one troupe each. The Australians had one troupe per division.[5] *Hints on Training* issued by XVIII Corps in May 1918 positively recommended the running of divisional theatres.[6] These were found in the towns along the Lines of Communication which were generally used for rest periods, such as Rouen, Poperinghe and Lille. However, British servicemen's concert parties were found in every battle zone. The Pierrot troupe and regimental band of the 2/5 Hampshire Regiment put on a performance at the Laik-ud-Dowla Theatre, India, in February 1916. This performance received glowing reviews in the Indian press, including the *Madras Mail*, the *Daily Post, Bangalore*, the *Madras Times* and the *Southern Indian Observer*.[7]

Many concert parties were established by servicemen with the support and encouragement of their commanders. The Guards Division did not have a divisional concert party, but in 1916, this 'omission' was remedied by the 3rd Battalion, Coldstream Guards who formed a theatrical company called 'The Lilywhites'. The idea for this group appears to have come from men of all ranks in the unit, and was encouraged by their commander, Lieutenant-Colonel R. B. Crawford.[8] The 'Iron Rations' Concert Party & Orchestra of the 71st and 83rd Motor Transport Companies (ASC) was also formed on the initiative of the men. Their 'little show' was formed after a suggestion by Major C. A. Crawley-Boevey, following a 'free and easy sing-song, held one night in the rain at Camps en Amienois, that the column possessed 'sufficient talent' to form the nucleus of an organised group. Volunteers for this purpose were called for and several promptly came forward'. The enterprise was funded by a loan from the Canteen Fund, to be repaid by the profits from performances, which eventually went to make a considerable profit for the unit. The first performance by the 'Iron Rations' was given on a wet and windy evening, on Sunday 22 October 1916, at Woincourt. Adjoining a barn, the stage was made of petrol can cases stacked together, covered with a tarpaulin, and an orchestra 'pit' was dug into ground which proceeded to fill with water. The varied programme was a mixture of comedy and song, concluding with a 'burlesque pantomime' version of *Robinson Crusoe,* for which the music was composed by Private C. 'Titch' Hull, who was 'mercifully, a very competent musician'. The group went on to perform in a range of venues in France and Belgium, including Monchy La Gache, Cayeux, Estree en Chausee, Avroult and Monchain. They sometimes were able to use buildings such as the Casino at Mers-Les-Bains, the town hall at St Pol and the YMCA hut at the Base Hospital in Le Treport. A 'command performance' was given at

Divisional Headquarters, Nobescourt Farm, in front of several members of the High Command, including General Cavanagh of the Cavalry Corps.[9]

In the 'Liverpool Pals', the 17th Battalion of the Kings Regiment, a group formed by Billie Bray performed to the regiment while they were stationed at the Prescot Barracks, at Christmas 1914. This group became known as 'The Optimists' and became the concert party (Figure 10.1).[10] On 28 May 1915, at the camp of the 30th Division at Belton Park, Grantham, it was reported that 'Billy Bray's Boys (of the 17th Service Battalion Liverpool Regiment)' were performing for 'the amusement of the troops'.[11] In June 1915, at a Red Cross fundraising concert, the same ensemble 'brought the house down with a successful military burlesque entitled "Captain's Memoranda"'. This was a parody of military life and, 'to the military it appealed in great style, for it certainly was one of the cleverest skits that they could wish to see, and civilians, too, could not fail to follow the trend of events which led up to a most humorous animation, and an extraordinary climax'.[12] By the spring of 1916, the 17th Service Battalion Liverpool Regiment were on the Western Front. On 1 July 1916, with many other Pals battalions, the unit successfully attacked and held Montaauban with fewer than seventeen casualties. All of the 30th Division's objectives are achieved. In August 1916, at Brigade Headquarters near Abbeville, the commander of the 17th battalion (Stanley) reported 'our entertainers', 'The Optimists', described as 'a sort of Pierrot troup [sic]' would be 'taken over lock, stock and barrel, by the Brigade, instead of their being a battalion show, and that we should have all of the arranging as regards their performances and who they should go and play to. Also, that we should have the transporting of them, and in fact, that they should be attached to Brigade Headquarters.'[13]

Several regimental histories indicate a resentment that the Divisional concert parties 'were for the most part wholly professional' and that 'their members were exclusively employed on concert work'.[14] However, it was a matter of some pride that members of concert parties like the 'Iron Rations' and 'The Optimists' were not excused from any of their military duties. The Guards Division underlined that 'the players in this troupe' were 'men of the battalion' who 'were not struck off the strength' to perform.[15] The Motor Transport Companies (ASC) felt that this fact 'is deserving of record' when the men undertook rehearsals and performances in their own time, 'often at great personal inconvenience' after 'long, tiring days at the wheel of a lorry or at a workshop bench'.[16] In response to resentments of this nature aired at the time, Stanley underlined that of 'The Optimists' it was to be 'clearly understood that . . . when

Figure 10.1 'The Optimists', concert party of the 17th Battalion of the King's Regiment, ('Liverpool Pals'). © Tony Lidington.

the questions came of work of a military nature, they were to take their share just as much as anybody else'. He reported that 'throughout they have done most willingly; in fact, they made it a point of honour that any job they were given to do should be carried out more than well. It did not matter what it was; whether it was the forming of dumps or acting as runners, or innumerable other jobs of that description, they always earned a good name for themselves.'[17]

Second Lieutenant Harper Seed was appointed Officer in Command of the 39th Divisional Concert Party, 'The Tivolies', in December 1916. Seed, from Sheffield, had been a student of the Royal Academy of Music in London when war was declared. He had enlisted with the 17th Battalion (Sherwood Foresters), arriving on the Western Front in September 1916.[18] After fighting on the Somme and at the Battle of the Ancre, the 39th Division moved from the Thiepval area to the French border with Belgium for a period of rest until a few days before Christmas 1916 when they moved to positions by the Ypres canal. It was at this point that a message was sent to all battalions in Seed's division that an officer was wanted to lead the divisional concert party. Seed's commanding officer had been 'very charmed' with Seed's rendering of *Tit Willow* during a sing-song in the mess, and put him forward for the post, which he appeared glad to accept.[19] Lieutenant Seed was kept very busy with his theatrical work. It was his job to maintain the theatre, source costumes and props, manage the publicity and takings, and coordinate the performers' availabilities according to their military duties and casualty rates. In January 1917, he describes his daily schedule as:

Up in the morning 7.30, breakfast 8.15, there indents had to be made for rations, fuel, oil, carbide, coal, nails etc. Rehearsal from 9.00 until 12.30 for a new and original revue . . . I also had to keep an eye on the cleaner at work in the hall and a carpenter who was patching up the proscenium & later making seats. After dinner I had 3 hours shopping – buying ladies blouses, skirts etc (details verboten) also false hair to make up into wigs. Then came tea at 5 oclock [sic] I had to chase men round so that all lights shall be ready & hall attendants at their various posts by 5.25 when doors opened. The performance went on till 8 pm when I had to count up the takings book them & make up accounts for the week [sic]'.[20]

Seed was relieved when the first shows went well as 'the General is pleased & the performers a real good humour [sic]'.[21] Seed was responsible for eighteen men, a number which he expected to grow, and he was in charge of 'pay, discipline, rehearsal, dress & everything else'.[22] The second revue he produced was '*Ave a Drop o' Gin*. Half the performers were professional, but Seed wrote that 'I wish they all were'. His biggest problem was acquiring suitable props, but he was given the use of a car and driver make the forty-kilometre journey to go shopping for items at a 'seaside town'. At this point he admitted that 'time is brief & what I have to spare is taken up with inventing means of improving our show'. Feeling the competition with a neighbouring division with a concert party in town, which had been running for four months, Seed relayed that 'it wants a lot of beating but we are out to *do* it'.[23] At the end of January 1917, Seed observed that he is 'getting away from the practical side of the war to more sordid things such as the musical, & financial'.[24] He is clearly finding his feet as a theatrical impresario:

I suppose I am as new a theatrical manager as anyone in the British Army can be. But as my men are soldiers drawing soldiers' pay & yet set free from the discipline of their Units – and moreover suffering under the delusion that they are indispensable artists, it requires a good deal of manoeuvring to keep all the works in good running order. An artist's temperament is an awful nuisance you know [sic].[25]

Seed relayed that his men are mostly happy and in the habit of having an 'after concert' after the main performance, though he would have preferred that they 'reserve their efforts for the rehearsal tomorrow morning'.[26] In March 1917, the concert party moved with the unit to a nearby camp. They were given a hut which they proceed to fit up as a proper working theatre with a larger stage, proscenium, painted scenery and electric lighting.[27] However, the move resulted in a hiatus which suspended performances and, seemingly as a punishment, Seed was transferred to the post of Divisional Burial Officer.[28]

The Canadian musician Gitz Rice was another officer who found himself taking on the additional important service of organising and performing in stage shows, to entertain his fellow soldiers. Rice met the performer Lieutenant Basil Green, of the 8th Infantry Battalion, Canadian Expeditionary Force, in the course of his concert party work while his unit was at rest near Bailleul in November 1915. As a trained musician, Green had been selected to perform in the Brigade Concert Party, which he did until he returned to front line duty in March 1916. Together, Green and Rice made the Casse D'Epergne at Bailleul into a theatre, sharing it with a cinema and the 3rd Canadian Field Ambulance minstrel show, for which Rice played the piano. Rice later accompanied the Princess Patricia's Canadian Light Infantry Comedy Company, formed in May 1916. Rice and other soldier-entertainers wrote and rehearsed new material during lulls in active duty. It was in this way that, in addition to singing and playing the piano for the concert parties, Rice turned his hand to songwriting. Following the Battle of Somme, Rice created a committee to develop concerts to entertain soldiers. After he was gassed at Vimy Ridge in 1917, Rice returned to Canada to oversee the entertainment of approximately 70,000 troops per week.[29]

Professional performers were eventually enlisted for Divisional Concert parties. In the British Army, for example, 'The Follies' (4th Division), 'The Whizz Bangs' (5th Division), 'The Fancies' (6th Division) and 'The Crumps' were largely made up of professional performers.[30] In the RFC/RNAS, professional musicians who had joined the service established their own troupes. 'The Be(e)s' concert party were all professional musicians, and professional musicians made up the majority of 'The Balloonatics' (Balloons Section) (Figure 10.2), 'The Antiques' (13 Squadron), 'Ye Dud Knights' (101 Squadron) and 'The Hispano Suizas' (56 Squadron). Others, such as 'The Aero Lights' contained airmen who were keen musicians. This group included Lieutenant [later Lord] Rhodes and observer Jack Warner, who had sung semi-professionally in France before the war. Warner was particularly proud of his parody of the song *I Hear You Calling Me* entitled *I Hear You Stalling Me*.[31] RFC/RAF concert parties generally took advantage of their accommodation in hangars or Nissen huts on aerodromes, and Warner recalled that they would often perform for soldiers coming out of the trenches on their way behind the lines.[32] In addition, after 1917, American concert parties would also tour around certain locations, something recalled by the letters of Chaplain Leonard who described an American 'jazz band' performing for one of his squadrons.[33]

Several very well-known entertainers served in the RFC/RAF. Captain Basil Hallam, better known among the troops as 'Gilbert the Filbert', served in No.21 Kite Balloon section, and Sub-Lieutenant David Ivor Davies, better known as Ivor Novello, served in the RNAS and the RNVR. Novello had taken part in the second Lena Ashwell concert tour in the spring of 1915, listed as a tenor. On 18 June 1916, he joined the Royal Naval Air Service (RNAS) training depot at Crystal Palace as a probationary flight sub-lieutenant. Novello continued to write songs while serving in the RNAS. During his training at Chingford he took part in various entertainments on the base, such as 'The Chingford Review' put on by 'The Conspirators' on 4 December 1916. The ensemble was a combination of men from the Royal Navy and RNVR, which included Sub-Lieutenant Davies [Novello].[34] The Revue's original 'Opening Chorus' was composed by Davies, RNVR. It was 'interrupted' by the 'Vicar' (Flight Commander B. Travers, R.N.), 'whose humorous Address was a veritable "scream", its topical allusions being exceptionally clever'. Another favourite of the reviewer 'was "Sunday Afternoon", a tuneful portrayal of the doings of two "Querks" in connection with a lady visitor, and their desertion by the Fair One who seemed to prefer a real flying Staff

Figure 10.2 PC96/269/4: 'The Balloonatics' concert party, RFC. © RAF Museum.

Officer. The Pilot, however, crashes before her eyes, much to the joy of the P.F.O.s who again regain possession of the Fickle One.' There was 'A

Pukka song, sweetly sung by the composer, Ivor Novello, who played his accompaniment, received a well-deserved encore.' Following this, '[a] delightful burlesque on the American and Russian dances was given by Flight Commanders Travers and Irving, who caused great amusement by their antics.' There was also an 'Ape' who 'did some very neat dancing steps, and was quite an acquisition to the number'.[35] Despite the cachet of having Novello in their concert party, his service record shows that by January 1917, he was 'not making satisfactory progress and it is considered that he will not become an efficient Pilot'. His work as an observer was described as 'satisfactory' if only as 'second rate'.[36] By May 1917, he failed to report for duty, and on 4 June, he was hospitalised with neurasthenia with a stay in Haslar Hospital in Gosport.[37] Records show that 'a submission was put forward' that Davies would be discharged from the RNAS and transferred to the RNVR, retaining his rank and uniform but without pay from naval funds.[38] He took up his administrative post Cockspur Street, as a Sub-Lieutenant in the RNVR, in London on 19 June 1917.[39]

The RAMC were musically active wherever they served. On a hospital ship in the Mediterranean, for example, the talent among the medical staff was such that a concert party was formed and took its variety show over to other ships in the vicinity. The padre of the ship recalled that the Matron took a great deal of persuading to sing in front of her colleagues, but that she brought a certain tone to the whole affair and received several encores.[40] In 1916, with a number of 'mental cases' on board among survivors from Kut, the sergeant in charge was in the padre's opinion, 'a very comical bird' and 'the source of much fun'. The sergeant performed several original sketches, including one called *Peace in 1980*. The padre relayed that this skit described a Grandfather telling his grandson how the war had been fought in his day, 1914–16, and made a parody of their present-day arrangements. It was said that 'everybody and everything came under review – O.C.s and sergeant-majors, matrons and sisters, rations and ship-cooks, hospital ships and conscription. Even padres were shown to have improved by 1980!'[41] Fresh material was welcome. The padre related that 'some of us are tiring at being "artistes" ... *Blasé* is the only word to describe our attitude to one another's *repertoires* nowadays.' When he dared to ask the Matron to choose another less-performed song she smartly told him that she had recently sat through another of his old sermons without protest, so he might do the same.[42]

The members of the 85th Field Ambulance (3rd London, 28th Division) acquired a reputation for producing excellent musical entertainments, producing three annual pantomimes.[43] Pantomimes 'were especially popular as entertainment in the armed forces, for reasons which were both psychological and practical'.[44] They were an established feature of civilian life, particularly at Christmastime, and this tradition was continued on the fighting fronts during the Great War. The panto-mime form, with its penchant for comic melodrama and cross-dressing, was a perfect fit for servicemen's entertainment. At Lille, Leslie Henson and Bert Errol led a company of professional performers to give the pantomime *Aladdin*. Chaplain Leonard wrote that 'you wouldn't find a better show in town, and we sat and roared the whole time'.[45] At Christmas 1915, in Salonika, the 85th Field Ambulance put on their production of *Dick Whittington*.[46] On hearing about the production dur-ing a tour of the trenches, Major-General C. J. Briggs, commanding officer of the 28th Division, went to see the performance for himself. He records that he was 'so amused and charmed' that he asked the company to take the piece on a tour of the Division 'so that all the men might have the same pleasure and enjoyment'.[47] It was written by Frank Kenchington who wrote that 'apart from the attentions of the enemy' it was difficult to find a quiet spot in a Balkan camp to work on composition.[48]

In Macedonia at Christmas 1917, the 28th Division put on the third of their annual Christmas productions, *Bluebeard*.[49] The music and lyrics were written by G. G. Horrocks, and original music was com-posed by C. H. B. Jaques. Major-General H. L. Croker of the 28th Division wrote that 'the whole Pantomime Company' had repaid 'the trouble and anxiety that such a theatrical enterprise entails'.[50] *Bluebeard* was performed at the Kopriva Palace Theatre within the range of Turkish guns.[51] The commanding officer, Lieutenant-Colonel R. Henvy, underlined that the production ran for a five-month season and was seen by over 30,000 people, estimated to be 80 per cent of the Division. Henvy also emphasised that members of many units had contributed to the success of the venture, including the Royal Engineers, the ASC, and the EFC. The director was Corporal W. H. Drury and the orchestra was made up of twelve musicians from the 'regimental Bands of the Division' conducted by Private G. Thorne. The pantomime opens at Bluebeard's house, which for this production was based in Salonika. At Christmas 1918, the 52nd Brigade concert party presented their version of *Aladdin*. It was set in the Ypres area with the action taking place between 1914 and 1918 and included two characters, Mick and Muck, who are revealed as German spies. On their re-enactment of the declaration of war, Abanazah becomes a recruiting sergeant, and Aladdin is enlisted, promoted to Captain, and then denounced as a deserter after finding the magic lamp in a German trench near Ypres.[52]

Lieutenant George Miller Johnstone was the Principal of the Birmingham Conservatoire of Music shortly before war was declared.[53] He documented very little detail of the musical life of his wartime experience, but he does however describe the informal ways in which musicians from civilian life were identified by their abilities and then formed performance groups themselves. To celebrate receiving their commissions, Johnstone and his fellow RFC recruits held a concert in the Mess. It was recalled that 'everyone came out of his shell and displayed unsuspected talent'. Excerpts from Grand Opera were given 'by two fellows who had been studying music professionally when war broke out. One of them stilled his audience to a silence that was homage to his art.' The next moment, 'the same audience were all bawling some raucous chorus with equal enjoyment'.[54] In some units, however, there was an understandable reluctance to take on extra, non-military duties of this kind, particularly where there was a lack of will or talent among the ranks. In some cases, however, this was done begrudgingly and treated as another duty to be fulfilled.[55] Certainly, by August 1916 on Malta, Corporal Johnson William Double wrote that after another performance he was 'absolutely fed up with concerts, it is a bit too thick, never know where to get new stuff to put on'.[56] Double and his orchestra at Ghain Tuffieha convalescent camp were giving concerts outside the British military headquarters at Vallarta to crowds of approximately 2,000 troops most days of the week. In addition, they had two practice sessions every day except Saturday, and played at two church parades every Sunday. He was still officially classed as a convalescent, and unfit for duty, but his diary shows he was constantly being asked to play by the YMCA and Church Army, plus private engagements for officers.

Chaplains, particularly those who were of a similar age to the men under their care, quickly became aware that with no fixed programme of work they had to develop their own schedules and methods of connection. Wesleyan chaplain the Reverend Herbert Cowl learned that 'his full concentration needed to be focused not only on the spiritual, moral and mental, but also the physical and medical needs of the men he was assigned to serve'. Cowl's unit saw its first action in the trenches at Laventie from the middle of September 1915. Like so many other Army Chaplains, 'he would discover that his work would become critical in maintaining a high level of general morale within the Army'. On 19 October 1915, Cowl wrote to his parents that he was 'beginning to find my feet and to get the measure of my opportunity, which is a great comfort to me. I don't mind anything so long as I can "get busy" for the Great Master. Short of that, I'm miserable.'[57] Chaplains were often tasked with getting a unit's concert party off the ground. This became a cause for concern among the Army Chaplaincy Department. In his 1918 publication *Tips for Padres: A Handbook for Chaplains,* Everard Digby emphasised that chaplains were attached officers not under direct command. In this regard he advised that chaplains should not get too involved in the administration of recreational work:

If you are really good at any sport, play for the Battalion team, but don't take on committee work, and never be the secretary. Certainly sing at the concerts, if you can sing well, but don't be responsible for the entertainments. It is not your job; you are not 'the only man with nothing to do in the Battalion,' although the Commanding Officer may think so, and you have not the time for these things, unless your work is to be neglected.[58]

The boxing, rugby-playing, concert-cinema-organiser Chaplain Patrick Leonard could well have been used by Digby as a prime example of everything a chaplain should have avoided. Leonard was Anglican chaplain to the King's Own from the winter of 1914, serving in and around the trenches of Flanders and Picardy before he was one of four chaplains posted to the Royal Flying Corps in November 1917. Leonard wrote to his parents that on active service the chaplain is 'a jack of all trades, and has a finger in every pie'. He described how he ran the mess, censored letters, organised concerts and sports matches. He maintained that most chaplains had a similar experience. It was 'not that we have any more experience or skill than anyone else, but simply that we have, or are supposed to have, more time'.[59] Leonard recognised that the men needed diversion. On 1 November 1915, while the Kings Own were resting behind the lines, he wrote that he was going 'to try and get up a concert for the Battalion tomorrow night. Poor boys, they have nothing to do here except sit in their barns and gamble.'[60] Periods described as 'rest' were anything but, and Leonard asserted that 'there isn't a single man who wouldn't rather remain where he is than go back for a month's constant fatigues and parades. It's like exchanging the freedom of Oxford for the restraint and discipline of school.' He did however say that 'it will be a relief not to hear a gun for four solid weeks'.[61]

Despite some post-war protestations to the contrary, members of the High Command were not left without entertainments. Near General Headquarters in Montreuil, there was a theatre which was 'usually given up to cinema shows but occasionally visited by the variety companies which were organised for the amusement of the troops'. It was said to have been well patronised on special occasions.[62] Key ports such as Le Havre and St Omer offered theatre buildings in which concert parties could perform. Towns through which servicemen moved up to forward positions, such as Bethune and Armentieres, were home to more makeshift entertainment facilities in tents and barns, often supported by one of the voluntary-aid organisations. Poperinghe was a key location for servicemen's recreation, including music, cinema, food, drink and shopping. Chaplain Noel Mellish recalled that it was 'a pleasant place for officers and men with restaurants where you could have good dinners with plenty of champagne'.[63] Although the town was well within firing range Poperinghe afforded a very welcome change from the trenches. It had a cinema and a theatre run by the 6th Division, and it was also the location for 'Toc.H.', the everyman's club established by Reverend 'Tubby' Clayton.

While the Guards were in the area of the Second Army, encamped around the town of Poperinghe, they were able to further develop their provisions for entertainments. Their history records that they acquired a large hall near the railway station and converted it into a theatre capable of accommodating 1,000 people. The divisional staff installed a cinema and a canteen was established. Entertainments lasting from 2.30 pm to 6.30 pm were given every day and the hall was invariably crowded. It is underlined that it was 'an enormous boon to all ranks when they came out of the mud and squalor of the trenches to be able to go to a place in which they could find rest and refreshment, listen to good music and witness a show which was both instructive and amusing'. In addition to the cinema entertainment, the bands of the various Guards regiments, which came out in turn to France, gave many excellent concerts. Bandmaster Rogan of the Coldstream Guards added to these concerts by bringing with him a giant gramophone with a trumpet attachment which enabled songs by Melba, Caruso, Clara Butt and others to be heard all over the Hall.[64] In December 1915, on a visit to Poperinghe, Leonard went to see the 6th Division's concert party, the 'Fancies':

The party consists of five officers, one private and two Flemish girls called Vaseline and Glycerine who sing English songs in broken English.... They made me howl with laughter.... The hall is a big showroom, I think, lighted by acetylene motor lamps – for gas and electric light is cut off so near the front. The stage effect is splendid all homemade so to speak. The first half of the programme is a pierrot entertainment, the stage & hangings all jet black, the pierrots in white and black, the stools on which they sit black and white check – very striking and novel, and the singing and fooling absolutely first rate. The second half of the show is a sort of revue, screamingly funny and very topical.... It is quite the best two francs' worth I've ever had.[65]

Leonard was inspired. He returned to his battalion and arranged their first concert party which was described as 'a strange event' because he could not obtain a piano. However, 'the performers didn't seem to mind the absence of an accompaniment but warbled away sweetly and keeping the time extraordinary successfully'. Leonard relayed that 'Tommy loves his emotions to be tickled.' He wrote that there are 'only two kinds of songs Tommy likes, the sentimental type of thing which tells of the white-haired mother and her darling child, sitting by the fire or starving in the attic, and the vulgar comic'. He advised that 'whether its sentimentality or vulgarity it's got to be laid on thick, and the thicker it is the more Tommy enjoys himself'.[66] Leonard builds on this initial success and at the end of January 1916, he is busy organising more concerts alongside the battalion's coffee bar, which he also runs.[67] By February 1916, Leonard was acting as President of Regimental Institutes – handling money for services, as well as overseeing the catering and menu plans of the officer's mess. He commented that '[s]o far from being a spiritual pastor, it seems I am being initiated into the mysteries of commerce. When the war is over, what I won't know about feeding and lubricating a Battalion won't be worth knowing.'[68]

Leonard also secured the services of the Mudlarks, their 'Divisional pierrot party'. Leonard recalled that it took 'a good deal of blarney to persuade them to leave their comfortable billets for the rough accommodation of our hut, and I had to tell them the tale of how when the prophet was unable to go to the mountain, the mountain was patriotic enough to come to the prophet'. All the members of the Mudlarks were professional entertainers, and Leonard relayed that the men enjoyed 'perfect feats of wit and pathos, sentiment and humour, all neatly set to music, to say nothing of sleight of hand, for among the artists was a first rate card manipulator who performed prodigies of magic with hard-boiled eggs and silk handkerchiefs and tissue paper'. At the end of the show, Leonard 'doled out the usual tea and rum'. He proposed three cheers for the Mudlarks, 'and sent all home with an inward glow of satisfaction and contentment, which I am sure was worth untold reinforcements in the trenches next day'.[69] Chaplain Mellish believed that 'this kind of relaxation, with baths and clean clothes, made it possible for men to carry on and keep their splendid cheerfulness'[70] On returning from an assault on the 'Bluff' by the Ypres-Comines canal in March 1916, Leonard wrote that the men had 'have been through the furnace of affliction ... seen sights which we would fain forget [and] lost many good men and true'. The men had lived in a 'world of blood and fire, and now we come back here ... to recover from a mental and spiritual bruising and pick up again the old threads of peaceful trench life and weekly concerts and coffee bars and all the other adjuncts of normal existences out here'.[71]

In the weeks immediately after Easter 1916, Leonard took advantage of a spell of good weather to arrange an open-air concert. He found 'a field which forms a natural amphitheatre – a nice semi-circular grassy slope on which the Battalion will recline at ease, while the piano and performers will be mounted on a wagon drawn up in the middle'.[72] To decide on the cast for the performance, Leonard held auditions. He recalled how he 'waded through a great host of would be vocalists'. He found that it was 'extraordinary how many men fancy themselves as sentimental singers, and I am afraid there was a good deal of heart burning among the unsuccessful applicants for a place in the programme'.[73] Later in the week they had 'a great Brigade entertainment in the cinema hall' which was also being used as a dormitory by the RFC. They had the Divisional band, a concert party, and some 'very spirited boxing jumbled together to entertain the assembled generals and privates. All the big bugs were there in their scarlet and gold, and as many men as could be packed into the rather limited space.'[74] Not long after his transfer to the RFC in November 1917, Leonard was 'roped in' as the house manager of the concert party of 7 Squadron. Known as 'The Joysticks', Leonard was responsible for advertising and the selling of tickets. The best groups of performers were highly sought after, and there was a good deal of cross-fertilisation between concert party troupes and between those in the Army and the RFC. In December 1917, on attachment to four RFC squadrons, Chaplain Leonard detailed going into Poperinghe 'to get some hints' for his squadron's troupe: 'This particular Divisional group does an excellent Revue in a barn near the station. The station is the target of the Bosch [sic] gunners and Bosch airmen, so our pleasure was punctuated by "wind up" every time a "bonk" sounded particularly near. The next day I arranged for the concert party . . . to give a performance to one of my outlying squadrons.'[75]

By Christmas 1917, after the attack on Cambrai, Mellish recalled that 'everyone was tired and there was a feeling of depression all over us. . . . we sang some Carols in the evening, but without enthusiasm – "See amid the Winter's snow" was too real to sing about it.'[76] To lighten this atmosphere, during the unit's Christmas dinners and entertainments near Arras, their concert troupe debuted – the 'Elegant Extracts' under the supervision of Major Winnington Barnes, who was 'a soldier of fortune, amazing good company and very popular'. Mellish first met him 'swinging down through the Menin Gate on my return to the battalion, his jovial face beaming with a smile which almost engulfed one'. Barnes 'had great histrionic talent' and under his and the Padre's tuition 'the company was very successful'.[77] Mellish recounted that the star turn was 'Doris the girl, (not according to the flesh). He (or she) cultivated the part with such success that even on parade as a Lewis Gunner he was sometimes known to blush and pout and when suitably made up he was really charming.'[78] He also remembered that 'Curly' was another talented member of the troupe who in civilian life had worked as a boxing partner in the East End. However, former taxi driver Miller 'was the most valuable of all because he could always make his audience rock with laughter simply by looking at it'. Mellish described him as 'a little man, with a lean, sad face ... he would have made a good understudy for Charlie Chaplin'.[79]

Finding facilities for concerts was a challenge. In the rural areas of France and Belgium a barn could be found and made suitable, particularly if a unit was already in possession of the building. Leonard recalled that one of the companies in the Kings Own was billeted in a large straw thatched barn which he thought would 'do quite admirably'. The only stipulation the company made was that Leonard's unit had to provide new straw after the concert. There was no seating accommodation. Leonard outlined that 'the audience will have to sit on the floor like tailors, with nothing but a few whisps of straw between their trousers and the cold hard beaten earth'.[80] Chaplain Mellish described a similar situation while his battalion was resting behind the lines. Underlining the importance of 'quiet and calm after the incessant noise and strain of the front', a local priest gave Mellish's unit the use of a schoolroom where they could hold services in the morning, reading and writing in the afternoon, and concerts in the evening on rotation by different regiments of the brigade.[81] As would be expected in war zones, the makeshift theatres created by the concert parties were often damaged. In January 1917, for example, while the 30th Division were at Halloy for a month's training, their theatre – 'an old barn with a bit of stage and forms in it' caught fire. 'The Optimists' lost theatrical props, scenery, costumes and their recently purchased piano. However, 'thanks to their excellence, [the] "Optimists" were able to get engagements up and down the line, and within a short time were able to make enough money to wipe out that loss'.[82] In April 1918, the unit was stationed at Villers-St Christophe. They were expecting the Germans to attack at any time, but they were determined to give a dinner party with 'The Optimists' to follow, 'intending to have a real good evening, even if the Boche attacked next day'. On 20 April, they had their dinner party. Stanley recalled that it was 'a most cheery evening, and all of us laughed a great deal, being under no false illusions as to what we were in for the next day ... "The Optimists" were in their best form, and we kept it up till about 12 o'clock', shortly before the Germans opened their bombardment that evening.[83] On the afternoon of 29 April, at Estrees (HQ), 'The Optimists' gave an outdoor concert 'in their ordinary, and very mud-stained, clothes. All their kit and "properties" had been lost and fallen into the hands of the Boche at Esmery Hallon.' The concert was a great success, both with British and French troops, 'who poured into the village. In the middle of the concert the "Alerte" were sounded for the French, and off they went. All sorts of vague rumours were flying about, but one thing was certain, which was that the Boche had got into Braches.'[84]

The Grand Fleet had its own recreational spaces, primary among them being the SS *Gourko*. The sister vessel of the canteen ship SS *Borodino*, the *Gourko* was a 'Theatre Ship' with 'her 'tween deck and for'ard utilised for that purpose'.[85] Based at Scapa Flow and around the North Sea, it was said that '[m]any excellent shows have been given by ships' companies, for the benefit of the entire Fleet ... performances that would have done credit to many a London house'. One performance by the crew of HMS *Iron Duke* was recalled as particularly good, and that 'one would never have dreamt the "ladies" on stage were in reality the "snotties" from the flagship!' It was said that Admiral Jellicoe 'kept coming in and out quietly' to check for urgent messages 'apparently enjoying the play before him'.[86] The canteen ship SS *Borodino* had a piano in its lounge, and the crew maintained its own concert party.[87] Indeed, when the *Borodino* went alongside a ship the men would come aboard and avail themselves of the facilities, with many making straight for the piano. The crew of HMS *Benbow* developed a reputation on the *Borodino* for being particularly quick to gather around the piano to sing 'all the latest music hall songs'.[88]

When out on operations, it was a commonly held belief that sailors had 'far fewer chances of recreation and entertainment'.[89] However, the men of the Royal Navy were just as keen and competent as their land-based comrades in providing for their own amusements. In the years immediately before the Great War, it was said that Jack Tar 'lives hard, works hard, but instead of bemoaning his fate, his rollicking, devil-may-care good humour, is ever at the surface waiting for an outlet'.[90] Sailors loved to dance: 'Perhaps of all Jack's forms of amusement none is so popular as dancing, his favourite dance being a waltz; and no sooner is music of this sort struck up than each side of the fo'castle is cleared, men choose their partners, and round and round they go with an energy that seems untiring'.[91] However, sailors would never perform the sailor's hornpipe while afloat: 'step dancing of any description is rarely seen on board our ships of war, for Jack reserves all his efforts in this direction until he gets on shore, where, mounted on a stage in some "sing-song" house, he is willing to entertain the audience until sheer exhaustion induces him to cry halt'.[92] The absence of women on board was no impediment. In September 1916, an officer serving on HMS *Agamemnon* in the Mediterranean wrote to his mother that 'the wardroom had a kind of impromptu dance, but there weren't enough ladies to go round. So we danced with each other.'[93] Marine bands generally produced the orchestra for ships' concerts and the bandmaster often produced the whole show. This included panto-mimes at Christmas, occasional musical comedies and frequent concerts. Bandsman A. C. Green achieved such fame with a series of shows that word reached the RNSM Director of Music who wrote to congratulate him: 'Such performances do credit to this Institution and do a great deal of good. Given the same numbers our bands can compare favourably with the Divisional Marines Bands, a fact that wants to be known and this is the way to do it.'[94] Many of the Royal Navy's commanding officers took a great interest in the musical lives of their ships. All Naval Officers who had been to the colleges at Dartmouth or Osborne were, for example, 'well acquainted' with the operas of Gilbert and Sullivan as these produc-tions would take place at the end of term. This was of particular interest to the commanding officer of HMS *Donegal*, Captain Warren Hastings Doyly, the brother of the owner of the Doyly-Carte Opera Company who specialised in Gilbert and Sullivan operas. Marine Bandsman Reed recalled that during practice hours 'the Captain would come to our room and describe each song and the way it should be played or sung. ... "Ruddigore", was not in our library, he at once sent off for the full score. Naturally, one of these selections were included in our programme for dinner, when we played for Ward-Room or Gun-Room Officers'.[95]

The Navy had their own concert party troupes; for example, on board the aircraft carrier HMS *Vindex*. While the nature of the land-based war meant that the British Army had to expand substantially during the war, creating many new battalions of civilian-soldiers, the Royal Navy did not undergo such a dramatic expansion in its forces. The ship, as the naval equivalent of a battalion, is at its basic level one self-contained unit of men who remain serving together on board. Each ship would generally have its own concert party and perhaps a Royal Marines Band, thereby following a long-standing tradition of self-made entertainment. While the Navy very much enjoyed seeing the professional concert parties, they were by no means starved of music or entertainment of various kinds. Indeed, 'Music making of one form or another has always been an integral part of the official and social life of the Navy.'[96] Smoking concerts were as popular with the sailors as the soldiers. In March 1915, the Chatham Battalion on Special Service at sea 'rendered great assistance in supplying the things necessary for the comfort of the artistes and audience ... the various turns were highly appreciated'. This included songs, a 'Comic Yarn', recitations, 'Exhibition in Weight-Lifting' and a musical selection by the subaltern officers.[97] Instruments were also found on board. When

an officer moved from HMS *Lion*, commanded by Vice-Admiral Sir
David Beatty, to HMS *Cumberland*, the ship's magazine published
a humorous poem 'Noisy', alluding to his 'boisterous, cyclonic' nature:
'Surely you must regret the pianola,/That placid beast of burden for the
feet,/Which you have driven like a Brooklands racer,/Until at last it
couldn't even bleat.'[98]

In January 1916, the officers of HMS *Lion* produced a revue called 'All
Bosch'. It was the subject of 'considerable rehearsal' and was performed
on at least two occasions to 'a very crowded house'. Lieutenant Chalmers
acted as manager, and the whole company put on a 'quite exceptional
performance, which went through without a hitch in spite of the difficulties involved by a 40-knot gale'. The ship's company 'showed, by their
generous applause, that they enjoyed every minute of it'.[99] The vessel's
magazine, *Searchlight*, outlined that the production of a revue, as opposed
to 'a time-honoured Sing-Song' appeared to be impossible. However, the
idea was popular, and two officers, Chalmers and Burghersh, 'decided
that the various obstacles could be surmounted, and undertook the
proposition'. The dialogue was composed by several officers, and the
musical setting was arranged by Mr P. J. Whelan. The scenery was
painted by Gunner Glendinning RMA 'whose fine artistic work added
greatly to the finished appearance of the stage'. Stage and props built by
Mr Dailey and his staff. The first performance was given before 'a distinguished audience, consisting of the Vice-Admiral [Beatty], Flag
Officers, Captains, and Officers of the ships present'. The performance
opened with the chorus, *Here We Are Again*. 'The Beauty Chorus' comprised a number of officers dressed in 'the highest traditions of the
theatre' who 'danced and sang charmingly'. Various comical scenes
followed, including one which 'brought us "Home Again" with a vivid
touch of reality. To see the bluejacket "on leaf" (Selby), revived memories
of Pompey in those halcyon days of peace in no uncertain manner.' An
ensemble sang *Four Jolly Sailormen* 'in a seamanlike manner', and a skit
'On the Music Hall Stage, 1900 AD' featured 'Rebecca, the showman's
daughter (Payne), [whose] pink dress and flaming hair produced quite
a sensational thrill throughout the audience'. Officers Haines and
Alderson played the part of the pantomime horse 'with skill and pluck'.
A parody called 'The German Submarine U 19' had a 'stage effect worthy
of Drury Lane' and featured officers appearing as Von Tirpitz and two
scared German sailors. A burlesque on a cinema play featured a chase
scene 'in which the majority of the entire company took part in their
efforts to get to grips with the villain'. Three popular songs, with choruses,
formed 'a sparkling finale to the Revue'. In reviewing the production *All
Bosch* 'it would be ungenerous to describe it as merely successful. The

Revue was more than that. It was, in fact, in its own particular way, a triumph for the whole company.'[100]

Many servicemen appreciated the playing of classical music, and the lilting melodies of traditional folk songs, but the majority of those serving in the forces found significant emotional and physical release in belting out the more bawdy popular tunes in the company of their fellow men. This was recognised by the touring professionals:

Tommy is still more at home in the free and easy sing-song which is peculiarly his own ... Talent is always available, since all classes are in the ranks, and a packed house is invariably the rule ... For many days the artistes are in serious training, and patriotic songs are utterly taboo ... so sentiment and fun have full sway ... stalls are borrowed chairs, and are usually reserved for the officers ... The place is full of smoke and smiles. Here are hundreds of men who have faced death to-day, and will do the same tomorrow. Many present will never raise a chorus again! A giant of wag is giving 'I'm a Navvy Working on the Line' ... An Irish Fusilier ... sings 'My Prarie Mary' with droll interpolations of his own, and an orchestra of thirty mouth-organs to support him. 'My Home in Dixie', 'A Ragtime Christening' and 'The Little Grey Home in the West' succeed each other, and set the house rocking with sheer emotional joy.[101]

When the performer Julius Harrison toured British bases around the coast of Normandy with a Lena Ashwell concert party in May 1917, he was struck by the enthusiasm the British servicemen had for ensemble singing. He spoke of the 'intoxicating champagne of chorus-songs'. In the singing of songs such as *Here We Are Again!* and *Are We Downhearted?*, 'Beethoven, Brahms and Wagner were all forgotten ... there was real genius in these despised rag-times. Could you but hear those music-starved men shouting out these songs with full lung-power.' The ragtime songs 'seem to quicken the pulse of the soldier in an extraordinary way ... to be the external expression of his whole emotional being'.[102]

On the island of Malta in 1916, Corporal Johnson William Double was regularly called to play for the sergeants' and officers' messes. On 20 March, his diary records that he 'played for a concert in No.2 Sgts. Mess ... Some very good turns resulted. I don't know how these chaps get to know the good ones but they fine 'em somehow.'[103] Four days later, he played in the sergeants' mess again, and there their favourite songs were the *Bedouin Love Song* and *If Those Lips Could Only Speak!*[104] On Sunday 29 October, after the morning church service in which he accompanied the hymns, Double and his band colleagues were taken to St Pauls Island for the entertainment of Officers and their ladies at a picnic. He appears to have enjoyed the excursion: 'You can bet we had a good time an although we had a fair amount of work to do we managed to enjoy ourselves ... We arrived in camp about 7.30 having been on the go since breakfast time, except when stopping for meals. Therefore think our 1/- was well earned today.'[105] Double, like many soldiers, especially those with musical training, were very discerning about the concert parties in which he performed or which he heard. On 7 April 1916, he attended a concert given by a troupe called 'The Strafers'. Double commented that 'they were however no better received than our own chaps, even if so well, which is doubtful. There were only two good artists among them.'[106]

Servicemen were always a very honest audience, particularly when the performers were their own comrades rather than a touring group of professionals. On 18 April, Double and his colleagues gave 'a splendid concert in the tent this evening. 16 items which were all well received, only had one artist make an ass of himself and he was an ass and no mistake. The fellows began blowing a whistle at the back causing roars of laughter.'[107] As he was based on Malta, Double attended several naval concert parties. Of the performance given by the men of HMS *Harrier* on 25 October, Double thought they were '[a] somewhat weak company compared to ours'.[108] At Christmas 1917, on the Western Front, the men of the RFC issued 'a snowball barrage' to acts they did not like. Chaplain Leonard relayed that this method 'of giving a performer to understand you don't like him and wish to discourage him from staying longer is extremely efficacious, but somewhat detrimental to the scenery'.[109] Servicemen's concert parties could be raucous occasions. In a squadron based in the Middle East, an RFC concert party utilised many of the features seen in the ensembles of the Army and Navy. The Flight Sergeant 'surprised everyone with his excellent singing and imitations of Harry Lauder', the orchestra was 'quite as good as the best London Theatre Orchestra':

The *piece de resistance* was a surprise, especially in a place where there were no women: you may guess our astonishment when a fresh, handsome young English girl appeared, dressed beautifully in an all-white creation, with a bunch of red roses at her breast. She looked a picture in the lime-light, with her beautiful auburn hair and fresh pink and white complexion, and when she walked on everyone gasped with astonishment and commenced whispering 'Where did they find the "Bird"?' The Staff in the front row perked up to a man and recovering from their initial surprise, led the welcoming applause to which she responded with a full curtsey.

She was a great Artist and stilled and enthralled her audience, singing beautifully in a sympathetic, rich contralto. In response to vociferous applause she had an encore, which brought down the house: this she followed with a vigorous rendering of 'For We Don't Want to Lose You'.

While acknowledging her final ovation, she put her hand down the front of her dress and removed one of her chest rotundities ... a small orange, which she proceeded to eat, as laconically, swinging wig in one hand s(he) walked off the stage ... The uproar lasted nearly lasted five minutes and spoiled the next turn, which had to be curtained and re-commenced. He was an inimitable past master of female impersonation: his entire make-up was perfect. He had obtained his dress from a first-class French shop in Alexandria and his wig ... came from the Opera House, Cairo. Altogether he was a stunning success.[110]

Many commanding officers of the RFC/RAF were adept at organising their unit's musical activities (Figure 10.3). Cecil Lewis recalled that Major Richard Bloomfield, who served as one of the early commanding officers of 56 Squadron, was a firm believer in the importance of music to keep up the spirit of his men. Lewis wrote that '[t]o keep fighting pilots on their toes there must be an A1 morale. For this there was nothing like music; the squadron must have its own band. The Major got scouts out round the depots, and whenever a saxophone player or a violinist turned up, he swapped one of his own men of equal rating for the man who was a musician as well. A sergeant who had been a theatre-orchestra conductor was put in charge, and later, in France, whenever things were not quite as bright as they might be, out came the squadron band.'[111] As well as the best orchestra, the star members of 56 Squadron had musical leanings too. William Fry, who had served in 11 Squadron with Captain Albert Ball, recalled that the famous fighting 'ace' was: '[w]ithdrawn and not sociable in the Mess he would escape to his hut as soon as he could, where he could be heard sometime practicing his violin. He always played his piece in Squadron concerts ... the old stand-by "Humouresque".'[112] Ball's colleague in 56 Squadron, James McCudden, had joined the Royal Engineers as a bugler before transferring to the RFC. McCudden was particularly fond of musical theatre and like many servicemen, when he was able, he frequented the shows in London's West End such as *Chu Chin Chow*, *Maid of the Mountains* and *The Bing Boys Are Here*. McCudden would buy the sheet music for the shows' main numbers and take them home for his sister Mary to play on the piano.[113]

In April 1918, a troupe of Chinese Labourers gave a concert in one of the aerodromes. Chaplain Leonard did not appear to enjoy it, saying that '[a]s a show it was priceless and cause howls of suppressed laughter. Ever since everybody has been rehearsing a "Chinese concert" for the next Mark 1 Binge'.[114] On the same day, a Belgian regimental string band gave a concert 'in the spare hangar and wonderfully fine it was. ... The Belgian may have his drawbacks but he certainly can play.'[115] Even better, in Leonard's opinion, was the concert party formed of 'Yanks from the American division in the neighbourhood'. Leonard described that it was 'the most refreshing show [he'd] seen from many a long day – all the performers were professionals and really excellent'. The accompaniment

Figure 10.3 RFC/RAF concert party members, RAF Museum.

was supplied by 'a small orchestra, a fiddle, a piano, a banjo and a ukulele … and the noise they made was remarkable … especially when they played typical American ragtimes. Then the banjo and ukulele got intoxicated with their own music, and carried the audience away to the limit of enthusiasm.' The show was of 'the usual song, dance and recitation variety, and yet "usual" is the one word which couldn't be applied to it [because] from start to finish it was absolutely original and unusual'. The first item was a dance, '*a pas de seul*', by 'an accomplished tango expert'. This was followed by 'a fellow who told stories in a typically American way'. Their female impersonator was 'perfect, and so on – and nobody ever sang more than one verse of the song, or worried the audience to sing the chorus against their will'.[116]

After their wartime service, it would be the choruses of the song servicemen sung on the fighting fronts which would be imprinted on their memories. Furthermore, the singing of wartime songs and regimental tunes would form an important part of the veterans' own rituals around reunions and remembrance practices. The melodies of 1914–18 would also be preferred by the next generation as they fought the war that those who lived and lost through the Great War had hoped would never happen. The music did not stop after the Armistice.

11 After the Armistice

At Menin, on 10 November 1918, Chaplain Leonard and the officers of 7 Squadron had dinner in a former German Flying Corps mess. The room was decorated with a German flying song 'which the Bosch had painted on the wall over the mantelpiece. It was the usual hot air about fearing neither death nor foe; and how when the wind did not blow that was the time they particularly liked to cleave the air with their wings.'[1] The next morning, the guns were silenced by the signing of the Armistice. However, music continued to be important to the British armed forces in the post-war period as millions of military personnel moved into Germany as the Army of Occupation, and fighting continued in the East. The voluntary-aid organisations found themselves stretched as they accompanied the troops into Germany, expanded their provision to German prisoners of war, and continued to provide services for servicemen, including Chinese and Indian labourers, who were engaged in the clearing of the battlefields and digging of graves creating the 'concentration' cemeteries we see today. These agencies also played significant roles in helping care for returning prisoners of war and demobilised soldiers, many of whom were dissatisfied with the slow process of demobilisation, in addition to their disappointing prospects regarding employment and welfare. The work of Basil Dean in the British military camps at home, combined with the obvious benefit of civilian performers such as Seymour Hicks, Ellaline Terriss, Lena Ashwell and Harry Lauder, would develop in 1939 into ENSA.[2] However, the Navy and Army Canteen Board (NACB) – which would later become the Navy Army Air Force Institute (NAAFI) – made no attempt to integrate the work of other organisations which had provided indispensable canteen and recreational services on the fighting fronts.[3]

The tenor of the first post-war Christmas was said to have been celebratory. The Gramophone Company believed that '[t]he world had changed indeed; with it, public taste … Nostalgia with a jazz flavour took over from flag-waving and drum-beating'.[4] However, the final human cost of the war was being counted. The voluntary-aid organisations which had done so much to support Britain's armed forces were not immune from this loss. Two workers with the Church Army, James Kershaw and F. B. Leighton, were killed during 1917. They are both buried in Commonwealth War Graves cemeteries; Kershaw in Noex-Les-Mines near Arras, and Leighton in St Sever, Rouen. The Salvation Army lost five of their officers in France, not including the thousands of their members who had enlisted to serve in the forces. Thirty-eight YMCA workers died as a result of their war service with the organisation. After fighting in the Boer War, losing his two brothers and spending over a year playing music on Malta, Corporal Johnson William Double was killed at Passchendaele on 22 August 1917. Double's body was never found, and he is commemorated at Tyne Cot Cemetery.[5] Second Lieutenant Harper Seed, manager of 'The Tivolies' concert party, was killed by a sniper on 20 September 1917, during an advance at Zillebeke at the Battle of the Menin Road Bridge.[6] He is buried in Duhallow ADS Cemetery, and commemorated on the war memorial of the Royal Academy of Music. Captain Basil Hallam Radford, known as 'Gilbert the Filbert', died when he fell from an observation balloon near Calais on 20 August 1916, and is buried at Couin British Cemetery.[7] Lieutenant George Butterworth was killed on 5 August 1916, at the battle of the Somme. He is commemorated on the memorial to the missing at Thiepval, and on the war memorial at the Royal College of Music. The deaths did not stop after the guns were silenced. Two performers with a Lena Ashwell-YMCA concert party, Emily Pickford and Frederick Taylor, drowned in the Somme as a result of a car accident returning from a concert in Guoy on 7 February 1919. They are buried in the Abbeville Extension Cemetery.

Of the approximately 5,000 chaplains who served with the British armed forces in the Great War, 179 died in the course of their duties.[8] After being severely injured by a shell near Armentières in 1915, the Reverend Herbert Butler Cowl survived the torpedoing of the hospital ship *Anglia*, and as a result of his actions that day he was the first Wesleyan Army chaplain to receive the Military Cross for exemplary gallantry. In August 1916, Cowl was reassigned to the Portsmouth Garrison where he led services in the King's Theatre at Southsea and survived the war.[9] Chaplains Julian Bickersteth, Pat Leonard and Noel Mellish returned home to their parishes. Leonard continued to work with 'Tubby' Clayton for Talbot House. Bandsman Victor Shawyer of the Rifle Brigade was injured by a sniper, evacuated to Southampton and survived the war. Marine Bandsman Herbert Reed also survived and continued to serve with the Royal Marines Band Service. Harry Lauder was knighted for his wartime efforts in 1919, performing through the interwar period, and worked with ENSA in the Second World War. Seymour Hicks was twice awarded the *Croix de Guerre* for his work entertaining the troops in both world wars, and he was knighted in 1934. Ellaline Terriss continued to appear on the stage and in British films, and with Hicks she went to the Middle East with ENSA to perform for troops in the Second World War. After touring with the second Lena Ashwell-YMCA concert party in 1915, Ivor Novello enlisted in the RNAS before his transfer to the RNVR. He became internationally celebrated for his appearances in popular films and for his work in British musical theatre. His song *We'll Gather Lilacs*, composed during the Second World War, never attained the popularity of *Keep the Home Fires Burning*, which was widely sung in Britain's second total war. Former PoWs who survived internment returned home. After their attempted escape from Holzminden PoW camp in July 1918, Jack Shaw and James Whale rejoined civilian life, with Whale going on to become a leading film director in Hollywood. A fictionalised treatment of the tunnel escape from Holzminden was filmed as *Who Goes Next?* (1938), directed by Maurice Elvey and starring Barry K. Barnes.

Folk dance instructor Daisy Daking travelled with twelve of her team with the Army of Occupation, with whom she worked for two years before the YMCA ran out of funds.[10] The YMCA discussed giving up their residency at Ciro's on the signing of the Armistice. However, as the club had been an 'outstanding success' they looked for new premises to continue what they had started at the club.[11] By February 1919, the YMCA was discussing the possibility of renting Ciro's to continue the concert parties which had been so well received on the Western Front.[12] Music became a staple feature of the physical, mental and emotional rehabilitation of returning servicemen. Indeed, the American YMCA performer Paula Lind Ayers became known as 'the girl who sang away shellshock'.[13] In Britain, charitable funds were established to provide musical instruction and instruments to patients; for example, at the Star and Garter Hospital in 1919, for soldiers whose spinal injuries resulted in paralysis below the waist to play violins, 'cellos and banjos.[14] Lieutenant-Colonel Sir Frederick Mott donated a piano to the Maudsley Hospital and, as a founder member of the Society of English Singers, argued that choral singing would 'prove for convalescent soldiers an uplifting mental diversion, which by promoting cheerfulness and healthy recreation could not fail to beget that sense of well-being so essential for mental and bodily recuperation'.[15] In 1919, Mott published *Treatment by Speech and Song*, a post-war continuation of work he had published in 1909.[16] The two main areas Mott described were '[v]oice production as a general hygienic measure to promote convalescence and recovery of invalid and disabled soldiers', and 'the restoration and re-education of soldiers suffering with shell shock or war neuroses, in whom mutism, aphonia, stammering, stuttering, and speech defects are prominent symptoms'.[17] Part-singing was deemed to be particularly effective in servicemen's recovery. Mott believed that 'the singing classes do more than help stammers, they improve the sense of well-being and promote an atmosphere of cure in hospital'. Concerts held by the men were encouraged and, continuing what he had started with the NMMU, Mott promised to give a cup for the best performance by a hospital department.[18] Inspired by this work, a Vocal Therapy Fund was established by Lady Canarvon and supported by Henry Balfour, to raise money for vocal teachers to continue working with patients and convalescents. This would be one of many post-war initiatives to raise money for the rehabilitation of wounded veterans. A Decca gramophone record was recorded by men from the Queen Mary's Hospital for Limbless Men in Roehampton; entitled *The Supreme Sacrifice*, it was recorded at a concert given under the auspices of the Stock Exchange War Wounded Entertainment Fund.[19]

Military musicians were busier than ever: Bandmaster Rogan called 1919 a 'hectic year of peace'.[20] The band of the Brigade of Guards played for troops returning from Cologne at railway stations, playing them to the barracks at London, Windsor and Caterham in addition to their normal duties such as guard-mounting, investitures and other ceremonies.[21] On 3 June 1919, the first Trooping of the Colour since the outbreak of war took place. On Empire Day, there was a concert at Hyde Park, and on 19 July 1919, the Victory March took place in London. Orders for the Victory March were issued through Haig, and Rogan was responsible for overseeing all of the military music. The Coldstream and Scots Guards bands were stationed at the saluting point, opposite the Victoria Memorial, and they played 'patriotic music' for a couple of hours before the march began. Approximately 20,000 servicemen from the Allied armies passed, and the Massed Pipers played for their own units as they went by. For the 1914 Expeditionary Force, they played *Tipperary* and *The Boys of the Old Brigade*.[22] Later that evening, the Massed Bands were ordered to play in Hyde Park in combination with the Imperial Choir.[23] The wartime Coldstream Band, twenty-nine musicians averaging between twenty and thirty years' service, were invalided out or discharged.

The Marine Band Service was reorganised. In November 1919, an internal memo outlined how standards were being raised and that '[u]ndesirables, insufficients and backward boys are being sent out of the Service faster than some of them relish by the present C.O.'[24] Rogan's last appearance as Bandmaster took place on 24 March 1920, at a Buckingham Palace dinner party. He was invited to have a private audience with the King shortly afterwards, who thanked Rogan for his service to British military music. Rogan retired as the highest-ranking soldier musician – Lieutenant Colonel and Royal Victorian Order.[25] Sir Alexander Mackenzie wrote to Rogan telling him that his work and career had helped military music directors and bandmasters 'to dignify their positions and to secure them chances of promotion which, until quite recently, were not within their reach. The Bandmaster's status has been raised to one more befitting and worthy its importance.'[26] *The Times* wrote that Rogan was missed as 'the wonderful march music that Rogan made still in memory thrills us and makes the heart beat quicker'.[27] He remained active in retirement, giving lectures at RUSI, the Royal Academy of Music and the Queen's Hall, trying to encourage British composers to write specifically for military bands.[28]

Lena Ashwell was awarded an OBE in 1917. She published her wartime memoir, *Modern Troubadours*, in 1922, in which she underlined that it 'by the provision of entertainment, the savagery of the soldier has been curbed'.[29] Ashwell regretted that she was not officially allowed to help the American YMCA. There had been some work between the two branches, but Ashwell's offers were refused. Nevertheless, British concert parties at Abbeville, Paris and Amiens were often requisitioned for American troops.[30] Ashwell recalled that America 'had great schemes for the organization of magnificent entertainment, but there were obstacles which prevented much of their work materializing'. German submarines prevented the easy transport of women, on which concert parties depended. Secondly, it was 'not possible to organize on a large scale ... work which has been considered of no national importance'.[31] She continued to work in the theatre, publishing her memoirs and texts of lectures given on British culture.

The composer Percy Scholes was one of the first people to recognise the possibilities of the gramophone as an aid to knowledge and understanding of music. Influenced by his experiences of teaching music on the fighting fronts, his *First Book of the Gramophone Record* (1924) lists fifty records of music from the sixteenth to the twentieth century, with a commentary on each; a *Second Book* followed in 1925. From 1930 onwards, Scholes collaborated with the Columbia Graphophone Company in *The Columbia History of Music by Ear and Eye*; this included eight 78rpm records specially made for the series. Employed in February 1918 by YMCA headquarters in London, the composer John Foulds (Figure 11.1) continued to organise special Sunday concerts of dedicated and sacred music at Ciro's. The last of these were held on 15 June 1919. Until January 1923, Foulds gave a regular talk called 'An hour with the great

Figure 11.1 YMCA/K/1/8/131: John Foulds conducting the Central Orchestra of the YMCA. © YMCA England and the Cadbury Research Library.

composers' in addition to organ recitals, midday concerts and accompanying the hymns at Central YMCA meetings. He continued his work with the YMCA's amateur orchestra and choral society, Centymca, until 1923 when the Central YMCA could no longer afford to keep paying him as Musical Director.[32] It was during his time working for the YMCA, and his continued contact with servicemen at Ciro's, that Foulds composed his *World Requiem*. This would be performed in the first Festivals of Remembrance, 1923–26.

Music and Remembrance

The first Festivals of Remembrance were staged every Armistice Night from 1923, with performances of John Fould's *World Requiem* (Opus 60).[33] Foulds, a theosophist, conceived of the *World Requiem* as an empty tomb, 'a cenotaph in sound', which would touch and therefore heal the grieving and bereaved. With a running length of approximately two hours, the *World Requiem* was written for 1,200 singers and instrumentalists. It was agreed that the royalties from the annual performances would be donated to the British Legion for an initial term of five years. The citation in the score reads 'A tribute to the memory of the Dead – a message of consolation to the bereaved of all countries.' The piece used texts from multiple literary sources, including the Bible, *Pilgrim's Progress*, Hindu poetry and some contemporary free verse. Foulds' work also pioneered the use of the quarter-tone, and an Indian instrument called the sistrum was played publicly in Britain for the first time. The first performance took place on Armistice Night 1923, at the Royal Albert Hall. It was attended by the King and Queen, and by the Prince of Wales in his role as patron of the British Legion. Foulds was congratulated by the Price of Wales and Field Marshal Sir Douglas Haig. The latter was unable to attend the concert as he was unveiling the war memorial at Berwick, but he wrote of 'the splendid reception which the public gave to the Requiem'.[34]

However, the ways in which the war should be commemorated in Britain became increasingly contentious. By 1927, it was felt by the Home Office, War Office and Admiralty that the ex-service community should be more fully represented at the Cenotaph. Foulds' piece was dropped from the national programme of remembrance as too middlebrow for the establishment, too elitist for many of the veterans and general public, and too expensive for the British Legion to stage. In its place, the *Daily Express* secured the Royal Albert Hall for its own Armistice Night concert. The newspaper's two-year tenureship of the event marks a clear change in tone of the character of British national remembrance during Armistice Night. British Legion Headquarters were asked to organise ex-service parade past the Cenotaph.[35] The *Daily Express* approached the Legion suggesting there should be a corresponding evening event – a reunion rally of ex-servicemen and women in the Albert Hall. The Legion's National Executive Council agreed to the evening event. Billed as a festival of 'remembrance', it would include the singing of congregational hymns. Indeed, the principal feature of the Festival was 'community singing', an activity that the *Daily Express* had started to popularise in October 1926 with its Community Singing Movement.[36] The *British Legion* magazine informed its readership that 'all the old war-time songs will be revived and sung together by many of those who knew them so well on the various battle-fronts'. The Bands and Pipers of the Foot Guards, and Trumpeters of the Life and Horse Guards would be joined by the 10th Hussars. The Prince of Wales would be in attendance and 'has promised to address his old comrades'.[37] Following the successful BBC broadcast of the Legion's Whitsun parade at the Cenotaph earlier that year, the reunion rally was to be broadcast by BBC radio. The *British Legion* was glad that the music of the evening would enable the thousands of those who could not be present to 'nevertheless enjoy the programme and take a part ... in the doings of the evening'. The night's schedule also included a torchlight procession from the Royal Albert Hall to the Cenotaph, to be led by the Prince of Wales, where a wreath would be laid.[38]

The coming together of ex-servicemen in organised singing allowed them to continue to define their identities as combatants which could then be reinforced in pageants, memorials, rituals and community singing.[39] There was a widespread call for tickets for the rally in 1927. Owing to demand, places had to be limited to those who had served in war areas, and British Legion Headquarters allotted seats for the event by Divisions, 'a system which provided many instances of men meeting again, war-time pals whose very existence had in some cases been forgotten since a "blighty" had parted them "somewhere on the Western" or other "Front"'.[40] The reunion element was a particular draw for the event, and recollections of the event are effusive. The writer and war veteran H. V. Morton, whose review was printed in both the *Daily Express* and the *British Legion*, bubbles over with nostalgia underpinned by a strong justification of the importance of comradeship in war the veterans felt. Ten thousand people, the majority men, stood in the Albert Hall under flags which had been used in the war. Some of them 'mere shreds of cloth', they included Admiral Jellicoe's flag from HMS *Iron Duke* at Jutland, and the royal box was draped in the Union Jack which had flown over the Menin Gate at Ypres. The Prince of Wales was the star turn, and at his first appearance at the gathering the assembly sung *For He's a Jolly Good Fellow*. Once *Pack Up Your Troubles* opened the programme, Morton recalled that he and his fellow ex-servicemen 'found ourselves back in 1914':

how intense is the emotion stored in these strange songs: for strange they are, strange as the British temperament, full of self-satire, pungent with humour directed against our own dignity. We did not realise until last night that the songs we sang in the Army are bits of history. In them is embalmed in that comic fatalism which carried us through four years of hell.... Thirteen years fell from us. We ceased to see the Albert Hall and the thousands of white faces in the arc lights; we looked into an abyss of memories where the long columns passed and repassed over the dusty roads in France, where the grotesque, unthinkable things of war happened day and night – the brief joys, the sharp sorrows of those days, the insane injustices of Fate, and, above all, the memory of the men we knew so well, men better than we were, nobler, finer, more worthy of life, who slipped into the silence of death.[41]

Morton pleaded that the event 'must not die ... Every year we must sing these songs again. In singing them we draw nearer to the men who died; in singing them we show to the world a thing that is visible only once a year – the splendid heart of England.'[42] Once the singing was finished the assembly filed out of the Albert Hall for a torch lit 'All London' march to the Cenotaph. Led by the Prince of Wales, once the procession reached Knightsbridge the 'immense column' was joined by a large number of veterans who had gathered in Hyde Park. On the way to the Cenotaph the *British Legion* reported that the column had been joined by 'enthusiastic and appreciative Londoners' which swelled the column's numbers and was proof of the public's support that 'the people of London had risen in their masses to march with the British Legion'.[43] However, Armistice Night 1927 was the only time the running of the Festival was in the sole hands of the *Daily Express*. Serious concern about the march and the Prince's safety meant that the following year the event was organised by the British Legion's General Secretary. Nevertheless, the desire of ex-servicemen to gather together and revisit their wartime memories through music and song had been established. The songs of 1914–18 were regularly sung at football matches and became central to the Community Singing movement led by the *Daily Express*.[44] Many of these melodies became foundation stones in the aural architecture of the memory of 1914–18, key topographical features in the landscape of Britain's memory, a central part of the 'thick description' of Britain's modern memory of the conflict.[45]

Conclusion

This book has shown that all types of music are integral to the history of the Great War. In periods of work, rest and play, servicemen's formal and informal musical activities were important aspects of their wartime experiences. Each musical encounter worked in conscious and unconscious ways to support combatant motivation and decrease the sense of dislocation with servicemen's pre-war lives. There are many aspects to the music provided for and by servicemen on the fighting fronts in political, economic, cultural and diplomatic terms. Military bands were an outward symbol of Britain's military heritage. The diplomatic visits of the Guards' bands in Paris and Rome were used as a projection of strength to inspire confidence in Britain's allies as well as for the members of the forces themselves. That the M.P. and pensions activist James Hogge joined Harry Lauder on his tour of the Western Front to help make men aware of the efforts made to secure pensions and welfare after the war shows how the recreational spaces of the Great War enabled large numbers of men to gather together and consider their lives once their wartime service was over. Existing dramatic and musical forms, such as music hall songs and pantomimes, were used to express their cause for war. Pantomime villains were cast as German or Turkish, and scenes, dialogue and music were transposed to the servicemen's everyday reality of the fighting fronts to buttress their ideas of fighting a just war.

For many civilian performers, musical activities for servicemen combined patriotic duty with job creation and economic protectionism. Groups such as the Three Arts Club, Music in War-Time Committee and Soldiers' Entertainment Fund worked not only to entertain the troops but also to provide employment for performers whose livelihoods were compromised by the conflict. This sense of national purpose in wartime can be seen in the efforts of individuals and organisations who worked with the British armed forces during the Great War. The power of music to console, educate and entertain was particularly effective when the work of individual musicians and performers combined with the logistical might of the YMCA. The YMCA and the Salvation Army were particularly effective at combining their own brands of practical Christian philanthropy and ministry to servicemen. They recognised very early on that the war was a great opportunity to reach men they struggled to contact in civilian life. Chaplains identified that, by their 'ministry of presence', their helping facilitate and supply music and light relief was a method of caring for men's wellbeing. As this book has shown, chaplains' duties extended far beyond worship as they were very often involved in the coordination of leisure and recreational activities, providing essential links between voluntary-aid organisations, commanders, local civilians and those at home.

Music of all kinds prompted the emotional remembrances of home by linking back to the sound worlds of comfort and family. Whether it was a bawdy music hall tune, the phrases of a Chopin piano piece or the strains of their own native instruments, through music the soldiers were reminded of the homes for which they were fighting. In its most basic forms, music was a portable commodity that required minimal equipment. Tunes could be carried in men's minds and sung or whistled from memory. Musical instruments could be improvised by inventive servicemen indicating their desire to create music wherever and whenever they could. Fundraising to send instruments to the men, such as mouth organs and gramophones, was a principal method of letting the men know they were remembered by friends and family awaiting their safe return. Those who organised and performed music on the fighting fronts understood their *raison d'etre* as taking the music of home to the men for the servicemen's enjoyment, but also their intellectual, physical and moral well-being, as well as emphasising that Britain's cause was just in France, Belgium, Mesopotamia, Egypt and beyond. The importance of music and entertainment was evidenced in supplies sent out by the Red Cross, both for PoWs and for hospitals and convalescent homes. Hospitals at base camps were usually permanent structures with facilities for performances, and could be delivered to large numbers of patients where performers could visit hospitals on rotation. This book has also considered the therapeutic applications of music, from the provision of gramophones in hospital wards through to concert parties, convalescent rehabilitation and the treatment of neurasthenia. That veterans' recorded oral histories are peppered with recollections of the bugle calls, and the words and music to their regimental songs more than fifty years after they had last heard them, indicates the powerful links between music and memory.

This book has shown how the wartime endeavours of British musicians served their king and country at every stage of the Great War. Music was not in any way ephemeral; it was unmatched in its power to cajole, console, cheer and inspire during the conflict and its aftermath.

Notes

INTRODUCTION

1. See for example Kate Kennedy & Trudi Tate, 'Literature and Music of the Great War', *Great War Studies*, 2:1, 2011; Jeffrey Richards, *Imperialism and Music: Britain 1876–1953*, (Manchester: Manchester University Press, 2001); Glenn Watkins, *Proof through the Night: Music and the Great War*, (California: University of California Press, 2003); Toby Thacker, *British Culture and the Great War*, (London: Bloomsbury, 2014)
2. John Mullen, *The Show Must Go On! Popular Song in Britain During the Great War*, (Ashgate: Farnham, 2015), p. 8. Also see Trevor Herbet (ed.), *The British Brass Band: A Musical and Social History*, (Oxford: Oxford University Press, 2000) and Stephen Etheridge, 'Southern Pennine Brass Bands and the Creation of Northern Identity c.1840–1914: Musical Constructions of Space, Place and Region', *Northern History*, September 2017, 54:2, pp. 244–261
3. Mullen, *The Show Must Go On!*, p. 9
4. Timothy Bowman & Mark Connelly, *The Edwardian Army: Recruiting, Training and Deploying the British Army, 1902–1914*, (Oxford: Oxford University Press, 2012), p. 1
5. *Evening News,* 21 October 1909, p. 4
6. Samuel Hynes, *A War Imagined: The Great War and English Culture*, (London: Pimlico, 1990), p. 57
7. Nicholas Hiley, 'Ploughboys and Soldiers: The Folk Song and the Gramophone in the British Expeditionary Force 1914–1918', *Media History*, 1998, 4:1, 61–2
8. Ibid., pp. 61–2
9. Samuel Hynes, *A War Imagined*, p. 57
10. W. R. Colton as quoted Hynes, p. 58
11. Rupert Brooke, '1914', in Geoffrey Keynes (ed.), *The Poetical Works (Poets of the Great War)*, (London: Faber & Faber, 2014)
12. Richards, *Imperialism and Music,* p. 10
13. F. A. Hadland, 'Music and the Great War', *The Strad*, April 1916, p. 2
14. IWM, LBY 09/71, Lena Ashwell Special Collection: *Pall Mall Gazette,* 28 October 1914, npr
15. Ibid.
16. IWM, LBY 09/ 71, Lena Ashwell Special Collection: *Era,* 7 October 1914, npr

17. Elizabeth Crawford, *The Women's Suffrage Movement: A Reference Guide, 1866–1928*, (London: Routledge, 2001), pp. 423–4

18. Baker, Anne Pimlott. 'Moore, (Lilian) Decima (1871–1964)', oxforddnb .com, Oxford University Press, September 2004 (accessed 18 May 2018). The WEC also established several leave clubs. The flagship of these clubs was the British Navy, Army and Air Force Leave Club in Paris, of which Decima Moore acted as director general. From the WEC derived the Women's Volunteer Reserve, the Women's Legion, the National Food Fund and the Women's Emergency Canteen, attached to the French Army from 1915

19. Harry Lauder, *A Minstrel in France*, (New York: Hearst's International Library Co., 1918); Lena Ashwell, *Modern Troubadours: A Record of Concerts at the Front*, (London: Glydendal, 1922); Ada Ward, *My Greatest Adventure*, (Leonor edition, Bibliolife, 2018); Ellaline Terriss, *By Herself and With Others*, (London: Cassell, 1928) and Ellaline Terriss, *Just a Little Bit of String*, (London: Hutchinson, 1955). Also see Ashwell's biography, Margaret Leask, *Lena Ashwell: Actress, Patriot, Pioneer*, (Hertfordshire: University of Herfordshire Press, 2012)

20. Sir Walter Raleigh, *The History of the War in the Air, 1914–1918*, (Barnsley: Pen & Sword, 2014 [1922]), p. 4

21. Sholto Douglas, *Years of Combat*, (London: Collins, 1963), p. 13

22. R. H. Mottram's *Spanish Farm Trilogy* (1924), quoted in Douglas, p. 13

23. Emma Hanna, 'Memory and the Aural Landscape of 1914–18', in Krista Cowman & Angela Smith (ed.), *Landscape and Voices of the Great War*, (London: Routledge, 2017), pp. 41–57

24. Pierre Nora (ed.) *Lieux de Mémoire*, (Paris: Gallimard, 1984–92)

25. Dan Todman, *The Great War: Myth & Memory*, (London: Hambledon, 2005)

26. F. T. Nettleingham, *Tommy's Tunes: A Comprehensive Collection of Soldiers' Songs, Marching Melodies, Rude Rhymes, and Popular Parodies, Composed, Collected and Arranged on Active Service with the B.E.F. Tommy's Tunes*, (London: Erskine Macdonald, 1917), pp. 14–15

27. IWM LBY 09/71: Lena Ashwell Special Collection, *The Globe*, 7 April 1915, npr

28. John Brophy & Eric Partridge, *The Long Trail: What the British Soldier Sang and Said in The Great War of 1914–18*, (Tonbridge: Andre Deutsch, 1965 [1930])

29. Ibid.

30. C. H. Ward-Jackson, *Airman's Song Book: Being an Anthology of Squadron, Concert Party, Training and Camp Songs and Song-Parodies [...]*, (London: Sylvan, 1945), p. vi

31. H. E. Adkins, *Treatise on the Military Band*, (London: Boosey & Co.,1931); George Farmer, *Memoirs of the Royal Artillery Band* (London: Boosey & Co.,1904)

32. Jason Wilson, *Soldiers of Song: The Dumbbells and Other Canadian Concert Parties of the First World War*, (Waterloo: Wilfred Laurier Press, 2012); Robert Holden, *And the Band Played On: How Music Lifted the Anzac Spirit in the Battlefields of the First World War*, (London: Hardie Grant, 2014)

33. See Jeffrey Richards, *Imperialism and Music: Britain 1876–1953*, (Manchester: Manchester University Press, 2001); Nalini Ghuman, *Resonances of the Raj: India in the English Musical Imagination, 1897–1947*, (Oxford: Oxford University Press, 2014); Emma Hanna, 'Musical Entertainment in the British Empire, 1914–1918', Michael Walsh & Andrekos Vanava (eds.), *Empire and the Great War*, (London: Ashgate, 2016)

34. Theodore Adorno, *Essays on Music*, (Berkeley: University of California Press, 2002), p. 445

35. Mullen, *The Show Must Go On*, pp. 1–4

36. Peter Martland, *Recording History: The British Record Industry, 1888–1931*, (London: Scarecrow Press, 2013); Nicholas Hiley, 'Ploughboys and Soldiers: The Folk Song and the Gramophone in the British Expeditionary Force 1914–1918', *Media History*, 1998, 4:1, 61–76

37. Royal Engineers Museum: Index to *The Sapper*, preface written by Captain Henry W. Corke (Ret.), June 1977

38. Timothy Bowman, *Irish Regiments in the Great War: Discipline and Morale*, (Manchester: Manchester University Press, 2003), p. 26

39. The 'Ensuring We Remember' campaign, led by the Chinese in Britain Forum, is currently working to raise awareness of CLC history, and generating funds for a memorial to the Chinese Labour Corp in Britain: http://ensuringweremember.org.uk (accessed 21 February 2019)

40. See J. G. Fuller, *Troop Morale and Popular Culture in the British and Dominion Armies*, (Oxford: Clarendon, 1990)

41. Jeffrey S. Reznick, *Healing the Nation: Soldiers and the Culture of Caregiving during the Great War*, (Manchester: Manchester University Press, 2011); Michael Snape, *The Back Parts of War: The YMCA Memoirs and Letters of Barclay Baron, 1915–1919*, (Boydell & Brewer, 2009)

42. Charles H. B Jacques, *Music from Macedonia*, Introduction by Second Lieutenant F. Kenchington, (Abbots Langley: no publisher or date)

43. Preface by Major-General John Bernard Seely in Lieutenant-Colonel J. Mackenzie-Rogan, *Fifty Years of Army Music*, (London: Methuen, 1926), p. v

44. Tony Mason & Eliza Reidi, *Sport and the Military: The British Armed Forces 1880–1960*, (Cambridge University Press, 2010); L. J. Collins, *Theatre at War, 1914–18*, (London: Jade, 2004)

45. Robert Holden, *And the Band Played On: How Music Lifted the Anzac Spirit in the Battlefields of the Great War*, (London: Hardie Grant, 2014); Jason Wilson, *Soldiers of Song: The Dumbells and Other Canadian Concert Parties of the Great War*, (Waterloo: Wilfrid Laurier University Press, 2012)

46. See also Emma Hanna, 'Say it with Music: Combat, Courage and Identity in the Songs of the RFC/RAF, 1914–1918', *British Journal for Military History*, 4:2, February 2018

47. Adolf Lukas Vischer, *Barbed-Wire Disease: A Psychological Study of the Prisoner of War*, (London: John Bale & Danielson, 1919). See also A. J. Brock, 'Boredom and Barbed-Wire Disease', *British Medical Journal*, 1940, 1: 744, and John Yarnall, *Barbed Wire Disease: British and German Prisoners of War, 1914–1919*, (History Press, 2011).

48. See also Emma Hanna, 'Putting the Moral into Morale: YMCA Cinemas on the Western Front, 1914–1918', *Historical Journal of Film, Radio & Television*, October 2015, 35:4, 615–630

MUSIC IN BRITAIN, 1914

1. The Tattoo: the sounding of the 'First Post' with drums and fifes, a selection of music consisting of marches and other pieces, followed by the 'Last Post' then 'Lights Out' at the closing call of the day.
2. Lieutenant-Colonel J. Mackenzie-Rogan, *Fifty Years of Army Music*, (London: Methuen, 1926), pp. 1–5
3. Ibid., p. 7
4. NAM 1978-08-80-1: Memoirs of Bandsman Sergeant Victor Shawyer, Foreword
5. John Trendell, *A Life on the Ocean Wave: The Royal Marines Band Story*, (Dover: A. R. Adams & Sons, 1990), p. 28
6. Ibid.
7. Ibid., pp. 2–3
8. Gordon Turner & Alwyn W. Turner, *The Trumpets Will Sound: The Story of the Royal Military School of Music, Kneller Hall*, (Tunbridge Wells: Parapress, 1996), p. 15
9. Ibid., pp. 17–22
10. Trevor Herbert & Helen Barlow, *Music in the British Military in the Long Nineteenth Century*, (Oxford: Oxford University Press, 2013), pp. 319–20
11. Ibid.
12. Ibid.
13. John Ambler, *The Royal Marines Band Service*, (Portsmouth: Holbrooks, 2003), p. 1
14. Ibid., p. 29
15. Ibid., pp. 6–7
16. Ambler, p. 1
17. Ibid., p. 2
18. RMM: Letter from W. R. Hoare, Training Ship *'Mercury'*, Hamble, Southampton, October 1902
19. Rogan, *Fifty Years of Army Music*, pp. 9–10
20. Ibid., pp. 10–11
21. Ibid., pp. 122–3
22. Ibid., p. 54
23. Ambler, p. 4
24. However, this move did not take place and the RNSM remained at Eastney until its move to Deal in 1930.
25. See George Farmer, *The Military Band*, (1912), Bandmaster of Portsmouth Division 1884–1917, and *Military Music* (1950)
26. RMM 11/13/28: Memoirs of a Royal Marine Bandsman, H. J. Reed, p. 8
27. Ibid.
28. Ibid.
29. Ibid., p. 9

30. Ibid., p. 11
31. NAM 1978–08-80–1: Memoirs of Bandsman Sergeant Victor Shawyer, p. 29
32. Ibid., p. 55
33. Ibid., p. 57
34. Ibid., p. 61
35. Ibid., p. 62
36. Ibid., p. 57
37. Ibid., p. 62
38. Ibid., p. 65
39. Charles Nalden, pupil of Adkins, quoted in Gordon Turner & Alwyn W. Turner, *The Trumpets Will Sound: The Story of the Royal Military School of Music Kneller Hall*, (Tunbridge Wells: Parapress Ltd, 1996), p. 55. Adkins would be appointed as Director of Music at Kneller Hall in 1921 until his retirement in 1943.
40. NAM 1978–08-80–1: Memoirs of Bandsman Sergeant Victor Shawyer, pp. 114–15
41. G. J. H. Evatt, *Our Songless Army: A Proposal to Develop the Singing of Marching Songs, Unison Singing, Part-Songs, and Choral Societies by the Soldiers of Our Regular Army, Militia, Yeomanry, Volunteers, Cadet Corps, and Boys' Brigades*, (London: J. Curwen & Sons, 1907)
42. Ibid., Section 1.
43. Ibid.
44. Ibid.
45. Ibid.
46. Ibid., Section 3.
47. Ibid., Section 1.
48. Ibid., Section 1.
49. Ibid.
50. Ibid., Section 2.
51. Ibid.
52. Ibid.
53. Ibid.
54. Ibid., Section 3.
55. Monthly Musical Notes by 'Sackbut', *Dover Express and East Kent News*, 8 October 1909, p. 6
56. *Evening Telegraph & Post*, 24 July 1911, p. 4
57. John Farmer (ed.), *Scarlet & Blue: Or, Songs for Soldiers and Sailors*, (London: Cassell, 1909, 1898)
58. Colonel B. R. Ward, *The Organisation of the Naval and Military Musical Union: Being a Paper Read at Aldershot by Col. B.R. Ward, R.E., to the Members of the Marlborough Lines Literary and Debating Society, November 1911*, (London: Whiteman & Co./Organization Society, 1912), p. 4
59. Ibid.
60. Ibid.
61. Ibid., p. 5
62. Ibid.
63. Ward, *The Organisation of the Naval and Military Musical Union*, p. 6

64. Ibid.
65. Ibid., p. 5
66. Ibid., p. 6
67. Ibid.
68. TNA: ADM 196/61/275: Service record of Lieutenant Colonel Charles Hope Willis
69. *Evening News,* 21 October 1909, p. 4
70. *Evening News,* 8 October 1912, p. 4
71. *Evening News* 8 August 1913, p. 4
72. *Evening News* 12 May 1914, p. 4. See TNA: HO 144/1318/252301: 'Title Royal: Naval and Military Musical Union Refused'
73. TNA: ADM 196/61/275: Service record of Lieutenant Colonel Charles Hope Willis
74. *Western Daily Press,* 25 January 1915, p. 7
75. John Mullen, *The Show Must Go On! Popular Song in Britain During the First World War,* (Ashgate: Farnham, 2015)
76. Catriona Pennell, *A Kingdom United: Popular Responses to the Outbreak of the First World War in Britain and Ireland,* (Oxford: Oxford University Press, 2014), p. 98
77. *Portsmouth Evening News,* 17 May 1915. I am grateful to Katarina Henderson and the archivists of the Kings Theatre for this example.
78. *Portsmouth Evening News,* 26 May 1915, npr
79. IWM 495: James Pratt, Reel 2, recorded 1974
80. TNA: KV 1/74 (1915): Music score with secret writing by the spy Courtenay de Rysbach
81. TNA HO 45/10727/254753: Activity of enemy agents, 1914–16
82. Arthur Jacobs, *Henry J. Wood: Maker of the Proms,* (London: Methuen, 1994), p. 149
83. Ibid., p. 148
84. John Williamson & Martin Cloonan, *Players' Work Time: A History of the British Musicians' Union, 1893–2013* (Manchester: Manchester University Press, 2016)
85. Jane Angell, 'Music and Charity on the British Home Front during the First World War', *Journal of Musicological Research,* 2014, 33:1–3, 184–205
86. Royal Academy of Music: *The RAM Club Magazine,* No.43, November 1914, p. 22
87. See the AHRC-funded project *Music Making in Manchester During World War I* led by Professor Barbara Kelly at the Royal Northern College of Music: www.rncm.ac.uk/news/music-in-manchester-world-war-1/ (accessed 20 February 2019)
88. RMM: *Globe and Laurel,* No.227, Vol. XXI, 7 September 1914, p. 149
89. Quoted in Ambler, p. 18
90. RMM 11/13/28: Memoirs of a Royal Marine Bandsman, H. J. Reed, p. 16
91. Trendell, *A Life on the Ocean Wave,* p. 41
92. RMSM: Kneller Hall, Diary, 4 August 1914
93. Turner & Turner, *The Trumpets Will Sound,* p. 54
94. Ibid., p. 55

95. Rogan, *Fifty Years of Army Music*, p. 182
96. NAM 1978–08-80–1: Memoirs of Bandsman Sergeant Victor Shawyer, p. 146
97. Ibid., p. 147
98. Ibid.
99. Ibid.
100. Ibid., pp. 150–1
101. Ibid., pp. 152–3
102. RMM: *Globe and Laurel*, No.227, Vol. XXI, 7 September 1914, p. 149
103. NAM 1978–08-80–1: Memoirs of Bandsman Sergeant Victor Shawyer, p. 154
104. Ibid., p. 155
105. Ibid., p. 158
106. Ibid., pp. 164–5
107. Ibid., p. 166
108. Ibid., p. 170
109. RMM: *Globe and Laurel*, No.228, Vol. XXI, 7 October 1914, p. 167
110. RMM: *Globe and Laurel*, No.234, Vol. XXII, 7 April 1915, p. 70
111. EFDSS: George Butterworth, *Diary & Letters*, pp. 18–19
112. Rogan, *Fifty Years of Army Music*, p. 182
113. SAIHC: *The Bandsman, Local Officer & Songster*, No.389, Vol.VIII, 12 September 1914, p. 586
114. Ibid., p. 584
115. SAIHC: *The Bandsman, Local Officer & Songster*, No.385, Vol.VIII, 15 August 1914, p. 520
116. SAIHC: *The Bandsman, Local Officer & Songster*, No.386, Vol.VIII, 22 August 1914, p. 531
117. SAIHC: *The Bandsman, Local Officer & Songster*, No.384, Vol.VIII, 8 August 1914, p. 501

RECRUITMENT AND FUNDRAISING

1. Captain James E. Agate, *Lines of Communication: Being the Letters of a Temporary Officer in the Army Service Corps*, (London: Constable & Co. Ltd., 1917), p. 3
2. Gerard DeGroot, *Back in Blighty: The British at Home in World War I*, (London: Vintage, 2014), p. 70
3. NAM 9601–32: Parliamentary Recruiting Committee, 'Patriotic Song Sheet', Leaflet 11, October 1914
4. IWM, LBY 09/71, Lena Ashwell Special Collection: *Nineteenth Century*, August 1915, p. 345
5. Lieutenant-Colonel J. Mackenzie-Rogan, *Fifty Years of Army Music*, (London: Methuen, 1926), p. 183
6. Ibid.
7. Ibid.
8. Ibid., p. 184
9. Ibid., pp. 183–4

10. Ibid., p. 184
11. Rudyard Kipling quoted in Rogan, *Fifty Years of Army Music*, pp. 184–5
12. IWM, LBY 09/71, Lena Ashwell Special Collection: *Daily Telegraph*, 25 February 1915, npr
13. IWM, LBY 09/71, Lena Ashwell Special Collection: *Music Student*, 22 April 1915, npr
14. IWM, LBY 09/71, Lena Ashwell Special Collection: *Daily Telegraph*, 25 February 1915, npr
15. Rogan, *Fifty Years of Army Music*, p. 185
16. IWM, LBY 09/71, Lena Ashwell Special Collection: *The Times*, 2 March 1915, npr
17. IWM, LBY 09/71, Lena Ashwell Special Collection: *Pall Mall Gazette*, 12 July 1915, npr
18. IWM, LBY 09/71, Lena Ashwell Special Collection: *Evening News*, September 1915, npr
19. IWM, LBY 09/71, Lena Ashwell Special Collection: *Daily Chronicle*, 30 July 1915, npr
20. L. J. Collins, *Theatre at War 1914–18*, (Oldham: Jade, 2004), pp. 8–9
21. Quoted in L. J. Collins, *Theatre at War 1914–18*, p. 12
22. *The Saturday Review*, 18 September 1915, p. 279
23. Rogan, *Fifty Years of Army Music*, p. 186
24. Ibid., p. 185, emphasis in original
25. Ibid., p. 186
26. Ibid.
27. Ibid., pp. 186–7
28. J. Aulich & J. Hewitt, *Seduction or Instruction? First World War Posters in Britain and Europe*, (Manchester: Manchester University Press, 2007), p. 98
29. Harry Lauder, *A Minstrel in France*, (New York: Hearst's International Library Co., 1918), pp. 35–6
30. Ibid., p. 37
31. Ibid., p. 38
32. Stephen J. Hornsby, 'Patterns of Scottish Emigration to Canada, 1750–1870', *Journal of Historical Geography*, October 1992, 1:4, 397–416
33. Andrew G. Ralston, *Lauchlan MacLean Watt: Poet, Preacher & Piping Padre*, (Glasgow: Society of Friends of Glasgow Cathedral, 2018)
34. Ellaline Terriss, *By Herself and with Others*, (London: Cassell, 1928), p. 212
35. Jane Angell, 'Music and Charity on the British Home Front during the First World War', *Journal of Musicological Research*, 2014, 33:1–3, 184–205
36. Ibid., pp. 187–8
37. Ibid., pp. 192–6
38. Ibid.
39. Collins, p. 82
40. IWM Documents: Lena Ashwell Special Collection: Memo from the Women's Emergency Corps relating to the Three Arts Emergency Relief Fund, August 1914
41. Ibid.

42. IWM, LBY 09/71, Lena Ashwell Special Collection: *Nineteenth Century*, August 1915, p. 344
43. IWM, LBY 09/71, Lena Ashwell Special Collection: *Musical Herald*, August 1915, npr
44. IWM, LBY 09/71, Lena Ashwell Special Collection: Memo from the Women's Emergency Corps relating to the Three Arts Emergency Relief Fund, August 1914
45. Ibid.
46. Ibid.
47. IWM, LBY 09/71, Lena Ashwell Special Collection: newspaper cutting – no title, date or page reference, estimated October 1914
48. IWM, LBY 09/71, Lena Ashwell Special Collection: programme, 3 February 1915
49. IWM, LBY 09/71, Lena Ashwell Special Collection: *Daily Chronicle*, 15 January 1915, npr
50. Lena Ashwell, *Modern Troubadours*, p. 5
51. 'The Morals of London', *The Times*, 7 August 1916, p. 3
52. Ibid.
53. Jerry White, *Zeppelin Nights: London in the First World War*, (London: The Bodley Head, 2014), p. 50. See also Stephen McKenna, *While I Remember*, (New York: G. H Doran Company, 1921), pp. 84–5; Arthur Marwick, *The Deluge: British Society and the First World War*, 2nd edition (London: Macmillan, 1996 [1965]), p. 90; Adrian Gregory, *The Great War: British Society and the First World War*, (Cambridge: Cambridge University Press, 2008), pp. 160–1
54. SAIHC: *The Bandsman, Local Officer & Songster*, No.388, Vol.VIII, 5 September 1914, p. 573
55. Angell, 'Music and Charity', pp. 204–5
56. IWM LBY 09/71, Lena Ashwell Special Collection: *Windsor Magazine*, no date, p. 366
57. IWM, LBY 09/71, Lena Ashwell Special Collection: *Evening Standard*, 23 April 1915, npr
58. IWM, LBY 09/71, Lena Ashwell Special Collection: *Musical News*, 28 August 1915, p. 195
59. Ibid. pp. 195–6
60. IWM 17198: Correspondence relating to the *Daily Express* 'Cheery Fund'. See Peter Grant, *Philanthropy and Voluntary Action in the First World War*, (London: Routledge, 2014)
61. IWM, LBY 09/71, Lena Ashwell Special Collection: *My Call*, Spring 1915, npr
62. IWM, LBY 09/71, Lena Ashwell Special Collection: *Truth*, 31 March 1915, npr
63. IWM, LBY 09/71, Lena Ashwell Special Collection: *Evening Standard*, 23 April 1915, npr
64. Ibid.
65. Quoted in IWM, LBY 09/71, Lena Ashwell Special Collection: *Nineteenth Century*, August 1915, p. 352

66. Ibid.
67. IWM, LBY 09/71, Lena Ashwell Special Collection: *Nottingham Express*, ? March 1916, npr
68. YMCA: *The YM*, 30 June 1916, p. 602
69. IWM Documents 15459: Gordon Williams, text of letter in *Southport Visitor*, August 1916
70. IWM Documents 15459: Gordon Williams, lecture notes introduction
71. Ibid., undated and untitled newspaper cutting of Gordon William's lecture in Southport
72. Ibid., lecture notes
73. Ibid.
74. RMM: *Globe and Laurel*, No.234, Vol. XXII, 7 April 1915, p. 70
75. RMM: *Globe and Laurel*, No.230, Vol. XXII, 7 January 1915, p. 13
76. Rogan, *Fifty Years of Army Music*, p. 226
77. Ibid., p. 227
78. Ibid.
79. Ibid.
80. RMM 11/13/28: Memoirs of a Royal Marine Bandsman, H. J. Reed, pp. 27–8
81. Ibid., p. 204
82. Ibid., p. 200
83. Film footage of the bands and Carrie Tubb outside the venue in Paris: www .iwm.org.uk/collections/item/object/1060005363
84. Rogan, *Fifty Years of Army Music*, p. 204
85. Ibid., p. 205
86. NAM 2016/10/23/245/8: Sir Francis Lloyd, correspondence and reports, 1917–1918
87. Rogan, *Fifty Years of Army Music*, p. 205
88. Ibid., p. 207
89. Ibid.
90. Ibid., p. 210
91. Ibid., p. 217
92. Ibid., p. 218
93. Ibid.
94. Ibid., p. 217
95. Ibid., p. 219
96. Ibid., p. 225
97. Ibid., p. 217
98. Ibid., p. 225

INSTRUMENTS OF WAR

1. RMM: 'A Short History of Drummers, Buglers & Fifers in the Royal Marines, B.R.13, *The Bugler's Handbook*, pp. 1–2
2. Trevor Herbert & Helen Barlow, *Music & The British Military in the Long Nineteenth Century*, (Oxford: Oxford University Press, 2013), p. 29
3. Alwyn W. Turner, *The Last Post: Music, Remembrance and the Great War*, (London: Aurum Press, 2014), pp. 7–10

4. IWM 374: Charles Harry Ditcham
5. Henry Newbolt, 'The Toy Band: A Song of the Great Retreat' was published in *The Times* in December 1914. Cecil D. Eby, *The Road to Armageddon: The Martial Spirit in English Popular Literature, 1870–1914*, (London: Duke University Press, 1987), pp. 105–6
6. IWM 8172: Major John Frederick Ford
7. EFDSS: George Butterworth, *Diary & Letters*, p. 32
8. Max Arthur, *Forgotten Voices* (London: Ebury Press, 2002), p. 32
9. IWM 8172: Major John Frederick Ford
10. John Brophy & Eric Partridge, *Songs and Slang of the British Soldier: 1914–1918* (London: Eric Partridge, 1931), p. 184
11. IWM 374: Charles Harry Ditcham
12. IWM 777: Alfred Walter Hedges
13. TNA WO 162/3: Commander in Chief and War Office: Adjutant General's Department. New Armies, Organization
14. Ibid.
15. Ibid.
16. Ibid.
17. IWM 9428: Tommy Keele
18. *Highland Light Infantry Chronicle*, Vol.XV, Issue 1, 1 January 1915, p. 4
19. *1st C. B. Royal Fusiliers Chronicle*, Issue 1, 1 April 1915, pp. 11–12
20. IWM 10457: Turville Kille
21. IWM 16268: Personal papers of Chaplain M. P. G. Leonard, 11 February 1916, Flanders
22. Alwyn W. Turner, *The Last Post: Music, Remembrance and the Great War*, (London: Aurum Press, 2014), p. 12
23. John Bourne, 'The Working Man in Arms' in Hugh Cecil (ed.), *Facing Armageddon*, (London: Pen & Sword Select, 2003), p. 338
24. *Manchester Guardian*, 18 May 1916
25. Bourne, 'The Working Man in Arms', p. 345
26. IWM 11341: Donald A Hodge
27. IWM 314: Percy Snelling
28. IWM 7831: Private Papers of J J McGale
29. IWM 8270: Percy Valentine Harris
30. NAM 1978–08–80–1: Memoirs of Bandsman Sergeant Victor Shawyer, p. 28
31. IWM LBY 11119–1: C. A. Atherley, *Trumpet and Bugle Sounds for the Army with Words also Bugle Marches*, (Aldershot: Gale and Poulden, 1915)
32. IWM 8270: Percy Valentine Harris
33. Ibid.
34. John Brophy & Eric Partridge, *Songs and Slang of the British Soldier: 1914–1918* (London: Eric Partridge Ltd, 1931), p. 184
35. Turner, *The Last Post*, p. 12
36. Bourne, 'The Working Man in Arms', p. 338
37. The Somme Times, 31 July 1916, Vol.1, Issue 1, pp. 1–2
38. CA: *Church Army Gazette*, 11 November 1916, p. 4
39. John Norris, *Marching to the Drums: A History of Military Drums and Drummers*, (Stroud: Spellmount, 2012), p. 133

40. Ibid., p. 134
41. *London Gazette*, 18 February 1915, p. 1699
42. TNA WO 95/1219/2: 1 Battalion Coldstream Guards, War Diary, 22 August 1915
43. TNA WO 95/1218/3/030: 2 Guards Brigade, Headquarters, War Diary, Appendix 15, 13 February 1916
44. TNA WO 95/1219/2: 1 Battalion Coldstream Guards, War Diary, 23 August 1915
45. TNA WO 95/1218/3/050: 2 Guards Brigade, Headquarters, War Diary, 14 June 1917
46. *Illustrated War News*, 12 August 1914, p. 17
47. *The Grey Brigade (Camp Journal of the Great War 1914–1916)*, Issue 3, 26 March 1915, p. 1
48. Thomas Greenshields, Unpublished paper delivered to the 'Pack Up Your Troubles: Performance Cultures in the First World War' conference, University of Kent, March 2016
49. Lauchlan Maclean Watt, *In France and Flanders with the Fighting Men*, (London: Hodder & Stoughton, 1917), p. 2
50. IWM, LBY 09/71: *Windsor Magazine*, no date, pp. 373–4
51. *Highland Light Infantry Chronicle*, Vol.XVIII, Issue 2, 1 April 1918, p. 63
52. *The Fifth: The Magazine of the Fifth London (City of London) Military Hospital, St Thomas*, Vol.1, Issue 2, 1 January 1917, pp. 44–45
53. CA: *Church Army Gazette*, 11 December 1915, p. 1
54. Andrew G. Ralston, *Lauchlan MacLean Watt: Poet, Preacher & Piping Padre*, (Glasgow: Society of Friends of Glasgow Cathedral, 2018). Watt published accounts of his wartime experiences, *In Time of War: A Padre with the Bagpipes* (Edinburgh: Turnbull & Spears, 1915) and *In France and Flanders* (1917).
55. *Highland Light Infantry Chronicle*, Vol.XVI, Issue 1, 1 January 1916, p. 44
56. *The Outpost, Troon*, Issue 4, 1 May 1915, p. ix
57. *The Royal Sussex Herald*, Vol.4, Issue 43, 7 September 1918, p. 2
58. *The Wing*, Issue 39, 22 December 1917, p. 19
59. *The Ducal Weekly*, Issue 4, 18 October 1914, p. 4
60. IWM 16268: Personal papers of Chaplain M. P. G. Leonard, 25 January 1916
61. Ibid., 6 February 1916
62. Ibid., 29 July 1917
63. RAM: Letters of 2nd Lieutenant Harper Seed of the 17th Btn Sherwood Foresters, 17 August 1917
64. H. E. Adkins, *Treatise on the Military Band*, (London: Boosey & Co., 1931), p. 6
65. IWM, LBY 09/71: *Windsor Magazine*, no date, p. 367
66. Trendell, p. 41
67. Ibid.
68. Ambler, p. 16
69. IWM, LBY 09/71: *Evening News*, September 1915, npr

70. Gilbert A. Singleton, *Music in Blue: Uniforms of Musicians in the Royal Air Force and its Predecessors – A Photographic History* (Maidenhead: Eagle & Lyre Publications, 2007) p. 7
71. Singleton; also see Lewis McCudden & Alex Revell, *High in the Empty Blue* (Mountain View, CA: Flying Machines Press, 1995)
72. Reviews of their concerts in *The Piloteer* station magazine
73. FAAM: *The Piloteer* station magazine, November 1917
74. *The Fledgling: The Monthly Journal of the No. 2 Royal Flying Corps Cadet Wing*, 1 September 1917, Vol.1, No.4, p. 128
75. SAIHC: *Under the Colours*, October 1915, Vol.XIX, No.10, p. 117
76. *London Gazette*, 21 June 1916, p. 6157
77. *Daily Express*, 23 June 1916, p. 2
78. Ibid.
79. *Daily Express*, 24 June 1916, p. 2
80. Malcolm J. Doolin, *The Boys of Blackhorse Road: The Story of an Elementary School War Memorial*, (London: Astra Publications, 2016)
81. Sarah Reay, *The Half-Shilling Curate: A Personal Account of War and Faith 1914–1918*, (Solihull: Helion, 2016), p. 89
82. IWM, LBY 09/71: *Birmingham Picture World*, 10 August 1915, npr
83. RAF X003-0400/001: Letter from Second Lieutenant Alfred Severs, No.25 squadron, 10th Wing RFC, 30 December 1916
84. Lieutenant-Colonel J. Mackenzie-Rogan, *Fifty Years of Army Music*, (London: Methuen, 1926), pp. 210–11
85. IWM, LBY 09/71: *Blackwood's Magazine*, December 1916, npr
86. IWM, LBY 09/71: *Musical Times*, 1 July 1915, p. 401
87. RMM: *Globe and Laurel*, No.230, Vol.XXII, 7 January 1915, p. 13
88. NAM 1978-08-80–1: Memoirs of Bandsman Sergeant Victor Shawyer, p. 171
89. IWM 17246: Private papers of J. W. Double, Diary
90. The award was made by the King on 11 January 1915 and announced in *The Edinburgh Gazette*, 15 January 1915, p. 104
91. *The Edinburgh Gazette*, 15 January 1915, p. 104
92. *The London Gazette*, 25 August 1915, p. 8509
93. NAM 1978-08-80–1: Memoirs of Bandsman Sergeant Victor Shawyer, pp. 203–4
94. RMM: *Globe and Laurel*, No.229, Vol.XXI, 7 December 1914, p. 215
95. RMM 11/13/28: Memoirs of a Royal Marine Bandsman, H. J. Reed, p. 17
96. Ibid., p. 18
97. Ibid., p. 19
98. Ibid., p. 32
99. Jon Sumida, 'British Naval Administration and Policy in the Age of Fisher', *The Journal of Military History*, January 1990, 54:1, pp. 1–26. I am grateful to Rear Admiral RAN James Goldrick for this reference.
100. Ibid., pp. 11–12
101. H. P. K. Oram, *Ready for Sea*, (Annapolis: United States Naval Institute, 1974)

102. John Trendell, *A Life on the Ocean Wave: The Royal Marines Band Story*, (Dover: A.R. Adams & Sons, 1990), p. 43
103. RMM: *Globe and Laurel*, No.231, Vol.XXII, 7 January 1915, p. 13
104. RMM: *Globe and Laurel*, No.233, Vol.XXIII, 7 March 1915, p. 30
105. RMM: *Globe and Laurel*, No.234, Vol.XXII, 7 April 1915, p. 70
106. Gordon Turner & Alwyn W. Turner, *The Trumpets Will Sound: The Story of the Royal Military School of Music Kneller Hall*, (Tunbridge Wells: Parapress Ltd, 1996), p. 55
107. Rogan, *Fifty Years of Army Music*, p. 188
108. TNA WO 95/1219/2: 1 Battalion Coldstream Guards, War Diary, 12 November 1915
109. TNA WO 95/1219/2: 1 Battalion Coldstream Guards, War Diary, 25 June 1916
110. Rogan, *Fifty Years of Army Music*, p. 188
111. Ibid.
112. Ibid., p. 189
113. Ibid.
114. Ibid.
115. Ibid.
116. Ibid.
117. Ibid., p. 190
118. Ibid.
119. Ibid.
120. Ibid., p. 195
121. IWM 17246: Private papers of J. W. Double, Diary
122. Ibid., 6 March 1917
123. Ibid., 24 February 1917
124. Ibid., 28 October 1917
125. C. E. Wurtzburg, *The History of the 2/6th (Rifle) Battalion "The King's" (Liverpool Regiment)*, (Aldershot: Gale & Polden, 1920), p. 93. I am grateful to Jim Beach for sending me this reference.
126. IWM 16268: Personal papers of Chaplain M. P. G. Leonard, 1 May 1916
127. Ibid., p. 197
128. Ibid., p. 200
129. Ibid., p. 199
130. Ibid., p. 211
131. TNA WO 339/6477: Long Service Papers, Lieutenant Colonel John Mackenzie Rogan
132. TNA AIR/2/93: Postwar Establishments for RAF Music; TNA AIR 2/80: Establishment for RAF School of Music; TNA AIR 2/90: RAF School of Music; TNA AIR 2/131: RAF Music Services and Bands
133. Gilbert A. Singleton, *Music in Blue: Uniforms of Musicians in the Royal Air Force and its Predecessors – A Photographic History* (Maidenhead: Eagle & Lyre Publications, 2007). For example, see the scathing article 'An Aerial School of Music' in *Truth* on 23 April 1919.
134. Singleton, p. 3. However, plans for new bands petered out and the central band was disbanded in February 1919.

SONGS, IDENTITY AND MORALE

1. IWM, LBY 09/71: *Windsor Magazine*, no date, pp. 365–6
2. Charles Purday, (ed.), *The Royal Naval Song Book* (London, 1867); G. W. Bishop (ed.), *The Royal Naval Song Book* (London, 1890); George Farmer (ed.), *Scarlett & Blue: Songs for Soldiers and Sailors*, (London: Cassell, 1896)
3. *The Organisation of the Naval and Military Musical Union: Being a Paper Read at Aldershot by Col. B.R.Ward, R.E., to the Members of the Marlborough Lines Literary and Debating Society, November 1911*, (London: Whiteman & Co./ Organization Society, 1912)
4. IWM Library: *Marching Songs and Tommy's Tunes: A Handbook for Our Soldiers*, (London: Stanley Paul, 1914), preface
5. Ibid.
6. SAIHC: *The Bandsman, Local Officer & Songster*, No.384, Vol.VIII, 8 August 1914, p. 460
7. IWM Library: National Service League, *Songs for Our Soldiers* [undated, estimated c.1914–15]
8. Henry Walford Davies (ed.), *Songs Old and New: For Use in Wartime* (London: S. Roirden, 1915); Henry Walford Davies (ed.), *The Aldershot Song Book for Regimental Choirs: Thirty-Eight Songs for Camp Concerts*, (London: J. Curwen & Sons, 1916)
9. NAM 9512–170: Private papers of E. W. Jones, Private in the 20th Middlesex (Artists's) Rifles in 1904, Second Lieutenant Royal Sussex Regiment from 1917.
10. Arthur Ainger, *Marching Songs for Soldiers* (London: Ascherberg, Hopwood & Crew, 1914)
11. *The Times*, 1 October 1914, p. 7
12. John Brophy & Eric Partridge, *The Long Trail: What the British Soldier Sang and Said in The Great War of 1914–18*, (Tonbridge: Andre Deutsch, 1965 [1930]), pp. 14–24
13. For an analysis of themes in popular songs of the Great War, see John Mullen, *The Show Must Go On! Popular Song in Britain During the First World War*, (Ashgate: Farnham, 2015), p. 87
14. SAIHC: *The Bandsman, Local Officer & Songster*, No.384, Vol.VIII, 8 August 1914, p. 460
15. *Twenty Years After: The Battlefields of 1914–18: Then and Now*, Part 12, (George Newnes Publication), p. 429
16. C. H. Ward-Jackson (ed.), *Airmen's Songbook: Being an Anthology of Squadron, Concert Party, Training and Camp Songs and Song-Parodies [...]*, (London: Sylvan, 1945), p. xi
17. *Liverpool Echo*, 4 February 1916, p. 6
18. Nicholas Hiley, 'Ploughboys and Soldiers: The Folk Song and the Gramophone in the British Expeditionary Force 1914–1918', *Media History*, 1998, 4:1, p. 66
19. IWM, LBY 09/71: *Windsor Magazine*, no date, pp. 365–6
20. *Musical Times*, 1 December 1914, p. 697
21. Brophy & Partridge, *The Long Trail*, p. 213

22. Thomas Tiplady, *The Soul of the Soldier: Sketches from the Western Battle-Front*, (London: Fleming H. Revell, 1918), pp. 61–2
23. IWM 8270: Percy Valentine Harris, Reel 1
24. Ibid.
25. *The Era*, 25 August 1915, p. 9
26. *Liverpool Echo*, 4 February 1916, p. 6
27. *The Spectator*, 18 August 1917, p. 8
28. Lieutenant-Colonel J. Mackenzie-Rogan, *Fifty Years of Army Music*, (London: Methuen, 1926), pp. 14–15
29. RMM: 'The Spirit of the Navy', E. Hallam Moorhouse, *The Fleet*, 1 September 1914, p. 296
30. RMM: 'The Man Behind the Gun', From *Ballads of the Blue*, by a Bluejacket, *The Fleet*, 7 September 1914, p. 312
31. RMM: *The Fleet*, No.118, Vol. XJ, December 1914, pp. 442–4
32. RMM: *Globe and Laurel*, No.234, Vol. XXII, 7 April 1915, p. 71
33. EFDSS: George Butterworth, *Diary & Letters*, pp. 18–19
34. IWM, LBY 09/71: *Windsor Magazine*, no date, p. 367
35. Private E. Todd quoted in IWM Podcast: www.iwm.org.uk/history/voi ces-of-the-first-world-war-wartime-leisure-and-entertainment   (accessed 15 August 2018)
36. YMCA/K/6/1: Percy A. Scholes, 'Music and the Fighting Man', *The Red Triangle*, Vol.2, September 1917 – August 1918, p. 192. Emphasis in original.
37. CA: *Church Army Gazette*, 3 March 1917, p. 5
38. Collins, p. 81
39. YMCA/K/6/1: Major H. Walford Davies 'Music and Arms', *The Red Triangle*, Vol.1, September 1917 – August 1918, p. 97
40. CA: *Church Army Gazette*, 26 August 1916, p. 5
41. *Twenty Years After: The Battlefields of 1914–18: Then and Now*, Part 12, (George Newnes Publication), p. 429
42. Ibid.
43. NAM 1978–08–80–1: Memoirs of Bandsman Sergeant Victor Shawyer, p. 227
44. *Liverpool Echo*, 2 November 1917, p. 3
45. 'Rice, Gitz' in Helmut Kallmann, et al. (eds.), *Encyclopedia of Music in Canada*, 2nd edition, (Toronto: University of Toronto Press, c1992), p. xxxii. Also see www.collectionscanada.gc.ca/gramophone/028011–1027-e.html
46. Liddle/WW1/GS/1088: letter from Mellish printed in his parish magazine: *St Pauls, Deptford, Parish Church Magazine*, 19 August 1915.
47. IWM Documents 16268: Personal papers of Chaplain M. P. G. Leonard, 14 June 1916, France
48. YMCA: 'Songs and Stories of the Front', *The YM*, 23 June 1916, p. 565
49. F. T. Nettleingham, *Tommy's Tunes: A Comprehensive Collection of Soldiers' Songs, Marching Melodies, Rude Rhymes, and Popular Parodies, Composed, Collected and Arranged on Active Service with the B.E.F. Tommy's Tunes*, (London: Erskine Macdonald, 1917), p. 26
50. SAIHC: *The Bandsman, Local Officer & Songster*, No.405, Vol.IX, 2 January 1915, p. 10
51. EFDSS: George Butterworth, *Diary & Letters, Appreciations*, p. 100

52. Maud Karpeles, *Cecil Sharp: His Life and Work*, (London: Routledge & Kegan Paul, 1967)
53. John J. Niles, *Singing Soldiers*, (New York/London: Charles Scribner's Sons, 1927), pp. vii–viii
54. IWM LBY K. 06 /2608: Private Sam Naishtad (SAI Brigade), *The Great War Parodies of the East, Central African and Flanders Campaigns*, undated
55. TNA AIR 76/369/4: Service record of F. T. Nettleingham
56. Nettleingham, *Tommy's Tunes [. . .]*, p. 14
57. Ibid.
58. *The Spectator*, 24 November 1917, p. 19; *New Statesman*, 13 October 1917, p. 40; *Musical Herald*, 1 November 1917, p. 337
59. Nettleingham, *Tommy's Tunes [. . .]*, p. 13
60. Ibid.
61. Ibid., p. 21
62. Ibid., p. 28
63. Tiplady, The Soul of the Soldier, p. 59
64. Lionel Yexley, *The Inner Life of the Navy*, (London: Pitman & Sons, 1908), pp. 199–200
65. IWM 8270: Percy Valentine Harris, Reel 1
66. Ibid.
67. Ibid.
68. See Emma Hanna, 'Say it with Music: Combat, Courage and Identity in the Songs of the RFC/RAF, 1914–1918', *British Journal for Military History*, 4:2, February 2018: (http://bjmh.org.uk/index.php/bjmh/article/view/214)
69. Ward-Jackson, *Airmen's Songbook*, pp. 2–3
70. Sholto Douglas, *Years of Combat*, (London: Collins, 1963), p. 66
71. Imperial War Museum (IWM) 16: Gascoyne, James V (Oral history): Reel 4
72. Douglas, *Years of Combat*, p. 66
73. Clémentine Tholas-Disset & Karen A. Ritzenhoff, *Humour, Entertainment and Popular Culture in World War I*, (London: Palgrave Macmillan, 2015), p. 3
74. Martin Francis, *The Flyer: British Culture and the Royal Air Force, 1939–1945*, (Oxford: Oxford University Press, 1998), p.106
75. YMCA/K/6/1: Percy A. Scholes, 'Music and the Fighting Man', *The Red Triangle*, Vol.2, September 1917 – August 1918, p. 192
76. IWM, LBY 09/71: *Windsor Magazine*, no date, p. 366
77. IWM Documents 17246: Private papers of J. W. Double, Diary, 28 September 1915
78. IWM Documents 15993: Private papers of Private H. Molsom
79. Ibid., p. 110
80. Ibid., p. 106
81. Ibid., pp. 109–10
82. IWM Documents 24991: Private Papers of Captain G. Miller Johnstone, *Any Fool Can Fly*, p. 92
83. Nettleingham, *Tommy's Tunes [. . .]*, p. 49.
84. Lynsey Shaw Cobden, 'The Nervous Flyer: Nerves, Flying and the First World War', *British Journal for Military History*, February 2018, 4:2, 121–142: http://bjmh.org.uk/index.php/bjmh/article/view/215

85. Also see Michael Collins, 'A Fear of Flying: Diagnosing Traumatic Neurosis among British Aviators of the Great War', *First World War Studies*, 6:2, (2015), 187–202; Martin Francis, *The Flyer: British Culture and the Royal Air Force*, (Oxford: Oxford University Press, 2011); and Mark Wells, *Courage and Air Warfare: The Allied Experience of the Second World War*, (London: Frank Cass, 1995)

86. Shaw Cobden, 'The Nervous Flyer'

87. Douglas, *Years of Combat*, pp. 64–5; Alex Revell, *The Happy Warrior: James Thomas Byford McCudden VC*, (Aeronaut Books, 2015), p. 30

88. Douglas, *Years of Combat*, pp. 66, 163–4

89. Maryam Philpott, *Air and Sea Power in World War I: Combat and Experience in the Royal Flying Corps and Royal Navy*, (London: I.B.Tauris, 2013), pp. 75–6

90. Alan Clark, *Aces High: The War in the Air over the Western Front 1914–18*, (London: Weidenfeld & Nicolson, 1973), pp. 30–1

91. IWM Documents 16268: Letters of Reverend M. P. G. Leonard, 28 November 1917, France, Letter 132

92. Ibid., pp. 6–7

93. Charles Quinnell quoted in IWM Podcast: www.iwm.org.uk/history/voi ces-of-the-first-world-war-wartime-leisure-and-entertainment (accessed 15 August 2018)

94. Ward-Jackson, *Airmen's Songbook*, p. 14

95. Rogan, Fifty Years of Army Music, pp. 195–6

96. REM: *The Sapper*, August 1915, p. 14. *In Memoriam*, lyrics by Minnie Coles Windsor, music by John Mainwaring

97. *Daily Mirror*, 17 July 1915

98. *Daily Express*, 18 December 1915

99. *The Era*, 27 September 1916, p. 8

100. Lieutenant the Hon. Esmund Elliot, fourth son of Lord Minto, died of wounds received while he was in command of 'G' Company, 2nd Battalion Scots Guards at Steenbeck River, Langemark, 6 August 1917, age 22. He is buried at Mendinghem Military Cemetery in West Flanders. CWGC Graves Registration Report Form, 29 April 1921

101. Rogan, Fifty Years of Army Music, p. 215

102. RAF PC73/60/189: *A Song of Stunting*, 1918. The aircraft to which this song is dedicated is probably the Avro 504.

103. Tiplady, *The Soul of the Soldier*, pp. 69–70

104. Edward Madigan, '"Sticking to a Hateful Task": Resilience, Humour, and British Understandings of Combatant Courage, 1914–1918', *War in History*, 20:1, (2013), pp. 76–98

CAPTIVITY

1. Fourth Geneva Convention (1949) Chapter V, Article 94, pp. 200–1: www .un.org/en/genocideprevention/documents/atrocity-crimes/Doc.33_GC-IV -EN.pdf (accessed 8 June 2018)

2. Matthew Stibbe, *British Civilian Internees in Germany: The Ruhleben Camp, 1914–1919*, (Manchester: Manchester University Press, 2013);

John Yarnall, *Barbed Wire Disease: British and German Prisoners of War, 1914–1919*, (Stroud: History Press, 2011)

3. Oliver Wilkinson, *British Prisoners of War in First World War Germany*, (Cambridge: Cambridge University Press, 2017), p. 29

4. BRCA: *The British Prisoner of War*, Vol.1, No.7, July 1918, p. 79

5. F. W. Harvey, *Comrades in Captivity: A Record of Life in Seven German Prison Camps*, (London: Sidgwick & Jackson Ltd., 1920), pp. 140–1

6. Ibid., p. 141

7. See Niall Ferguson, *Pity of War*, (London: Penguin, 2009), pp. 367–94; Tim Cook, 'The Politics of Surrender: Canadian Soldiers and the Killing of Prisoners in the Great War', *Journal of Military History*, 2006, 70:3, 637–65; Heather Jones, *Violence Against Prisoners of War in the First World War: Britain, France and Germany, 1914–1919*, (Cambridge: Cambridge University Press, 2011)

8. TNA WO/161: Committee on the Treatment of British Prisoners of War, Interviews and Reports

9. NAM 2005–05-51: Letters of Oliver Lenz, 2nd Rifle Brigade, Soltau PoW Camp

10. IWM, LBY 09/71: *Musical News*, 2 October 1915, npr

11. Harvey, p. 144

12. Ibid., p. 170

13. Adolf Lukas Vischer, *Barbed-Wire Disease: A Psychological Study of the Prisoner of War*, (London: John Bale & Danielson, 1919). See also A. J. Brock, 'Boredom and Barbed-Wire Disease', *British Medical Journal*, 1940, 1: 744; and Yarnall, *Barbed Wire Disease*

14. Harvey, p. 28

15. BRCA: *The British Prisoner of War*, Vol.1, No.1, January 1918, p. 4

16. Harvey, p. 84

17. BRCA: *Reports by the Joint War Committee and the Joint War Finance Committee of the British BRC Society and the Order of St John of Jerusalem in England on Voluntary Aid rendered to the Sick and Wounded at Home and Abroad and to British Prisoners of War 1914–1919, with Appendices* (London: His Majesty's Stationery Offices, 1921), Part I, p. 1

18. BRCA: *The British Prisoner of War*, Vol.1, No.1, January 1918, p. 1

19. BRCA: *The British Prisoner of War*, Vol.1, No.12, December 1918, p. 137

20. BRCA: *The British Prisoner of War*, Vol.1, No.1, January 1918, p. 4

21. BRCA: *The British Prisoner of War*, Vol.1, No.6, June 1918, p. 62

22. BRCA: *The British Prisoner of War*, Vol.1, No.7, July 1918, p. 78

23. BRCA: *The British Prisoner of War*, Vol.1, No.8, August 1918, p. 86

24. Ibid.

25. Ibid.

26. BRCA: *The British Prisoner of War*, Vol.1, No.10, October 1918, front page

27. Harvey, p. 25

28. Ibid., pp. 25–6

29. BRCA: *The British Prisoner of War*, Vol.1, No.8, August 1918, p. 96

30. Ibid.

31. Harvey, pp. 70–80

32. Ibid., p. 77. This song is sometimes referred to as *Captain Stratton's Fancy*, the name of the poem by John Masefield.
33. Ibid., p. 311
34. Ibid., p. 83
35. Ibid.
36. TNA WO 339/50028: Lieutenant William Leefe Robinson VC, Worcestershire Regiment and Royal Flying Corps
37. TNA AIR 79/2503/287271: Second Lieutenant Frank Ernest Hills was seconded from the Royal Garrison Artillery to the RFC in August 1916, *The London Gazette*, 25 August 1916, p. 8405
38. BRCA: *The British Prisoner of War*, Vol.1, No.12, December 1918, p. 143
39. TNA WO 372/8/133001: Medal card of Lieutenant B.M.Greenhill, Household Battalion
40. TNA AIR 76/92/150: Service record of C.A.Clifford, RFC/RAF
41. TNA AIR 76/337/3: Service record of R.B.Martin [note not R.E.], RFC/RAF
42. TNA ADM 240/82/1335: Service record of Lieutenant-Commander Wybrants Olphert, Royal Naval Reserve
43. BRCA: *The British Prisoner of War*, Vol.1, No.12, December 1918, p. 143
44. Ibid., p. 144
45. Harvey, p. 237
46. Ibid., p. 238
47. *The Barb*, 22 December 1917, 6, p. 28
48. Liddle/WW1/POW/016: V. C. Coombs, transcription, p. 8
49. This could have been Captain James Dyson of the Royal Army Chaplain's Department. His service record is available at TNA: WO 374/21603
50. BRCA: *The British Prisoner of War*, Vol.1, No.3, March 1918, pp. 34–5
51. Ibid., p. 35
52. Ibid., pp. 27–9
53. Ibid.
54. IWM 10767: Oral history of Joe Fitzpatrick
55. This could be Percival Leslie Norman whose service record is available at TNA: AIR 79/1422/158258
56. BRCA: *The British Prisoner of War*, Vol.1, No.7, July 1918, p. 74
57. TNA – details not found. He is mentioned in Roger Hutchins, *British University Observatories, 1772–1939*, (London: Routledge, 2008)
58. Harvey, pp. 235–6
59. Ibid., pp. 302–3
60. Ibid., pp. 87–9
61. Ibid., pp. 91–4
62. Ibid., p. 94 (emphasis in original)
63. Ibid., p. 83
64. Ibid., pp. 83–4
65. Liddle/WW1/POW/016: V. C. Coombs, transcription, p. 8
66. BRCA: *The British Prisoner of War*, Vol.1, No.7, July 1918, p. 81
67. Harvey, p. 84
68. Ibid., p. 202

69. BRCA: *The British Prisoner of War*, Vol.1, No.8, August 1918, p. 87
70. Harvey, p. 225
71. Ibid., pp. 226–7
72. Ibid., p. 230
73. TNA ADM 339/1/38674: Service record of Cecil Arthur Tooke (1884–1966), Able Seaman, Royal Naval Volunteer Reserve. They also published *The Link: A Souvenir Book Published by British Prisoners of War Interned at Doeberitz, Germany, 1914–17*, Edited by A. E. Barter, J. Power, C. A. Tooke.
74. BRCA: *The British Prisoner of War*, Vol.1, No.8, August 1918, p. 88
75. Ibid., p. 89
76. Harvey, p. 36
77. TNA AIR 79/33/2556: Service record of John [Harold] Chapman
78. RAF X006-4186/005: Prisoner of War journal of Second Lieutenant John Chapman, July 1917
79. RAF X006-4186/005: Prisoner of War journal of Second Lieutenant John Chapman, December 1917
80. BRCA: *The British Prisoner of War*, Vol.1, No.11, November 1918, p. 125
81. Ibid.
82. BRCA: *The British Prisoner of War*, Vol.1, No.8, August 1918, p. 95
83. Ibid.
84. IWM 23157: Tom Mapplebeck
85. TNA AIR 76/333/56: Service record of Captain Thomas George Mapplebeck, RFC
86. IWM 23157: Tom Mapplebeck
87. TNA WO 372/18/20265: Medal card of Lieutenant Jack Shaw, Oxfordshire and Buckinghamshire Light Infantry
88. TNA WO 374/73337: Service record of Lieutenant James Whale, Worcestershire Regiment
89. BRCA: *The British Prisoner of War*, Vol.1, No.3, March 1918, p. 26
90. BRCA: *The British Prisoner of War*, Vol.1, No.6, June 1918, p. 62
91. BRCA: *The British Prisoner of War*, Vol.1, No.7, July 1918, front page
92. BRCA: *The British Prisoner of War*, Vol.1, No.12, December 1918, front page

RELIGION AND PASTORAL CARE

1. See Sir Arthur Keysall Yapp, *The Romance of the Red Triangle; The Story of the Coming of the Red Triangle and the Service Rendered by the Y.M.C.A. to the Sailors and Soldiers of the British Empire*, Library of Congress (31 December 1918)
2. Michael Snape, *God and the British Soldier: Religion and the British Army in the First and Second World Wars*, (Oxford: Routledge, 2005); Michael Snape, 'Church of England Army Chaplains in the First World War: "Goodbye to All That"', *Journal of Ecclesiastical History*, April 2011, 62:2, 371–403; Michael Snape & Edward Madigan (eds.), *The Clergy in Khaki: New Perspectives on British Army Chaplaincy in the First World War*, (Farnham: Ashgate, 2013)
3. Quoted in Stuart Bell, *Faith in Conflict*, p. 32

4. Stuart Bell, *Faith in Conflict: The Impact of the Great War on the People of Britain*, (Solihull: Helion, 2017)
5. *The Era*, 25 October 1916
6. RMM 11/13/28: Memoirs of a Royal Marine Bandsman, H. J. Reed, p. 32
7. William J. Allen, *SS Borodino, M.F.A. No.6: A Short Account of the Work of the Junior Army and Navy Stores' Store Ship with H.M. Grand Fleet, December 1914– February 1919*, (London: Fleetway Press, 1919), pp. 19–21
8. Ibid.
9. IWM 16268: Letters of Reverend M.P.G.Leonard, 5 December 1917
10. Leonard, 15 March 1918, Belgium
11. Lena Ashwell, *Modern Troubadours: A Record of Concerts at the Front*, (London: Gyldenhal, 1922), p. 86
12. Lieutenant-Colonel J. Mackenzie-Rogan, *Fifty Years of Army Music*, (London: Methuen, 1926), p. 197
13. Leonard, Third Sunday after Epiphany 1916
14. Leonard, 13 August 1916
15. Sarah Reay, *The Half-Shilling Curate: A Personal Account of War and Faith 1914–1918*, (Solihull: Helion, 2016), p. 76
16. Ibid., pp. 83–4
17. Thomas Tiplady, *The Soul of the Soldier: Sketches from the Western Battle-Front*, (London: Fleming H. Revell, 1918), p. 45
18. YMCA K/2/4: YMCA War Work, France, 1915–1918
19. Tiplady, *The Soul of the Soldier*, p. 47
20. 'The Padre', *Fifty Thousand Miles on a Hospital Ship: A Chaplain's Experiences in the Great War*, (London: Religious Tract Society, 1917), pp. 248–9
21. Geoffrey Winthrop Young, *A Story of the Work of the Friends' Ambulance Unit*, (London: Newnham, Cowell & Gripper, 1915); Meaburn Tatham & James E. Miles (eds.), *The Friends' Ambulance Unit, 1914–1919: A Record*, (London: Swarthmore Press, 1920); Olaf Stapledon, 'Experiences in the Friends' Ambulance Unit' in Julian Bell (ed.), *We Did Not Fight 1914–18: Experiences of War Resisters*, (London: Cobden-Sanderson, 1935), pp. 359–74; Jessica Meyer, 'Neutral Caregivers or Military Support: The British BRC, the Friends' Ambulance Unit, and the Problems of Voluntary Medical Aid in Wartime', *War and Society*, 2015, 34, 105–20; Linda Palfreeman, *Friends in Flanders: Humanitarian Aid Administered by the Friends' Ambulance Unit During the First World War*, (Eastbourne: Academic Press, 2017); Rebecca Wynter, 'Keeping the Peace: Working Relationships and the Friends' Ambulance Unit in the First World War', *Ieper*, January 14, 2006
22. For example, see Liddle/WW1/GS/1088: Typescript recollections of Noel Mellish; IWM 16268: Personal papers of Chaplain Pat Leonard; Wartime experiences of the Reverend Herbert Butler Cowl in Sarah Reay Leonard, *The Half-Shilling Curate: A Personal Account of War and Faith 1914–1918*, (Solihull: Helion, 2016)
23. Snape, God and the British Soldier; Snape, 'Church of England Army Chaplains'; Snape & Madigan, The Clergy in Khaki
24. BRCA: *Reports [...]* p. 311

25. Jeffrey S. Reznick, *Healing the Nation: Soldiers and the Culture of Caregiving in Britain During the Great War*, (Manchester: Manchester University Press, 2004)
26. Ibid., p. 5
27. RMM: *Globe & Laurel*, November 1914, p. 395
28. Allen, SS Borodino, p. 16
29. Agnes Weston, *My Life Among the Bluejackets*, (London: James Nisbet, 1909)
30. Lionel Yexley, *Charity and the Navy: A Protest against Indiscriminate Begging on Behalf of 'Poor Jack'*, (London: The Fleet Ltd, 1911), p. 8
31. RMM 11/13/28: Memoirs of a Royal Marine Bandsman, H. J. Reed.
32. SAIHC: *The Bandsman, Local Officer & Songster*, No.388, Vol.VIII, 5 September 1914, p. 569
33. Ibid., p. 568
34. CA: *Church Army Gazette*, 12 September 1914, p. 3
35. SAIHC: *The Bandsman, Local Officer & Songster*, No.386, Vol.VIII, 22 August 1914, p. 531
36. EFDSS: George Butterworth, *Diary & Letters*, p. 32
37. Ibid., p. 29
38. YMCA/K/1/7: Green Book No.5, Photographs Illustrating the emergency war work of the YMCA (Germany, Holland, India, Italy)
39. SAIHC: *The Bandsman, Local Officer & Songster*, No.396, Vol.VIII, 31 October 1914, p. 696
40. Reverend G. Vernon Smith, *The Bishop of London's Visit to the Front*, (London: Longmans, 1915), p. 78–9
41. Liddle/WW1/GS/1088: letter from Mellish printed in his parish magazine: *St Pauls, Deptford, Parish Church Magazine*, 16 July 1915
42. Michael Young, *Army Service Corps 1908–1918*, (Barnsley: Leo Cooper, 2000)
43. Arthur Yapp and F. A. McKenzie quoted in Michael Snape, *The Back Parts of War: The YMCA Memoirs and Letters of Barclay Baron, 1915–1919*, (Woodbridge: Boydell & Brewer, 2009), pp. 20, 21
44. SAIHC: *The Bandsman, Local Officer & Songster*, No.385, Vol.VIII, 15 August 1914, p. 520
45. SAIHC: *The Bandsman, Local Officer & Songster*, No.399, Vol.VIII, 21 November 1914, p. 739
46. SAIHC: *The Bandsman, Local Officer & Songster*, No.427, Vol.IX, 5 June 1915, p. 360
47. SAIHC: *The Bandsman, Local Officer & Songster*, No.397, Vol.VIII, 7 November 1914, p. 714
48. Ibid.
49. SAIHC: *The Bandsman, Local Officer & Songster*, No.394, Vol.VIII, 17 October 1914, p. 665
50. IWM Documents 17246: Private papers of J. W. Double, Diary
51. SAIHC: *The Bandsman, Local Officer & Songster*, No.407, Vol.IX, 16 January 1915, p. 58
52. CA: *Church Army Gazette*, 22 July 1916, p. 5
53. SAIHC: *Under the Colours*, April 1915, Vol.XIX, No.4, p. 99

54. CA: *Church Army Gazette*, 18 March 1916, p. 5
55. SAIHC: *Under the Colours*, April 1915, Vol.XIX, No.4, p. 82
56. CA: The Church Army 'Blue Book: Report, 1913–1915', p. 114
57. YMCA: *The YM*, 7 January 1916, p. 1244
58. SAIHC: General W. Bramwell Booth quoted in *The Bandsman, Local Officer & Songster*, No.392, Vol.VIII, 3 October 1914, p. 632
59. CA: *Church Army Gazette*, 19 December 1915, p. 6
60. Captain James E. Agate, *Lines of Communication: Being the Letters of a Temporary Officer in the Army Service Corps*, (London: Constable & Co. Ltd., 1917), p. 88
61. Leonard, 28 July 1918
62. Leonard, 17 January 1916
63. Leonard, 19 June 1918
64. Leonard, 14 June 1916
65. Leonard, 30 October 1918
66. Leonard, 22 May 1916
67. Liddle/WW1/GS/1088: Typescript recollections of Mellish, E Noel, p. 29
68. Liddle/WW1/GS/1088: Letter from Mellish to *St Pauls, Deptford, Parish Church Magazine*, 16 July 1915
69. RAMC/CF/4/3/92/PRAY, 'A Form of Prayer to be used at Open-Air Services'
70. CA: *Church Army Gazette*, 1 May 1915, p. 3
71. Tiplady, *The Soul of the Soldier*, pp. 68–9
72. CA: *Church Army Gazette*, 31 March 1917, p. 1
73. SAIHC: *The Bandsman, Local Officer & Songster*, No.391, Vol.VIII, 26 September 1914, p. 616
74. CA: *Church Army Gazette*, 21 August 1915, p. 5
75. CA: *Church Army Gazette*, 10 October 1914, p. 2
76. CA: *Church Army Gazette*, 20 February 1915, p. 1
77. *The Bystander*, 29 March 1916, p. 593; *The Illustrated Sporting and Dramatic News*, 6 May 1916, p. 274
78. Michael Snape, 'British Army Chaplains and Capital Courts Martial During the First World War' in Kate Cooper & Jeremy Gregory (eds.), *Retribution, Repentance and Reconciliation*, (Martlesham: Ecclesiastical History Society, 2004), pp. 357–68. The oral testimony of Leonard Martin-Andrews is available at IWM 4770 (1981).
79. TNA WO 95/2954/2, War Diary of 1/12 Battalion, London Regiment (Rangers), 1 February 1916–31 January 1918
80. John Bickersteth (ed.), *The Bickersteth Diaries: 1914–1918*, (London: Leo Cooper, 1995), pp. 189–94. The condemned man was No. 47431, Rifleman Walter Yeoman, aged 22 of the 1/12th Battalion, London Regiment, 168th Brigade, 56th Division. He was executed on 3 July 1917 for desertion. He was buried at Achicourt Road Cemetery, 2 miles southwest of Arras, France. Walter Yeoman's trial record can be found at TNA WO 71/566.
81. TNA WO 95/2963/1, War Diary of 1/9 Battalion, London Regiment (Queen Victoria's Rifles), 1 February 1916–31 January 1918

82. Bickersteth, *Bickersteth Diaries*, pp. 224–5. The soldier was No. 393923, Rifleman Harry Williams, of 1/9th Battalion, London Regiment (Queen Victoria's Rifles), 169th Brigade, 56th (London) Division. He was executed on 28 December 1917 for desertion, and buried in Roclincourt Military Cemetery, 2 miles north of Arras, France.

83. SAIHC: *The Bandsman, Local Officer & Songster*, No.387, Vol.VIII, 29th August 1914, p. 547

84. IWM Documents: Lena Ashwell Special Collection, *Windsor Magazine*, no date, p. 369

85. RLCM: J8822/e 38: *Carry On: The Official Journal of the EFC Section of the Army Service Corps on Service* [undated], 'Our Daily Routine and a few well-known Hymns', p. 4

86. NAM 9702-13: Personal papers of Lieutenant-Colonel Sir Hoel Llewellyn, 'This is the orders for the day' [sic]

87. F. T. Nettleingham, *Tommy's Tunes: A Comprehensive Collection of Soldiers' Songs, Marching Melodies, Rude Rhymes, and Popular Parodies, Composed, Collected and Arranged on Active Service with the B.E.F. Tommy's Tunes*, (London: Erskine Macdonald, 1917), pp. 42–4

88. C. H. Ward-Jackson (ed.), *Airman's Song Book: Being an Anthology of Squadron, Concert Party, Training and Camp Songs and Song-Parodies . . .*, (London: Sylvan, 1945), p. 10

89. CA: *Church Army Gazette*, 3 March 1917, p. 5

90. Ibid.

91. SAIHC: *Under the Colours*, October 1914, Vol.XVIII, No.10, p. 5

92. SAIHC: *The Bandsman, Local Officer & Songster*, No.395, Vol.VIII, 24 October 1914, p. 675

93. Reznick, *Healing the Nation*, p. 3

94. Ambler, *The Royal Marines Band Service*, p. 25

95. Double, 12 March 1916

96. Double, 13 February 1916

97. Double, 27 October 1916

98. Double, 2 November 1916

99. Double, 29 March 1916

100. Double, 3 March 1916

101. Double, 20 April 1916

102. Double, 16 April 1916

103. David Lazell, *Gypsy from the Forest: A New Biography of the International Evangelist Gipsy Smith (1860–1947)* (CITY: Gwasg Bryntirion Press, 1997), p. 152

104. YMCA/ACC2: YMCA Unofficial Papers: Papers of Gipsy Smith, scrapbook, p. 3, p. 15

105. Lazell, p. 37

106. SAHC: *Bandsman, Local Officer & Songster*, 22 July 2016

107. SAIHC: *The Bandsman, Local Officer & Songster*, No.402, Vol.VIII, 12 December 1914, p. 792

108. YMCA: Report by L. G. Pilkington, Havre, 31 December 1915

109. YMCA: 'The Red Triangle in a Rest Camp', R. H. Miller (Calais) undated, p. 2
110. J. G. Fuller, *Troop Morale and Popular Culture in the British and Dominion Armies*, (Oxford: Clarendon, 1990), p. 81
111. IWM, LBY 09/71: *Pall Mall Gazette*, 12 April 1915, npr
112. TNA 10 95 4120 1: No.5 Convalescent Depot, Wimereaux, War Diary, 22 September 1916
113. YMCA: Major-General A. A. Chichester, 2nd Army HQ, to Oliver McCowen, 1 March 1916
114. YMCA/K/1/7: Green Book No.5, Photographs Illustrating the emergency war work of the YMCA (Germany, Holland, India, Italy)
115. Liddle/WW1/GS/1088: letter from Mellish printed in his parish magazine: *St Pauls, Deptford, Parish Church Magazine*, 16 July 1915
116. CA: *Church Army Gazette*, 3 March 1917, p. 5
117. YMCA/K/6/1: Percy A. Scholes, 'Music and the Fighting Man', *The Red Triangle*, Vol.2, September 1917–August 1918, p. 192
118. YMCA/K/6/1: 'The Music Department and its Resources', *The Red Triangle*, Vol.6, September 1917–August 1918, p. 207
119. Ibid.
120. Ibid.
121. *The Musical Times*, 1 October 1918, p. 475
122. YMCA/K/6/1: Helen Mott, 'Good Music and the Soldier', *The Red Triangle*, Vol.1, September 1917–August 1918, pp. 367–8
123. Ibid.
124. IWM, LBY 09/71: *Blackwood's Magazine*, December 1916, npr
125. Also see Catherine Hindson, *London's West End Actresses and the Origins of Celebrity Charity, 1880–1920*, (Iowa City: University of Iowa Press, 2016), p. 198
126. IWM, LBY 09/71: *Illustrated Sunday Herald*, 28 March 1915, npr
127. YMCA/K/1/8/31: Minutes of the Finance and War Emergency Committee, 24 April 1917 and 22 May 1917
128. Hon. Mrs Stuart-Wortley, 'What We Are Doing at Ciro's', *The Red Triangle*, 25 May 1917, p. 467
129. YMCA/K/1/8/31: Minutes of the Finance and War Emergency Committee, 26th June 1917
130. YMCA/K/6/1: *The Red Triangle*, 15 June 1917
131. YMCA Education Committee, Music Sub-Committee, Minutes, 21 February 1923
132. IWM Documents 15459: Private Papers of Gordon Williams, diary, July 1917, pp. 10–11
133. EFDSS: D. C. Daking, 'A Report', *English Folk Dance and Song*, March-April 1940, pp. 44–5
134. Ibid. Regarding Étaples, Daking wrote that 'there was a colonel who applied for a couple of folk dancers for one week as his men rather wished to have a meeting'. In her papers in the EFDS she has crossed out the word 'meeting' and written in the word 'mutiny'.
135. Ibid.

136. YMCA: *Yearbook of the Young Men's Christian Association in England, Ireland and Wales, [. . .] 1914–1920* (London: YMCA, 1921), pp. 8–9
137. YMCA K/1/7: War Emergency Work; Germany, Holland, India, Italy
138. YMCA K/2/4: YMCA War Work in France, 1915–18 – Work for Indians in France
139. YMCA: *Red Triangle Bulletin*, No.58, 18 September 1918, npr
140. YMCA K/1/7: War Emergency Work; Germany, Holland, India, Italy
141. YMCA: Reverend A. W. McMillan, *The Indian Labour Corps in France*, p. 12
142. YMCA: *The World*, 5 February 1918, p. 135
143. YMCA: *The Indian Labour Corps in France*, p. 7 and *The World*, 5 February 1918, p. 135
144. YMCA: *The Red Triangle*, No.3, November 1917, p. 82
145. YMCA: *The Red Triangle*, February 1920, p. 211
146. TNA WO 107/37: Distribution of Labour Battalions and Companies. For more on the CLC, see Gregory James, *The Chinese Labour Corps 1916–1920*, (Hong Kong: Bayview Educational, 2013) and Michael Summerskill, *China on the Western Front*, (Norwich: Page Bros, 1982)
147. YMCA: *Yearbook of the Young Men's Christian Association in England, Ireland and Wales [. . .] 1914–1920*, (London: YMCA, 1921) p. 7
148. Yapp, *Romance of the Red Triangle*, pp. 164–5
149. CA: *Church Army Gazette*, 30 October 1915, p. 8
150. YMCA/K/6/1: Percy A. Scholes, 'Music and the Fighting Man', *The Red Triangle*, Vol.2, September 1917–August 1918, p. 192
151. IWM, LBY 09/71: *Blackwood's Magazine*, December 1916, npr

MEDICINE AND THERAPY

1. IWM, LBY 09/71: *Daily Star*, 20 March 1915, npr
2. Letter from Bruce Porter, Colonel Commanding, 3rd London General Hospital, to Annette Hullah, 29 March 1917, 'Record of the MIWTC, IWM', p. 14
3. BRCA: *Reports [. . .]*, Part I, p. 2
4. Alfred Harmsworth Northcliffe, *At the War*, (London: Hodder & Stoughton, 1916)
5. BRCA: *Reports [. . .]*, p. 16
6. Ibid., p. 61
7. Ibid., p. 158
8. Ibid., p. 232
9. Ibid., pp. 208–9
10. Ibid., pp. 209–10
11. Ibid., pp. 261–2
12. Ibid., p. 236
13. Ibid., p. 277
14. Ibid., pp. 98–9
15. Ibid., p. 100
16. Ibid., p. 99
17. Ibid., p. 293

18. Ibid.
19. Ibid., p. 294
20. Ibid.
21. Ibid., p. 296
22. Ibid.
23. Ibid.
24. Ibid.
25. Ibid.
26. Ibid.
27. Ibid.
28. Ibid.
29. Ibid.
30. Ibid.
31. Ibid., p. 358
32. Ibid., pp. 355–6
33. Ibid., p. 356
34. Ibid.
35. Ibid.
36. Ibid.
37. Ibid., p. 357
38. Ibid.
39. Ibid.
40. Ibid.
41. Ibid., p. 358
42. Ibid.
43. Ibid.
44. Ibid., p. 410
45. Ibid.
46. Ibid., pp. 410–11
47. Ibid., p. 411
48. Ibid., p. 412
49. IWM 17246: Private papers of J. W. Double, Diary, 18 June 1915
50. Ibid., 19 June 1915
51. BRCA: *Reports [. . .]*, p. 426
52. Ibid., p. 428
53. BRCA: *Reports [. . .]*, p. 472
54. YMCA-sponsored Lena Ashwell performers recalled being driven in BRC ambulances, for example, the young violinist Gwendoline Teagle: IWM, LBY 09/71: *Queen*, 17 July 1915, npr
55. BRCA: *Reports [. . .]*, p. 311
56. SAIHC: *Under the Colours*, February 1915, Vol.XIX, No.2, p. 20
57. *The Fledgling: The Monthly Journal of the No.2 Royal Flying Corps Cadet Wing*, 1 September 1917, 1, 4, p. 128
58. *Daily Sketch*, 31 December 1914, front page
59. Ellaline Terriss, *Just a Little Bit of String*, (London: Hutchinson, 1955), p. 221
60. IWM, LBY 09/71: *Daily News*, 26 September 1915, npr

61. MMM: QARANC/P6/1/107/BLAI, Miss M. A. C. Blair, p. 10
62. IWM, LBY 09/71: *The Globe*, 7 April 1915, npr
63. MMM: QARANC/P6/1/107/BLAI, Miss M. A. C. Blair, p. 11
64. IWM, LBY 09/71: *Bradford Weekly Telegraph*, 6 August 1915, npr
65. IWM, LBY 09/71: *Manchester Guardian*, 4 June 1915, npr
66. IWM, LBY 09/71: *Musical Times*, 1 July 1915, p. 401
67. IWM, LBY 09/71: *Dublin Evening Herald*, 20 July 1915, npr
68. IWM 22371: Private Papers of E. B. Pierpoint. Letter from C. W. James, 3 January 1917
69. IWM, LBY 09/71: *Daily News*, 26 September 1915, npr
70. IWM, LBY 09/71: *Queen*, 17 July 1915, npr
71. Harry Lauder, *A Minstrel in France*, (New York: Hearst's International Library Co., 1918), p. 143
72. IWM, LBY 09/71: *Musical Times*, 1 July 1915, p. 401
73. IWM, LBY 09/71: *Dublin Evening Herald*, 20 July 1915, npr
74. Lieutenant-Colonel J. Mackenzie-Rogan, *Fifty Years of Army Music*, (London: Methuen, 1926), p. 190
75. Ibid., p. 193
76. Ibid.
77. IWM, LBY 09/71: *The Gentlewoman*, 27 November 1915, p. 352
78. Lauder, *A Minstrel in France*, pp. 40–1
79. IWM, LBY 09/71: *The Globe*, 7 April 1915, npr
80. IWM Documents 15459: Gordon Williams, diary, July 1917, p. 18
81. IWM, LBY 09/71: *Musical News*, 3 April 1915, npr
82. IWM, LBY 09/71: Minute from Director of Medical Services to the Governor of Malta (Methuen) published by the *Malta Daily Chronicle*, 11 March 1916
83. BRCA: *Reports [. . .]*, p. 392
84. Ibid.
85. Ibid.
86. Ibid., p. 393
87. IWM 17246: Private papers of J. W. Double, Diary, 28 March 1916
88. Ibid., 3 April 1916
89. Ibid.
90. Ibid., 4 April 1916
91. Ibid., 24 April 1916
92. Ibid., 23 May 1916
93. TNA WO/372/6/69654: Medal card of Double, Johnson W.
94. BRCA: *Reports [. . .]*, p. 405
95. Ibid., p. 398
96. Ibid., pp. 399–400
97. Ibid., p. 400
98. Ibid.
99. Ibid.
100. Ibid.
101. Ibid., p. 401
102. Ibid.

103. TNA 10 95 4120 1: No.5 Convalescent Depot, Wimereaux, War Diary, 8 August 1915
104. Ibid., 20 August 1915
105. Liddle/WW1/GS/1088: Typescript recollections of Mellish, E Noel, p. 1
106. TNA 10 95 4120 1: No.5 Convalescent Depot, Wimereaux, War Diary, 18 September 1915
107. Ibid., 16 January 1917
108. Ibid., p. 11. A Lieutenant Anthony Arrigone is listed as having served in The King's Own (Yorkshire Light Infantry) and his service papers are found at TNA WO 339/28770.
109. Ibid., p. 12
110. Ibid.
111. Ibid., pp. 12–13
112. Ibid., p. 13
113. Ibid., p. 8
114. Ibid., p. 13, emphasis in original.
115. TNA 372/11/103105: Medal card of Trooper Michael Kearns, Guards Machine Gun Regiment
116. TNA WO 95 4121 4: No.13 Convalescent Depot, Trouville, War Diary, p. 20
117. Ibid., p. 15
118. Ibid., p. 15. There is a photograph of an open-air performance in front of a large audience of troops by the 'Bohemians' of No. 14 Convalescent Depot at Trouville. The stage has been erected in the shell of a ruined building, 16 August 1918: IWM Q 11503.
119. IWM, LBY 09/71: *Dublin Evening Herald*, 20 July 1915, npr
120. Jenny Hazelgrove, 'Spiritualism after the Great War', *Twentieth Century British History*, 1999, 10, 404–30. See also Jay Winter, *Sites of Memory, Sites of Mourning*, (Cambridge: Cambridge University Press, 1995)
121. James G. Mansell, 'Musical Modernity and Contested Commemoration at the Festival of Remembrance, 1923–1927', *The Historical Journal*, 2009, 52:2, 435
122. Annie Besant, *Religion and Music*, p. 20 and Cyril Scott, *Music, Its Secret Influence throughout the Ages* (1933) both quoted in Mansell 'Musical Modernity and Contested Commemoration at the Festival of Remembrance, 1923–1927', p. 439
123. IWM, LBY 09/71: *Daily Express*, 18 June 1915, npr
124. IWM, LBY 09/71: *Liverpool Courier*, 7 September 1915, npr
125. Ibid., p. 254
126. Ibid.
127. Ibid., pp. 254–5
128. Ibid., p. 255
129. Ibid.

THE GRAMOPHONE

1. NHC: *Talking Machine News and Journal of Amusements*, Vol.VII, No.205, January 1915, p. 42

2. IWM LBY 09/71: Lena Ashwell Special Collection, *Windsor Magazine*, no date, p. 366
3. Peter Martland, *Recording History: The British Record Industry, 1888–1931*, (London: Scarecrow Press, 2013), p. 208
4. NHC: *Talking Machine News and Journal of Amusements*, Vol.VII, No.205, January 1915, p. 42
5. Ibid., pp. 41–42
6. Ibid., p. 41
7. NHC: *His Master's Voice Records of Patriotic Songs: National Anthems of the Allies, Military and Naval Airs, Songs about Tommy Atkins and Jack*, c.1917–18
8. NHC: *Talking Machine News and Journal of Amusements*, Vol.VII, No.205, January 1915, p. 44
9. Ibid., p. 42
10. Ibid., p. 44
11. NHC: *HMV: The Catalogue* of Records, September 1916
12. NHC: *Talking Machine News and Journal of Amusements*, Vol.VII, No.205, January 1915, p. 42
13. Ibid., p. 44
14. Ibid., p. 1
15. Ibid., p. 42
16. RMM: November 1914, p. 395
17. NHC: *Talking Machine News and Journal of Amusements*, Vol.VII, No.205, January 1915, p. 44
18. *The Sketch*, 4 August 1915, 91, 1175, p. II
19. *The Graphic Summer Number*, 10 June 1916, 93, 2428, p. 756
20. *Answers*, 23 September 1916, 57, 17, p. 322
21. *The Machine Gun Corps Magazine*, 1 May 1918, 2, p. 14
22. Ibid.
23. Ibid.
24. Ibid.
25. *The Bystander*, 1 December 1915, 48, 626, p. 383
26. Ibid.
27. *The Graphic Summer Number*, 10 June 1916, 93, 2428, p. 756
28. *The Bystander*, 27 January 1915, 45, 582, p. 132
29. NHC: *Edison Bell Discaphones Catalogue*, 1915–16 season, Introduction
30. *The Sketch*, 29 December 1915, 92, 1196, p. 290
31. NHC: *Edison Bell Discaphones Catalogue*, 1915–16 season, pp. 7 and 11
32. *The Sketch*, 4 August 1915, 91, 1175, p. II
33. *The Sketch*, 29 December 1915, 92, 1196, p. 290
34. Ibid.
35. Ibid.
36. *The Musical Standard*, 25 February 1911, 35, 895, p. 123
37. Ibid.
38. *Answers*, 23 September 1916, 57, 17, p. 322
39. Ibid.
40. Ibid.

41. Quoted in *The Graphic Summer Number*, 10 June 1916, 93, 2428, p. 756
42. *The Graphic Summer Number*, 10 June 1916, 93, 2428, p. 756
43. Ibid.
44. *Answers*, 23 September 1916, 57, 17, p. 322
45. Captain James E. Agate, *Lines of Communication: Being the Letters of a Temporary Officer in the Army Service Corps*, (London: Constable & Co. Ltd., 1917), p. 85
46. *The Sketch*, 29 December 1915, 92, 1196, p. 290
47. NAM 2013/05/1: Letters of Lieutenant Jack Wood, 15th Middlesex Regiment, 21 September 1915
48. IWM 9927: Arthur Hemsley, Reel 7
49. IWM 9535: George Cole, Reel 3
50. *The Sphere*, 16 December 1916, 67, 882, p. viii
51. IWM 6482, 19/16/1: War Diaries of Lieutenant R. P. E. Roberts, Royal Field Artillery
52. *The Saturday Review*, 16 February 1918, p. 133
53. Ibid.
54. Ibid., p. 134
55. Agate, Lines of Communication, p. 83
56. Ibid.
57. Ibid., p. 84
58. *Answers*, 12 August 1916, 57, 11, p. 201
59. Enid Bagnold published an account of her hospital experience in *A Diary Without Dates* (1917). Bagnold then went on to serve as a driver, publishing *The Happy Foreigner* in 1920.
60. *Reveille*, 1 August 1918, p. 90
61. Ibid., p. 91
62. Ibid.
63. Ibid.
64. Ibid.
65. *The Listening Post*, 7th *Canadian Infantry Battalion (1st British Colombia Regiment)*, 1 April 1918, p. 6
66. Ibid.
67. Ibid.
68. Ibid.
69. Lieutenant-Colonel J. Mackenzie-Rogan, *Fifty Years of Army Music*, (London: Methuen, 1926), p. 210
70. *The Machine Gun Corps Magazine*, 1 May 1918, 2, p. 14
71. Ibid.
72. Ibid.
73. TNA WO 339/2518: Service record of Major Hope Brankston Viney, Army Service Corps
74. *With the Colours: A Record of Service for King and Country at Home and Abroad by Employees of Hazell, Watson and Viney Ltd.*, 1 December 1916, p. 96
75. BRCA: *The British Prisoner of War*, Vol.1, No.6, June 1918, p. 66
76. IWM 16268: Personal papers of Chaplain M. P. G. Leonard, 12 December 1915

77. Ibid., 17 January 1916
78. NHC: Letter from Lieutenant Richard Noble to his wife, 3 February 1916, p. 3. Noble's service record is at TNA WO 374/50748.
79. NHC: Letter from Lieutenant Richard Noble to his wife, 13 February 1916, p. 1
80. NHC: *Edison Bell Discaphones Catalogue*, 1915–16 season, Introduction
81. *The Machine Gun Corps Magazine*, 1 May 1918, 2, p. 14
82. *The Barb*, 22 December 1917, 6, p. 28
83. RAF X006-4186/005: Prisoner of War journal of Second Lieutenant John Chapman, July 1917
84. BRCA: *The British Prisoner of War*, Vol.1, No.6, June 1918, p. 66
85. IWM 17246: Private papers of J. W. Double, Diary
86. BRCA: *Reports by the Joint War Committee and the Joint War Finance Committee of the British Red Cross Society and the Order of St John of Jerusalem in England on Voluntary Aid rendered to the Sick and Wounded at Home and Abroad and to British Prisoners of War 1914–1919, with Appendices* (London: His Majesty's Stationery Offices, 1921), p. 294
87. Ibid., p. 297
88. Ibid., pp. 402–3
89. Ibid., p. 402
90. Ibid., p. 471
91. Ibid., pp. 471–2
92. Ibid., pp. 518–19
93. Ibid., pp. 520–1
94. *The Silver Lining or Sister's Smiles: A Journal for the Patients of the 42nd C.C.S.*, 1 October 1916, 1, p. 8 [emphasis in original]
95. *Burgoo! The Gazette of the 3rd London General Hospital, Wandsworth*, 2, 4, 1 January 1917, p. 111
96. Ibid.
97. Ibid.
98. *The Gazette of the 3rd London General Hospital, Wandsworth*, 1 September 1916, p. 314
99. Cutherbert Headlam, *The History of the Guards Division in the Great War, 1915–18* (London: John Murray, 1924)
100. Mackenzie-Rogan, Fifty Years of Army Music, p. 191
101. Ibid.
102. *Stand Easy: Being the Journal of the 2/7 Manchester Regiment*, 1 October 1916, p. 60
103. IWM 16268: Leonard, 17 December 1915
104. Leonard, 17 November 1915
105. Leonard, 21 November 1915
106. Cecil Lewis, *Sagittarius Rising* (London: Peter Davis, 1936), p. 227
107. IWM, LBY 09/71: *Evening News*, September 1915, npr
108. Gramophone Company, *Gramophone Records of the First World War: An HMV Catalogue 1914–18*, Introduced by Brian Rust, (Newton Abbot: David & Charles, 1975)

CIVILIAN CONCERT PARTIES

1. Basil Dean, *Theatre at War*, (London: George Harrap, 1956), chapter 1
2. Letter from the secretary of John Broadwood & Sons to Annette Hullah, 30 June 1919
3. Ellaline Terriss, *By Herself and with Others*, (London: Cassell, 1928), p. 211
4. Ellaline Terriss, *Just a Little Bit of String*, (London: Hutchinson, 1955), p. 216
5. *The Times*, 23 December 1914, p. 11
6. Terriss, *Just a Little Bit of String*, p. 216
7. Ibid.
8. Terriss, *By Herself and with Others*, p. 212
9. Terriss, *Just a Little Bit of String*, pp. 216–17
10. Ibid., p. 217
11. Ibid.
12. Sir John French's telegram quoted in Terriss, *Just a Little Bit of String*, p. 217
13. Ibid.
14. Ibid.
15. Ibid.
16. Ibid., p. 218
17. Ibid.
18. *The Times*, 22 December 1914, p. 5
19. Terriss, *Just a Little Bit of String*, p. 218
20. Ibid., p. 219
21. *The Times*, 22 December 1914, p. 5
22. Terriss, *Just a Little Bit of String*, pp. 219–20
23. *The Times*, 28 December 1914, p. 3
24. Ibid.
25. Terriss, *Just a Little Bit of String*, p. 221
26. *The Times*, 29 December 1914, p. 6
27. *The Times*, 28 December 1914, p. 3
28. Terriss, *Just a Little Bit of String*, p. 222
29. *The Times*, 31 December 1914, p. 11
30. Terriss, *Just a Little Bit of String*, p. 221
31. *The Times*, 29 December 1914, p. 6
32. Terriss, *Just a Little Bit of String*, p. 222
33. Ibid.
34. *The Times*, 30 December 1914, p. 8
35. Ibid.
36. Terriss, *Just a Little Bit of String*, p. 222
37. Ibid., p. 223
38. *The Times*, 31 December 1914, p. 11
39. Ibid.
40. Ibid.
41. Harry Lauder, *A Minstrel in France*, (New York: Hearst's International Library Co., 1918), p. 109
42. Ibid., p. 109–10
43. Ibid., p. 111

44. For more on James Hogge's work for servicemen's pensions see Emma Hanna, 'Veterans' Associations (Great Britain and Ireland)', in *1914–1918-Online: International Encyclopedia of the First World War*, Ute Daniel, Peter Gatrell, Oliver Janz, Heather Jones, Jennifer Keene, Alan Kramer & Bill Nasson (eds.), (Berlin: Freie Universität, 2015)
45. Ibid., p. 240
46. IWM 7256: Lendon Fitz Payne, oral history
47. IWM 11794: Diary of W. J. Reynolds, Royal Naval Division
48. Lauder, *A Minstrel in France*, p. 251
49. Ibid., p. 323
50. IWM, LBY 09/71: *Blackwood's Magazine*, December 1916, npr
51. Lena Ashwell, *Modern Troubadours: A Record of Concerts at the Front*, (London, 1922), p. 5
52. Ibid.
53. IWM, LBY 09/71: *Nineteenth Century*, August 1915, p. 346
54. Ashwell, *Modern Troubadours*, p. 7
55. IWM, LBY 09/71: *De Rouen*, 25 February 1915, npr
56. Ibid.
57. IWM, LBY 09/71: Letter from Theodore Flint to Lena Ashwell, 21 February 1915
58. IWM, LBY 09/71: Letter from Frederick Hudson to Lena Ashwell, 19 February 1915
59. IWM, LBY 09/71: *Daily Star*, 20 March 1915, npr
60. IWM, LBY 09/71: Letter from I.G.Pilkington (YMCA) to Lena Ashwell, 20 February 1915
61. IWM, LBY 09/71: *Leeds Mercury*, 8 March 1915, npr
62. IWM, LBY 09/71: *Daily Star*, 20 March 1915, npr
63. IWM, LBY 09/71: Flyer for YMCA Grand Concerts, 22–27 March 1915
64. IWM 22371: Private Papers of E. B. Pierpoint, YMCA Map
65. IWM, LBY 09/71: *Nineteenth Century*, August 1915, p. 346
66. IWM, LBY 09/71: *Bradford Weekly Telegraph*, 6 August 1915, npr
67. 'G.S.O.', *G.H.Q. (Montreuil-sur-Mer)*, (London: Philip Allan & Co., 1920), p. 60
68. LIDDLE/WW1/GS/1088: Typescript recollections of Mellish, E Noel, p. 1
69. IWM, LBY 09/71: *Daily Chronicle*, 13 March 1916, npr
70. Ibid.
71. Ashwell, *Modern Troubadours*, p. 80
72. IWM, LBY 09/71: Schedule, Firing Line parties
73. IWM, LBY 09/71: *Musical Times*, 1 July 1915, p. 401
74. IWM, LBY 09/71: *Daily Chronicle*, 13 March 1916, npr
75. Ibid.
76. Ibid.
77. YMCA: 'On Tour in the Mediterranean'. *The YM*, 9 June 1916, p. 519
78. Ibid.
79. Ibid.
80. IWM Documents 12735: H. W. Williams, RN: L. H. W. Williams (ed.), *Fat's War: His Letters, Journals and Diary*, pp. 151–2

81. YMCA: 'On Tour in the Mediterranean'. *The YM*, 9 June 1916, p. 519
82. Ibid.
83. IWM 17246: Private papers of J. W. Double, Diary
84. IWM, LBY 09/71: *Daily Malta Chronicle*, 9 March 1916, npr
85. IWM 17246: Private papers of J. W. Double, Diary
86. IWM 22371: Private Papers of E. B. Pierpoint
87. Ibid., 18 April 1916
88. Ibid., 20 April 1916
89. IWM 22371: Letter from E. A. Pleasance, YMCA Calais, 12 August 1916
90. IWM 22371: Letter from E. A. Pleasance, YMCA Calais, 26 April 1917
91. IWM 22371: Private papers of J. W. Double, Diary, 22 December 1916
92. Ibid., 29 December 1916
93. IWM 22371: Private Papers of E. B. Pierpoint
94. IWM 15459: Private Papers of Gordon Williams, Diary, July 1917, pp. 10–11
95. IWM 15459: Private Papers of Gordon Williams
96. Ibid., Diary, July 1917, p. 14
97. Ibid., p. 15
98. Ibid., p. 14
99. Ibid., Diary, July 1917, p. 15
100. Rose Venn-Brown, letter to home 16th February 1918, p. 81
101. Rose Venn-Brown, Diary of the Great War, p. 32
102. IWM 15459: Private Papers of Gordon Williams, Diary, July 1917, p. 17
103. Ibid., p. 14
104. Ibid., Diary, p. 24
105. IWM, LBY 09/71: *Blackwood's Magazine*, December 1916, npr
106. IWM, LBY 09/71: *Daily News*, 30 July 1915, npr
107. IWM 15459: Private Papers of Gordon Williams, Diary, July 1917, p. 16
108. Ibid.
109. Ibid., p. 19
110. Ibid.
111. Ibid.
112. Ibid., p. 20. The monkey was probably Jeffery, owned by Captain Vernon William Blythe Castle, a Norwich-born dancer who was living in American and enlisted as a pilot in the Royal Flying Corps in 1915. His service record is available at TNA: WO 339/55743.
113. Ibid., Diary, p. 20
114. Ibid., p. 21
115. Ibid., p. 21
116. Ibid., Diary, August 1917, p. 23
117. Ibid., p. 22
118. Ibid., pp. 23–4
119. Ibid., p. 24
120. Ibid., p. 25
121. Ibid., text of letter in newspaper cutting, December 1917, no newspaper title given
122. Ibid.

123. IWM, LBY 09/71: *Musical News*, 3 April 1915, npr
124. IWM, LBY 09/71: *Beckenham Journal*, 17 July 1915, npr
125. IWM, LBY 09/71: *Nineteenth Century*, August 1915, p. 345
126. IWM, LBY 09/71: *Manchester Guardian*, 4 June 1915, npr
127. For more on this see Emma Hanna, 'Putting the Moral into Morale: YMCA. Cinemas on the Western Front, 1914–1918', *Historical Journal of Film, Radio & Television*, October 2015, 35:4, 615–30
128. Ibid.
129. Siegfried Sassoon, *Memoirs of an Infantry Officer*, (London: Faber & Faber, 1930), p. 65

SERVICEMEN'S CONCERT PARTIES

1. See J. G. Fuller *Troop Morale and Popular Culture in the British and Dominion Armies 1914–1918*, (Oxford: Clarendon, 1990), p. 102
2. RAM: Letters of John Barbirolli to his father, 1918
3. George A. Birmingham, 'Sweet Lavender' in *Told in the Huts: The YMCA Gift Book*, (London: Jarrold & Sons, 1916), p. 20
4. IWM 16268: Personal papers of Chaplain M.P.G. Leonard, 15 November 1915, France
5. Fuller, p. 96
6. Collins, p. 109
7. Liddle/WW1/EP/066: Private papers of Lieutenant Robertson
8. Cuthbert Headlam, *The History of the Guards Division in the Great War, 1915–1918*, (London: John Murrray, 1924), p. 132
9. Stanley J. Levy, *Memories of the 71st & 83rd MT Companies, RASC*, (London, printed for private circulation, 1931) pp. 137–47
10. F. C. Stanley, *History of the 89th Brigade 1914–1918*, (Liverpool: Daily Post Printers, 1919), p. 54
11. *Grantham Journal*, 1915 Belton Park show
12. *The Era*, Red Cross concert, 1915
13. Graham Maddocks, *Liverpool Pals: 7th, 18th, 19th, 20th (Service) Battalions, The King's (Liverpool) Regiment*, (Barnsley: Pen & Sword, 2015), pp. 96, 223
14. IWM: Levy, *Memories*, p. 138
15. Cuthbert Headlam, *The History of the Guards Division in the Great War, 1915–1918*, (London: John Murray, 1924), p. 132
16. Levy, *Memories*, p. 137
17. Stanley, *History of the 89th Brigade 1914–1918*, p. 177
18. TNA WO 339/46799: Service record of 2nd Lieutenant Harper Seed
19. RAM: Letters of Second Lieutenant Harper Seed, 25 January 1917
20. Ibid., 6 January 1917
21. Ibid.
22. Ibid., 17 January 1917
23. Ibid.
24. Ibid., 25 January 1917
25. Ibid.
26. Ibid.

27. Ibid., 13 March 1917
28. Ibid., 2 May 1917
29. 'Rice, Gitz' in Helmut Kallmann, et al. (eds.), *Encyclopedia of Music in Canada*, 2nd edition, (Toronto: University of Toronto Press, c1992), p. xxxii. Also see www.collectionscanada.gc.ca/gramophone/028011-1027-e.html
30. Liddle/WW1/GA/EEN/5: Private papers of Lance-Corporal P. E. Coffin
31. Liddle AIR 336: J. Waters (Jack Warner), typescript of tape recordings, 344–9, pp. 6–7
32. Ibid., pp. 11–12
33. IWM 16268: Personal papers of Chaplain M.P. Leonard, 14 April 1919, Letter 213
34. Ivor Davies adopted part of his mother's maiden name, 'Novello' as his professional surname, although he did not change it legally until 1927.
35. Fleet Air Arm Museum: 'Concerning the Conspirators', *The Chingflier*, p. 33
36. TNA: ADM 273-9-143, Service record of David Ivor Davies
37. TNA: ADM 337-123-443, Service record of David Ivor Davies
38. TNA: ADM 273-9-143, Service record of David Ivor Davies
39. TNA: ADM 273-16-145, Service record of David Ivor Davies
40. 'The Padre', *Fifty Thousand Miles on a Hospital Ship: A Chaplain's Experiences in the Great War*, (London: Religious Tract Society, 1917), pp. 250–1
41. Ibid., pp. 258–9
42. Ibid.
43. The music from these productions was collected and published by Charles H. B Jacques, *Music from Macedonia*
44. L. J. Collins, *Theatre at War 1914–18*, (Oldham: Jade, 2004), p. 3
45. IWM 16268: Personal papers of Chaplain M.P. Leonard, 23 January 1919. Several photos of this, see www.iwm.org.uk/collections/item/object/205235950 and www.iwm.org.uk/collections/item/object/205235952
46. MMM: RAMC/PE/2/2/273/WHIT, Programme for *Dick Whittington*, Christmas 1915
47. Ibid., foreword by Major-General C. J. Briggs
48. Jacques, *Music from Macedonia*
49. MMM: RAMC/PE/2/2/274/BLUE, Programme for *Bluebeard*, Christmas 1917
50. Ibid., foreword by Major-General H. L. Croker
51. Jacques, *Music from Macedonia*
52. MMM: RAMC/PE/1/BRYO/63: Miscellaneous Pamphlets, Programme for *Aladdin*, Christmas 1918
53. TNA WO 339/105668: Service record of Lieutenant George Miller-Johnstone (RFC) and TNA AIR 76/261/182: Service record of Lieutenant George Miller-Johnstone (RAF)
54. IWM 24991: Memoirs of Captain G. Miller Johnstone, *Any Fool Can Fly*, pp. 25–6
55. Ibid.
56. IWM 17246: Private papers of J. W. Double, Diary, 9 August 1916

57. Sarah Reay, *The Half-Shilling Curate: A Personal Account of War and Faith 1914–1918*, (Solihull: Helion, 2016), p. 72
58. Everard Digby quoted in Michael Snape, *Clergy Under Fire: The Royal Army Chaplain's Department, 1796–1953* (Woodbridge: Boydell, 2008), p. 209
59. IWM 16268: Letters of Reverend M. P. G. Leonard, 18 August 1916, Picardy
60. Ibid., 1 November 1915, France
61. Ibid., 6 February 1916, Flanders
62. 'G.S.O.', *G.H.Q. (Montreuil-sur-Mer)*, (London: Philip Allan & Co., 1920), pp. 50–1
63. LIDDLE/WW1/GS/1088: Typescript recollections of Mellish, E Noel, p. 14
64. Cutherbert Headlam, *The History of the Guards Division in the Great War, 1915–18* (London: John Murray, 1924)
65. IWM 16268: Personal papers of Chaplain M.P.G. Leonard, 6 December 1915, Belgium
66. Ibid., 17 January 1916
67. Ibid., 31 January 1916
68. Ibid., 6 February 1916
69. Ibid., 20 March 1916
70. LIDDLE/WW1/GS/1088: Typescript recollections of Mellish, E Noel, pp. 15–16
71. IWM 16268: Personal papers of Chaplain M.P.G. Leonard, 14 March 1916
72. Ibid., 28 April 1916
73. Ibid.
74. Ibid.
75. Ibid., 8 December 1917
76. Liddle/WW1/GS/1088: Typescript recollections of Mellish, E Noel, p. 72
77. Ibid.
78. Ibid., pp. 72–3
79. Ibid.
80. IWM 16268: Personal papers of Chaplain M.P.G. Leonard, 14 February 1916
81. LIDDLE/WW1/GS/1088: Mellish
82. Stanley, *History of the 89th Brigade 1914–1918*, p. 185
83. Ibid., p. 255
84. Ibid., p. 273
85. William J. Allen, *SS Borodino, M.F.A. No.6, A Short Account of the Work of the Junior Army and Navy Stores' Store Ship with H.M. Grand Fleet, December 1914–February 1919*, (London: Fleetway Press, 1919), p. 46
86. Ibid.
87. Ibid., p. 67
88. Ibid., pp. 56–7
89. YMCA: *The YM*, 30 June 1916, p. 602
90. K. McLean & P. McDonald, *The Log of H.M.S. Caesar, 1900–1903 Mediterranean Station*, (London: Westminster Press, 1903), p. 66
91. Ibid.
92. Ibid.

93. IWM 12735: Captain H. W. Williams, RN: L. H. W. Williams (ed.), *Fat's War: His Letters, Journals and Diaries*, pp. 151–2
94. John Ambler, *The Royal Marines Band Service*, (Portsmouth: Holbrooks, 2003), p. 25
95. RMM 11/13/28: Memoirs of a Royal Marine Bandsman, H. J. Reed, p. 17
96. John Trendell, *A Life on the Ocean Wave: The Royal Marines Band Story*, (Dover: A. R. Adams & Sons, 1990), p. 28
97. RMM: *Globe and Laurel*, No.234, Vol.XXII, 7 April 1915, p. 76
98. RMM: *HMS Lion's Searchlight*, 1 April 1916, p. 4
99. Ibid., p. 5
100. Ibid., pp. 13–15
101. IWM, LBY 09/71: *Windsor Magazine*, no date, p. 374
102. IWM, LBY 09/71: *Musical Times*, 1 July 1915, p. 401
103. IWM 17246: Private papers of J. W. Double, Diary, 20 March 1916
104. Ibid., 24 March 1916
105. Ibid., 29 October 1916
106. Ibid., 7 April 1916
107. Ibid., 18 April 1916
108. Ibid., 25 October 1916
109. IWM 16268: Personal papers of Chaplain M. P. Leonard, 26 December 1917
110. IWM 24991: Private Papers of Captain G. Miller Johnstone, pp. 25–6
111. Cecil Lewis, *Sagittarius Rising*, (London: Peter Davis, 1936), p. 165
112. Fry quoted in Colin Pengelly, *Albert Ball VC*, (London: Pen & Sword, 2010)
113. Alex Revell, *The Happy Warrior: James Thomas Byford McCudden VC*, (Reno, NV: Aeronaut Books, 2015) p. 82
114. IWM 16268: Personal papers of Chaplain M. P. Leonard, 8 April 1918
115. Ibid.
116. Ibid., 28 July 1918

AFTER THE ARMISTICE

1. IWM 16268: Personal papers of Chaplain M. P. Leonard, 11 November 1918
2. Eric Taylor, *Showbiz Goes to War: World War 2 Military Forces Entertainments*, (London: Hale, 1992)
3. L. J. Collins, *Theatre at War, 1914–18*, (London: Jade, 2004), p. 92
4. Gramophone Company, *Gramophone Records of the First World War: An HMV Catalogue 1914–18*, Introduced by Brian Rust, (Newton Abbot: David & Charles, 1975), p. 220
5. CWGC Index No. M.R.30, Tyne Cot Memorial, Part VII (UK)
6. TNA: WO 372/17/218428, medal card of Second Lieutenant Harper Seed. His service record is at TNA WO 339/46799.
7. CWGC: Grave Registration Reports, 12 March 1920
8. Sarah Reay, *The Half-Shilling Curate: A Personal Account of War and Faith 1914–1918*, (Solihull: Helion, 2016), Foreword by Hugh Pym, p. xii
9. Ibid., p. 124

10. At the outbreak of war in September 1939, Daking applied to the EFDS to once again take up her work with servicemen in using folk music and dancing for the upkeep of morale in the war effort. However, her suggestion was given a lukewarm reception by the chairman of the EFDSS. In the spring of 1940, she published a substantial report in the EFDSS journal *English Dance and Song* recalling the work she had done in the First World War and of the benefits which were to be gained from using folk music and dance. Shortly afterwards, on 2 May 1940, Daking's journal recalled that a staff officer in YMCA badges arrived at the EFDSS HQ and enquired about teaching folk dancing to the 'women's army' after one of his superiors recounted seeing one of Daking's demonstrations in 1917. On 10 May 1942, she took her own life by drinking Lysol in the toilets at Charing Cross station. She was fifty-five years old.
11. YMCA/K/1/8/31: Minutes of the Finance and War Emergency Committee, 12 November 1918 and 26 November 1918
12. YMCA/K/1/8/31: Minutes of the Finance and War Emergency Committee, 25 February 1919
13. Alaine E. Reschke-Hernandez, 'Paula Lind Ayers: "Song Physician" for Troops with Shell Shock During World War I', *Journal of Music Therapy*, 2014, 51:3, 276–91
14. *The Spectator*, 13 December 1919, p. 14
15. Frederick Mott, *War Neuroses and Shell Shock*, (London: Henry Frowde, 1919), p. 297; Edgar Jones, '"An Atmosphere of Cure": Frederick Mott, Shell Shock and the Maudsley', *History of Psychiatry*, 2014, 25, 412
16. Frederick Mott, *The Brain and the Voice in Speech and Song*, (London and New York: Harper and Bros., 1909)
17. Frederick Mott, 'Treatment by Speech and Song', *Reveille*, 1 February 1919, 432–9
18. Ibid., p. 439
19. www.iwm.org.uk/collections/item/object/80032710: Track 1: 'O Valiant Hearts' (George Baker and chorus) Track 2: Community Singing: 'It's a Long Way to Tipperary'; 'Pack up Your Troubles'; 'There's a Long, Long Trail'
20. Lieutenant-Colonel John Mackenzie-Rogan, *Fifty Years of Army Music*, (London: Methuen, 1926), p. 232
21. Ibid., p. 231
22. Ibid., p. 233
23. Ibid.
24. RMM: Confidential memo from T.R.Porteous, RNSM, to All Bandmaster Afloat, 6 November 1919
25. Rogan, *Fifty Years*, p. 247
26. Ibid., p. 248
27. Ibid.
28. Ibid., p. 249
29. Lena Ashwell, *Modern Troubadours: A Record of Concerts at the Front*, (London: Gyldenhal, 1922), p. 124
30. Ibid., p. 68
31. Ibid.

32. BLM 56482: Foulds' correspondence
33. James G. Mansell, 'Musical Modernity and Contested Commemoration at the Festival of Remembrance, 1923–1927', *The Historical Journal*, 2009, 52:2, 433–54. For more on the music of Foulds and MacCarthy, see Nalini Ghuman, *Resonances of the Raj: India in the English Musical Imagination, 1897–1947*, (Oxford: Oxford University Press, 2014)
34. BLM 56482: Letter from Douglas Haig to John Foulds, 14 November 1923
35. RBL: General Secretary's Monthly Circular for November 1927 and *British Legion*, Vol.7, No.5, November 1927, p. 1
36. *Daily Express*, 5 October 1926, p. 9. See also Adrian Gregory, *The Silence of Memory: Armistice Day 1919–1946*, (Oxford: Berg, 1994)
37. RBL: *British Legion*, Vol.7. No.5, November 1927, p. 1
38. Ibid.
39. Eric Leed, *No Man's Land: Combat and Identity in World War I*, (Cambridge: Cambridge University Press, 1979), p. 212
40. *British Legion*, Vol.7. No.6, December 1927, p. 1
41. Ibid., p. 149
42. Ibid.
43. Ibid.
44. Emma Hanna, '"When Words Are Not Enough" Memory and the Aural Landscape of 1914-18', in Krista Cowman & Angela Smith (ed.), *Landscape and Voices of the Great War*, (London: Routledge, 2017), pp. 41–57
45. Clifford Geertz, *The Interpretation of Cultures*, (New York: Basic Books, 1973)

Sources and Select Bibliography

Borthwick Institute for Archives, University of York
MacCarthy-Foulds Archive

British Library Manuscripts
MS 56469–56483: John Foulds Collection

British Red Cross Archives
The British Prisoner of War
Reports by the Joint War Committee and the Joint War Finance Committee of the British Red Cross Society and the Order of St John of Jerusalem in England on Voluntary Aid Rendered to the Sick and Wounded at Home and Abroad and to British Prisoners of War 1914–1919, with Appendices (London: His Majesty's Stationery Offices, 1921)

Cadbury Special Collections, University of Birmingham
YMCA/K/6/1: YMCA Publications 1914–1918
YMCA K/2/4: YMCA War Work, France, 1915–1918
YMCA K/1/7: War Emergency Work; Germany, Holland, India, Italy
YMCA/ACC2: Unofficial Papers: Gipsy Smith, scrapbook
YMCA/K/1/8/31: Minutes of the Finance and War Emergency Committee
YMCA K/2/4: YMCA War Work in France, 1915–18, Work for Indians in France
YMCA J25: Education Committee

Cambridge University Library Manuscripts
Church Army Collection

English Folk Dance & Song Society
Daisy Caroline Daking Manuscript Collection
George Butterworth Manuscript Collection
English Folk Dance and Song

Fleet Air Arm Museum

The Piloteer

Imperial War Museum

Documents

IWM 17198: Correspondence relating to the *Daily Express* 'Cheery Fund'

IWM 17246: Personal papers of J. W. Double, Diary

IWM 16268: Personal papers of Chaplain M. P. G. Leonard

IWM 15459: Personal Papers of Gordon Williams

IWM PST 13607: Irish recruiting poster, 1915–16, author unknown

IWM 7831: Personal Papers of J. J. McGale

IWM 24991: Private Papers of Captain G. Miller Johnstone

IWM 15993: Private papers of Private H. Molsom

IWM 22371: Private Papers of E. B.Pierpoint

IWM 6482, 19/16/1: War Diaries of Lieutenant R. P. E. Roberts

IWM 11794: Private Papers of W. J. Reynolds

IWM 12735: H. W. Williams

IWM, LBY 09/71: Lena Ashwell Special Collection

Oral Histories

IWM 9535: George Cole

IWM 374: Charles Harry Ditcham

IWM 10767: Joe Fitzpatrick

IWM 8172: Major John Frederick Ford

IWM 16: James V. Gascoyne

IWM 8270: Percy Valentine Harris

IWM 777: Alfred Walter Hedges

IWM 9927: Arthur Hemsley

IWM 11341: Donald A Hodge

IWM 9428: Tommy Keele

IWM 10457: Turville Kille

IWM 23157: Tom Mapplebeck

IWM 4770: Leonard Martin-Andrews

IWM 7256: Lendon Fitz Payne

IWM 495: James Pratt

IWM 314: Percy Snelling

Liddle Collection, University of Leeds

Liddle/WW1/GS/1088: Typescript recollections of Noel E. Mellish

Liddle/WW1/EP/066: Private papers of Lieutenant E. Robertson

Liddle/WW1/GA/EEN/5:   Private   papers   of   Lance-Corporal
P. E. Coffin
Liddle/WW1/POW/016: Private papers of V. C. Coombs
Liddle AIR 336: Private papers of J. Waters (Jack Warner)

Museum of Military Medicine

MMM: RAMC/CF/4/3/92/PRAY, 'A Form of Prayer to Be Used at
Open-Air Services'
MMM: QARANC/P6/1/107/BLAI, Miss M. A. C. Blair
MMM: RAMC/PE/2/2/273/WHIT, Programme for *Dick Whittington*,
Christmas 1915
MMM: RAMC/PE/2/2/274/BLUE,   Programme   for   *Bluebeard*,
Christmas 1917
MMM: RAMC/PE/1/BRYO/63: Programme, *Aladdin*, Christmas 1918

National Army Museum, London

NAM 1978–08-80–1: Memoirs of Bandsman Sergeant
Victor Shawyer
NAM 9601–32: Parliamentary Recruiting Committee
NAM 9512–170: Private papers of E. W. Jones
NAM 2005–05-51: Letters of Oliver Lenz
NAM 9702–13: Personal papers of Lieutenant-Colonel Sir Hoel
Llewellyn
NAM 2013/05/1: Letters of Lieutenant Jack Wood
NAM 2016/10/23/245/8: Sir Francis Lloyd, correspondence and
reports, 1917–1918

Nicholas Hiley Collection

NHC: *Talking Machine News and Journal of Amusements*, Vol.VII,
No.205, January 1915, p. 42
NHC: *HMV: The Catalogue* of Records, September 1916
NHC: *His Master's Voice Records of Patriotic Songs: National Anthems of
the Allies, Military and Naval Airs, Songs about Tommy Atkins and Jack*,
c.1917–18
NHC: *Edison Bell Discaphones Catalogue*, 1915–16 season,
Introduction
NHC: Letters of Lieutenant Richard Noble, 1916

Royal Academy of Music

The RAM Club Magazine
Letters of John Barbirolli
Letters of Second Lieutenant Harper Seed

Royal Engineers Museum

The Sapper

Royal Air Force Museum

RAF X003-0400/001: Letters of Second Lieutenant Alfred Severs
RAF PC73/60/189: *A Song of Stunting*, 1918
RAF X006-4186/005: Prisoner of War Journal of Second Lieutenant
John Chapman

Royal Logistics Corps Museum

RLCM: J8822/e 38: *Carry On: The Official Journal of the EFC Section of
the Army Service Corps on Service* [undated], 'Our Daily Routine and
a few well-known Hymns', p. 4

Royal Marines Museum

RMM: Letter from W. R. Hoare, Training Ship *Mercury*
RMM 11/13/28: Memoirs of a Royal Marine Bandsman, H. J. Reed
RMM: *The Fleet*
RMM: *Globe and Laurel*
RMM: B.R.13, *The Bugler's Handbook*
RMM: *HMS Lion's Searchlight*

Royal Military School of Music, Kneller Hall

Kneller Hall, Diary

Salvation Army International Heritage Centre

The Bandsman, Local Officer & Songster
Under the Colours

The National Archives

War Diaries

TNA 10 95 4120 1: No.5 Convalescent Depot, Wimereaux
TNA WO 95 4121 4: No.13 Convalescent Depot, Trouville
TNA WO 95/1218/3/030: 2 Guards Brigade, Headquarters
TNA WO 95/1219/2: 1 Battalion Coldstream Guards
TNA WO 95/2954/2, War Diary of 1/12 Battalion, London Regiment
(Rangers)
TNA WO 95/2963/1, War Diary of 1/9 Battalion, London Regiment
(Queen Victoria's Rifles)

Personnel Records

TNA 372/11/103105: Medal card of Trooper Michael Kearns
TNA ADM 240/82/1335: Service record of Lieutenant-Commander
Wybrants Olphert
TNA ADM 339/1/38674: Service record of Cecil Arthur Tooke

TNA: ADM 196/61/275: Service record of Lieutenant Colonel Charles Hope Willis

TNA: ADM 273–9-143, TNA: ADM 337–123-443: Service records of David Ivor Davies

TNA AIR 76/333/56: Service record of Captain Thomas George Mapplebeck

TNA AIR 76/337/3: Service record of R. B. Martin,

TNA AIR 76/369/4: Service record of F. T. Nettleingham

TNA: AIR 79/1422/158258: Service record of Percival Leslie Norman

TNA AIR 76/92/150: Service record of C. A. Clifford

TNA AIR 79/2503/287271: Second Lieutenant Frank Ernest Hills

TNA AIR 79/33/2556: Service record of John [Harold] Chapman

TNA WO 339/105668, AIR 76/261/182: Service records of Lieutenant George Miller-Johnstone

TNA WO 339/2518: Service record of Major Hope Brankston Viney

TNA WO 339/28770: Service record of Lieutenant Anthony Arrigone

TNA WO 339/46799: Service record of Lieutenant Harper Seed

TNA WO 339/50028: Lieutenant William Leefe Robinson VC

TNA WO 339/6477: Long Service Papers, Lieutenant Colonel John Mackenzie Rogan

TNA WO 372/18/20265: Medal card of Lieutenant Jack Shaw

TNA WO 372/8/133001: Medal card of Lieutenant B. M.Greenhill

TNA WO 374/50748: Service record of Lieutenant Richard Noble

TNA WO 374/73337: Service record of Lieutenant James Whale

TNA WO/372/6/69654: Medal card of Johnson William Double

TNA: WO 339/55743: Service record of Captain Vernon William Blythe Castle

TNA: WO 374/21603: Service record of Captain James Dyson

Miscellaneous

TNA AIR/2/93: Postwar Establishments for RAF Music

TNA AIR 2/80: Establishment for RAF School of Music

TNA AIR 2/90: RAF School of Music

TNA AIR 2/131: RAF Music Services and Band

TNA HO 45/10727/254753: Activity of enemy agents, 1914–16

TNA: HO 144/1318/252301: 'Title Royal: Naval and Military Musical Union Refused'

TNA WO 107/37: Distribution of Labour Battalions and Companies

TNA WO 162/3: Commander in Chief and War Office: Adjutant General's Department

TNA WO/161: Committee on the Treatment of British Prisoners of War: Interviews and Reports

Wartime Memoirs

Agate, Captain James E., *Lines of Communication: Being the Letters of a Temporary Officer in the Army Service Corps*, (London: Constable & Co., 1917)

Allen, William J., *SS Borodino, M.F.A. No.6: A Short Account of the Work of the Junior Army and Navy Stores' Store Ship with H.M. Grand Fleet, December 1914-February 1919*, (London: Fleetway Press, 1919)

Ashwell, Lena, *Modern Troubadours: A Record of Concerts at the Front*, (London: Glydendal, 1922)

Barter, A. E., J. Power & C. A. Tooke (eds.), *The Link: A Souvenir Book Published by British Prisoners of War Interned at Doeberitz, Germany, 1914–17*, (Berlin-Schöenberg: Doeberitz Edition, 1917)

Brophy, John, & Eric Partridge, *The Long Trail: What the British Soldier Sang and Said in The Great War of 1914–18*, (Tonbridge: Andre Deutsch, 1965 [1930])

Corbett-Smith, Arthur, *A Memoir*, (Herne Bay: Ridout & Son, 1945)

Douglas, Sholto, *Years of Combat*, (London: Collins, 1963)

"G.S.O." [Frank Fox], *G.H.Q. (Montreuil-sur-Mer)*, (London: Philip Allan & Co., 1920)

Harvey, F. W., *Comrades in Captivity: A Record of Life in Seven German Prison Camps*, (London: Sidgwick & Jackson Ltd., 1920)

Lauder, Harry, *A Minstrel in France*, (New York: Hearst's International Library Co., 1918)

Levy, Stanley J., *Memories of the 71st & 83rd MT Companies, RASC*, (London, printed for private circulation, 1931)

Lewis, Cecil, *Sagittarius Rising*, (London: Peter Davis, 1936)

Mackenzie-Rogan, Lieutenant-Colonel John, *Fifty Years of Army Music*, (London: Methuen, 1926)

Northcliffe, Alfred Harmsworth, *At the War*, (London: Hodder & Stoughton, 1916)

Oram, H. P. K., *Ready for Sea*, (Annapolis: United States Naval Institute, 1974)

'The Padre', *Fifty Thousand Miles on a Hospital Ship: A Chaplain's Experiences in the Great War*, (London: Religious Tract Society, 1917)

Sassoon, Siegfried, *Memoirs of an Infantry Officer*, (London: Faber & Faber, 1930)

Smith, Revered G. Vernon, *The Bishop of London's Visit to the Front*, (London: Longmans, 1915)

Tatham, Meaburn, & James E. Miles (eds.), *The Friends' Ambulance Unit, 1914–1919: a Record*, (London: Swarthmore Press, 1920)

Terriss, Ellaline, *By Herself and with Others*, (London: Cassell, 1928)

Terriss, Ellaline, *Just a Little Bit of String*, (London: Hutchinson, 1955)

Tiplady, Thomas, *The Soul of the Soldier: Sketches from the Western Battle-Front*, (London: Fleming H. Revell, 1918)

Ward, Ada, *My Greatest Adventure*, (Leonor edition, London: Methuen and Co., 1918)

Watt, Lauchlan Maclean, *In France and Flanders with the Fighting Men*, (London: Hodder & Stoughton, 1917)

Wells, Mark, *Courage and Air Warfare: The Allied Experience of the Second World War*, (London: Frank Cass, 1995)

Yapp, Arthur Keysall, *The Romance of the Red Triangle: The Story of the Coming of the Red Triangle and the Service Rendered by the Y.M.C.A. to the Sailors and Soldiers of the British Empire*, (Library of Congress, 31 December 1918)

YMCA, *Yearbook of the Young Men's Christian Associationin England, Ireland and Wales, [. . .] 1914–1920*, (London: YMCA, 1921)

YMCA, *Told in the Huts: The YMCA Gift Book*, (London: Jarrold & Sons, 1916)

Young, Geoffrey Winthrop, *A Story of the Work of the Friends' Ambulance Unit*, (London: Newnham, Cowell & Gripper, 1915)

Songbooks and Collections

Ainger, Arthur, *Marching Songs for Soldiers*, (London: Ascherberg, Hopwood & Crew, 1914)

Anon., *Marching Songs and Tommy's Tunes: A Handbook for Our Soldiers*, (London: Stanley Paul, 1914)

Atherley, C. A., *Trumpet and Bugle Sounds for the Army with Words also Bugle Marches*, (Aldershot: Gale and Poulden, 1915)

Bishop, G. W. (ed.), *The Royal Naval Song Book*, (London, 1890)

Davies, Henry Walford (ed.), *Songs Old and New: For Use in Wartime*, (London: S. Roirden, 1915)

Davies, Henry Walford (ed.), *The Aldershot Song Book for Regimental Choirs: Thirty-Eight Songs for Camp Concerts*, (London: J. Curwen & Sons, 1916)

Farmer, John (ed.), *Scarlet & Blue: Or, Songs for Soldiers and Sailors*, (London: Cassell, 1909 [1898])

Jacques, Charles H. B., *Music from Macedonia*, (Abbots Langley: no publisher or date)

Naishtad, Private Sam (SAI Brigade), *The Great War Parodies of the East, Central African and Flanders Campaigns*, (undated)

National Service League, *Songs for Our Soldiers*, (undated, estimated c.1914–15)

Nettleingham, F. T., *Tommy's Tunes: A Comprehensive Collection of Soldiers' Songs, Marching Melodies, Rude Rhymes, and Popular Parodies, Composed, Collected and Arranged on Active Service with the B.E.F. Tommy's Tunes*, (London: Erskine Macdonald, 1917)

Nettleingham, F. T., *More Tommy's Tunes: An Additional Collection of Soldiers' Songs [. . .]*, (London: Erskine Macdonald, 1918)

Purday, Charles (ed.), *The Royal Naval Song Book*, (London, 1867)

Ward-Jackson, C. H., *Airman's Song Book: Being an Anthology of Squadron, Concert Party, Training and Camp Songs and Song-Parodies [. . .]*, (London: Sylvan, 1945)

Personal Collections

Rose Venn-Brown, unpublished, reproduced courtesy of Sandra Venn-Brown

Books

Adkins, H. E., *Treatise on the Military Band*, (London: Boosey & Co., 1931)

Adorno, Theodore, *Essays on Music*, (Berkeley: University of California Press, 2002)

Ambler, John, *The Royal Marines Band Service*, (Portsmouth: Holbrooks, 2003)

Arthur, Max, *Forgotten Voices*, (London: Ebury Press, 2002)

Aulich, J., & J. Hewitt, *Seduction or Instruction?: First World War Posters in Britain and Europe*, (Manchester: Manchester University Press, 2007)

Baade, Christina L., *Victory through Harmony: The BBC and Popular Music in WW2*, (Oxford: Oxford University Press, 2012)

Bell, Julian (ed.), *We Did Not Fight 1914–18: Experiences of War Resisters*, (London: Cobden-Sanderson, 1935)

Bell, Stuart, *Faith in Conflict: The Impact of the Great War on the People of Britain*, (Solihull: Helion, 2017)

Bickersteth, John, (ed.), *The Bickersteth Diaries: 1914–1918*, (London: Leo Cooper, 1995)

Bowman, Timothy, *Irish Regiments in the Great War: Discipline and Morale*, (Manchester: Manchester University Press, 2003)

Bowman, Timothy, & Mark Connelly, *The Edwardian Army: Recruiting, Training and Deploying the British Army, 1902–1914*, (Oxford: Oxford University Press, 2012)

Cecil, Hugh, (ed.), *Facing Armageddon*, (London: Pen & Sword Select, 2003)

Clark, Alan, *Aces High: The War in the Air over the Western Front 1914–18*, (London: Weidenfeld & Nicolson, 1973)

Collins, L. J., *Theatre at War, 1914–18*, (London: Jade, 2004)

Cooper, Kate, & Jeremy Gregory (eds.), *Retribution, Repentance and Reconciliation*, (Martlesham: Ecclesiastical History Society, 2004)

Cowman, Krista, & Angela Smith (eds.), *Landscape and Voices of the Great War*, (London: Routledge, 2017)

Crawford, Elizabeth, *The Women's Suffrage Movement: A Reference Guide, 1866–1928*, (London: Routledge, 2001)

DeGroot, Gerard, *Back in Blighty: The British at Home in World War I*, (London: Vintage, 2014)

Doolin, Malcolm J., *The Boys of Blackhorse Road: The Story of an Elementary School War Memorial*, (Woodbridge: Astra Publications, 2016)

Eby, Cecil D., *The Road to Armageddon: The Martial Spirit in English Popular Literature, 1870–1914*, (London: Duke University Press, 1987)

Evatt, G. J. H., *Our Songless Army: A Proposal to Develop the Singing of Marching Songs, Unison Singing, Part-Songs, and Choral Societies by the Soldiers of Our Regular Army, Militia, Yeomanry, Volunteers, Cadet Corps, and Boys' Brigades*, (London: J. Curwen & Sons, 1907)

Farmer, George, *Memoirs of the Royal Artillery Band*, (London: Boosey & Co., 1904)

Fennell, Jonathan, *Combat and Morale in the North African Campaign: The Eighth Army and the Path to El Alamein*, (Cambridge: Cambridge University Press, 2014)

Francis, Martin, *The Flyer: British Culture and the Royal Air Force, 1939–1945*, (Oxford: Oxford University Press, 1998)

Fuller, J. G., *Troop Morale and Popular Culture in the British and Dominion Armies*, (Oxford: Clarendon, 1990)

Geertz, Clifford, *The Interpretation of Cultures*, (New York: Basic Books, 1973)

Ghuman, Nalini, *Resonances of the Raj: India in the English Musical Imagination, 1897–1947*, (Oxford: Oxford University Press, 2014)

GramophoneCompany, *Gramophone Records of the First World War: An HMVCatalogue 1914–18*, Introduced by Brian Rust, (Newton Abbot: David & Charles, 1975)

Grant, Peter, *Philanthropy and Voluntary Action in the First World War*, (London: Routledge, 2014)

Gregory, Adrian, *The Great War: British Society and the First World War*, (Cambridge: Cambridge University Press, 2008)

Hanna, Emma, 'Veterans' Associations (Great Britain and Ireland)', in *1914–1918-Online: International Encyclopedia of the First World War*, Ute Daniel, Peter Gatrell, Oliver Janz, Heather Jones, Jennifer Keene, Alan Kramer, & Bill Nasson (eds.), (Berlin: Freie Universität Berlin, 2015)

Headlam, Cutherbert, *The History of the Guards Division in the Great War, 1915–18*, (London: John Murray, 1924)

Herbet, Trevor (ed.), *The British Brass Band: A Musical and Social History*, (Oxford: Oxford University Press, 2000)

Herbert, Trevor, & Helen Barlow, *Music in the British Military in the Long Nineteenth Century*, (Oxford: Oxford University Press, 2013)

Hindson, Catherine, *London's West End Actresses and the Origins of Celebrity Charity, 1880–1920*, (Iowa City: University of Iowa Press, 2016)

Holden, Robert, *And the Band Played On: How Music Lifted the Anzac Spirit in the Battlefields of the First World War*, (London: Hardie Grant, 2014)

Hynes, Samuel, *A War Imagined: The Great War and English Culture*, (London: Pimlico, 1990)

Jacobs, Arthur, *Henry J. Wood: Maker of the Proms*, (London: Methuen, 1994)

James, Gregory, *The Chinese Labour Corps 1916–1920*, (Hong Kong: Bayview Educational, 2013)

Kallmann, Helmut, et al. (eds.), *Encyclopedia of Music in Canada*, (2nd edition, Toronto: University of Toronto Press, c.1992)

Karpeles, Maud, *Cecil Sharp: His Life and Work*, (London: Routledge & Kegan Paul, 1967)

Lazell, David, *Gypsy from the Forest: A New Biography of the International Evangelist Gipsy Smith (1860–1947)*, (Bridgend: Gwasg Bryntirion Press, 1997)

Leask, Margaret, *Lena Ashwell: Actress, Patriot, Pioneer*, (Hertfordshire: University of Hertfordshire Press, 2012)

McLean, K., & P. McDonald, *The Log of H.M.S. Caesar, 1900–1903 Mediterranean Station*, (London: Westminster Press, 1903)

Maddocks, Graham, *Liverpool Pals: 7th, 18th, 19th, 20th (Service) Battalions, the King's (Liverpool) Regiment*, (Barnsley: Pen & Sword, 2015)

Martland, Peter, *Recording History: The British Record Industry, 1888–1931*, (London: Scarecrow Press, 2013)

Marwick, Arthur, *The Deluge: British Society and the First World War*, (London: Macmillan, 1996 [1965])

Mason, Tony, & Eliza Reidi, *Sport and the Military: The British Armed Forces 1880–1960*, (Cambridge: Cambridge University Press, 2010)

Mullen, John, *The Show Must Go On! Popular Song in Britain During the Great War*, (Ashgate: Farnham, 2015)

Myerly, Scott Hughes, *British Military Spectacle: From the Napoleonic Wars through the Crimea*, (Cambridge, MA: Harvard University Press, 1996)

Hutchins, Roger, *British University Observatories, 1772–1939*, (London: Routledge, 2008)

Mott, Frederick, *The Brain and the Voice in Speech and Song*, (London and New York: Harper and Bros., 1909)

Mott, Frederick, *War Neuroses and Shell Shock*, (London: Henry Frowde, 1919)

Niles, John J., *Singing Soldiers*, (New York/London: Charles Scribner's Sons, 1927)

Nora, Pierre (ed.), *Lieux de Mémoire*, (Paris: Gallimard, 1984–92)

Norris, John, *Marching to the Drums: A History of Military Drums and Drummers*, (Stroud: Spellmount, 2012)

Palfreeman, Linda, *Friends in Flanders: Humanitarian Aid Administered by the Friends' Ambulance Unit during the First World War*, (Eastbourne: Academic Press, 2017)

Pengelly, Colin, *Albert Ball VC*, (London: Pen & Sword, 2010)

Pennell, Catriona, *A Kingdom United: Popular Responses to the Outbreak of the First World War in Britain and Ireland*, (Oxford: Oxford University Press, 2014)

Philpott, Maryam, *Air and Sea Power in World War I: Combat and Experience in the Royal Flying Corps and Royal Navy*, (London: I. B. Tauris, 2013)

Raleigh, Sir Walter, *The History of the War in the Air, 1914–1918*, (Barnsley: Pen & Sword, 2014 [1922])

Ralston, Andrew G., *Lauchlan MacLean Watt: Poet, Preacher & Piping Padre*, (Glasgow: Society of Friends of Glasgow Cathedral, 2018)

Reay, Sarah, *The Half-Shilling Curate: A Personal Account of War and Faith 1914–1918*, (Solihull: Helion, 2016)

Revell, Alex, *The Happy Warrior: James Thomas Byford McCudden VC*, (Reno, NV: Aeronaut Books, 2015)

Reznick, Jeffrey S., *Healing the Nation: Soldiers and the Culture of Caregiving during the Great War*, (Manchester: Manchester University Press, 2011)

Richards, Jeffrey, *Imperialism and Music: Britain 1876–1953*, (Manchester: Manchester University Press, 2001)

Sheffield, Gary, *Leadership in the Trenches . . .* , (Basingstoke: Macmillan, 2000)

Sheffield, Gary, *Command and Morale: The British Army on the Western Front*, (Pen & Sword, 2014)

Sheffield, Gary, & John Bourne (eds.), *Douglas Haig: War Diaries and Letters 1914–1918*, (London: Weidenfeld & Nicolson, 2005)

Singleton, Gilbert A., *Music in Blue: Uniforms of Musicians in the Royal Air Force and Its Predecessors – A Photographic History*, (Maidenhead: Eagle & Lyre Publications, 2007)

Snape, Michael, *God and the British Soldier: Religion and the British Army in the First and Second World Wars*, (Oxford: Routledge, 2005)

Snape, Michael, *The Back Parts of War: The YMCA Memoirs and Letters of Barclay Baron, 1915–1919*, (Woodbridge: Boydell & Brewer, 2009)

Snape, Michael, & Edward Madigan (eds.), *The Clergy in Khaki: New Perspectives on British Army Chaplaincy in the First World War*, (Farnham: Ashgate, 2013)

Stanley, F. C., *History of the 89th Brigade 1914–1918*, (Liverpool: Daily Post Printers, 1919)

Stibbe, Matthew, *British Civilian Internees in Germany: The Ruhleben Camp, 1914–1919*, (Manchester: Manchester University Press, 2013)

Summerskill, Michael, *China on the Western Front*, (Norwich: Page Bros, 1982)

Thacker, Toby, *British Culture and the Great War*, (London: Bloomsbury, 2014)

Tholas-Disset, Clémentine, & Karen A. Ritzenhoff, *Humour, Entertainment and Popular Culture in World War I*, (London: Palgrave Macmillan, 2015)

Todman, Dan, *The Great War: Myth & Memory*, (London: Hambledon, 2005)

Trendell, John, *A Life on the Ocean Wave: The Royal Marines Band Story*, (Dover: A. R. Adams & Sons, 1990)

Turner, Alwyn W., *The Last Post: Music, Remembrance and the Great War*, (London: Aurum Press, 2014)

Turner, Gordon, & Alwyn W. Turner, *The Trumpets Will Sound: The Story of the Royal Military School of Music, Kneller Hall*, (Tunbridge Wells: Parapress, 1996)

Lukas Vischer, Adolf, *Barbed-Wire Disease: A Psychological Study of the Prisoner of War*, (London: John Bale & Danielson, 1919)

Walsh, Michael, & Andrekos Vanava (eds.), *Empire and the Great War*, (London: Ashgate, 2016)

Ward, Colonel B. R., *The Organisation of the Naval and Military Musical Union: Being a Paper Read at Aldershot by Col. B. R. Ward, R.E., to the Members of the Marlborough Lines Literary and Debating Society, November 1911*, (London: Whiteman & Co./Organization Society, 1912)

Watkins, Glenn, *Proof through the Night: Music and the Great War*, (Berkeley, CA: University of California Press, 2003)

Weston, Agnes, *My Life among the Bluejackets*, (London: James Nisbet, 1909)

White, Jerry, *Zeppelin Nights: London in the First World War*, (London: The Bodley Head, 2014)

Wilkinson, Oliver, *British Prisoners of War in First World War Germany*, (Cambridge: Cambridge University Press, 2017)

Williamson, John, & Martin Cloonan, *Players' Work Time: A History of the British Musicians' Union, 1893–2013*, (Manchester: Manchester University Press, 2016)

Wilson, Jason, *Soldiers of Song: The Dumbells and Other Canadian Concert Parties of the First World War*, (Waterloo: Wilfred Laurier University Press, 2012)

Winter, Jay, *Sites of Memory, Sites of Mourning*, (Cambridge: Cambridge University Press, 1995)

Wurtzburg, C. E., *The History of the 2/6th (Rifle) Battalion "The King's" (Liverpool Regiment)*, (Aldershot: Gale & Polden, 1920)

Yarnall, John, *Barbed Wire Disease: British and German Prisoners of War, 1914–1919*, (Stroud: History Press, 2011)

Yexley, Lionel, *The Inner Life of the Navy*, (London: Pitman & Sons, 1908)

Yexley, Lionel, *Charity and the Navy: A Protest against Indiscriminate Begging of Behalf of 'Poor Jack'*, (London: The FleetLtd., 1911)

Young, Michael, *Army Service Corps 1908–1918*, (Barnsley: Leo Cooper, 2000)
Ziino, Bart (ed.), *Remembering the First World War*, (London: Routledge, 2014)

Articles

Angell, Jane, 'Music and Charity on the British Home Front during the First World War', *Journal of Musicological Research*, 2014, 33:1–3, 184–205

Brock, A. J., 'Boredom and Barbed-Wire Disease', *British Medical Journal*, 1940, 1: 744

Collins, Michael, 'A Fear of Flying: Diagnosing Traumatic Neurosis among British Aviators of the Great War', *First World War Studies*, 2015, 6:2, 187–202

Etheridge, Stephen, 'Southern Pennine Brass Bands and the Creation of Northern Identity c.1840–1914: Musical Constructions of Space, Place and Region', *Northern History*, September 2017, 54:2, 244–61

Hanna, Emma, 'Putting the Moral into Morale: YMCA Cinemas on the Western Front, 1914-1918', *Historical Journal of Film, Radio & Television*, October 2015, 35:4, 615–30

Hanna, Emma, 'Say It with Music: Combat, Courage and Identity in the Songs of the RFC/RAF, 1914-1918', *British Journal for Military History*, February 2018, 4, 2, 91–120

Hazelgrove, Jenny, 'Spiritualism after the Great War', *Twentieth Century British History*, 1999, 10, 404–30

Hiley, Nicholas, 'Ploughboys and Soldiers: The Folk Song and the Gramophone in the British Expeditionary Force 1914–1918', *Media History*, 1998, 4:1, 61–76

Hornsby, Stephen J., 'Patterns of Scottish Emigration to Canada, 1750–1870', *Journal of Historical Geography*, October 1992, 18:4, 397–416

Jones, Edgar, 'An Atmosphere of Cure': Frederick Mott, Shell Shock and the Maudsley, *History of Psychiatry*, 2014, 25, 412

Kennedy, Kate, & Trudi Tate, 'Literature and Music of the Great War', *Great War Studies*, 2011, 2:1, 1–6

Madigan, Edward, '"Sticking to a Hateful Task": Resilience, Humour, and British Understandings of Combatant Courage, 1914–1918', *War in History*, 20:1, 76–98

Mansell, James G., 'Musical Modernity and Contested Commemoration at the Festival of Remembrance, 1923–1927', *The Historical Journal*, 2009, 52:2, 433–54

Meyer, Jessica, 'Neutral Caregivers or Military Support? The British Red Cross, the Friends' Ambulance Unit, and the Problems of Voluntary Medical Aid in Wartime', *War and Society*, 2015, 34, 105–20

Mott, Frederick, 'Treatment by Speech and Song', *Reveille*, 1 February 1919, 432–39

Reschke-Hernandez, Alaine E., 'Paula Lind Ayers: "Song Physician" for Troops with Shell Shock during World War I', *Journal of Music Therapy*, 2014, 51:3, 276–91

Shaw Cobden, Lynsey, 'The Nervous Flyer: Nerves, Flying and the First World War', *British Journal for Military History*, February 2018, 4:2, 121–42

Sumida, Jon, 'British Naval Administration and Policy in the Age of Fisher', *The Journal of Military History*, January 1990, 54:1, 1–26

Snape, Michael, 'Church of England Army Chaplains in the First World War: "Goodbye to All That", *Journal of Ecclesiastical History*, April 2011, 62:2, 371–403

Wynter, Rebecca, 'Keeping the Peace: Working Relationships and the Friends' Ambulance Unit in the First World War', *Ieper*, January 14, 2006

Unpublished Papers and Theses

Greenshields, Thomas, paper delivered to the 'Pack Up Your Troubles: Performance Cultures in the First World War' conference, University of Kent, March 2016.

Websites

Baker, Anne Pimlott, 'Moore, (Lilian) Decima (1871–1964)', oxforddnb.com, Oxford University Press, September 2004, (accessed 18 May 2018)

Index